LEGAL DRAFTING

Process, Techniques, and Exercises
Second Edition

By

Thomas R. Haggard
Distinguished Professor of Law Emeritus
University of South Carolina School of Law

and

George W. Kuney
Professor of Law and Director
James L. Clayton Center for Entrepreneurial Law
The University of Tennessee College of Law

AMERICAN CASEBOOK SERIES®

THOMSON
WEST

Mat #40639528

American Casebook Series and West Group are trademarks registered in the U.S. Patent and Trademark Office.

© West, a Thomson business, 2003
© 2007 Thomson/ West
        610 Opperman Drive
        P.O. Box 64526
        St. Paul, MN 55164–0526
        1–800–313–9378

Printed in the United States of America

ISBN 978–0–314–18440–5

 TEXT IS PRINTED ON 10% POST CONSUMER RECYCLED PAPER

Dedicated To

*Bonnie, Sheba, Sandy, Fritz, Pearl,
Rudy, Hector, Max, Gus, Nubbin,
Nemo, Blackjack, and J.D.*

In Appreciation of Their Loyalty
and Friendship

Thomas R. Haggard
George W. Kuney

*

Preface

Many new lawyers are daunted by the prospect of drafting their first operative legal document. "What do I say first?" – as if the document will fail unless the prefatory chant has a particular pitch and intonation.

Every lawyer is forced to draft something eventually. And when that document, no matter how poor it is in form or substance, does not precipitate an immediate end to the world, the pendulum often swings to the opposite extreme. Unnecessary fear is replaced by dangerous indifference and unwarranted confidence. Drafting is regarded either as an inherent ability or merely a mechanical function that can be performed by emulating what is contained in form books or found on the Internet.

Discard both misconceptions. Drafting contracts, instruments, or legislation is neither a secret order into which one must be initiated by long and painful steps nor a skill acquired by osmosis from the label "attorney-at-law" on your stationery; and it is certainly not a matter of mindless imitation of the past. Drafting is, perhaps, the critical lawyering skill. Like other lawyering skills, drafting can be done well or poorly. Doing it well is something that can be taught, learned, and ingrained into one's habits.

Legal writing, including drafting, has enjoyed a rebirth of emphasis. Legal drafting courses are commonplace, covering both transactional documents and various forms of litigation. The skill is also increasingly taught across the curriculum in conjunction with contracts, property, trusts and estates, business associations, real estate, legislation, administrative law, and other courses involving transactional documents and instruments.

The practicing bar has awakened as well, realizing that the drafting habits and style of yesterday are inadequate in the new millennium. Clients appreciate and even demand documents that are clearly and simply written, that are captioned and organized with the user in mind, and that are free of hoary and obscure legalese.

The courts grow increasingly impatient with the unnecessary litigation that follows the trail of a badly drafted document. Courts are especially critical of statutes and regulations that are so obscure – and often intentionally so – that what they mean and the impact that they have on the citizenry remains unknown until they have undergone judicial interpretation. And in response to after the fact and somewhat far fetched claims about the meaning of a contract, courts are not hesitant to point out, testily, "Well, if you meant that, why didn't you say so?"

Even the legislatures and regulators have stepped in, passing laws that require certain kinds of documents to be written in plain English or satisfy some readability formula. Indeed, some legislatures have required that their own legislation and administrative regulations be drafted according to specific readability criteria.

This book deals with the process, techniques, and forms of expression used in drafted documents. It focuses on how one drafts private-law documents and legislation, not on the details of the substantive law that the drafter must deal with. Exactly what should be contained in a will, lease, partnership agreement, construction contract, contract for the sale of residential property, landlord-tenant statute, or any other type of drafted document is determined by substantive law of the jurisdiction, the subject-area expertise of the drafter, and the desires of the client. Texts that focus on substance rather than form exist for drafting these specialized documents.

The objective of this book is to enable the reader to produce documents that serve the needs of the client, that solve existing problems efficiently, that foresee and forestall future problems, that make for efficient governance, and that ease the tensions and uncertainties that are inherent in all forms of human social and economic intercourse. The accomplishment of those goals is the lawyer's highest calling.

This book reflects the drafting insights we have gained from our collective experience of approximately 60 years of practice and teaching legal drafting, both as a stand-alone course and as integrated into substantive courses like contracts, employment law, property, bankruptcy, and workouts & reorganizations. But in a greater sense, it also attempts to carry forward to a new generation the collective wisdom of the legal drafting community. Over the years, we have taught from or consulted many texts and articles, and those that have contributed the most to our courses and our books include those listed in the acknowledgments at the end of this book, before the index.

We thank the many students, practitioners, and teachers we have worked with over the years and whose comments and suggestions contributed enormously to this book. We also thank Joshua Ganz, Elizabeth Karb, Stacie Odeneal, and Peter Ripley, former students at the University of Tennessee College of Law, and attorney and Adjunct Professor Donna C. Looper of The University of Tennessee College of Law for their research and editorial assistance with this second edition. Professor Carl A. Pierce's comments on ethical issues were also greatly appreciated.

This book contains the full text of our Legal Drafting in a Nutshell, 3d Edition (2007), with additional exercises. Students should not purchase both titles.

THOMAS R. HAGGARD
Columbia, South Carolina
June 2007

GEORGE W. KUNEY
Knoxville, Tennessee
June 2007

Summary of Contents

PART IV.   ADDITIONAL EXERCISES   [p. 371]

Table of Contents

PART III.   DRAFTING TECHNIQUES

Page

LEGAL DRAFTING

Process, Techniques, and Exercises

Second Edition

*

Part I

INTRODUCTION

Chapter 1

A PHILOSOPHY OF DRAFTING

Imagine the following lawyer-client scenario:

Client: Hello. My name is Sam. I operate a small fruit stand down at Main and Pickens. I have been selling oranges and other fruit to the folks in the neighborhood for years, without any problems. But yesterday, a lawyer came in. He said he wanted to engage in an "orange transaction." I finally figured out he wanted to buy a pound of oranges. In a panic, I told him I needed to consult with my own lawyer first. He seemed to appreciate the need for that and said he would return "on or before 72 hours from now." Can you help me?

Lawyer: Sure. No problem. I'll draft you a contract.

The lawyer set aside the entire afternoon for the project and drafted the following:

CONTRACT, COVENANT, AND AGREEMENT OF SALE

KNOW ALL MEN BY THESE PRESENTS: Sam's Market, Inc., a Georgia corporation, doing business in South Carolina as Sam's Market, by and through Sam Jones, an individual, who is said Sam's Market, Inc.'s duly authorized and commissioned agent acting on its behalf pursuant to the applicable provisions of Georgia and South Carolina law (hereinafter referred to as "Seller"), in and for consideration of one dollar ($1.00) and other good, sufficient, and valuable consideration in hand paid this date by John Smith, an individual acting on his own behalf and not on behalf of Smith, Withe, and Deathe, LLC, of which he is a principal, (hereinafter referred to as "Purchaser"), the receipt whereof is hereby confessed and acknowledged by said Seller, does herein grant, sell, assign, transfer, alienate, and deliver unto said Purchaser, his heirs, successors, and assigns, from this time to have and to hold henceforth and forevermore, one (1) pound of each fruit named, denominated, and classified as a citrus sinensis (hereinafter referred to as "Orange"), together with all of the appurtenant rinds, skin, juice, pulp, and pits and with all rights and advantages therein.

Sam returned the next day with "said" John Smith. The contract was reviewed, signed, notarized, and recorded at the court house. The transaction was successfully consummated, with the pound of oranges being exchanged for $1.00. Sam was happy. John was happy. After being paid, Sam's lawyer was very happy indeed. And they all lived happily ever after.

Unfortunately, one does not have to look far to find actual documents that are drafted in a similar style to that parody. Briefs, office memoranda, client letters, and most especially drafted documents are full of the dull, ponderous, repetitive, pretentious nonsense that often passes for legal writing. The legal profession can no longer afford to indulge itself in this fashion.

Before we begin, you should know that every rule stated in this book is subject to exceptions. Legal drafting, like so many things, is subject to trends and fashion. Reasonable minds may differ on many of these matters. As with all legal writing and drafting, the point is communication. Remember, it is easier to tailor the form of your message to your audience than to try to force your audience to enjoy the form of your message. Use the rules, principles, and methods in this book as a default guide to contract drafting, but modify them to fit your audience and surroundings. It is best to remain flexible at all times.

A. THE CHARACTERISTICS OF GOOD LEGAL WRITING

The goal of the drafting process is to produce legally effective documents that can be easily understood by the legal and lay audience involved in the project. The words of the transactional document will govern the parties' relationship, rights, and duties. They will be considered to be the primary, and often only, evidence of the parties' intentions. Thus, carefully articulated documentation that clearly communicates its meaning to the parties, their counsel, and enforcing courts is the ideal end result.

A document can be drafted in plain English and still satisfy the requirements of the law and the purposes of the client. Avoid being a drafter who relies on less-than-plain language to achieve transactional ends. The plainer the language and the clearer the drafting organization, the more likely it is that the parties will not have differing interpretations of the contract. This should minimize the potential for litigation, or at least the risk of loss in litigation caused by a court adopting a different interpretation.

A contract drafted in this manner has at least four salient characteristics:

(1) It is *accurate,* meaning that it correctly expresses the deal.

(2) It is *complete,* meaning that all possibilities have been addressed. Look down the road, determine the range of different contingencies, and provide your client with rights and remedies to address contingencies if they occur. Focus on what could occur if one party fails to perform and is insolvent, injured, or dead. Include protections for your client addressing these possibilities.

(3) It is *exact,* meaning that it lacks *unintended vagueness* and *ambiguity.*

(4) Finally, *it is able to withstand hostile, critical review.* More likely than not, after the contract is executed, the next thorough review of its provisions will be by someone trying to break the contract or sue over the transaction. That person will focus on interpreting the docu-

ment in a vacuum, ignoring any evidence of the parties' intent not found within its four corners. Edit your contract with an eye to identifying and fixing unclear pronoun references, modifiers that may relate to one or all of the terms in a series, conjunctions that make a list conjunctive or disjunctive, introductions that make the list exclusive or inclusive, and classification or categorization systems that do not accurately reflect hierarchical relationships.

To address these elements, some drafters tend to be long and wordy. They use overlays of multiple synonyms, qualifying phrases, and arcane or legalistic prose in an attempt to be accurate, complete, and exact. All too often, the work product collapses under the weight of these techniques. It becomes filled with ponderous, repetitious sentences, paragraphs, and sections. Rather than using as many words as possible—the shotgun approach—strive to find the right word or words. This will involve considering the level of detail and generality of the words involved, as well as their potential multiple meanings and connotations.

Good legal writing, including drafting, features use of plain English and possesses five basic characteristics.

Characteristics of Plain English

1. Short sentences.
2. Definite, concrete, everyday language.
3. The active voice.
4. Presentation of complex or multi-factor information in subsections separating each element or factor.
5. Separate paragraphs and sections, with headings, for separate concepts.
6. The absence of overly legal jargon, highly technical business terminology, Latin, or other foreign terms.
7. The absence of double or multiple negatives.
8. The use of multiple columns of text if the font is small.

---

1. Accuracy

The most inexcusable inaccuracies in legal drafting are those that result from sheer carelessness, like writing "employee" when the drafter meant "employer," thus radically shifting the duty from one party to another. But accuracy involves more than careful proofreading. Unless the words are chosen with care and assembled into proper sentences and paragraphs, the safe and accurate communication of ideas will fail. For example, "My client has discussed your proposal to fill the drainage ditch with his partners" is, one hopes, not an accurate expression of the idea.

Lewis Carroll fully understood the need for accuracy in communication.

"You should say what you mean," the March Hare went on.

"I do," Alice hastily replied; "at least—at least I mean what I say—that's the same thing, you know."

"Not the same thing a bit!" said the Hatter. "Why, you might as just as well say that 'I see what I eat' is the same thing as 'I eat what I see.'!"

Meaning what you say but not saying what you mean can have devastating consequences. The poor selection and arrangement of words can prevent a letter from accurately advising a client what to do. It can prevent a contract from accurately expressing the intention of the parties. It can prevent a statute from accurately reflecting the legislative purpose. Accuracy is critical to everything a lawyer does.

Certainty is a component of accuracy and ambiguity is the opposite of certainty. Put differently, an ambiguous expression is capable of two or more accurate interpretations, depending on the perception of the reader. For example, if a will gives the executor authority to "pay Thomas and Sue $10,000," Thomas and Sue may accurately regard that as an instruction to pay each of them $10,000, construing the "and" in its several sense. But the remainder of the estate beneficiaries may accurately construe it as an instruction to give only a total of $10,000 to Thomas and Sue, to be held jointly. Which interpretation prevails is said to depend on the intent of the testator, but the will drafter should have reflected that intent with more certainty. After all, by the time the will "speaks," the testator is no longer with us to make his or her intent otherwise known.

2. Clarity

Poetic language is expected to mystify and challenge the reader's imagination. Thus, it is poor form for a lawyer. Uncertain referents, homonyms whose meaning must be determined from context, dangling modifiers, convoluted sentence structures, and stream-of-consciousness prose create an impenetrable swamp through which the reader must slog. These are examples of bad legal writing. The reader should be able to move rapidly and confidently through the document, understanding immediately the meaning of each word, phrase, sentence, and paragraph—and how they all tie together into a coherent whole. If the reader is left in a state of puzzlement over what the writer intended and has to go back and parse a sentence or ponder a paragraph, the legal writer has failed to communicate clearly.

Using the active voice promotes clarity. This is also accomplished by use of short sentences, writing with verbs instead of nouns or nominalizations, and keeping subjects close to verbs and verbs close to direct objects. It also helps to make the elements of a sentence parallel in structure, to be careful in word choice and usage, and to punctuate correctly.

3. Concision

Being concise means saying all that needs to be said with the fewest number of words. Concision should not be confused with brevity. A document can be concise, but not brief, if the document covers substantive terms that are both numerous and complex. And a document can be brief but not concise, if it omits necessary clarification and detail.

True concision is an essential element of good drafting. Lawyers, judges, clients, and other readers of legal writing are generally very busy people. They are not reading for pleasure. They have neither the time nor the patience to plod through page after page of excess verbiage. Nor do they need to be given information that is irrelevant to the purpose for which they are reading the document. As is true of all writing, legal writing must be done with the needs of the intended audience in mind.

If a word can be eliminated or if three words can be replaced by one without sacrificing the meaning of the sentence, do it. Similarly, if a sentence has effectively communicated the idea, then delete the second sentence that merely restates the idea in different words. Redundant paragraphs are an even greater shortcoming.

Concision is most easily achieved through judicious self-editing. At the initial stages of the writing process, the writer should focus primarily on substance and organization. After the manuscript has matured into the passable draft stage, the writer should put on an editor's hat and approach the manuscript with a critical eye and a red pen. The length of a document can often be reduced substantially by editing out wordy idioms, compound prepositions, expletives, nominalizations, redundant couplets, and passive voice constructions. The result will be a work product that is concise, crisp, and to the point. These attributes are particularly important in drafted documents.

4. Simplicity

To be "concise" means to say it in the fewest necessary words. Simplicity, in contrast, relates how those words are put together. The more substantively complex a document is and the greater the number of truly necessary words, the more important it is that they be presented in a straightforward, simple manner. A drafted document can and should emulate the simplicity of a good set of instructions: "Go to Lake Road. Turn left. Drive 3.5 miles. The house is on the right."

5. Tone

The Scylla and Charybdis of legal writing are folksiness and pompousness. The object is to steer a course between the two. Legal documents are about serious matters. They should not read like conversational English—with contractions, colloquialisms, sentence fragments, or editorial comments. Nor should lawyers ignore the conventions about what is offensive to the community, such as the use of gender-specific language. On the other hand, a legal document should not be written in stuffy, Edwardian English. Good legal writing has a professional tone.

B.   THREE TYPES OF LEGAL WRITING

Though all good legal writing possesses the attributes of accuracy, clarity, brevity, simplicity, and a proper tone, differences exist between the various forms of legal writing.

1.   Discursive Writing

In the legal context, "discourse" means speaking or writing authoritatively about a topic. The lawyer's discourse serves two different purposes—to inform and to persuade. Most documents contain an element of both. Client letters, legal memoranda, and judicial opinions are designed primarily to inform, presenting an accurate and objective statement of the law and its application to the facts at hand. Although these documents have a persuasive component, it manifests itself largely in the form of correct data and reasoning. On the other hand, briefs, memoranda in support of motions, and settlement letters are primarily intended to persuade someone to do something.

In either event, the literary form of legal discourse is that of an argument, consisting of premises from which a certain conclusion is drawn. In addition to being logically structured, this form of legal writing must also be easily readable and possess some degree of eloquence. Word choice, sentence structure, diction, cadence, and the smooth flow of ideas are all of critical importance.

2.   Litigation–Related Writing

Complaints, answers, motions, interrogatories, discovery requests, and the like are designed to satisfy both the formalities and the substantive ends of litigation. Statutes and court rules often dictate the exact form, order, and wording of pleadings.

These documents function primarily as triggering mechanisms, setting into motion the various phases of litigation. However, if done properly, these documents also inform, persuade, and channel the litigation to the writer's advantage. Although federal and many state rules of civil procedure allow for a highly abbreviated form of notice pleading, a good pleader will use every filed document to educate the court—each provides an opportunity to introduce or reinforce the theory of the case that is meant to drive the decision on the merits beneath the doctrine.

3. Normative Writing

Contracts, leases, wills, trust agreements, waivers, releases, by-laws, statutes, ordinances, and regulations all serve to establish, define, and regulate legal relationships. These documents are forward-looking and normative in character. They provide the rules that will control the behavior of the parties in the future.

Private documents like contracts, and public documents like statutes, differ from each other in some respects. The differences, however, are mainly cosmetic. The process and the necessary skills are basically the same, regardless of whether one is drafting an apartment lease or a noise ordinance. As will be discussed next, the consequences that attach when a lease is breached or an ordinance violated are also essentially the same. This book primarily addresses normative writing.

C. THE ULTIMATE CONSEQUENCE OF DRAFTED DOCUMENTS

One of the highest aims of government is to structure social relationships that are fair and just through laws that preserve individual rights and promote the common good. Drafted documents play a major role in this endeavor by creating legal obligations and remedies for those to whom a duty is owed and is unperformed. The law operates on the assumption that most people will honor their legal obligations most of the time. If the county enacts an ordinance (a public law) prohibiting the burning of leaves, we may grumble over the passing of a cherished rite of Fall, but we haul our leaves to the landfill like everyone else. If Sam contracts to sell an orange to John at a fixed price (a private law), Sam will probably honor that obligation even if he later discovers that he could have sold the orange to Betty at a higher price. If not, the law should provide a remedy or a penalty—there is no right without a remedy.

The potential for serious unintended consequences should always be in the back of the mind of every legal drafter, because its realization will instill in the drafter a strong sense of duty to be diligent, careful, cautious, thorough, and correct. A badly drafted leaf-burning ordinance, whose overbreadth of language makes it applicable to conduct that was not within the contemplation of county counsel, nevertheless constitutes the threatened use of physical coercion against anyone who deigns not to comply. A badly drafted contract of sale, through the omission of a significant condition subsequent that would have voided the transaction, nevertheless stands again as the source of and justification for the use of coercive force by the state against the unwitting and unwilling seller.

D. DRAFTING AS A FACILITATOR OF SELF–GOVERNMENT AND ECONOMIC ENTERPRISE

In a political society, especially a democracy, the laws are expected to be easily understood by the citizens, applied in an even-handed manner regardless of one's status or class, and consistent with both substantive and procedural due process. The government needs individuals with the training and aptitude to produce such laws. When one considers the chaos that results when a legislature enacts a poorly drafted law, it boggles the mind to think of the result that would inure if all laws were similarly flawed.

Similarly, a sophisticated and complex economy would be impossible without documents that provide for the future exchange of goods and services, and a legal system that makes the promises contained in those documents legally binding. A contractor would never build a house on the mere promise of future payment by the owner. And an owner would never part with the price of the construction in the mere expectation that the house would eventually be built. Commerce and enterprise could not exist. The legal drafter produces the documents that are the necessary conditions of a viable economy. It is said that our economic system depends on investors to provide the capital, workers to perform the labor, and managers to coordinate this combination of capital and labor. None of this would be possible without the drafter's assistance. The drafting skill and diligence that is required of the transactional lawyer is enormous, perhaps more than what is required of the legislative drafter.

E. DRAFTING AS A FORM OF PREVENTATIVE LAWYERING

Lawyers are primarily in the "problem" or "problem-solving" business. The buyer of a house has a problem with the condition of the house, and the seller has a problem with the buyer's refusal to close. The lawyers on both sides will attempt to resolve these problems, first by amicable negotiation, then, if that fails, through litigation. The value of the lawyers' involvement in this problem-resolution process cannot be ignored.

Though lacking the glory and glamour of the litigator, who is a backward-looking problem-resolver, the transactional drafter faces perhaps a more difficult task, that of the forward thinking problem-preventer. Although the peaceful resolution of an existing problem is a worthy endeavor, the better goal of the lawyer is to prevent problems from occurring in the first place. If done well, drafting helps accomplish that goal. If done poorly, it only creates more problems. Suppose that a manufacturer wants to retain a contractor to build a new production facility. This will be a massive, complex, expensive, and lengthy undertaking. If the drafter of the contract anticipates the problems and disagreements that are likely to arise during the course of construction and deals with them intelligently, the project will go forward to completion without difficulty. But if the contract is incomplete, ambiguous, unnecessarily vague, or unfairly favors one side, then the parties are likely to end up in litigation—while the partially constructed new plant sits in the middle of a muddy field.

F. DRAFTING AS AN INTELLECTUAL EXERCISE

Drafting is one of the most intellectually demanding of all lawyering skills. It requires a knowledge of the law, the ability to deal with abstract concepts, investigative instincts, an extraordinary degree of forethought, and organizational skills.

1. Knowledge of the Law

Drafting presupposes an extensive knowledge of both substantive and procedural law. The drafter uses the law in a manner unlike that of the brief writer, the memorandum writer, or the litigator. The brief writer uses the law to challenge or justify what has already happened. The memorandum writer uses the law to predict the legal consequences of what may happen. The litigator uses the law to determine how to characterize what has happened in its proper legal form and to then present it in court.

The drafter uses the law affirmatively, to accomplish the client's objectives. The client wants to ensure that a sales representative will not go to work for a competitor after the employment is terminated. This is not an especially easy objective to achieve. The law dealing with a covenant-not-to-compete is complex, and the drafter must work through the intricacies to produce an agreement that is both effective and enforceable. Or, the drafter may discover that a living will, in its mandated statutory form, will not accomplish all the client desires. The drafter may thus supplement it with a durable power of attorney.

In sum, the drafter must know how to use legal rules to meet the needs of the client. Although Chapter 8 more fully discusses how the drafter uses law in the drafting process, the basic principle is to harness the law by drafting clearly into or around existing legal rules and precedents.

2. Investigation

The client rarely, if ever, comes to the drafter with an already prepared, comprehensive list of facts the drafter will need to prepare the document. In part, this is because the client usually does not know what the document must contain to serve its desired purposes. The drafter must ferret out these facts through investigation.

The investigation usually begins with asking the client questions. The drafter must know what questions to ask. Checklists are an invaluable tool. In addition, the drafter must know how to ask the question so that the response provides an accurate reflection of what the client truly wants or needs. For example, "Do you want to impose any conditions on your duty to purchase this house?" might provoke a negative response. But the client is likely to respond favorably to, "Do you want to require the seller to provide a termite letter as a condition of your duty to purchase this house?''

The drafter's investigation, however, cannot be limited to the information provided by the client. The client may not know if the property being purchased has had environmental pollution problems, or even realize that this should be of concern. The drafter must anticipate this as a problem, discover the information from other sources, and draft accordingly.

The investigation required of a legislative drafter may be even more extensive. One cannot attempt to regulate a complex facet of human behavior, such as the issuance of corporate securities, without fully understanding the factual context and the problems that the legislation is designed to correct. Drafters of federal legislation usually have the luxury of committee hearings, where the facts are fully ventilated. And state legislative drafters are sometimes similarly blessed. But city ordinance drafters are often left to their own resources in the development of the facts that are necessary to produce legislation that accomplishes its purposes. These matters are discussed more fully in Chapter 9.

3. Conceptualization

Another fundamental intellectual skill required of the drafter is the ability to conceptualize—in terms of both law and facts. Simply put, conceptualizing involves knowing exactly what you are talking about and finding the right words to express it.

Legal conceptualization is the easiest to understand. Legal concepts, for the most part, come prepackaged. Negligence, agency, corporation, consideration, and a host of other legal concepts have fairly fixed meanings. The task of the drafter is to choose the concept that will accomplish the client's desires.

Occasionally, the statutory drafter is compelled to create a new legal concept. Often, this is caused by new technologies. Over a century ago, the advent of the railroad required the creation of some new tort concepts. Today, the information technology revolution has spawned many new forms of misbehavior, such as unauthorized access and theft by computer, that require careful conceptualization. Or, an amorphous form of previously unregulated conduct gradually becomes socially unacceptable, like sexual harassment. It cannot be prohibited, however, until it is first reduced to a concept with identifiable dimensions.

Factual conceptualization is a bit more difficult to understand. Briefly, it involves envisioning and expressing the facts with the proper degree of generality/specificity, vagueness/precision, and abstraction/concreteness. Choosing between these alternatives is an intellectually demanding and difficult task for the drafter.

Conceptualization will be discussed more fully in Chapter 10.

4. Forethought

Most drafted documents deal with events that will occur at a future date. The circumstances existing at the time the document is drafted and the circumstances existing at the time of actual performance may be radically different. The drafter must try to anticipate those changes and deal with them appropriately. The fundamental question of drafting is, "But what if . . . ?" A good drafter is like a chess player who sees three moves in advance. Anticipating the future must also be tempered with common sense. Drafting a specific provision contingent on the sun coming up in the east would be silly. Over-drafted documents violate the principle of simplicity.

In sum, the drafter must not only anticipate what might happen, but also make a judgment about whether the contingency is likely and important enough to be dealt with in the drafted document.

5. Organization

Contractual precision is achieved through good organization. Within a document, each section should address a specific subject or aspect of the transaction. Within each section, each subsection or paragraph should carry out one function. Within each subsection, each sentence should perform one sub-task. Do not hesitate to subdivide sections, subsections, paragraphs, and sentences as needed to break them into meaningful, digestible chunks.

The drafter's job is to create order out of chaos. Doing this requires a certain kind of intellect. A disordered document is often the product of a disordered mind. The skillful drafter must take the mass of information that is to be incorporated into the drafted document and divide it up into logically related and properly sequenced units.

Good organization is essential in making a document functional—that is, capable of being used easily by the intended audience. A tenant who wants to know what the landlord's various maintenance and repair duties are should be able to find that information in one place in the lease agreement, not scattered throughout six provisions. Or, consider the confusing disorganization of a criminal statute that states the prohibition in one section and a critical exception some sixteen sections later.

The organization of drafted documents is discussed more fully in Chapter 11.

G. DRAFTING AS A LITERARY EXERCISE

Drafting not only requires exceptional thinking abilities, it also requires exceptional writing abilities. Drafting involves a combination of architectural (design) and construction (assembly) skills, albeit of a linguistic variety. The basic units are words and punctuation, instead of bricks and mortar. The words and punctuation must not only be selected with care, they must also be carefully assembled so that the document does not become incoherent.

1. Words

Lawyers are word people. Words, phrases, sentences, paragraphs, sections, contracts, and briefs are their stock in trade. The contracts, instruments, and legislation that you draft must be clear, practical, and focused so that they work by guiding the course of performance or providing the foundation for a successful lawsuit. All that is for your client's sake.

The legal drafter should be very particular about words. At the thinking stage, the drafter has clarified the concepts that the client wants to deal with in the document. Then, the drafter must find exactly the right word or set of words to mirror that concept. The drafter must know the standard dictionary meaning of words, the conventional and specialized usages, and how they have been construed by the courts—all of which may be different.

Unlike most writers, however, the drafter is not limited to the existing storehouse of words with fixed meanings. Drafters have the extraordinary liberty of creating new words or giving old words new meanings. New words are the corollary of new concepts. A contract, for example, might empower the buyer to do A, B, and C—the combination of which has no given name. For ease of reference, the drafter thus creates a new word, Z, which is defined in terms of A, B, and C in combination. Unfortunately, some drafters abuse this liberty and use definitions to create a new and incomprehensible vocabulary unique to the document in question. Such documents could just as well have been written in code. The use and misuse of definitions is discussed more fully in Chapter 14.

The drafter must also choose words that will promote the objectives of good writing discussed earlier, especially those of accuracy, clarity, simplicity, and tone. Words that create legal consequences are particularly important, because this goes to the essence of the function of a drafted document. If the drafter uses "may,"—which merely creates a discretionary authority to act—when the drafter really intended to create an absolute duty—requiring the use of either "shall" or "will"—the drafted document will be flawed. This is discussed more fully in Chapter 15.

2. Sentences

In a brief or office memorandum, a dangling participle may merely mark the writer as a poor wordsmith. But in a drafted document this may produce an ambiguity or vagueness that cannot be resolved short of expensive litigation. The drafter must have a thorough knowledge of grammar, syntax, and punctuation. These are the nails that hold the individual words together and allow them to function as a sentence.

3. Other Word Construction Techniques

The legal drafter is not limited to sentences and paragraphs and can also use devices like lists, enumerations, charts, and tabbing to achieve greater clarity and readability. These are discussed in Chapter 16.

4. Headings

A drafted document is typically organized in outline form. Each major division and sub-division has a heading. The heading describes the substance of that portion of the document at a very high level of generality. Headings enable the reader to easily find in the document, whether a statute or a contract, the exact provision the reader wants to consult.

Writing an appropriate heading is a vastly under-appreciated skill. The heading cannot be over-or under-inclusive. If a heading carelessly refers to a class of entities that is broader than those that are specifically referenced in the substantive provision itself, this will produce a contextual ambiguity. The inclusion of matters that have nothing to do with the stated subject of the heading may also be legally ineffective—the misplacement of warranty disclaimers, for example. And notwithstanding the sometimes applicable rule that headings are not part of the statute, courts have been known to explicitly resolve uncertainties in the text by reference to the wording of the heading.

H.   DRAFTING AS AN ETHICAL EXERCISE

The drafter is faced with many ethical dilemmas. Whether it is solicitation, scope of permitted representation, conflicts of interest, confidentiality, destruction of documents, or some other aspect of professional ethics, all of the rules have special applications in the drafting context. But what the rules require is not always clear. Legal ethics operate principally from the perspective of the lawyer as a confrontational advocate of a single client. The manner in which these rules are applied in the context of the lawyer as a problem-preventer and facilitator of agreement is a matter of considerable dispute among the bar.

Even if what the client wants the drafter to accomplish is not illegal or fraudulent, it may offend the drafter's sense of morality, ethics, and common decency. The lawyer is not expected to accept representation of everyone who requests it. And, contrary to the popular image of lawyers as scavengers and sharks, most lawyers do exercise discretion over the kind of client and the nature of the representation they will accept.

The drafter-lawyer, however, has an opportunity that the litigator-lawyer often lacks. The litigator-lawyer is usually faced with conduct that has already occurred, and that lawyer's decision is between representation or not, to defend the conduct or challenge it. In contrast, the drafter-lawyer is usually brought into the process before the conduct occurs. This gives that lawyer the opportunity to gently suggest to the client that what the client proposes to do, while not illegal, may be questionable. And even if the client lacks even a shred of ethics, a realization that the behavior would not enhance his or her reputation and standing in the community may be sufficient, from a strictly pragmatic point of view, to deter the client from acting in that fashion. The drafter-lawyer's function as counselor cannot be underestimated. These matters are discussed more fully in Chapter 5.

I. THE COSTS OF BAD DRAFTING

A badly drafted document may impose tremendous costs on society, on clients, and on the drafter.

1. Social Costs

A badly drafted document is an invitation to litigation. Litigation is not just a private undertaking, fully funded by the participants. Everyone pays for it. Providing judges, clerks, staff, and courtroom facilities is a fundamental function of government funded by taxpayers. In addition, contract litigation caused by bad drafting clogs the dockets. It inures to the disadvantage of those for whom litigation is simply an unavoidable consequence of human interaction. Bad drafting contributes enormously to that litigation and the resulting social cost. A high percentage of all contract cases involve issues that could have been avoided by more careful drafting.

Statutory litigation provides an even more damning testament to the social costs that flow from bad drafting. Purely factual disputes are unavoidable. But the critical issue in statutory litigation is often not what the facts are, but whether the law as drafted applies to those facts or what the statute really means. Such litigation is evidence of bad drafting and the social cost of it is enormous. Further, poor drafting, especially of criminal statutes, leads to harms not effectively prevented and the unintentional criminalization of behavior that, in a free society, should go unregulated.

2.   Client Costs

People want lawyers to forestall or solve their problems, not to create them. If a document does not accomplish the client's objectives, this could be a very expensive drafting mistake indeed. A badly drafted contract will inevitably produce misunderstandings and ill-feelings that poison the relationship between the contracting parties. It may even prevent the relationship from arising again, causing the loss of an otherwise valuable customer, client, tenant, supplier, or subcontractor. Worse yet, a badly drafted document is an invitation to litigation, and litigation is extremely expensive for the parties. Someone always loses in litigation and often it can be said that all the parties have, in some sense, lost, no matter who wins. Damages can impose a significant and sometimes crushing financial hardship on an individual or business entity.

For the prevailing party, it is often a pyrrhic victory. The costs and attorneys fees of prosecuting a valid claim may equal or sometimes exceed the recovered amount. For the prevailing defendant, it is simply the minimalization of loss, but a loss nonetheless.

3.   Drafter Costs

The drafter who produces unworkable or litigation-producing documents will eventually pay for this ineptitude and sloppiness. At best, the attorney will suffer the loss of a client. Beyond that, upon discovering that their travails are the drafter's fault, many clients not only terminate the relationship, they also refuse to pay the bill and adopt a decidedly hostile "so sue me" attitude. There is also the spectre threat of a successful malpractice suit. The disappointed client will usually spread the word among friends, business associates, and even casual acquaintances.

Beyond the client, however, aspiring lawyers need to pay close attention to detail and take pride in all their written work product for their own sake. Each document you create—your work product—is your calling card. It is on this that you will be evaluated by your colleagues, clients, opponents, and others. Documents, including correspondence, that contain typos or substantive errors, that are badly formatted, or that do not convey an appearance of well-thought-out precision and accuracy will be held against you in the court of professional reputation.

All documents that go out over your name should be proofed, spellchecked, substantively correct, neat, and well-organized. This requires a level of attention to detail that few people other than lawyers, accountants, editors, and publishers give to writing. Each error that slips out can have a damaging effect upon the way others judge your professional competence, prudence, and attention to the matter at hand. The effect is cumulative. At some point—reached fairly quickly—mistakes add up to the reader, who assumes that the author is (a) not very smart, (b) not very careful, or (c) not paying attention. None of these impressions will advance your legal career.

J. DRAFTING FROM SCRATCH

Few documents are truly drafted from scratch. Rather, the drafter will rely on something from the firm's document files, a form book, or legislation from another jurisdiction, modified only with respect to the specific details of the transaction or regulated activity. These documents may not, however, conform to the style, usage, and terminology that modern drafting practice attempts to use and may contain provisions that are inappropriate for the matter at hand. Some of the substantive provisions of the prior contract may have been included because of a specific and unique aspect of that transaction. The current drafter is unaware of the purpose of the original provision, but includes it in the new contract on the assumption that it is probably essential, although the drafter could not possibly explain why to the client. The drafter then adds some provisions unique to the immediate transaction, and these in turn become part of the collective wisdom for that particular type of document. The one-size-fits-all documents often found in formbooks suffer from similar problems. It is necessary, when using precedent documents, to critically evaluate their structure and provisions to determine if they are appropriate for the current matter. The drafter must "reset" the document's provisions. Better still is the ability to craft a document from scratch, after reviewing multiple precedent documents and understanding the context in which they were produced. Often, however, this is an unattainable luxury due to constraints of time and expense.

Chapter 2

CONTRACT DRAFTING

THE CONTEXT: THE DEAL TIMELINE: WHETHER BIG OR LITTLE, DEALS FOLLOW A PATTERN

A transaction generally follows a standard timeline or chain of events. First, the parties make contact and negotiate. A preliminary agreement is reached and they contact their lawyers, if they have not done so already. Although the key business issues have probably been addressed by the parties, there will often be significant issues left open, some of which will only become apparent to the client after consultation with counsel.

If possible, it is helpful for clients to meet with counsel prior to negotiating the basic business deal to explore the possible issues and structures for the contemplated transaction. A well prepared client can then bargain for an issue or structure with the other party from the very beginning. This may result in key issues being resolved in your client's favor with little or no discussion or quid pro quo. This might not be the case if the opposing party was just as prepared, left the issue open, followed up with his or her own counsel, and then negotiated the point.

As the parties proceed with full, formal documentation, due diligence (detailed factual and legal investigation), begins. Usually one party will produce documents and information relevant to representations and warranties that are being negotiated.

The definitive transactional documents are finalized and signed, and further due diligence and other pre-closing activities take place. Then the closing occurs. This is the point at which the majority of the consideration changes hands. Payments or deliveries may be made directly, party-to-party, or through an escrow, the preferred route for all but the most basic transactions. Escrows provide the parties with the security of knowing that although they have parted with their consideration, it will not be delivered to the other party until that party's deliveries are complete. In case of a dispute, the escrow agent can hold all consideration already delivered and maintain the status quo pending the dispute's resolution. There may be a post-closing adjustment period as well.

Contract negotiation and documentation is an exercise in *selling*. In the process, you are selling three things. You are:

(1) Selling the parties on executing the documents at the present time;

(2) Selling the parties on voluntary performance, after the document has been executed; and

(3) Selling a later court or other entity on enforcement, after voluntary performance has ceased.

These three sales goals undermine each other to some extent. Consider the tension between selling the parties on execution, which tends to imply documentation with few, if any, teeth, on the one hand, and selling the parties later on voluntary performance, which is furthered by fairly detailed documents that contain both carrot and stick provisions tailored to the particular parties. Balanced documents that accomplish all three sales goals require careful consideration before and during the negotiating and drafting process.

In the private law context, contracts are probably the most common form of drafted document. Wills, trust agreements, and various corporate and business documents—all of which are very substantive-law specific—comprise the remainder. Within the contracts sub-category, various types of contracts also tend to be very substantive-law specific. The desired substance of any particular type of document is beyond the scope of this book. Nevertheless, some generalizations are possible about contract drafting.

A. THE ROLE OF THE CONTRACT DRAFTER

Being a transactional lawyer involves a mode of analysis different from the litigation model that traditionally dominates law school, especially the first year curriculum. In the litigation model, one extracts rules of law from cases or statutes, examines a given set of facts, spots the issues, applies the law to the facts, and reaches a conclusion. (IRAC: Issue, Rule, Analysis, Conclusion). At every step of the way, one is dealing with "givens": facts that have already happened, laws that have already been made by legislatures and courts (even when one is arguing for a change in law). This is not to say that they cannot be argued, emphasized, or shaded in the advocacy process, but at core, they are fixed.

Transactional practice is different. It involves understanding the parties' deal and then translating the business terms into a transactional structure that uses contract, commercial, and other business law principles to govern the parties' relationship. It also involves making an appropriate record along the way as negotiations and documentation continue so that, should the deal break down and litigation ensue, litigation attorneys can present the case in the light most favorable to the client. The key here is that nothing, or at least very little, is a "given." There are notions of what is customary or what is the "market" approach or rate, and regulatory systems may affect what is possible to achieve with a given transactional structure. But the attorney is creating the structure and the provisions along the way in a manner that creates the most benefit for the client by harnessing applicable law and allocating risk and reward. This means determining what facts or states of nature should form the basis of conditions precedent to the transaction moving forward, what factual matters should be the basis for representations and warranties, when and how the transaction should terminate, if needed, and what sources of recovery should be available in the event of loss.

This is not to say that the same attorney cannot serve as a transactional lawyer and a litigator. Rather, the attorney should be conscious of which role is being played, and adjust his or her mode of thinking accordingly. Too often, especially with new attorneys, there is a tendency to look at transactional law and deal documents with the eyes of a litigator rather than a transactional planner. The transactional focus is on constantly improving the structure and utility of the documents.

B. RECURRING PROBLEMS IN CONTRACT DRAFTING

Transactional documents are an opportunity to prevent and plan for future litigation. You should think about how to integrate concepts from other sources and experiences into contracts. Transactional lawyers draft to fall within or to avoid the ambit of particular statutory or case law. What contract remedies would be available under the common law if the contract makes no provision for them? How can this common law result be altered in the contract? What is the evidentiary significance of various parts of the contract in later litigation? What can be done to render these portions admissible evidence? How can they be drafted so that they are favorable evidence for either party? Contract drafting provides an opportunity to use and reinforce a full range of substantive legal skills.

A review of the case law shows that contract litigation centers around the following problems, most of which are a result of poor drafting. If contract drafters consistently avoided these problems, contract litigation would diminish significantly. A great deal of this book is about the avoidance of these problems.

1. Unintended Contracts

Contract formation often begins with something that might appear to be an offer or even a full contract, but the originator intends it only to be a preliminary negotiation or an inquiry. The other party also frequently responds with something that is in appearance one thing, in intent another. Later, when it is to the advantage of one of the parties to do so, that party will claim that the correspondence was an offer/acceptance or a counter-offer/acceptance, thus creating a binding contract. Usually, objective appearance will prevail over subjective intent.

Drafters working with a client at the preliminary stages of a transaction should, if this is the client's intent, expressly indicate in the document itself that the letter or proposal is merely a preliminary inquiry, counter-inquiry, or an invitation to entertain offers and that the author reserves the right to terminate the negotiations at any time without prejudice. In other words, the terms stated in these documents are not necessarily intended to be the final terms of any agreement.

Often, however, even after the parties have agreed on all the principal terms, they still do not intend for their agreement to be binding until these agreed-upon terms are reduced to writing, the document is signed by both parties, and copies are exchanged. This preliminary document is sometimes referred to as a letter of intent. It should be conspicuously captioned as such and contain a comprehensive disclaimer of contractual intent, indicating that the document is neither a contract nor the memorial of an oral contract and that the parties do not intend to be bound until the designated formalities are followed. Even with these drafting safeguards, letters of intent are a minefield for the unwary. Many lawyers try to avoid them altogether.

An even more dangerous form of letter of intent is one that does in fact contain some binding promises, such as maintaining the status quo, keeping the negotiations secret, and not negotiating with anyone else until all the details are worked out. Here, the drafter must take particular care to indicate which provisions are binding and which are not. The better practice may be to make these two separate documents, one expressly binding, the other not.

2. Documents Intended to be Contracts that Fail

Regardless of the intent of the parties, the law will not necessarily enforce every promise that a person makes. Often the parties will sign a document intending to be bound by it, one of them will have a change of mind, and the other will discover that the promise is, indeed, unenforceable. The primary problems here are the lack of any recited or provable consideration and the incompleteness of the document.

With limited exceptions, to be enforceable, a contract must be supported by mutual consideration. There must be a bargained for benefit conferred or a detriment suffered by each party to the contract. Consideration takes a number of forms, including cash, promissory notes, letters of credit, transfers of property, services, transfers or surrender of rights, assumption of another's duty or liability, or mutual promises. Generally, lack of consideration is not an issue in real life, especially as the modern conception of consideration focuses on the "bargain test" rather than on notions of sufficiency or adequacy, yet it bears remembering. In some jurisdictions there are presumptions of consideration that arise when a written contract recites that consideration has been "had and received" or similar formulations.

Consideration is also an issue when one party's contractual obligations are supported by a third party's guaranty of payment or performance. In such a circumstance, the guarantor may not appear to be receiving consideration for the guaranty as the only parties receiving benefits are those to the contract being guaranteed; the guarantor appears merely to be gratuitously sticking its neck out for another. Some transactional lawyers put their minds at ease over the guaranty/consideration issue by ensuring that the guaranty states that it is being given by the guarantor to induce one or both of the parties to enter into the primary transaction and having the guarantor sign the guaranty *before* the parties execute the primary transactional documents.

The drafter can easily resolve consideration problems. Either ensure that the contract contains mutual promises, or recite that consideration has been paid to support the one-party promises contained in the contract. Do not leave it up to the courts to imply the return promise that is necessary to make the express promise enforceable. Consideration recitations should also be considered more than a formality. In some jurisdictions, proof that the consideration was not actually paid may defeat the contract. The drafter should ensure that it is paid. Similarly, if the promised exchange is one that might be construed as a gift, and the recited consideration is very small, then a court might regard it as nominal consideration—"consideration" in name only— which is to say it is not consideration at all. To be an enforceable contract, the document must also contain all of whatever the courts in that jurisdiction regard as the essential terms. Because of the liberality with which modern courts supply missing terms, few contracts fail completely for this reason anymore. But any contract that has to be salvaged in this way reflects poorly on the drafter.

3. Contracts Containing Gaps

A document may contain all of the essential terms of the transaction, thus qualifying as a contract, and yet be incomplete with respect to what turns out to be important details. Often, if the omission was unintentional, the parties acting in good faith can resolve these matters as the need arises. But sometimes, at the time of contracting, the parties will consciously decide to defer agreement on some matters and thus include an agreement-to-agree provision. To prevent such an agreement from being regarded as illusory, the drafter should either impose a good faith bargaining requirement, identify an objective basis for supplying the terms, or provide for mediation or binding arbitration.

In the absence of a later agreement between the parties, the missing terms must be supplied by a court. Extrinsic evidence may show that the parties had a contemporaneous understanding about this term that simply did not make it into the written contract. This presents a parol evidence problem. The UCC gap-fillers are available to supply some missing terms in commercial contracts. Beyond that, there are course of performance, course of dealing, and usage of the trade provisions that provide possible terms. And, there are some common law rules about what a court should imply if a contract is silent on a particular term.

So, the missing term can usually be supplied one way or another. However, it may be a term that one or even both of the parties would never have agreed to originally. And, it nearly always comes only after expensive litigation. This is a result the contract drafter must seek to avoid.

4. Ambiguous and Unnecessarily Vague Terms

The object of good drafting is to communicate clearly the meaning and legal significance of the provisions of the document, thus reflecting the purposes and intent of the parties. If the parties have honestly agreed in substance but the document does not reflect that agreement because of ambiguous or unintentionally vague terms, these drafting flaws may provide a way out when circumstances change to the disadvantage of one of the parties. In this way, ambiguity and unnecessary vagueness are common causes of contract litigation.

5. Unanticipated Events

Almost all contracts deal with what will happen at some future time, ranging from one day to many years. This causes the drafter two related problems. First, at the time of contracting, the parties may be operating on a set of assumptions that later turn out to be incorrect. The parties assumed that the subsoil was sandy loam, when it turns out to be solid rock. Second, at the time of contracting, the parties may have assumed that something was going to happen in the future, an assumption that turns out to be false. The parties assumed that the government would not impose an oil embargo, but the government did.

The contract law doctrines of mutual mistake, impossibility, commercial impracticability, and frustration-of-purpose allocate the risks of these unforeseen events, but they are a poor substitute for conscious risk-allocation by the parties themselves. Neither the parties nor the drafter can anticipate and deal with every possible contingency that might arise later. A surprising amount of contract litigation, however, deals with events that could have been anticipated, but were not. The conscientious contract drafter must always draft with the all-important "but what if. . .?" question in mind.

C. TYPES OF CONTRACTS

From the drafter's perspective, contracts come in three basic types. In the first, offer, acceptance, and performance are virtually simultaneous—buying an orange at Sam's fruit stand, for example. Drafted documents are often not used here, because no need exists for them. If, however, there are representations, warranties, covenants, or conditions that survive beyond the initial exchange, then drafted documents are appropriate for what is termed a "sign and close" deal.

In the second type, the contract is formed but performance is delayed. These transactions are said to be "delayed and closing" deals. The performance is still of a discrete variety. Once the transaction is complete, the parties generally have no further dealings with one another. In simple, day-to-day transactions, the contract is often oral and the professional drafter is not even involved. Dick agrees to sell Jane his used legal drafting book at the end of the fall semester. But quite apart from the requirements of the Statute of Frauds, contracts calling for the future performance of complicated and expensive obligations, like the sale and purchase of a corporate subsidiary, cannot safely be predicated on an oral agreement and a handshake. The drafter plays a critical role in the formation of this type of contract.

The third type of contract involves an ongoing relationship between the contracting parties, either for an extended or an indefinite period. Employment contracts, collective bargaining agreements, partnership agreements, joint ventures, and major construction contracts are examples of this type of contract. The skills of the drafter are acute in this type of contract, mainly because of the possibility of unexpected events. In deciding how many of an infinite number of contingencies should be dealt with in the contract, the drafter must assess the nature of the relationship between the parties, their past transactions, their reputations in the business community, and either count on the parties being able to resolve unforeseeable problems or provide an alternative mechanism, such a mediation or arbitration. The objective is simple: make it work, by whatever means are necessary.

D. THE PARTS OF A CONTRACT

Regardless of type or subject matter, the typical contract consists of the following parts:

1. Title.
2. Introductory paragraph, including the parties and the date of agreement.
3. Recitals or a Statement of Background Facts.
4. Definitions.

5. Core substantive provisions, including consideration, conditions, closing.

6. Representations, warranties, covenants, indemnities, guaranties, releases.

7. Events of default and remedies.

8. Boilerplate.

9. Signature Blocks.

10. Exhibits and Attachments.

The overall organization of a transactional document or group of transactional documents follows a group of rules:

- General provisions before specific ones.
- Important, central provisions before others.
- Rules before exceptions.
- Separate provisions or sub-sections for each concept.
- Technical, boilerplate, housekeeping, and miscellaneous provisions located last, before the signature blocks.

1. Caption or Heading

Generally, begin the first page of any transactional document with a title in all caps, centered, and in bolded type. The title should identify the type of contract using a generic term, such as "Lease," "Prenuptial Agreement," or "Asset Purchase Agreement." For example, **RESIDENTIAL LEASE, CONTRACT OF SALE,** or **EMPLOYMENT CONTRACT**.

2. Introductory Paragraph

The first paragraph of the agreement identifies the parties by their full legal names and the type of transaction they are documenting, indicates the defined term names that will be used later when referring to both the document and the parties, and provides a reference date for the document. Ensure that all parties' names and other information (such as state of incorporation) are correct—using defined terms means they will not come up again until the signature blocks. Beyond these items, there is no need for further detail. Leave that for the recitals and the body of the contract.

The introduction paragraph is not numbered. It should be in this form:[1]

> *This [Agreement, Lease, etc. as appropriate] ("[Defined Term]") dated [as of], 20xx, is between, [a Corporation, Limited Liability Company, General Partnership, an Individual, etc., as appropriate] ("[Defined Term]") and, [a Corporation, Limited Liability Company, General Partnership, an Individual, etc., as appropriate] ("[Defined Term]") [add additional parties as needed].*

For example:

> *This asset purchase agreement ("APA") dated September 21, 2010, is between Mayfield & Associates, LLC, a Delaware limited liability company, ("Buyer") and Bronson Construction, Inc., a California Corporation ("Seller").*

Note the, form used to define a term. These defined terms should be used consistently throughout the document. For ease of future use of this agreement as an exemplar for future transactions, choose generic defined terms like "Buyer," "Seller," "Landlord," "Tenant," etc. This allows a change of party name in the first paragraph to ripple or flow through the document automatically when the document is used as an exemplar in a subsequent matter.

3. Recitals

Preambles or recitals set the context for the agreement and are useful in later interpretation. They also provide a place to list related transactional documents and other things that may be part of the transaction as a whole but are otherwise not referenced in the particular agreement itself. Preambles or recitals do not need to be preceded by the word "whereas" and it is not necessary to title the section "Recitals," although you will no doubt run into those forms (and those who aggressively adhere to them) in practice.

The recitals section provides the premises on which the contact is based. Some courts have stated that recitals are not part of the contract. This is not correct. Recitals are as much a part of the contract as everything else in the

---

1. Bracketed—[ ]—text in examples is optional language or language needing replacement when drafting a specific provision. Brackets should be deleted when using these provisions.

document. The difference is that recitals are not promissory in form; they are statements of fact or belief. However, they serve other important functions and should be drafted with care. Each recital should be written in plain English, and should be preceded by a capital letter numbering or ordinal system (just like this section of this text). In the recitals, include facts that will help a later reader grasp the nature, purpose, and basis for the agreement.

A recital might explain the purpose of the contract. This could be important if one of the parties later tries to avoid the contact under the doctrine of frustration of purpose. Or, a recital might state a mutual understanding of fact. This could later pave the way for avoidance of the contract under the doctrine of mutual mistake. Facts stated as a recital might also be relevant to whether a breach qualifies as a material breach, since the recital will establish what is important to the parties. For example, if a particular brand of pipe is important to the owner of a house being constructed, then the recital should indicate this and, to further ensure that a court will strictly enforce the contract, explain why. If the body of the contract contains a "time is of the essence" clause, include a recital that demonstrates why time is so important. Neither the clause nor the recital will ensure that the courts treat lateness as a material breach, but these provisions will certainly help.

Recitals are powerful medicine. Some courts have held that recitals are conclusive evidence of the facts they state. Recitals often provide background information that becomes relevant in the computation of damages. For example, a contract recital might list the profits that the enterprise has enjoyed over a certain period, thus easing proof of damages in the form of lost profits. Examples of appropriate facts for recitals include: (i) the relationship and goals of the parties, (ii) the nature of the transaction, and (iii) other transactional documents and things associated with the transaction. Take care to be accurate and not to include unnecessary facts in the recitals—they may be used later in litigation to prove that which they state. When in doubt, be more general than specific in the recitals. Avoid the temptation to recite everything.

An appropriately drafted recital may also prevent a contract from being declared unconscionable for either procedural or substantive reasons. If a particular provision could appear to a judge to be harsh or unfair to one of the parties, and thus subject to a later unconscionability challenge, the recital should explain why the provision was included and indicate that the apparently disfavored party fully understands its implications.

Recitals, like definitions, should not contain obligations or promises. If an assertion of fact is unilateral, and is in essence a warranty by one of the parties, then it should be in the substantive sections of the contract with other warranties and be correctly labeled.

4. Statement of Consideration and Agreement

Most contracts include a statement of consideration near the beginning of an agreement. Examples of statements of consideration include the following (which range from archaic and legalistic to plain English):

> *NOW, THEREFORE, premises considered and in consideration of the mutual covenants and agreements hereinafter set forth and in consideration of one dollar ($1.00) paid by Seller to Buyer, the receipt and adequacy whereof is hereby acknowledged, the Seller and Purchaser hereby covenant and agree as follows:*

—or—

> *In consideration of the mutual promises set forth in this Agreement, the parties agree [as follows]:*

—or—

> *[Accordingly] The Parties agree:*

The second formulation is preferable to the first or third, as it retains the notion of agreement and bargain and transitions a reader from the recitals to the main body of the agreement. Further, it strips out all the excess verbiage that seems to elevate form over substance by suggesting that this recital of consideration will make the contract enforceable even if it is not true. Although this may be correct in limited circumstances–option contracts (Restatement (Second) of Contracts § 88), for example–the law is not uniform in this regard, and the lengthy chant about consideration may give false courage, a sort of whistling in the dark while walking by a graveyard. Better is the short statement of agreement that follows recitals that describe the transaction, including the bargained for nature of the exchange of covenants and other provisions that can aid in interpretation or demonstrate consideration.

5. Definitions

Defined terms are powerful tools that can decrease the length and increase the readability of substantive provisions. They allow you to lay out the full meaning of a complicated concept that must be addressed without cluttering the substantive provisions with litanies of near-synonymous terms. At the same time, they increase the readability of your document by unpacking your provisions. In the same way that nicknames can make it easier to refer to a person, defined terms simplify reference longer, more detailed concepts.

For example, one definition of the word "claim" might be: "Any right to payment, whether or not such right is reduced to judgment, or is liquidated, fixed, contingent, matured, disputed, legal, equitable, or secured, or a right to an equitable remedy for breach of performance whether or not such right to an equitable remedy is reduced to judgment, fixed, contingent, matured, disputed, or secured." If this definition is provided for separately in the document, the single word "Claim" can be used when needed in the contract's substantive provisions and its broad meaning is included without need for the litany.

This example raises another issue, because this definition was taken from the Bankruptcy Code, specifically 11 U.S.C. § 101(5). If there is a body of law that covers the concept you are trying to express, consider incorporating this law into your contract. In doing so, you must consider the effects of future amendments or repeals of the statute. Should you define the term with a reference to the citation of the statute alone? Or would your contract be more effective with a recitation of the current statutory definition because the citation will likely change? In any event, should you include the phrase, "as it may be amended from time to time"?

Terms may be defined throughout the contract "on the fly," as it were. This is especially appropriate for terms that are used only in one section or group of sections. If they are used more widely or if there are many of them, provide a defined term section at the beginning of the contract (after the recitals and statement of consideration) rather than at the end. For easy reference, put definitions in alphabetical order.

6. Substantive Provisions

This is the main body of the contract. It contains the promises that each party has made. The provisions should be tightly organized, so that everything dealing with a particular aspect of the transaction is brought together in one place. It should contain informative headings and sub-headings, using proper outlining techniques.

Substantive provisions are constructed out of five basic types of provisions: covenants or promises, conditions, representations, warranties, and waivers or releases. These basic building blocks of contracts, covered in depth in Chapter 15, are the mechanisms that give all the substance to the contract. Covenants establish rights and duties of the parties; conditions trigger, excuse or modify those rights and duties; representations and warranties capture statements of fact made by one party and relied upon by another party; and waivers and releases extinguish rights and duties.

Notes, leases, and other contracts that govern continuing relationships feature specific sections that delineate events of default, procedures for declaring a default, and the remedies available to a non-defaulting party upon declaration of default. These provisions are the special concern of the lawyers because, at the front end of the deal, the negotiation and documentation stages, the clients are primarily focused on performance, not on default.

7. Housekeeping Provisions

These provisions deal generally with the administration of the contract. Some of them, but not all, are what is known as boilerplate. The term "boilerplate" is derived from the word for flat-rolled steel used to make steam engine boilers and the hulls of ships. In the early days of newspaper syndication, the term was also used to describe the plates of non-movable type that publishers delivered to local newspapers and which contained the syndicated text and advertising that the local paper would adopt in full, adding its own stories and advertising to supplement the syndicator's standard material. The term was first used in the legal context in the mid–1950s, as a reference to standard clauses found in most contracts. That is the salient characteristic of good boilerplate—it contains language that allows it to be used in a variety of documents. Unfortunately, many people, lawyers and non-lawyers, similarly believe in the inviolability of the wording of whatever boilerplate they are familiar with, however hoary with age the verbiage might be. This is nonsense. Boilerplate terms can be worded in a variety of ways. There is no reason why these provisions cannot be as well drafted as the rest of the document.

These provisions are routine, but like real boilerplate making up a boiler in the hull of a ship, or a local paper, they are very important. Without good boilerplate, the boiler explodes and the ship sinks, or the paper consists only of local interest stories and farm reports. To refer to these provisions as "housekeeping" provisions, as we do here, as when labeling anything "miscellaneous," tends to denigrate their importance. The term "boilerplate," when understood, reflects their fundamental importance as well as their routine nature.

Boilerplate provisions commonly come into effect when there is a problem or disagreement between the parties, so they must be carefully considered and drafted to ensure that they work correctly when they are needed most. They represent another opportunity for prelitigation planning, something that every lawyer must keep in mind when drafting documents.

Although it is fine for a lawyer to prepare boilerplate in advance that can be inserted without change into almost any document, the lawyer should always consider whether the needs of the client would be better served if the provision in question were individualized. The standard no-assignment clause, for example, could be modified to allow assignments under certain conditions or to a designated class of potential assignees.

Never take boilerplate for granted or simply incorporate standard provisions without thought and analysis. When reviewing contracts drafted by others, do not just skim the boilerplate: Much mischief can be hidden there. Students and lawyers that do not have a transactional practice sometimes claim that this advice is hypertechnical and exaggerated. But transactional lawyers confirm the import and potential mischief of boilerplate. Just as beginning litigators are advised never to agree to the "standard stipulations" in a deposition without knowing what those stipulations are, transactional attorneys are cautioned against taking the other side's boilerplate for granted.

The more common housekeeping provisions include the following:

Severability Clause. This clause states that if a court declares any part of the contract void, the remainder of the contract is unaffected. The converse of a severability clause is a prohibition against severance and partial enforcement. Whether the clause allows or prohibits severance, in most cases it simply mirrors the contract law default rule that would be applied even in the absence of a clause. That is, if a court has declared one provision void or unenforceable, the court will usually treat the other provisions of the contract as still in force unless doing so would destroy the purpose of the contract or create unfairness. If, however, there is any question about how the default severability rule would be applied if a particular term in the contract is declared void, then the drafter should, by all means, make this express.

Choice of Law. This identifies which state or national law the parties want the court to use in construing and enforcing the contract. Conflicts law provides a default choice. Before deciding whether to alter that, the drafter should carefully compare the law in the various jurisdictions that might qualify. Although the courts generally defer to the desires of the parties on this matter, choice-of-law provisions are subject to certain limits. Since a court might refuse to defer to the parties choice of law, the drafter should always draft with the default choice in mind.

Modification. Most written contracts require that any changes, amendments, or modifications also be in writing. Although UCC § 2–209(2) recognizes the efficacy of these no-oral-modification provisions, the courts in both sales and non-sales contract contexts are often quite liberal in finding a waiver of the provision. This notwithstanding, NOM clauses may serve a useful prophylactic effect.

No Waiver. The contract may provide that the failure of a party to insist on strict performance in one instance does not constitute a waiver of the right of that party to insist on strict performance if another default occurs. Again, although these provisions are useful in some situations, the courts often circumvent them by finding that the parties implicitly modified the contract through a course of performance. The duty of the drafter here is to advise the client of the possible consequences of non-enforcement, the contract language notwithstanding.

Merger Clause. This clause indicates that the contract is the final and complete agreement of the parties with respect to this transaction. If properly drafted, a merger clause will prevent a party from even alleging that the agreement also includes some additional or different terms from another source—usually oral. The common law parol evidence rule performs the same function, but to prevail under that approach usually requires litigation, while a merger clause may forestall such litigation.

Assignment and Delegation. The parties may want to expressly prohibit or permit the assignment of contract rights or the delegation of contract duties to a third party. Dealing with the issue in this manner is much easier than litigating it under the murky common law rules on assignment and delegation. Although a reference to an assignment of the contract is frequently construed as referring to both rights and duties, the drafter should deal separately with the assignment of rights and the delegation of duties.

Survivability. This provision deals with the effect the incapacity or death of one or more of the parties will have upon the continued validity of the contact and who may enforce it.

Notices. If the contract requires notices, this provision will describe to whom the notice must be sent, where, and by what means.

Liquidated Damages. This is one of the most important of the various boilerplate provisions. Some drafters prefer to put liquidated damages provisions in their own section, along with other remedy provisions such as one expressly stating that a decree of specific performance is appropriate and consented to. Liquidated damages clauses, however, may not be viewed with favor by all courts and the drafter should review the controlling law of the jurisdiction to ensure that the provision is enforceable and will not be construed as a penalty. It should also specify whether or not the liquidated damages are the parties' sole remedy in case of default or breach.

Force Majeure. This clause will excuse delay or discharge the duty of performance altogether if certain extraordinary events occur. Natural disasters, war, governmental actions, labor disputes, and unavailability of transportation are commonly included in the list. Formbook *force majeure* clauses vary enormously, however. Before borrowing a *force majeure* clause from a commercial formbook, the drafter should carefully review each item on the list to ensure that excusing delay on that basis is consistent with the intent and objectives of the client and that nothing has been omitted.

The drafter should also ensure that the list is consistent with other provisions of the contract. For example, the *force majeure* clause must be consistent with the liquidated damages clause or a cost-overrun provision. The contract cannot simultaneously provide for liquidated damages per day of delay or an enhanced fee and also excuse the delay entirely.

Other Matters. In specialized contracts, the housekeeping section might include some other matters. This section, however, should not be used as a catch-all for provisions that do not fit anywhere else. A housekeeping section that is full of miscellaneous substantive matters is evidence of poor conceptualization and organization. Either create a separate section for these other substantive provisions or include them in the section that relates most closely to their substantive content.

8. Signature Blocks

This provides a place for the parties and witnesses to sign. Type the name and title below the signature line. Signatures should not be on a separate page if possible; include some of the text of the contract on the page on which the signatures appear. In addition, on extremely important documents, the parties should initial each page at the bottom.

Before the signature blocks, there is usually some introductory language. Like other standard provisions in agreements, there is a tendency for this language to become ossified and to exhibit dated legalese. It is better to delete phrases such as "In Witness Whereof" and "as of the date that first appears above" and use a modern, plain English provision.

The Parties agree to the terms of this Agreement, above.

-or-

To show that they have agreed to the terms of this agreement, the Parties have executed this Agreement below on [the date stated on page 1 or the date(s) indicated below].

-or-

Agreed.

To avoid inconsistent dating of documents, the introductory language to a signature block often refers to a date appearing on the first page or paragraph of the document. This is fine, as long as that date is filled in. Too many times, in the heat of closing, the parties simply flip to the last page of the agreement (which they have already reviewed many times before in negotiations), and fail to note that the date on page 1 has been left blank. In another form that is common in practice, the agreement is dated "as of" a date contained on the first page (filled in early in the drafting process) and the signature blocks are undated or contain the dates of execution by the parties. In such a case, it is a good idea for the contract to specify which date is the effective date.

Take care with party names and make sure you get them *exactly* right. Especially easy to miss are issues of punctuation, such as commas and periods, and descriptors of limited liability status, such as "LLC" or "Inc." For example "Allen Bates & Lebowitz LLP" could be a limited liability partnership that is the successor to "Allen, Bates & Lebowitz" a general partnership and is legally distinct from the former entity, a general partnership including professional corporations. Many jurisdictions do not prohibit the formation of entities with very similar names, which might differ only by a comma or spelling out the word "and" rather than using an ampersand (&). Train your eye to notice details of this nature. It is embarrassing when the client catches the mistake at the closing. It is even worse when the error is not uncovered until it is the subject of later litigation.

9. Date

If the date was not included in the lead paragraph, include it here.

10. Notarization

If the contract is to be notarized, the notary's statement or "jurat", signature, and seal come last, before any appendices, exhibits, schedules, or other attachments.

11. Appendices, Exhibits, Schedules

Many complex commercial, financial, and corporate contracts include an appendix containing exhibits and schedules. An exhibit usually consists of a document that is relevant to, but not a part of, the agreement itself. In a multi-party transaction, the contract between Acme Corporation and Beta Corporation may build on or interface with the contract between Beta Corporation and Charlie Corporation, which could be attached as an exhibit to the Acme/Beta contract. A schedule, on the other hand, is properly a part of the agreement. It may consist of a list of persons to whom certain notices must be sent, list of contracts, leases, or other assets, important but tedious technical data, computation formulas, and even standard boilerplate provisions promulgated by government regulation or industry trade groups.

Certain sections of agreements are designed to elicit information from the parties to the agreement, such as lists of existing indebtedness, contracts, subsidiaries, etc. Those items should be included as a schedule to the agreement or identified as having been delivered under the agreement. Identification of the schedules can be by sequential numbering or lettering, or may correspond to the numbers of the sections addressing this information in the agreement. Rather than leaving the form of schedules as an open issue to be resolved after the parties have signed the main transactional documents, negotiate and agree to them up front. This will avoid later disputes when one party will have gained or lost negotiating leverage. This establishes that everyone knows what is expected and helps to avoid later, disruptive disputes.

Where an agreement calls for the execution and delivery of instruments or other, related documents, consider attaching forms of these documents as consecutively numbered or lettered exhibits ("in substantially the form of Exhibit A to this Agreement.") As with schedules to an agreement, it is the best practice to negotiate the form of supplemental documents up front, rather than leaving them for negotiation and preparation after execution of the main agreement. Among other things, this will force the parties and counsel to really think through all aspects of the deal and make appropriate arrangements for all foreseeable contingencies. This practice can make for bulky documents. However, the benefits generally outweigh the extra work and paper expended on the front end to prevent disputes later.

Consider including complicated provisions dealing with special aspects of the transaction (complex valuation or pricing formulas, for example) as exhibits. This is common practice in real estate transactions, where a meets and bounds description of property can be long and cumbersome. It is often used in purchase contracts, where pricing formulas and worksheets can be complex, but its use can be expanded into many other areas of practice.

Reference appendices, exhibits, and schedules in the table of contents.

The appendix should have its own table of contents and be consecutively paginated, even if some of the enclosed documents have their own internal pagination.

E.   EXEMPLAR CONSIDERATIONS

To save time and expense, maintain exemplars from prior deals so that they can be accessed and tailored for a new transaction quickly. This is most easily accomplished by maintaining files in word processing format in separate folders on your computer system along with an index listing file names, document title, and comments (e.g. "LeaseLL.txt, Lease of Real Property, Landlord Oriented"). When a similar matter arises, you will be able to consult the index, pull up the exemplar, and proceed to tailor the document to the specifics of the new deal. This technique will greatly speed your revision of the document. If your agreements use generic defined terms for parties and other deal specifics you can then change these items in the preamble and definitions sections, and proceed to review and modify the substantive provisions. Remember, laws and practices change, exemplars do not. Always understand what substantive provisions and legal phrases mean. Do not simply parrot a document. It may be outdated.

Finally, remember that an exemplar from a prior transaction was, at best, right for that transaction, not the current one. It represents a negotiated compromise of issues that were in play in that prior deal. Said another way, it represents an allocation of risk and reward, benefit and burden, between those parties at that time. This being the case, it is best to view the exemplar with a critical, not an accepting, eye and reset the provisions to a neutral position or one that favors your client before proposing the document to the other side.

F.   AMENDING CONTRACTS

Often, contracts and other transactional documents require amendment after they have been executed. There are three basic methods of amending a contract.

The first is crude but effective: the parties manually change the provisions by hand, striking out or inserting text on the original document and then initialing each change. It may be a good idea to add new signature blocks at the end of the document, or on a separate sheet, where the parties re-execute the agreement as amended.

The second method is to prepare a second document, entitled "Amendment Number to [name original document]," and then to specify the amendments that are being made, perhaps including recitals that give context to the amendment for later use in understanding what went on and why the document was amended. In essence, this sort of amendment acts as an instruction sheet for later use in virtually cutting and pasting the two documents together into the new, resulting agreement.

The third method is called "amending and restating" the document. Using this method, the original contract terms, as amended, are written out or typed fresh as a new contract. The contract can be prepared to reflect the original contract date, the amendment date, or both. This is the best method for situation where there are many amendments to be made at once. Sometimes, an original agreement has been amended piecemeal many times using the second method described above, and it may make sense to amend and restate the amendments. This would result in the original agreement accompanied by a consolidated amended and restated set of amendments.

In choosing the method used, consider how often the document will be referred to by the parties for guidance. If the answer is seldom, then either of the first two methods may be used effectively. If it will be reexamined often, amending and restating, or restating amendments is appropriate. The major risk in embarking on a complete restatement of a document is that it may reopen issues for negotiation that had been previously settled.

Amending an existing contract can require as much care, thought, and skill as drafting one. First, if the existing contract has a clause that not only prohibits oral modifications but also dictates the form of any modification, then those form requirements must be satisfied.

Second, the drafter must ensure that the modification is either supported by consideration or, if the modification affects UCC Article 2 goods, that it meets the "good faith" test of UCC § 1–203. Contract modification is perhaps the most important time that the issue of consideration comes up. A contract to modify an existing contract must generally be supported by mutual consideration. It is good practice to make sure this is the case by providing for consideration on both sides of the deal (the one-dollar-had-and-received formulation of yore), even if your jurisdiction has done away with the common law pre-existing duty rule (requiring more than a pre-existing duty to support a contract). *See, e.g.,* U.C.C. § 2–209(1) (preexisting duty rule repealed by UCC for sales of goods).

Third, the drafter must consider how changing one part of the contract may affect other parts. If paragraph 6(a) is changed from "January 15, 2008" to "January 15, 2015," and if an unmodified paragraph 67(c)(iii) still refers to "the date provided in paragraph 6(a)" as the triggering date for something else, does the amendment of paragraph 6(a) operate as an implied modification of the second provision as well?

Fourth, the amendment should identify exactly what in the existing contract is being modified and what the change is. An amendment should *not* merely say:

> *The contract dated October 23, 2008, between Able and Betty is amended to provide as follows:*
>
> (a) *Able will deliver the Series 7 drill presses on January 15, 2010.*
>
> (b) *Able is not required to ship the drill presses using the Seattle Kluless Trucking Company.*
>
> (c) *If Betty requires any additional drill presses meeting the Series 7 specifications for a period of one year following delivery, Betty will purchase those presses from Able.*

Rather, the amendment should specify what is being changed, what is being added, and what is being deleted.

> *The contract dated October 23, 2008 between Able and Betty, is amended to provide as follows:*
>
> (a) *The "January 15, 2009," date in paragraph 6(a) is changed to read "January 15, 2010." [changing the date]*
>
> (b) *Paragraph 10 is deleted in its entirety. [deleting the mode of delivery requirement]*
>
> (c) *Paragraphs 11, 12, and 13 are renumbered 10, 11, and 12 respectively.*

(d) A new paragraph 13 is added, as follows:

> *If Betty requires any additional drill press-*
> *es meeting the Series 7 specifications, for a*
> *period of one year following delivery Betty*
> *will purchase those presses from Able. [add-*
> *ing a new provision]*

When the amendment is complete, ensure that it is distributed to all those that have or had the original document and ask them to include the amendment with their copy of the original documents. When amending documents that have been filed or recorded with governmental offices, it is probably necessary for the amendments, an amended and restated document, or, at a minimum, an abstract of them, to be filed with the same office to be perfected or "good against the world." This is generally the case with recorded deeds, encumbrances, lease abstracts, UCC–1 financing statements, and the like. In refiling, thought must be given to the effect of intervening filings by the parties or third parties, and the effect of those filings and the new filings on lien priority and similar issues. Title policy endorsements are available to provide "no loss of priority" protection in some cases.

Chapter 3

LEGISLATIVE DRAFTING

Public law documents—broadly referred to as "legislation"—include codes, statutes, ordinances, regulations, rules, and anything else of a command nature that emanates from an agency of government.

A. WHO DRAFTS LEGISLATION?

Legislation comes from several classes of drafters, with varying degrees of expertise and competence. Federal and most state legislative bodies have full-time staff attorneys who do nothing but draft and revise proposed legislation on behalf of the elected representatives. The President and most governors have staff members whose sole job is to draft legislation for the administration. Administrative agencies within the executive branch nearly always have a section in the legal department that does nothing but draft agency regulations. Cities and counties usually rely on their appointed or elected attorneys, for whom drafting is only one of a myriad of duties and who sometimes work on a part-time basis. Unfortunately, some legislators and other officials, many of whom are not lawyers, think that because they were elected to enact laws they are also competent to draft them.

In recent years, there has also been an increase in the amount of legislation that was initially drafted by private sector attorneys. Trade associations and labor unions frequently use experienced in-house drafters to prepare legislation favorable to their special interests. Law firms that provide lobbying and legislative oversight services nearly always have attorneys who are competent to translate a client's desires into proper statutory form.

Those are the people who may initially draft a piece of legislation. At this stage, drafting can be a thoughtful, reflective, careful, and painstaking process. Lawmaking, however, is not very tidy; the results of this initial drafting process rarely survive intact. Once a bill is introduced, it becomes fair game and everyone is free to take a shot at it. Typically, a bill will be sent to a committee, where the amending and rewriting process begins. Whatever emerges from committee is subject to further tinkering by the full legislative body. As a matter of both style and substance, the drafting done at this stage is often—but not always—inferior to the initial proposal.

B. THE FUNCTION OF THE LEGISLATIVE DRAFT-ER

Legislation starts with an idea and ends with words on paper. The legislative drafter's primary function is not to come up with the idea. Lawyers working for a legislative drafting service are almost never expected to produce the idea; they draft what they are asked to draft. But many of the other classes of drafters discussed above do play an integral role in the development and formulation of the client's policies—whether it is those of the President, the governor, the Securities and Exchange Commission, the AFL–CIO, or the Chamber of Commerce.

On the other hand, even if formulating the idea is not within the drafter's bailiwick, the legislative drafter does more than merely ensure compliance with the technical composition and formatting rules of drafting. In between the idea and the legislation attempting to implement it lies a long and complex period of gestation. The idea or policy usually exists initially only as a vague generality; making it clear requires a host of subordinate policy choices. Even if the original idea is generally a good one, bad choices with respect to the details and implementation can quickly convert well-intentioned legislation into an instrument of oppression.

The primary function of the legislative drafter is to be instrumental in promoting good rather than bad choices at this critical stage of the process—realizing that the ultimate choice is the client's. The legislative drafter, thus, must thoroughly understand the problem being addressed, its sources and impact, and the alternative techniques and approaches that are available for addressing it. More specifically, the legislative drafter should usually consider, in consultation with the sponsor or client, some or all of the following:

- Is the legislation really needed; or can social and market forces deal with it more quickly and efficiently?

- Will the legislation deal with the problem or simply drive it underground?

- What will be the secondary effects of the legislation? For example, what will people do instead of the prohibited conduct? It could be as bad, or worse.

- What will be the long-term effects of the legislation?

- Exactly who will be benefited or hurt, and how?

- Can the law be enforced as written?

- If so, what are the costs of that enforcement, in time, money, and personnel? Are those resources available?

- What is the fundamental philosophical premise of this legislation and can it withstand the test of general application?

If the legislative client has thought through the hard questions and is determined to proceed in a particular manner, then the legislative drafter should effectuate that intent. Subverting the intent through subtle drafting techniques is one of the most unethical things a legislative drafter can do. Unfortunately, it does occur occasionally.

C. LEGISLATION COMPARED TO PRIVATE–LAW DOCUMENTS

All drafted documents serve essentially the same function. They establish the rights, duties, privileges, immunities, and other legal relations of and between the parties that are subject to the jurisdiction of the document. This is as true of a criminal code as it is of a construction contract.

Moreover, the investigatory and thinking process of creating drafted documents is basically the same, as are the rules of organization, style, and precision that are used in contract drafting.

Thus, the preparation, form, and content of the portions of a condominium lease dealing with limits on the use of the leased premises might not differ appreciably from the comparable regulations of a Housing Authority. Both are law. The lease represents the private law between two parties who have each specifically consented to its terms. The regulation represents public law between the sovereign and its subjects, whether they specifically consent to it or not.

Private law documents that are in the form of rules likewise bear a striking similarity to statutes—an employer's work rules or condominium homeowners association rules, for example. Indeed, many regard private law documents of this type as being essentially legislative in form. This chapter, however, uses the terms legislation and legislative to refer to public-law documents exclusively.

Although they share basic similarities, legislation differs from private law documents in several material respects. This difference affects how each is drafted.

1. Nature and Size of the Audience

Most private law documents have a relatively limited audience. Often, they address the relationship between only two people, with other users being secondary. This means that the drafter needs to focus only on the identity, objectives, and circumstances relating to these particular people and need not worry about other people, their objectives, or their circumstances.

Legislation, however, typically applies to a very large class of persons. It may include everyone in the country, the state, the county, or the city. Even a limited class including only the registered owners of handguns living in incorporated areas is larger than the class directly affected by the typical private law document.

To accommodate this larger audience, the legislative drafter may do one of three things. The first option is to draft at a higher level of generality than is customarily used in a private law document. This is necessary to ensure that the broad harm to be prevented or the good to be promoted, varying only in its factual detail, is covered by the legislation. This approach, however, may fail to recognize that while the intended audience shares a primary characteristic, important subsidiary differences also exist. A one-size-fits-all piece of legislation inevitably encounters difficulties of enforcement, efficacy, and fairness.

The second option is to draft a complex set of rules or exceptions to deal with these differences. It is almost impossible, however, to get all of these details right in the first instance. Experience and a better understanding of the problem and the various possible solutions frequently suggest the need for alterations. However, the legislative process is cumbersome; amendments fine-tuning the legislation may be impractical.

The third option is to draft in fairly general terms, but also to empower an administrative agency to fill in the details with regulations, which are much easier to enact and change than the legislation itself. The drafter following this alternative, while giving the agency sufficient discretion to deal with the complexities of the problem, must also provide guidance to prevent the agency from taking the legislation beyond its intended limits.

Legislation also has an audience that private-law documents lack. The parties to the transaction usually initiate the enforcement of private law documents by filing a lawsuit; a court or arbitrator then makes the enforcement decision. This is also true of some legislation, such as a statute establishing a tort unknown to the common law or one creating additional damages for some types of contract breach. But, the enforcement of most statutory law is initiated by a third party—either a police officer, a government official, or an administrative agency. Legislation must be drafted with this audience in mind. If a criminal statute is so complex and obscure that a police officer cannot understand it, the statute may end up being enforced in a draconian fashion or not at all.

In addition, many administrative agencies not only initiate the enforcement process, through the filing of a charge or complaint; the agency also initially adjudicates it, with limited judicial review. Although this involves some technical separation-of-powers problems that the drafter must also address, the point is that the adjudicator pathos of an administrative agency may differ from that of a court. The drafter, thus, must understand and draft with that audience characteristic in mind.

2.   The Need for Precision

Vagueness can be a viable technique in drafting private law documents. The transaction costs of being completely thorough on every detail may outweigh the advantages. The parties may be content to rely on each other's good faith and their ability to work out details and disagreements later. The legislative drafter does not, or should not, enjoy the same degree of latitude. Whether civil or criminal, a statute is a command by the sovereign to do or refrain from doing certain things, with sanctions for noncompliance. Fundamental fairness requires that a citizen be on notice of what is required. Criminal statutes that do not meet this test may be void-for-vagueness. The courts are more tolerant of civil statutes that are unduly vague; but such statutes reflect both poor drafting and poor governing.

3.   Policy Considerations

The drafter of private law documents has a limited duty to discuss the broader social and policy implications with the client. Serving the client's interest is the primary concern. The legislative drafter's involvement in policy is usually somewhat broader. In a sense, the public is that drafter's ultimate client. The legislative drafter, however, can assist the proximate client—whether it is an individual legislator, a committee, or the head of an administrative agency—in making the correct policy choices.

4.   The Need for Factual Data

Because of the wider audience, the more precise focus, and the policy considerations, the legislative drafter usually requires more facts than the average private law document drafter does. Often, this factual data is developed in legislative hearings, which the drafter must then study and assimilate into the drafting process. At lower legislative levels, the drafter is often the one who does the investigation.

5. Political Considerations

The legislative drafter working for a specific legislator, committee, or agency can never ignore the political opposition. The drafter must assess what they are likely to object to, how strong they are, and what they might compromise on. The ultimate decision will be made by the client. But, the drafter can assist by suggesting alternative provisions that basically meet the client's objectives, but that are also more palatable to the opposition.

The drafter should warn the client about crippling amendments. Complex legislation involves an interaction between the various provisions. Section 2 may be essential to the structural integrity of the statute. If it is deleted by floor amendment, this might render the entire statute incoherent. Thus, if Section 2 is likely to have significant opposition, then that opposition should be accommodated before the bill is introduced if possible. Alternatively, the drafter should have a substitute bill prepared that both accommodates the opposition and still advances the objectives of the client, albeit perhaps to a lesser degree.

Sometimes, political pressures will force the drafter to abandon the standards of the profession. This often occurs when the opposing political factions are at deadlock over a particular provision but agree in principle on everything else. The drafter is thus instructed to draft an ambiguous provision that could be construed either way, leaving it to the courts to sort the mess out. This is drafting in one of its most degenerate forms.

6. Fitting the Document into an Existing Body of Law

Sometimes, the parties to a private law document will have other existing relationships (also created by private law) that the drafter must take into account and accommodate to ensure consistency in the legal relationship. Similarly, some of the rights and duties that will inure to the transaction may have already been the subject of statutory regulation—a landlord-tenant statute, for example. The private law drafter must take that into account and draft accordingly.

This task of accommodating the new document with existing documents and laws, and making sure it all fits together, is much more difficult for the legislative drafter, because there is so much more to consider. The drafter must take into account everything touching on the proposed legislation—constitutional provisions, existing statutes, administrative regulations construing that legislation, court opinions on that and related subjects, attorney general opinions, existing statutes in other jurisdictions, common law rules, and even learned treatises and law reviews.

7. Legal Limits

Distinct from "making it all fit together" is ensuring that the newly drafted document is within the limits imposed by superior law. The private-law document drafter is bounded by numerous legal constraints with respect to substance. A waiver of rights under the Age Discrimination in Employment Act must contain certain things to be effective. The inclusion of some provisions in a consumer loan agreement may render it void.

The legislative drafter is subject to fewer such constraints. The principal limits are those imposed by the hierarchy of legal authority and the scope of delegated powers. Federal and state constitutions are the highest legal authority. In addition to establishing the structure of government, their principal function is to limit legislative authority. The most important limits are like those contained in the Bill of Rights. No conscientious drafter should draft legislation that patently infringes upon an individual's freedom of speech. Other constitutional provisions are more technical in nature. State constitutions, for example, often prohibit statutes dealing with more than one subject. Although the concept of a subject virtually defies identification, the legislative drafter should be cautious before including in an ordinance on the location of mobile homes a provision also dealing with the tax consequences of certain municipal bonds. The more important constitutional limits are the substantive ones. Unfortunately, legislative clients often instruct the drafter not to worry about possible constitutional limits, erroneously believing this to be an exclusive function of the judiciary.

Similarly, within the hierarchy of authority, federal law generally overrides inconsistent state law and state law controls over inconsistent local law. Drafters working at one of these subordinate levels of government must draft with the superior law in mind.

At the federal level, a great deal of legislative law is not in the form of statutes; it is in the form of administrative rules and regulations. State administrative law is also fairly extensive. Administrative agencies, however, do not have inherent power to enact law. The existence and scope of their authority depends on a delegation from the legislature. The administrative drafter must always keep the scope of that delegation in mind, because rules that go beyond it will be declared void.

The administrative drafter must also comply with administrative procedure acts that dictate the procedure an agency must follow when promulgating a rule or regulation. The statute that created the agency may impose additional procedural requirements. And since administrative agencies are generally considered a part of the executive branch of government, they are often subject to executive orders as well. In sum, the administrative drafter must be aware of a myriad of both substantive and procedural limits.

The courts and their administrative offices are a final source of legislation-like rules. Here, the principal limits flow from the doctrine of separation of powers. The question is whether the court has the authority—constitutional, inherent, or statutory—to promulgate a particular rule or whether this is exclusively a legislative function. The judicial rule drafter must draft within those often uncertain constraints.

8. Legislative History

Bargaining history is sometimes used in contract litigation to determine the intent of the parties. So, too, with legislation. The person who drafted the legislation will frequently write the committee report or a summary explaining the bill. If the drafter is a part of a legislator's staff, the drafter may also prepare the remarks the sponsor will make when introducing the legislation. These reports, comments, and speeches can put a gloss on the legislation that may not be apparent from the words themselves. Because of the fictional nature of legislative intent and its capacity for abuse, many courts take a decidedly jaundiced view toward this manufactured evidence of intent. Nevertheless, it remains an important part of the legislative drafting game.

9. Form, Style, and Usage

Within limits, the private law document drafter is free to adopt whatever conventions of form, style, and usage that meet that drafter's fancy. A failure to follow sound drafting principles may cause difficulties in interpretation and enforcement; but it generally is not going to disqualify the document. The legislative drafter does not enjoy that freedom. Legislatures, legislative drafting services, administrative agencies, and even the various court systems frequently use drafting manuals and rules that explicitly dictate the form, the style, and the usage that must be adhered to when drafting legislation. The content of these manuals and rules may differ in material respects, and some of them are better than others. Nevertheless, the in-house legislative drafter must adhere to these manuals or risk being terminated. A private attorney drafting on behalf of a client should follow these rules because the document will eventually be brought into compliance anyway—and there is a significant risk of a mistranslation occurring during that process.

D.   THE PARTS OF A STATUTE

Statutes typically consist of several discrete parts, as follows:

1. Title

Statutes and constitutions frequently require that legislative enactments contain a title that describes the purpose of the legislation, identify the statutes that are being amended or repealed, and comply with other formalities.

A BILL TO AMEND CHAPTER 3, TITLE 16, CODE OF LAWS OF SOUTH CAROLINA, 1976, BY ADDING SECTION 17 SO AS TO PROHIBIT HARASSMENT AND STALKING, TO PROVIDE DEFINITIONS, TO PROVIDE PENALTIES, AND

TO AUTHORIZE TEMPORARY RESTRAINING
ORDERS; AND TO REPEAL SECTION 16–3–1070,
RELATING TO THE CRIME OF STALKING.

As in this example, titles are usually fairly long and are
typed in all-caps, making them difficult to read. The title of
a bill, however, is not to be taken lightly. Legislation without
a proper title may be void.

2. Enacting Clause

Constitutions or statutes also often prescribe the exact
language of enacting clauses. Under federal law, legislation
must be introduced with the following:

Be it enacted by the Senate and House of Representa-
tives of the United States of America in Congress
assembled.

The exact wording of enacting clauses varies from state to
state. Legislation that does not contain these magic words is
void.

3. Short Title Section

This indicates how the legislation is to be referred to
colloquially.

This chapter may be cited as the "Fair Labor Standards
Act of 1938."

4. Findings

Comprehensive enactments frequently contain a section
outlining the legislative body's findings. These may consist
of specific facts, an identification of the problems to be
corrected or purposes to be served, the underlying policy,
how the law is to be construed, and other matters of a
general nature.

Some findings are of critical importance. For example, if
a bill states that Congress has found a particular type of
transaction to impose a burden on interstate commerce, then
the courts are likely to accept that finding without further
proof in any individual case. In the absence of such a
finding, however, a court might resolve the issue differently.

Legislative findings are also relevant to the question of
intent, which determines how the courts will construe the

substantive provisions. If the literal words of a section are capable of two interpretations, then the stated purpose or policy of a statute may determine which controls. The legislative drafter, however, should not rely on the findings section to salvage what is an otherwise poor job of drafting.

5. Definitions

As in private law documents, definitions in statutes are usually consolidated into one section. However, in a statute with many chapters, if a term is used in only one chapter, that is probably the best place to put the definition.

6. Substantive Provisions

The core of a statute is an identification of the conduct that is prohibited, required, allowed, disallowed, or made a condition of a particular entitlement.

7. Enforcement Mechanisms

Unless it is a criminal statute, where enforcement is presumed to be by the attorney general or district attorneys, a statute will generally contain a provision indicating who may enforce it, how, where, and under what time limits. If enforcement is primarily by a government official or agency, the statute should indicate whether it also creates a private cause of action and, if so, on whose behalf. A statute should contain a limitations period and indicate whether the limitations period is jurisdictional and thus not subject to waiver, estoppel, and tolling. It should indicate whether jurisdiction lies in federal court, state court, or both. If an administrative agency will be involved in the application or enforcement of the statute, then the statute will need to contain provisions dealing with its establishment, powers, duties, and procedures. The statute should also indicate, directly or indirectly in the provision dealing with civil suits, whether plaintiffs are required to exhaust these administrative procedures. Of increased importance is whether alternative dispute resolution mechanisms, if agreed to, must be used to enforce the statute.

8. Remedies or Penalties

Whether criminal or civil, the penalties, sanctions, and other remedies that are available for violations of the statute are usually contained in a separate subtitle or subchapter. The availability of attorneys fees should also dealt with here.

9. Housekeeping Provisions

These typically include the following:

Effective Date. This presents a more complicated drafting problem than might appear at first. A provision simply stating that the statute is effective when signed is inadequate, since it does not indicate what the consequence of effectiveness is. For example, a change in procedural law could be construed (1) as applying only to cases that are filed after the signing date; (2) as applying also to cases that are pending and have not gone to final judgment at the time of signing; or (3) as even applying to cases that are already on appeal or still subject to appeal.

Similarly, a change in substantive law could be construed as applying only (1) to operative events that occur after signing; (2) to all operative events, regardless of when they occurred, except those on which the statute of limitations has run or which have already been litigated and are barred by the doctrine of *res judicata* or collateral estoppel; or (3) to operative events that occurred prior to signing that are, however, subject to pending litigation at the time of signing.

The courts have construed the effective date of statutes in all of these ways, and possibly others. Whatever the legislative intent with respect to retroactivity, that intent should be made express.

Savings Clause. A savings clause preserves rights and duties that have matured and proceedings that have begun before the effective date of the statute. A cause of action that has accrued or a crime that has been committed remains actionable, even if the underlying statute is being repealed by the new one.

Repeals. If one statute is replacing another, the existing statute must be repealed—subject to a savings clause discussed above. Older statutes sometimes contained a general repeal: "All laws that conflict with this law are hereby repealed." This is sloppy drafting since it suggests that the drafter does not know what existing laws are in conflict. It is also extremely dangerous. It presents the courts with the difficult task of determining when a conflict exists. If the two statutes can be reconciled by giving each of them a particular construction, should the court do that? Or should it declare a conflict and treat the earlier statute as repealed? The drafter should not leave these matters to chance. If a proposed statute conflicts with a prior statute, the legislative client should decide whether to amend the proposal, modify one or both of the statutes to resolve the conflict, or repeal the prior statute in whole or in part.

Termination Date. Occasionally, a statute will contain a date certain for termination. More common are specific provisions stating that particular sections lapse after a certain period of time.

Severability. As is true with private law document severability provisions, these are generally unnecessary in legislation because the courts already have the inherent power to sever illegal provisions and enforce the remainder. Conversely, courts also have the power to ignore a severability provision and to declare the entire statute void if severance of a key provision would render the statute arbitrary or unenforceable. Nevertheless, most statutes contain a severability clause.

Appropriations. This provision will indicate the amount, the source, and the recipient of any monies necessary to enforce the statute. Unfortunately, it is a trick of the political process to enact conspicuously a popular piece of legislation but quietly fail to include any money for implementation.

Preemption. Although general rules exist for determining when a federal statute preempts a state statute or a state statute preempts a local ordinance, an express provision will avoid litigation over the issue.

E.   AMENDING STATUTES

1.   When Are Amendments Drafted?

Often the drafter will be asked to draft amendments to an existing statute. Here, there is no reason why the drafter cannot devote as much time and effort to the planning and investigating functions as is spent in drafting a statute in the first instance. As a matter of substance, the drafter should also be sensitive to the broader ramifications of the amendment. Will it create internal inconsistencies? To make it workable, will other provisions also have to be amended? Will it create insurmountable enforcement problems? These and other problems of this type should at least be brought to the attention of the sponsor.

The professional drafter may also be called upon to prepare an amendment to proposed legislation when the bill is either in committee or as something to be proposed as a floor amendment. Time and sponsor-demands permitting, the drafter should again take as much care in the wording and content of the amendment as the original drafter did. This is not always possible. Legal drafters are often asked to prepare amendments during the heat of battle, as it were, while the legislation is being actively considered by committee or the legislature itself. These "yellow pad" amendments are rarely great examples of the drafting art—but that is not the fault of the drafter.

2. The Parts of an Amendment

Amendments consist of two parts. The first part contains what is called "vehicular language." This simply indicates that the bill is amending an existing statute.

Section 1. The Fair Labor Standards Act is amended by adding the following new section:

This is then followed by the substance of the amendment, with the new section being put in quotes:

"Section 405. An enterprise located in the District of Columbia that is engaged in the manufacture of...."

3. What Amendments Do

An amendment generally does one of three things. First, it may add language to an existing statute. This may consist of an entirely new section (use *adding*), as in the above example, or merely a word or phrase in a particular section (use *inserting*), as in the following:

Section 1. Section 15–4–2006(c) is amended by inserting "or mules" after the word "horses."

Second, an amendment may remove a word or phrase or an entire section (use *striking*), as in the following:

Section 16. Section 401(k) is amended by striking the words "unless otherwise provided for by state law."

-or-

Section 16. Section 401 is amended by striking subsection (k).

If Section 401 contains sub-sections following (k), these will have to be redesignated, as follows:

Section 17. Section 401 is amended by redesignating subsections (l) through (t) as subsections (k) through (s) respectively.

If an entire title, chapter, or major portion of a statute is going to be deleted by an amendment, this is usually dealt with in terms of repeal.

Section 7: Title V of the Livestock Inspection Act of 1943 is repealed.

Third, an amendment may both add and delete, as in these examples:

Section 3. Section 499(c)(4) is amended by striking the word "children" and inserting "dependent minors."

Section 10. Section 15–678–2000 is amended by striking subsection (4) and by inserting the following:

"(4) Homestead property that is located in a Class IV city is subject to a tax rate of . . . ."

It is unnecessary to add "in lieu thereof" or "in its place" since it is assumed that the insertion will replace the deleted material.

Amendments that deal only with the specific language that is being added or deleted can be very confusing since the reader must constantly move back and forth between the original text and the amendments. An alternative approach, and one that is most appropriate when numerous changes are being made to a particular provision, is to present the amendment in the form of a complete restatement of the amended section.

Section 13. Section 647 of the Livestock Inspection Act is amended to read as follows:

"Section 647 . . . . ."

Although this gives the reader a clear understanding of what the amended section will do, it does not put the reader on notice of the specific changes that have been made. Thus, some legislative rules require that amendments be in both the specific and the restatement form.

4. Amendments Changing a Judicial Interpretation or Construction

Decisions by a court of last resort construing a statute may precipitate an amendment if the legislature disagrees with the court's interpretation. Some of these disagreements are fairly technical in nature, with the amendment resolving the matter cleanly and clearly.

But corrective legislation is far more difficult to achieve, and the end result more problematic, when the court's interpretation (often reflected in a series of decisions) radically alters the meaning or scope of a significant piece of social legislation. This requires the legislature to re-determine its own policy and find ways of expressing it in ways that the Court cannot ignore. If the matter is of widespread public concern, legislature must also accommodate the political demands of the public—which produces all kinds of strange things. It is not surprising that amendments of this type are often poorly conceptualized, obtusely worded, and thus the source of a whole new generation of litigation designed to determine exactly what the new law means.

Ideally, a legislative body that is attempting to enact this kind of amendatory legislation should, through its drafting staff, do several things. First, if the alleged objective is to codify the law as it was before the offending decision, then a legislature and its drafters must have a thorough understanding of what the law was generally thought to be before the decision in question. But frequently there will have been a variety of views among the various courts of appeals, with the court of last resort taking its own approach. Congress must decide which, if any, of the other views it wants to codify and find words that will do that accurately.

Second, drafting this kind of amendatory legislation requires a thorough understanding of what the court did in its offending decision. Congress and its drafters must know exactly what the problem is before they can purport to correct it.

Third, watershed decisions by courts of last resort not only affect the meaning of the specific statute before the Court, they nearly always have a ripple effect on similar statutes, with the lower courts assuming that the court was articulating a broad principle of interpretation. The legislative drafter, thus, must determine the scope of this ripple effect and deal with it. Suppose, for example, that the court determines that Provision A in Statute 1 means X–Y. But before the legislature can gear up for an amendment, which usually takes several years, the lower courts felt compelled to construe provisions in substantively related statutes in a similar fashion. If the legislature, in specific response to the court decision itself, later amends Provision A in Statute 1, what effect does this have on that kind of provision in the other statutes? Some courts will say that if the legislature wanted to amend these other statutes, it could and should have done so expressly. Other courts will imply an intent that the amendatory language to Statute 1 also apply to these other statutes.

One familiar with statutory law does not have to look far to find amendatory statutes that were enacted by legislatures without a sufficient amount of the understanding referred to above. Inevitably, this results in enormous legal confusion and years of clarifying litigation.

Chapter 4

THE RULES OF INTERPRETATION

Rules of statutory interpretation that are imposed by statute are usually quite specific and the courts apply them like any other rule. But the common law rules of both statutory and contract interpretation are more like general principles or presuppositions. Moreover, many of these interpretive admonitions are capable of canceling each other out. For example, if one rule favors the statute dealing with a problem specifically over a statute that deals with the problem only generally, and another rule favors the most current statute, how should the courts deal with a general statute that is, however, more recent than the specific statute? Indeed, the invocation of a particular rule of interpretation often merely serves to justify an interpretation reached on a different basis; and sometimes the courts ignore the rules altogether when it suits them.

Although that view may possess some validity, the drafter cannot totally ignore these various rules of interpretation. They are, however, something to be drafted around rather than tools for achieving a particular result. Put differently, if a document is properly drafted, then a court will probably not need to rely on these rules when construing the document. Heed the advice of Voltaire: "Let all the laws be clear, uniform and precise: to interpret laws is almost always to corrupt them."

Most of these rules are applicable to both statutory and contract interpretation, although some are unique to a particular type of document. The rules of interpretations have two sources: statutory and common law.

A. STATUTORY RULES

Many codes contain an umbrella interpretation or construction provision that applies to all the statutes within the code. For example, Chapter 1 of Title 1 of the United State Code provides, in part, as follows:

> *In determining the meaning of any Act of Congress, unless the context indicates otherwise—*
>
> > *words importing the singular include and apply to several persons, parties, or things;*
> >
> > *words importing the plural include the singular;*
> >
> > *words importing the masculine gender include the feminine as well....*

Some of the state statutory rules of interpretation are modeled after the Uniform Statutory Construction Act. Often, these rules are in the form of mandated definitions. For example:

> *The term "person" includes corporations, companies, associations, firms, partnerships, societies, and joint stock companies.*
>
> *A "quorum" of a public body is a majority of the number of members fixed by law.*
>
> *Words importing the singular include the plural.*

A legislative drafter in a jurisdiction with such a statute must draft with these rules and definitions in mind. Sometimes, a statute itself will expressly dictate how it is to be construed.

> *The rule that statutes in derogation of the common law are to be strictly construed does not apply to this Act.*

Perhaps the most bizarre example of a legislatively mandated judicial rule of interpretation is contained in the Civil Rights Act of 1991. It provides:

> *No statements other than the interpretive memorandum appearing at Vol. 137 Congressional Record S 15276 (daily ed. Oct. 25, 1991) shall be considered legislative history of, or relied upon in any way as legislative history in construing or applying, any provision of this*

Act that relates to Wards Cove–Business necessity/cumulation/alternative business practice.

One is not surprised to discover that the referenced memorandum is totally unenlightening on the issue—which apparently was the intent of Congress.

B. COMMON LAW RULES

The more frequently used rules of interpretation are those that have been fashioned by the courts themselves.

1. Intent Controls

This is the cardinal rule of interpretation. Intent controls, whether it is the intent of the legislature in passing a statute, the intent of the testator in writing a will, or the intent of the parties in making a contract. But intent is really a conclusion, not a fact. The question is: How should a court determine intent? The courts follow two radically different approaches in answering that question.

a. The Plain Meaning or Four Corners Rule.

Under this rule, a court must interpret a document by the plain meaning of the words that lie within the four corners of the document. Common words are given their ordinary dictionary meaning, technical words are given their specialized meaning, and sentences are construed by reference to the rules of grammar and punctuation. Under this approach, a court construing the words of a statute will not look at the legislative history, the purpose of the statute, the harm to be avoided, the good to be achieved, or any other extraneous evidence of legislative intent. Similarly, a court construing a contract or other private-law document will not look at the negotiating history, statements either party may have made, the course of performance under the contract, course of dealing under other contracts between these parties, usage of the trade, or other evidences of intent. Although the courts frequently acknowledge the plain meaning or four corners rule, they rarely apply it so strictly.

Moreover, the rule has two exceptions—ambiguity and absurd results. The first of these is not so much an exception as it is a corollary of the rule. If a statute or contract is ambiguous—which is just another way of saying that it has no plain meaning—then the courts have no choice but to look to external sources to determine intent and thus resolve the ambiguity.

Similarly, if the plain meaning of a provision would lead to what the courts regard as an absurd result, then the courts will ignore that interpretation and adopt a more reasonable one. Suppose, for example, a city ordinance requires all bars to close at midnight. Sam closes his bar at midnight and then opens five minutes later. The bar is closed at midnight. Sam has not violated the statute, literally construed. This, however, would be an absurd result.

The trouble with this rule is that one person's absurdity may be another person's reasoned judgment. In one case, for example, the lower court held that a particular construction of the statute was "unthinkable." The court of appeals disagreed and proceeded to adopt that construction: "Quite obviously, the result we reach cannot be unthinkable; we have thought it." *Simmons v. Robinson*, 399 S.E.2d 605, 611 n. 5 (S.C. Ct. App. 1990).

b. The Mischief Rule and Other Evidences of Intent. Justice Oliver Wendell Holmes once noted that a "word is not a crystal, transparent and unchanged, it is the skin of a living thought and may vary greatly in color and context according to the circumstances and the time in which it is used." Holmes and his band of jurists did not think much of the plain meaning rule. Rather, they believed that if intent is the controlling consideration, then everything relevant to ascertaining that intent should be considered. As the Restatement of Contracts, Second, puts it, "Words and other conduct are interpreted in the light of all the circumstances...."

Chief among the circumstances this school of interpretation relies on in construing statutes is the harm or mischief the legislation was intended to correct or the good it was designed to achieve. Indeed, an extreme variant of the mischief rule goes beyond direct purpose and looks at the spirit of the legislation. This approach is sometimes referred to as the "Holy Trinity Church Doctrine," named after a case involving a New York City church that retained the services of a new rector and prepaid his passage from England to the

United States, in violation of the literal words of a federal statute that was apparently intended to stem the tide of immigration. The Court dismissed the indictment, holding that "a thing may be within the letter of the statute and yet not within the statute, because not within its spirit...." *Holy Trinity Church v. United States*, 143 U.S. 457 (1892).

Courts construing contracts and other private law documents also frequently go beyond the plain meaning and four corners of the document in search of intent, looking at the purpose of the document, bargaining history, contemporaneous memoranda, and other matters. Indeed, under the Uniform Commercial Code, usages of the trade, prior dealings, and course of performance are themselves a part of the contract and can be used to determine intent.

c. Effect on Drafters. The drafter should keep both the plain meaning rule (with its exceptions) and the mischief rule in mind and recognize that it is impossible to predict which approach a court might take in any particular case. The drafter's object, however, is to control the outcome. This has several consequences.

First, the plain meaning rule imposes an obligation on the drafter to use language that does indeed have a plain meaning. This effect in itself is a highly desirable one. Speaking to Justice Sandra Day O'Connor about an interpretation the Supreme Court gave a certain federal statute, Senator Warren Rudman said, "Congress gets very upset sometimes when you interpret statutes exactly as we have written them."

Second, if the drafter intends for the courts to take a plain meaning approach to the interpretation of the document, then the drafter should consider using express words to that effect. This can be done with a simple statement that the words of the document are to be given their ordinary meaning and by specifically excluding other possible evidences of intent.

Third, the drafter must try to imagine every possible situation that the literal words of the statute might encompass. A drafter should never count on a plausible linguistic interpretation being discounted merely because of its apparent absurdity to the drafter. Conversely, if the drafter is dealing with something in a novel manner, producing a result that might appear absurd to someone who disagreed with it, then the drafter should take special care to ensure that the client's intent is clearly and unequivocally expressed.

Fourth, if the drafter intends for the court to have broader discretion in the interpretation of the document, then the drafter should consider providing the resources for the exercise of that discretion within the document itself. This can often be done in the preamble of a statute or the recitals of a contract.

2. The Rule of Strict Construction

The courts traditionally construe certain kinds of statutes strictly or narrowly, as follows:

a. Criminal Statutes. The reason for strict construction of criminal statutes is that citizens are entitled to have advance notice of the sovereign's commands. In one case, for example, an individual had been convicted of doing something involving an airplane under a statute that made it illegal when done with a "motor vehicle," which was defined as "an automobile, automobile truck, automobile wagon, motor cycle, or any other self-propelled vehicle not designed for running on rails." Justice Holmes opined that although an airplane fit within the literal words of the "or any other" clause of the statute, an ordinary citizen would not normally think of an airplane when pondering the meaning of a "self-propelled vehicle not designed for running on rails." The drafter of criminal statutes thus needs to operate at an elevated level of clarity and precision.

b. Statutes in Derogation of the Common Law. One reason for the rule of strict construction of statutes in derogation of the common law dates back to the time when most law was judge-made rather than statutory, and the courts were jealous of their law-making prerogatives. The common law does not enjoy the same prominence today and judges are less inclined to resent legislative intrusions into the law-making process.

A less partisan reason for the continued vitality of the rule relates to the nature of the common law itself. Common law rules operate at a very high level of factual generality, and are relatively unstructured and interconnected—the seamless web. A carelessly drafted statute that alters one common law rule may have unanticipated effects on other common law rules, unless the alteration is narrowly construed.

The drafter of statutes in derogation of the common law needs to fully understand the common law rule the statute will affect and draft with a pin-point focus.

c. Statutes Depriving a Court of Jurisdiction. Here, judicial prerogatives continue to assert themselves. The courts are an equal branch of government and do not look kindly upon legislative encroachment. Indeed, the United States Constitution and state constitutions define the jurisdiction of courts. As Chief Justice John Marshall established early on, what those provisions mean is a matter for the courts to decide.

The drafter of a jurisdictional statute must be aware of both the constitutional limits and the proclivity of the courts to protect their respective jurisdictions. And even if the constitution, state or federal, allows the legislature to allocate jurisdiction, the drafter should draft limiting statutes with special care and precision.

d. Statutes in Derogation of Sovereignty. Sovereignty, the power to issue and effectively enforce commands within a given geographical area, is the factual predicate on which all law is based. Take it away, and no law exists. In the United States, this sovereignty is divided between state and federal governments and, within each, between the three branches of government. The courts, as one branch of the larger sovereignty, are thus suspicious when an equal branch purports to surrender some of that sovereignty. Alternatively, the surrender of sovereignty is regarded as an extraordinary occurrence. Thus, for either reason or both, the courts construe statutes in derogation of sovereignty strictly and narrowly.

State and federal tort claims acts are a typical example of the operation of this rule. Under the notion of sovereignty, it is axiomatic that "The King can do no [legal] wrong" and thus cannot be sued. Statutes allowing tort suits against government agents are thus narrowly or strictly construed. The drafter of these statutes must again take extra care to be specific and precise.

3. The Rule of Liberal Construction

The courts frequently state that a remedial statute must be liberally construed, so as to effectuate its object and purposes. Remedial statutes include any statute that creates or improves a remedy for an existing or newly created wrong. Most civil statutes are remedial in this sense. Thus, unless a statute falls within one of the categories covered by the rule of strict construction, the courts will liberally construe it. If that is what the legislative client desires, then everything is fine. Otherwise, the drafter must work with extraordinary precision to limit the scope of the enactment to its truly intended boundaries.

4. The Rule of *Expressio Unius Est Exclusio Alterius*

"The expression of one thing is the exclusion of another." This rule creates a negative inference that, when a document lists certain things, the list is exclusive. Suppose, for example, that a county ordinance gives Park Directors general powers to enact rules affecting the use of their parks. The ordinance also specifically provides:

> *A Park Director may prohibit motorcycles, mopeds, go carts, and other motorized vehicles on park trails that are within 100 yards of a camping area.*

Does a Park Director also have the power to prohibit non-motorized trail bikes on these trails? By implication, the answer might be no. The drafters of the ordinance appear to have gone out of their way to define what the Park Director may prohibit on certain park trails. Arguably, this was intended to be an exclusive list, despite the existence of the Park Director's general power to regulate.

In the statutory context, at least, the United States Supreme Court has limited the application of the *expressio unius* rule so that it can no longer be applied simply because something was omitted from a list. Rather, the nature of the omitted item must itself suggest that the omission was intentional. In the words of the Court, "The canon depends on identifying a series of two or more terms or things that should be understood to go hand in hand, which are abridged in circumstances supporting a sensible inference that the term left out must have been meant to be excluded." *Chevron U.S.A. Inc. v. Echazabal*, 536 U.S. 73 (2002) (citing E. Crawford, *Construction of Statutes* 337 (1940)).

In that case, a disability statute had expressly authorized employers to establish qualification standards. It stated that " 'qualification standards' may include a requirement that an individual shall not pose a direct threat to the health or safety of other individuals in the workplace." Using the *expressio unius* rule, some courts had read this as a prohibition against the exclusion from the workplace of an individual whose disability posed a risk only to that individual. The Supreme Court disagreed, noting first that risk to others was only an example of a qualification standard. But in addition, the Court found that risk to others and risk to self were not commonly paired items, so that the omission of one would not necessarily suggest a positive intent to exclude it as a permissible qualification standard. Since the disqualification of employees whose disability posed risks to themselves was otherwise "job related and consistent with business necessity," which was the broader test for a permissible qualification standard, the Court upheld the practice.

Nevertheless, the drafter should draft with the rule in mind. If a list is intended to be exclusive, then the drafter should state that expressly. If the list is not intended to be exclusive, then that should be expressed by appropriate language as well. To accomplish this, drafters frequently include the catch-all "and other" language. This, however, can also be extremely dangerous, as the next rule demonstrates.

5.   The Rule of *Ejusdem Generis*

When a sentence lists several specific items and concludes with a catch-all phrase like "and others," the rule of *ejusdem generis*—meaning "of the same kind"—provides that the general phrase is limited by the specific words that precede it. The rule is applied by identifying the common denominator of the specified items and then limiting "others" to entities also possessing that characteristic. The Federal Arbitration Act, for example, provides as follows:

> *Nothing herein contained shall apply to contracts of seamen, railroad employees, or any other class of workers engaged in foreign or interstate commerce.*

As a matter of constitutional law, foreign or interstate commerce is an extremely broad concept, covering even the farmer who grows grain for consumption by his own cattle. But for the purposes of this act, the courts have construed the phrase as applying only to workers who share a salient characteristic of those listed—namely, being literally engaged in the interstate transportation industry, like seamen and railway employees. A farmer's contract with a laborer to harvest wheat for local consumption would thus not be included in the exclusion from coverage.

The problem with the technique of finding the common denominator is that a collection of items may have several common denominators. For example, "automobiles, trucks, and buses" have all the following common characteristics: (1) they are generally driven by an internal combustion engine; (2) they operate primarily on public streets and highways; (3) they operate on land; and (4) they have rubber wheels. So what would the phrase "and similar vehicles" cover? It depends on what the operative common denominator is. If it is (1), then a horse drawn carriage is excluded, although it would not be excluded under the others. If the common denominator is (2), then a golf cart or dune buggy is excluded, but again not under the others. If it is (3), then boats and airplanes are excluded, as they would also be under (2); a boat would be excluded under (4) but an airplane would not. If it is (4), then a vintage World War II tank is excluded, although it would not be excluded under (1), (2), or (3).

To determine what is included or excluded by the phrase "and similar vehicles," a court would be required to determine the intended common denominator. But this is a power the drafter should not casually surrender to a court. It is the drafter's function, not that of the courts, to identify the common denominator and make its identity express. The application of the rule of *ejusdem generis* is, thus, evidence of bad drafting.

Some drafters, moreover, make the situation even worse by adding a phrase like: *or other vehicles [or whatever], without limitation or restriction to the generality of the foregoing.* All this does is give the courts a complete wild card in determining what is or is not included in the provision.

6. The Rule of *Noscitur a Sociis*

This means that a word is known by its associates. Put differently, the courts will construe words by reference to the context in which they appear. This is how the ambiguity that is associated with homonyms (words that are spelled the same but have more than one meaning) is frequently resolved. For example, a court rule might provide for the admission of the scientific testimony of competent witnesses. Here, "competent" is clearly being used in the sense of being an expert rather than in the sense of being sane.

The rule is also used to limit what would otherwise appear to be unqualified language. A workplace safety statute might provide:

> *In work areas, floors shall be painted with non-skid paint, yellow safety lines shall be drawn around all machinery, and all ceiling lights shall be 500 watts or greater.*

If the plant manager's office, which is certainly a work area, is carpeted, lacks a yellow line around the computer, and has a low intensity ceiling light, does this violate the statute? Probably not. The subject matter and context suggests that the requirements refer to production areas, not offices. The prudent drafter, however, should not intentionally rely on the rule as an excuse for sloppy drafting. If a word or phrase would be unclear except for the context, then clarify it. In this instance, for example, the drafter could have defined "work areas."

7. The Rule of *Reddendo Singula Singulis*

This means that the court will refer each item in a series to its corresponding item in a matched series.

> *Seller will begin the manufacture, assembly, and shipment of the goods on July 1, June 1, and August 1.*

This would probably be construed as meaning that the seller will begin the manufacture on July 1, the assembly on June 1, and the shipment on August 1, rather than the Seller would begin the entire process of manufacture, assembly, and shipment three times, on the dates indicated. The meaning of that provision would be clearer, however, if it were presented in list or chart form, thus obviating the need to rely on the rule of interpretation.

8.   The Rule of Last Modification

Under this rule, a qualifying phrase modifies only the immediately preceding word or phrase and not words or phrases more remote. Thus, "This section applies to cars, trucks, and vans that are red" imposes a color limit only on vans. The rule is intended to resolve an ambiguity of modification that the drafter should not be guilty of in the first instance. Even if that is the interpretation the drafter intended, this should have been made express by the techniques of enumeration or tabbing discussed in Chapter 16.

9.   The Rule That Handwritten Words Prevail Over Typed or Printed Words

Although all of the provisions of a contract should be consistent, the drafter should be especially cautious when some of the terms of an otherwise typed contract are added at the last minute in handwriting. If any ambiguity or inconsistency results, this rule gives the handwritten version priority. The theory is that the handwritten version reflects the conscious intent of the parties, who may not have read the typed or printed portion thoroughly. Sometimes, however, the inconsistency merely reflects last-minute carelessness. In any event, the drafter should carefully monitor the handwritten completion of a typed, printed, or word-processed contract to avoid any inconsistencies.

10.   The Rule That Written Amounts Prevail Over Arabic Number Amounts

Under this rule, if a contract provides that the price is "two thousand, five hundred and fifty-six dollars and eighty-nine cents ($20,557.89)," the lower written price might prevail. Yet, if this would be grossly unfair or clearly inconsistent with the intent of the parties, modern courts would probably ignore the rule. But if the difference was limited to the "...fifty-six" versus "$ ... 57" portion of the price, the rule would probably be strictly followed. This is a bit ironic, because studies have shown that, when confronted with both the written and the Arabic version of an amount, most people read only the Arabic version. The numerals, therefore, more likely reflect the mutual understanding of the parties.

The drafter can avoid the implication of this rule by simply presenting all dollar numbers in the Arabic form, and making sure that all the zeros and commas are correct. Numbers that do not reflect dollar amounts should be in either the written or Arabic form—but not both.

11.   The Rule That Specific Language Prevails Over General Language or Provisions

This rule means that if one statute or private law document, or a provision within those documents, deals with a subject in general terms and another document or provision deals with the subject in a specific and detailed way, the more specific document or provision controls. Thus, the drafter should be aware of any statute or private law document between the same parties that deals with the same subject matter and should make the relationship between the two statutes or documents express, rather than relying, on the court's invocation of this rule.

12.   The Borrowed Language Rule

Drafters in one state often borrow specific language, particular provisions, and indeed entire statutes from the laws of other states. Under the borrowed language rule of interpretation, a court will give great weight to how the courts of the sister state have construed their statute. This is true not only of constructions existing at the time of the borrowing, but also of later decisions. The legislative drafter should at least make the legislative client aware of this possibility. If the client wants to avoid having the statute saddled with an untenable interpretation of a court in another state, then the drafter should provide for this. A statement in the preamble, for example, could identify the source of the statute but indicate that the decisions of the courts in that state are not controlling or perhaps even relevant.

13. The Rule Favoring Agency Interpretation

Courts generally give considerable deference to the interpretation of a statute adopted by the agency charged with administering or enforcing that statute. For example, the *Interpretative Guidelines* of the Equal Employment Opportunity Commission have sometimes been treated almost as if they were formal regulations with independent legal effect. Those cynical about the rules of interpretation will note that the courts freely treat these *Guidelines* in an almost cavalier fashion when they adopt an approach the court disagrees with.

In any event, if a statute will be enforced or administered by an administrative agency, the drafter should take the agency's general viewpoint into account when drafting the statute or amendments to an existing statute. If, in the past, an agency has been casual in the application of certain procedural requirements and the legislature wants to give it jurisdiction over another matter, but also wants the procedural requirements to be strictly construed, then the drafter should take that into account. The procedural requirements should be stated in positive, mandatory, and perhaps even jurisdictional terms.

14. The Rule That a Document Must Be Read as a Whole

Under this rule, a court is governed not by the apparent meaning of words in one clause, sentence, or part of the document standing in isolation, but rather by the meaning of the document as a whole. The drafter must keep this rule in mind when reviewing a drafted document for internal consistency. The drafter may have used a vague term in one section of the document, not realizing that when the term is juxtaposed against what is contained in a later section, the vagueness resolves itself in one particular and not necessarily intended fashion.

15. The Rule of Construing Statutes *in Pari Materia*

This rule applies when two or more statutes deal with the same subject matter and have the same general purpose.

They are said to be *in pari materia*. Whether they truly are is the critical question. A statute dealing with hospitals from a tax perspective might not be *in pari materia* with a statute dealing with hospitals from a licensing perspective, even though they both deal with hospitals. Indeed, the term "hospital" might even have different meanings under the two statutes.

If the rule applies, it has several consequences. First, it requires the courts to construe two statutes in a way that renders them consistent. This variation is simply an expanded version of the rule that a single document should be read as a whole. Thus, if a statute could be construed as prohibiting certain conduct or not, a court would normally construe it as "not" if another statute affirmatively authorizes the conduct. If the two statutes cannot be reconciled, then the courts normally fall back on the rule that specific statutes prevail over general statutes.

In addition, if two statutes are *in pari materia*, then the courts will generally construe them in the same way. For example, after the courts clarified the nature and allocation of the "because of" burden of proof in a race discrimination case under the Civil Rights Act of 1964, the courts took the same approach to the "because of" proof of age discrimination under the Age Discrimination in Employment Act, since the two statutes were said to be *in pari materia*. Similarly, if one statute defines a term and an *in pari materia* statute does not, the definition in the first statute will be imported into the second.

The drafter must be acutely aware of the *in pari materia* rule during the research stage of legislative drafting. If an existing statute deals with the same general subject matter or uses terminology that the drafter intends to use in the new legislation, then the drafter should regard that other statute as being potentially *in pari materia* and deal with it accordingly. For example, since the Civil Rights Act of 1964 and the Americans with Disabilities Act both deal with employment discrimination, they have been construed *in pari materia* on several points. The drafters apparently anticipated this when they drafted the Disability Act. In one particular, thus, they chose to draft around the rule. Both statutes require "reasonable accommodation"—Title VII of religious practices and the Disability Act of handicapping conditions—if the employer can do it without "undue hardship." The Supreme Court has construed "undue hardship" under Title VII as meaning anything more than a *de minimis* cost. Since Congress intended the disability accommodation duty to be broader than that, the statute expressly defines "undue hardship" as an action requiring significant difficulty or expense. And the legislative history expressly states that the Title VII approach is not to be followed in construing this portion of the ADA.

16. The Rule Disfavoring Repeals by Implication

If a provision in one statute is arguably inconsistent with a provision in a later statute, an advocate seeking to avoid the application of the first provision might argue that it had been implicitly repealed—and, indeed, that may have been the inadequately expressed legislative intent. The other side, however, would invoke this rule. If the court accepts it, then the court will do whatever is possible to accommodate the two provisions, even if this results in a strained interpretation of both.

The message for the drafter is: Do not draft a statutory provision that is inconsistent with another statutory provision. If the intent is to repeal the earlier provision, do that expressly.

17. The Rule of *Lex Posterior Derogat Priori*

This means that a later statute takes away the effect of a prior one. Under this rule, if a 1960 statute prohibits conduct that a 1990 statute affirmatively authorizes, the 1990 statute will prevail—which is inconsistent with the rule that repeals by implication are not favored.

In its most extreme form, the rule also posits that the order of occurrence within a document controls, with a provision at the end of a statute prevailing over an inconsistent prior provision. This is also contrary to the rule that a document must be read as a whole.

18. The Rule of Construing a Document Against the Drafter

The party drafting the document usually has the advantage, in both choosing the terms to include and in wording them. Although the other party may have preferred other terms or that the terms be expressed differently, negotiating the changes sometimes does not seem to be worth the effort—except in retrospect. However, the other party can still exploit any ambiguity or vagueness by invoking this rule of interpretation. If successful, this turns the drafter's advantage into a disadvantage.

To avoid disagreements over who the drafter really was, the parties may want to include a provision stating that the document was drafted jointly and that this rule of interpretation has no application.

19. The Rule of Adopting a Construction That Favors Validity

If a particular interpretation of a contract would render it invalid or if the interpretation of a statute would make it unconstitutional, the court is unlikely to adopt that construction. For example, if a party is attempting to void a contract on the ground that its principal provision, as construed by this party, is inconsistent with the controlling statute, but the other party contends that this construction is erroneous and that the contract provision actually means something else, the court is likely to agree and uphold the validity of the contract. Similarly, if the attack upon the constitutionality of a statute is predicated only on a tenuous construction of the terms of that statute, a court is likely to reject that construction and adopt one that would be constitutional.

Draft in a way that is both unambiguous and substantively valid.

20. The Rule Favoring the Construction of Contracts in a Manner Consistent With Public Policy

Even if a relatively clear contract provision is not unconscionable or inconsistent with a common law or statutory requirement, on public policy grounds a court may refuse to enforce it or may construe it broadly or narrowly. This relatively recent development in contract law clearly demonstrates that the philosophy of contract interpretation and enforcement has moved from an emphasis on individual autonomy and responsibility, with the state playing a limited role with respect to the terms of the contract, to one of increased social control over both the process of contract formation and the substantive content of the resulting contract.

There is probably no way one can "draft around" this judicial proclivity. Rather, the drafter must simply attempt to divine what some court is later going to decide is consistent with public policy and draft with that possibility in mind.

Exercise 1

This exercise requires you to (1) identify the various rules of interpretation that a court might use, (2) specify what went wrong in the drafting process (thus making the use of these rules necessary), and (3) show how this might have been avoided by more astute drafting.

1. A provision in the State Administrative Procedures Act reads as follows:

> A petition for review of final agency decisions must be filed in Circuit Court within 30 days after the decision is rendered.

Assume that on September 1 the State Department of Environmental Control rendered a written decision denying James Joyce's application to construct a marina on Waller Creek. A copy of the decision was mailed to Mr. Joyce, but it was erroneously sent to "4567 Ulysses Street" rather than to "7654 Ulysses Street," which was the address Mr. Joyce used on his application. The person residing at the first address was in London at the time the mail was delivered and did not return until mid-October. However, she immediately sent the envelope to Mr. Joyce at his correct address and he received it on October 16. Mr. Joyce filed his petition for review on October 18.

What argument can you make that Mr. Joyce's petition is untimely and should be dismissed? What argument can you make to the contrary? How could the problem have been avoided by better drafting?

2. Assume that in 1941 the state legislature enacted a statute providing an exception to the state Blue Laws, as follows:

Notwithstanding Code § 356.1, it shall not be unlawful to exhibit publicly motion pictures, athletic sports and musical concerts and to engage therein from and after two p.m. on Sunday in counties where the United States Government has established and maintains permanent or temporary Army Forts, Naval or Marine bases.

The legislative history indicates that the statute was enacted at a time when the United States was inducting millions of individuals into the Armed Forces and providing almost around-the-clock training at facilities all over the county. Specifically, the legislature was aware that Sunday afternoon was the only time in which most members of the military were consistently free to engage in recreational activities. The statute was designed to allow them to engage in the activities listed.

The United States Government established an "Army Air Base" in Greenville County. Subsequently, the owner of the Majestic Theater in the City of Greenville was arrested for showing a movie on Sunday afternoon in violation of the Blue Laws.

What argument can you make that he should be convicted? What argument can you make that the exception applies? How could the drafters of this statute have avoided the problem?

3. A state job reference statute provides that an employer has an absolute privilege to provide certain types of information about former employees if the information is provided in writing.

George Jones, the Plant Manager at Acme Industrials, recently gave an oral job reference on Rae Bell Knight in which he stated that she had been suspended three times for being under the influence of drugs while at work. Jones had a reasonable, well-founded, and good faith belief that this was true. However, it was not true. Knight has sued Jones for defamation. Jones asserts his qualified common law privilege. Knight argues that the statute has superseded the common law rule. What argument can Jones make to the contrary? How could this problem have been avoided?

4. A federal statute bans the interstate shipment of any "obscene book, pamphlet, picture, motion-picture film,

paper, letter, writing, print, or other matter of an indecent nature." The owner of Melody Records has been arrested for sending admittedly obscene phonograph records across state lines. What argument can the owner make that phonograph records are not covered by the statute? What argument can the government make that they are? How could the statute have been drafted to avoid this problem?

5.   A state statute imposes an ownership tax on every "rifle, shotgun, archery bow, punt boat, and all-terrain vehicle that is used for hunting within the State." The money is designated for use by the State Wildlife Agency.

Sam Colt owns the rifle that his father used in World War II. He keeps it on a wall with other memorabilia of that War. He has never shot it or used it for hunting, although ammunition is still available. The State Department of Revenue has assessed a tax on the rifle, with penalties. What argument will the State make the rifle is subject to the tax? What argument will Colt make that the rifle is not covered? How could the statute be revised to make it clear that this rifle is not covered?

6.   Suppose the by-laws of a legal organization provide as follows:

> Law students and full-time faculty members may join the Law Student Division and Faculty Division by paying an additional $10 year.

Willy Wiseacre, a third year law student, has applied to join the Faculty Division. What rule of construction will prevent him from doing this?

7.   Susan Slick, representing Sam Seller, drafted a contract for the sale of goods between Seller and Bill Buyer. One provision reads as follows:

> After delivery, if Buyer determines that the goods are defective within 20 days Seller must replace them.

Thirty days after the goods were delivered Buyer determined that the goods were defective. Seller, however, refuses to replace them, claiming that the determination was not made within the requisite 20 days. What argument can Buyer make to the contrary?

8. A state attachment statute provides for a priority lien on "motor vehicles" in favor of anyone "injured or damaged by the negligent or reckless operation thereof." The object was to provide an *in rem* type of recovery. The statute does not define the phrase "motor vehicle." However, for the purposes of the state licensing and registration statute, the purpose of which is to enable an owner to establish title and to provide revenue to the state, the word "motor vehicle" is defined as "all vehicles independently propelled by gasoline, diesel, propane, any other explosive gas or liquid, steam, or electricity."

While Dave Dorset was driving his Mack Truck with an attached but detachable trailer, he carelessly turned a corner too quickly and swung the trailer into the car of Sarah Elizabeth, totally destroying her car and seriously injuring Sarah. Dave was given a ticket. He drove home, detached the trailer (which was only slightly damaged), got back into his Mack Truck and drove off—never to be seen again. Draggah Trailer Company has a lien on the trailer. Sarah, however, has used the state attachment statute to impose a lien on the trailer that is superior to that of Draggah. Draggah argues that a trailer is not a "motor vehicle" and the attachment statute does not apply.

What rule of construction will Draggah rely on? What rule of construction will Sarah rely on? Who do you think should win?

9. A state unfair trade practices act defines unfair trade practices and provides for damages to parties injured by them and for certain kinds of equitable relief. However, the statute expressly provides that "a Master in Equity shall not have the power to issue a preliminary injunction, prior to a trial on the merits, for any practice proscribed by this act." In the past, a preliminary injunction against certain types of business practices operated as a *fiat accompli*; it would put a competitor out of business and by the time of the trial on the merits, the issue would be moot.

Freddy Fender Bender Towing Service solicits business in a manner that not only arguably violates the unfair trade practices act, but also probably constitutes common law fraud. One of the victims of this practice, Straight Arrow Towing, has sued for damages under the act and also for common law fraud. Straight Arrow has sought a preliminary injunction against the practice. Freddy argues that the act prohibits the issuance of a preliminary injunction.

What rule of statutory construction can Straight Arrow rely on? What if Freddy argues that the statute preempts the field and that a fraud cause of action no longer exists for this?

10. A state statute prohibits anyone from bringing a "weapon" onto any publicly owned sports stadium, coliseum, or other facility in which sporting events are conducted. Elizabeth Borden has been arrested under this statute for possessing an ice pick at the Gotham City high school football stadium.

What rule of statutory interpretation will she invoke to challenge her conviction under this statute?

11. A law school regulation provides as follows: "Students with sight impairments, hearing impairments, or mobility impairments that have been certified as such by the Office of Student Affairs are entitled to the following rights and privileges:..." Hank Lugoff is totally blind, but his impairment has never been "certified as such" by the appropriate office. Nevertheless, he claims he is entitled to the listed rights and privileges. What rule of interpretation might he rely on to support that claim?

Chapter 5

DRAFTING ETHICS

Legal drafters are subject to the same ethical rules that govern the conduct of all lawyers. The discussion below is based generally on the ABA Model Rules of Professional Conduct, which in one version or another has been adopted in most jurisdictions. There are still some local deviations and differences of opinion about meaning. This chapter will focus more on an identification of the ethical problems facing the drafter than on providing anything more than very generalized answers to their resolution.

Concrete answers would be difficult to ascertain. Most of the ethical standards address dilemmas from the perspective of the lawyer as an advocate. The profession has not paid special attention to the ethical problems associated with drafting. Consequently, the legal drafter is comforted by less formal guidance in the form of ethics opinions and court decisions than other lawyers and must rely more on an internal ethical compass.

A. SOLICITATION

Drafters need to be concerned about several aspects of the general ethical limitations on solicitation.

1. Advertising Specialization or Concentration

Subject to the rules against false and misleading statements, a lawyer may generally communicate that the lawyer is a specialist, practices a specialty, or specializes in or concentrates on a particular area of the law. Drafters who primarily do estate work or real estate transactions can represent themselves as such. On the other hand, a lawyer may not represent that he or she has been "certified as a specialist" except under limited circumstances, although such identification is usually allowed when certification has been granted by a state agency or other organization.

2. Mass Mailings

Although advertising is generally allowed and personal solicitation is not, the line between the two is not always distinct. For example, mass mailings to strangers now seem to be permitted in some jurisdictions. Of particular interest to drafters is the question of mass mailings by real estate lawyers to real estate agents and home owners. The court decisions and ethical opinions reach different conclusions about the propriety of this practice.

3. Solicitation of Former Clients, Family, and Friends

A lawyer is generally permitted to suggest the need for legal services to former clients, family, and close friends. For example, the drafter of a will or other document may later communicate with the client and suggest the need for an update because of changes in the law or the client's circumstances. The communication with former clients must, however, be related to the former employment. A lawyer may also suggest to a family member the need for a will and then accept employment as the drafter of that will, subject to the conflict-of-interest problems discussed below.

B. COMPETENCE AND DILIGENCE

Some of the highest ethical duties of the lawyer are to be competent and diligent. The two are closely related. Mistakes often occur because the lawyer did not know any better and was too lazy to become better informed. Whenever a drafted document fails to produce the results the client expected, the client is likely to call the competence and diligence of the drafter into question. If incompetence or a lack of diligence exists, the drafter is not only guilty of an ethical violation—serious malpractice liability may also exist. Examples of drafting incompetence and lack of diligence, drawn from cases and ethical opinions, include the following:

- Giving a client a set of standard forms and instructions on how to fill them out, when the forms did not actually meet the needs of the client.

- Ignorance of the requirements of a Clifford Trust, thus creating a trust that deprived the client of the desired tax benefits.

- Failure to include the agreed upon one-year term in an employment contract, thus allowing the client-employee to be terminated before a year expired.

- Drafting a contract that violated the state usury law, creating liability for the client.

- Failure to provide properly for the intended beneficiaries of a will, thus creating liability to a third party.

- Drafting a contract containing an ambiguity that was later resolved against the client in litigation.

- Failure to obtain, in a timely fashion, a necessary signature on a mortgage, thus allowing the buyers to sell free and clear of the client's interests in the property.

The sole purpose of this book is to prepare students to be competent drafters when they enter the practice of law. Diligence is a trait that students must acquire on their own.

C. SCOPE OF REPRESENTATION

A lawyer is bound by the client's decisions concerning the objectives of the representation (unless they are criminal or fraudulent), but is only required to consult with the client regarding the means for achieving them.

1. Objectives and Means

The critical first step in the drafting process is to determine the client's objectives. The ethical corollary is that once those objectives are known, the drafter must generally honor them. If the drafter thinks these objectives are not in the client's own best interests or are of questionable legality, the drafter should discuss the matter with the client. This may be particularly troublesome when the drafter is representing an organization. In some instances, the drafter may be obliged to go over the head of the designated organizational representative and present the drafter's concerns to higher authority.

Depending on the nature of the relationship, the drafter may also want to discuss with the client the broader moral, economic, social, and political implications of a given objective. Clients may fail to realize that self-interest is often best served through decency and social responsibility; it is the lawyer's responsibility to make that point.

If the client is dedicated to achieving an objective that is deeply and morally offensive to the drafter, then withdrawal is the appropriate response. But under no circumstances may the drafter surreptitiously subvert the client's objectives or substitute the drafter's objectives for those of the client. The temptation to do this is particularly strong for the legislative drafter. These are generally career professionals, often with more tenure and experience in dealing with policy issues than those for whom they draft—whether the client is a specific legislator, a committee, or an administrative official. Indeed, the drafter is often asked to contribute to the formulation of agency or legislative policy. Ultimately, however, the drafter must defer to the wishes of the client. If the drafter disagrees with the proposed legislation, the drafter must still function as a competent technician, remain totally objective, and not allow his or her opinions about the wisdom of the legislation to subvert the client's objectives. If the drafter's social, political, and economic views are seriously at odds with those of the legislative client, then the drafter should possibly seek employment elsewhere.

As in other lawyering contexts, the drafter has more discretion and responsibility in selecting the most effective means of achieving the client's objective. Indeed, many clients leave that up to the drafter entirely. If, however, the client wants a transaction structured in a particular way and the drafter thinks that is not the best way to achieve the ultimate objective, then the drafter should discuss the matter with the client rather than ignoring the client's wishes.

2. Criminal, Fraudulent, and Otherwise Prohibited Transactions

The drafter who correctly advises a client that a particular transaction violates the criminal law and who later drafts the necessary papers is liable as an accomplice or conspirator. A drafter could not, for example, draft a contract of sale for goods known to be stolen. The "mere scrivener" defense was rejected centuries ago. Similarly, drafter participation in fraud may render the drafter liable in damages to the injured parties, although the courts are divided over some aspects of third-party liability.

An even more unsettled area of the law relates to drafter involvement with transaction documents that are neither criminal nor fraudulent, but that are otherwise unlawful, unenforceable, or a sham. For example, a business client might ask a lawyer to draft a covenant-not-to-compete that is geographically overbroad, hoping that the employee will not realize its unenforceability and will unwittingly comply with its limitations. The strategic use of *in terrorem* provisions that are either unconscionable or contrary to public policy also occurs, especially when the parties lack equal bargaining power and the weaker party is not represented by counsel. The weaker party is simply intimidated into compliance. Finally, a drafter might be called upon to draft documents that are a sham designed to circumvent some legal limit—such as a sale and resale arrangement in which the alleged profit is actually usurious interest.

A drafter, however, may not always know whether a particular provision is criminal, fraudulent, or otherwise illegal for some reason. The law is rife with uncertainty. Good faith predictions are often wrong and the lawyer who makes them, and who drafts documents on the basis of that prediction, is generally not regarded as being unethical. But between the two extremes of a good faith prediction that is wrong and conduct that is clearly illegal lies a very large gray area. For example, would it be unethical for a drafter to state, "I honestly think this provision violates the criminal law, but I can certainly make arguments to the contrary if the issue is litigated," and then proceed to draft the document on that basis? The legal ethical community is not of one mind on that matter.

Fraud is also a particularly slippery concept. For example, an attorney might be asked to draft a contract containing a term that is so indefinite that it will probably cause the contract to fail. The client intends to use this as an escape valve if performance under the contract later become unprofitable. Does that constitute fraud against the other party?

Similarly, in the legislative context an administrative agency may want a particular substantive requirement but also privately acknowledge that Congress would never consciously impose it. Is it unethical for an agency drafter to write the statute in such an obscure way that Congress will not realize the implications, thus allowing the agency to later interpret the statute to suit its fancy? Whether an actual ethical violation or not, most drafters would view this as a violation of the public trust and refuse to participate in such machinations.

Disclosure situations are also troublesome, from both a legal and an ethical perspective. The classic example is the purchaser who contracts to buy a piece of land, knowing that it contains buried treasure and that the current owner does not realize this. Compare that with the seller of property who contracts to sell without disclosing a latent defect to the buyer. Can the lawyer act as a drafter-participant in the transaction without insisting that the client disclose the information to the other party?

The drafter's duty of disclosure is fairly clear when mistakes find their way into the final written and signed version of a contract. If the parties have reached agreement and the lawyer for one of them is responsible for reducing the agreement to writing, that lawyer cannot intentionally and surreptitiously change the terms knowing that the other party is not going to catch it before signing. Moreover, if the later-discovered change or omission that favors the drafter's client was inadvertent, then the drafter should bring the matter to the attention of the other party and may probably do so without first consulting with the drafter's own client. Conversely, if an inadvertent clerical or mathematical error favors the non-drafting party, under the law of unilateral mistake the courts generally will not allow that party to snatch up the advantage and a lawyer should not advise that party to attempt to do so.

D. COMMUNICATION

A lawyer has the general duty to keep the client reasonably informed about the progress of the representation and to provide sufficient explanations to enable the client to make informed decisions. These client communication obligations affect the drafter in two ways.

First, if the drafter is also functioning as the negotiator of a contract, the drafter should keep the client appraised of the status of the negotiations, the nature of the counter-proposals, and the concessions that the drafter thinks are appropriate.

Second, if a lawyer has drafted a legally complex document for a client, the drafter should carefully explain to the client what the document contains and what its legal significance is. This is where the document summary discussed earlier plays an important role.

E. FEES

Ethical rules generally require that the lawyer's fee be reasonable. This, in turn, is dependent on such factors as the time and labor required, the novelty and difficulty of the representation, and the degree of skill that is required. But ethical rules also generally allow the fee amount to reflect the experience and reputation of the lawyer.

Sometimes, these two criteria may work against each other. Consider the lawyer who specializes in wills and estates. Over the years, through "from scratch" drafting of many estate planning documents, the lawyer has crafted provisions dealing with every possible contingency. These provisions are now incorporated into a computerized document assembly program. Basically, all the lawyer does now is obtain the necessary information from new clients, choose the appropriate previously drafted provisions, and merge the two. The time and labor involved in producing that specific document is minimal; but it reflects an enormous amount of experience, reputation, and ability on the part of the lawyer. Clearly, the drafter cannot bill for fictitious hours. The drafter may, however, adopt a value billing (set fee) approach as an alternative.

A similar problem that drafters face involves the use of essentially the same document for multiple clients. For example, a lawyer may draft a from scratch document for a client, at $75 per hour for ten hours, or $750. A few weeks later, another client needs an almost identical document. Now it takes the lawyer only an hour to produce it. Must the drafter charge only $75? Can the drafter charge another $750? Or is the correct fee somewhere in between? Again, the lawyer cannot bill the second client at a fictitious hourly rate; the drafter may, however, charge a flat fee for the document that is in excess of the normal hourly rate, as long as this is agreed-to in advance with the client.

F. CONFIDENTIALITY

Professional ethics require confidentiality. Client communications are also protected by the attorney-client privilege.

1. Ethical Requirements

The ethical rules all impose, to one extent or another, a duty of protecting the client's confidences and secrets. This impacts the drafter in several particulars.

For example, when drafting private documents, the drafter very often obtains personal information about individual clients and their families and commercially sensitive and trade secret information from business clients. A breach of the duty of confidentiality might be committed by the lawyer directly, for whatever reason, or it could be done by someone else privy to the information. Confidential information about socially prominent clients is sometimes leaked by office staff. A separation agreement between two movie stars, for example, might well contain many titillating, newsworthy tidbits of information. Confidential business information may also be leaked in this fashion, usually to the substantial financial benefit of the person possessing the information. The drafter has an affirmative obligation to educate secretaries, paralegals, and even couriers about the duty of confidentiality. Drafts of documents containing sensitive or confidential information should be shredded, not merely put in a trash can.

Not disclosing client information to third parties is only part of the ethical duty. The drafter's own use of the information is also limited. The drafter of corporate documents may not use the information when buying or selling stock in the company. Such insider trading is not only a breach of the canons of ethics, it may also violate state and federal securities law. Confidential client information is sometimes used for other forms of lawyer self-dealing. This is discussed further in the section dealing with conflicts of interest.

2. Attorney–Client Privilege

The duty of confidentiality also manifests itself in the form of an evidentiary privilege. In essence, a person who seeks legal advice or assistance from a lawyer may invoke an unqualified privilege not to testify about the contents of confidential communications with the lawyer. If asked to testify, the lawyer must also invoke the privilege on behalf of the client.

The privilege probably attaches to most of the information that an attorney would obtain when preparing to draft a document. Oddly enough, however, unless it contains information that would be privileged, the document itself is not generally privileged. The work-product privilege would also arise only in the unlikely circumstance of the document being prepared in anticipation of litigation.

The attorney-client privilege is subject to several exceptions of potential relevance to the drafter. First, the privilege does not arise when the lawyer is dealing with drafted documents in some capacity other than that as a lawyer, for example as a corporate officer, a business advisor, or a friend.

Second, lawyers drafting routine documents like deeds, who are acting on the instructions of a client and who are not giving any legal advice in connection with the drafting, have sometimes been referred to as "mere scriveners," meaning in this context that the privilege does not attach. The scope of this exception is unclear, however, since drafting even routine documents requires some degree of expertise, even if it is nothing more than knowing that a routine document will indeed suffice. The courts recognize the exception most often when the document is now unavailable and the purpose of the testimony is merely to establish that the document existed and what it contained.

Third, to be privileged, the information the drafter uses must come from the client, not third parties. This exception comes up most often in the corporate context, where the precise identity of the client is subject to considerable debate.

Fourth, the privilege does not apply to otherwise unprivileged client papers that substantially predate the relationship, even if they are given to the drafter for use in drafting a document that will cure whatever legal difficulty the papers present.

Fifth, when a lawyer is drafting a document for co-clients, information received from one client is generally not privileged from the other clients. This is another reason for declining to draft contracts on behalf of all the contracting parties.

Sixth, the privilege does not attach to information indicating a client's intent to engage in illegal or fraudulent conduct. This exception would apply if the drafter has been given information in connection with a request to draft a document to be used in a fraudulent transaction.

G. CONFLICT OF INTEREST

Ironically, the attorney-client relationship involves a conflict of interest at its very threshold: the conflict between the attorney who drafts the retainer contract and the client who is asked to agree to it. This is why attorney-client contracts are subject to fairly heavy regulation and scrutiny, especially with respect to fees. Moreover, any ambiguity in an attorney-client contract will nearly always be construed against the lawyer-drafter.

The other common conflict situations the lawyer-drafter faces are as follows:

1. Representation Against a Current Client

Lawyers are frequently asked to draft a contract for both parties, who say that they have agreed in principle and just want the lawyer to write it up in legal form. The representation of each may be representation against the other. This is because the parties' interests are almost always hostile to some extent, although they may not truly appreciate that fact. The question usually is whether the representation of one party will be materially limited by the lawyer's responsibility to the other party.

Many commentators believe that such a limitation is inherent in the drafting process. A skillful and conscientious drafter can nearly always draft in subtle ways that inure to the benefit of the client, and to the corresponding disadvantage of the other party, however minor. For example, if a lawyer is representing a buyer in a residential real estate transaction, that lawyer's ability to exercise drafting expertise is necessarily going to be materially limited by that lawyer's simultaneous representation of the seller in the same transaction. There are just too many provisions that could be drafted in a number of ways. For example, a provision dealing with a termite certification letter could be worded as a mere condition (favoring the seller) or as a promise (favoring the buyer). This would seem to qualify as a situation where the interests of multiple parties are fundamentally antagonistic to each other, which should preclude representation even if both parties consent.

On the other hand, other commentators think it is inefficient and unnecessary to turn every simple transaction into a federal case by requiring each side to retain separate counsel. Many ethics opinions allow lawyers to act on behalf of both parties in drafting relatively simple contracts where the parties have agreed to the basic terms.

Conflict questions also arise when a lawyer is asked to draft wills or other estate planning documents for members of the same family, such as a husband and wife. This particular conflict is illustrated by the following, oft-debated hypothetical. Meeting together, a husband and wife tell the lawyer how they want their individual property to be distributed—to each other, for example. Later, meeting alone with the lawyer, the wife indicates that she really wants her property distributed in a different way, but that she also does not want her husband to know about it because it would only make him angry. Can the drafter honor the wife's wishes and deceive the husband? Or should the drafter inform the husband and breach the wife's confidence and also precipitate marital discord? Or must the drafter decline to draft a will for either one of them? No easy answers exist to these questions.

Business lawyers frequently encounter drafting-related conflicts in the context of simultaneous representation of the corporation and that corporation's officers, directors, or stockholders. The lawyer's primary duty as counsel to the corporation is *always* to the corporate entity. A corporate lawyer, thus, cannot draft documents or otherwise assist stockholders in setting up a competing enterprise or draft a separation agreement on behalf of a departing officer.

Corporate takeovers are full of conflict possibilities. Each member of the corporation may have a different interest and may be giving different and conflicting instructions to the lawyer who is negotiating or drafting takeover documents. Ultimately, the drafter must defer to the wishes of the board of directors.

As a general rule, the courts are more tolerant of multiple representation in the context of a small, closely held corporation than in a large, publicly held corporation. Even in this context, however, if the venture sours and the interests diverge in fact, the lawyer can no longer represent anyone. If this occurs in the middle of drafting a complex document, the lawyer may be unable to even collect a fee for the work begun but not completed.

The ethical rule about avoiding conflicts applies not only to direct conflicts of interest, but also to broader conflicts of loyalty. A lawyer cannot engage in active representation against a current client even in unrelated matters if it would adversely affect the relationship. A lawyer who is drafting a complex construction contract for a Client A cannot represent Client B who is suing Client A in an unrelated tort action. Since loyalty is an essential element in the lawyer's relationship with a client, it would be a rare case indeed where the representation of Client B would not adversely affect the relationship with Client A.

Some transactions between an attorney and a client are subject to an almost total prohibition. Several are of particular importance to the drafter.

- A lawyer cannot enter into a business transaction with a client unless the terms are fair, the client has the opportunity to retain other counsel, and the client consents in writing. A lawyer's business contract with a client would be subject to intense scrutiny for over-reaching.

- A lawyer cannot use information relating to the representation of a client to the disadvantage that client. A lawyer who has drafted a purchase offer cannot use that information to submit a better offer on the drafter's personal behalf. It is unclear whether the ethical rules prohibit non-revelatory, non-adverse use of a client's information. For example, the drafter of a contract for the sale of land, knowing that its purchase and intended future use will increase the value of adjoining property, might be inclined to purchase an adjoining parcel. However, regardless of what the ethical rules say, general agency law restricts the agent's freedom to profit from the principal's business in that way, whether the use of the information harms the principal or not.

- A lawyer cannot draft a document, such as a will, giving that lawyer or a relative a substantial gift from the client, except where the client is related to the donee. Although it is not expressly prohibited, naming the will drafter the executor or administrator of the estate is filled with conflict.

- Prior to the conclusion of representation, a lawyer cannot negotiate or draft an agreement giving the lawyer literary or media rights to matters relating to the representation.

- A lawyer cannot negotiate or draft an agreement prospectively limiting the lawyer's liability for malpractice unless permitted by law and the client is represented by another attorney.

2. Representation Against a Former Client

The rules generally prohibit a lawyer who has previously represented a client from later representing another person in the same or a substantially related matter if the new client's interests are materially adverse to the interests of the former client, unless the former client consents to this. The application of this ethical duty to the drafter is fairly straightforward. Although a few decisions recognize a "mere scrivener" exception to the "substantially related" standard, usually, if a lawyer has represented a client in drafting a document, such as a contract or will, that lawyer cannot later represent another person in challenging the legality or efficacy of the document or in contesting the former client's conduct under that document.

3.   Imputed Disqualification

Lawyers generally practice in firms. This raises several difficult questions. For example, if one member, or former member, of the firm would be disqualified, is everyone in the firm similarly disqualified? At one time, the rules seemed to impose a virtually absolute disqualification. If Partner Abbott was disqualified from some form of representation in connection with a drafted document, then Partner Baker was as well—unless the original client consented. The current view is more permissive, but also more complicated.

First, for currently associated lawyers, imputed disqualification generally occurs only in four situations: (1) if it would involve a present-client conflict, (2) if it would involve assisting the client in making a prohibited gift to the primarily disqualified lawyer, (3) if it would offend the former-client conflict rule, or (4) if the primarily disqualified lawyer had previously served as an intermediary between the two clients.

Second, when the primarily disqualified lawyer has left the firm, the remainder of the firm is disqualified from representing a party with an interest that is materially adverse to that of the former client only if the matter is the same or substantially related to the prior representation *and* any lawyer remaining in the firm has confidential information relating to the matter. Thus, if Partner Abbott drafted a document for the client and Partner Baker's files still contain confidential information about this transaction, Partner Charles could not represent a client in a matter challenging the meaning or efficacy of that document.

An imputed disqualification generally does not follow a lawyer departing from a firm unless that lawyer actually acquired confidential information about the client. If Partner Abbott has drafted a will, Associate Darby probably could not, while still a member of the firm, represent another client challenging the will. But when Darby goes to work for another law firm, Darby is disqualified from such representation only if Darby acquired confidential information relating to the will. And even if Darby is disqualified, Partner Ethyl in the new firm may arguably still undertake the representation if Darby is sufficiently isolated from the representation. There is, however, considerable disagreement over that latter point.

4. Former Government Lawyer–Drafters

Lawyers who work for the government and then go into private practice face special conflict of interest problems. The general rule is that a lawyer cannot represent a private client in connection with a matter in which the lawyer participated personally and substantially as a public employee, without the consent of the appropriate government agency.

Insofar as the lawyer-drafter is concerned, the principal question is whether a government lawyer could draft a regulation and then, after leaving government service, advise clients about the regulation, file cases based on it, or even challenge its validity. This is a question that has not yet been finally resolved.

H. DEALINGS WITH THIRD PARTIES

Lawyers are often called upon to not only draft contracts, but also to negotiate the terms with the other contracting party. It is unethical for a lawyer to make a false statement of material fact or law. Unfortunately, the line between a misrepresentation of fact and the expression of opinion about value—mere "puffing"—is not always clear.

On the other hand, no ethical obligation normally exists to disclose a material fact unless nondisclosure would assist the client in doing a criminal or fraudulent act. The dimensions of that exception, however, are unclear. In addition, drafters inclined to take advantage of that privilege should be aware that it is subject to two legal limits. First, in some situations, nondisclosure of a material fact might make a contract unconscionable and thus unenforceable. Second, the common law rules of unilateral or mutual mistake could apply in some situations, thus making the contract voidable.

Another ethical concern of the lawyer-drafter involves dealing with another contracting party who is also represented by counsel. The rule is that direct contact with this party is impermissible unless the other lawyer has consented to it. A drafter could not, thus, submit a contract counter-proposal or suggested revision directly to the other party.

Conversely, if the lawyer-drafter is dealing with a party who is not represented by counsel, the ethical obligation is to ensure that this person fully understands that the lawyer is not disinterested and that the lawyer is representing only the interests of the client. The lawyer should take particular care not to give legal advice to an unrepresented person. Although the lawyer can explain the meaning of various contract provisions, the better practice is to advise third parties to retain their own lawyers for that purpose.

An odd kind of third party relationship exists between the legislative drafter and the general public. The politicians behind legislation sometimes have designs that would not withstand the light of day. They may thus commission the drafting of "Trojan Horse" legislation, innocuous and even meritorious on its face but containing deliberate ambiguities and vague terms that are clarified only by quietly prepared legislative history. This is probably not an actionable ethical violation, but the legislative drafter who participates in such chicanery is no more deserving of the public trust than the politician who commissioned it.

I. LITIGATION ETHICS

Drafted documents are often involved in litigation—a breach of contract case, for example. Clients frequently retain in their files documents containing information relating to the contract and, indeed, prior drafts of the contract itself. Sometimes, these documents are relevant to the litigation, and sometimes they contain information that is adverse to the interests of the party who has retained them.

It is widely considered unethical for a lawyer to destroy or conceal documents that have existing evidentiary value.

The simplest case arises when the opposing party has served a discovery request on the client for all documents relating to the contract. Clearly, the lawyer cannot advise the client to destroy incriminating documents, such as one indicating that the client had knowledge of a condition it was under a duty to disclose under a contract of sale. But whether the lawyer has a duty to affirmatively ensure that the client produces all relevant documents is not as clear.

Similarly, the ethics community seems divided over a client's pre-litigation destruction of documents. Assume, for example, that the lawyer has drafted documents involving a merger of two corporations. Although the lawyer believes the merger is legal, may the lawyer nevertheless advise the client to destroy certain documents that might tend to suggest the presence of an intent to monopolize, in violation of the antitrust laws? The answer to this question is not clear. The safest approach is to counsel the client to adopt a document retention-destruction policy that is based on some objective standard.

J. AIDING THE UNAUTHORIZED PRACTICE OF LAW

Lawyers cannot abet the unauthorized practice of law. It is still unclear, however, what constitutes the unauthorized practice of law. A legal drafter is likely to become involved in an unauthorized practice imbroglio in two situations. Do-it-yourself books and, more recently, computer programs that purport to enable lay persons to create their own legal documents generally do not constitute unauthorized practice, and entrepreneur lawyer-drafters may participate in the preparation of these materials. The courts, however, generally draw the line at giving advice that is personalized or directed at the specific problem of a designated or readily identifiable person. The inclusion of a telephone number or e-mail address that the consumer could contact for another lay person's assistance in completing the forms would thus be a form of unauthorized practice and a lawyer could not be involved in such an enterprise.

The second situation involves the age-old dispute over the role of real estate agents in preparing contracts and other documents involving the sale of land. A hold that simply filling in the blanks on a form contract constitutes the practice of law. Presumably, lawyers in those jurisdictions can not draft form documents that would be used in this manner. In the majority of states, however, realtors may fill out purchase contracts and other forms, provided they do not impose a separate charge for the service or give legal advice. In these states, thus, the lawyer could assist in the drafting of a form contract. Indeed, the real estate community would benefit from some competent drafting in that regard.

K. PROVIDING FREE DRAFTING SERVICES

The practice of law is a business, and it is not unethical for lawyers to treat it exclusively as such. The practice of law, however, is also a profession dedicated to the public good. Most lawyers aspire to provide a certain amount of free work. The drafter who is so inclined has two principal opportunities.

First, local bar associations frequently sponsor legal clinics where low-income persons can get legal advice on various matters. In addition, these clinics often provide simple contract and will drafting services. Second, churches and charities frequently urge their members and contributors to include a bequest to the institution in wills or to establish a trust on behalf of the institution. In both instances, the skilled drafter can provide an invaluable service, by drafting the necessary documents without cost.

Exercise 2

As your firm's resident expert in legal ethics, you are frequently asked to advise other members of the firm on various ethical issues. What advice would you give in the following situations? Why?

1. Attorney Anne has been contacted by an author (a non-lawyer) who is writing a do-it-yourself law book designed for a lay audience. He has asked her to draft some "simple," fill-in-the-blanks contracts—sale of a house, loan agreement, contract for services, sales agreement, and the

like. He also wants to list her as a contributor and as a "widely recognized specialist in legal drafting."

2. Attorney Bill has drafted lease agreement forms for the owners of several large apartment complexes and many individual landlords. None are considered currently active clients. The legislature recently enacted some legislation that makes several provisions in these leases illegal. A landlord who attempted to enforce them would be subject to a fairly substantial civil penalty in a suit bought by a tenant.

Bill wants to write all of these former clients a letter informing them of the change in the law and suggesting that their lease agreements be revised. In addition, since the firm is currently trying to encourage clients who are using the firm for one purpose (real estate transactions, for example) to also use the firm for other purposes (employment litigation, for example), Bill wants to include a paragraph that describes, in glowing terms, the firm's other areas of practice.

3. Attorney Charlie, who has just graduated from law school, tells you over lunch one day that his uncle, who is in the construction business, wants Charlie to draft a contract for the construction of a large shopping center, where the uncle's compensation will be in the form of a share of the ownership of the property rather than in cash, but with the other owners having an option to buy him out at the end of ten years. The uncle thinks he will incur substantial tax savings by doing it this way.

You ask Charlie if he is familiar with the construction business. He says "no," but that he figures he can find a construction contact in a form book. You ask him if he has looked into the tax angle. He says "no," but that his uncle said not to worry about that because his uncle was pretty sure it was legal. Charlie thinks this is a wonderful opportunity for him to make a name for himself in the firm. What do you think?

4. Attorney Danielle has been asked to draft a lease agreement containing some provisions that she knows will be void and unenforceable under the state landlord-tenant act—a provision, for example, in which the tenant agrees not to allow children to reside on the premises. She says she told

the client that these provisions could not be enforced, but the client wants them in the lease anyway (believing that the tenants will comply with them, unaware of their unenforceability).

5. Attorney Edgar is drafting a contract for his client involving the sale of several parcels of land within a large subdivision/condominium and golf complex that the client is developing. The client has agreed to sell and the buyer agreed to buy 103 separate parcels, but they cannot agree on some parcels that are located in one corner of the development, consisting partially of a parcel known locally as the Wilson tract and another known as the Woodrow tract. The parcels in question are shown below:

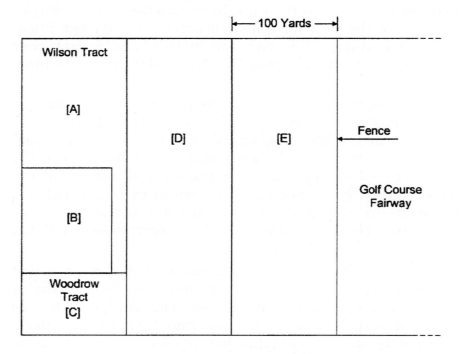

For convenience sake, Edgar and the client refer to the parcels by reference to the bracketed letters. The narrow, six-inch wide strip that is part of the Wilson tract is a result of sloppy surveying when the land was originally subdivided. Without seeing a plat, one would not even know it was part of the Wilson tract.

The client is willing to sell parcel D but wants to retain the other parcels for subdivision use. The buyer, however, is not interested in parcel D, but insists upon having the land contained in parcels B and E and may back out of the whole deal unless he gets them. Edgar has proposed to draft a provision identifying the land to be sold as "that land situated between the Wilson tract and the Woodrow tract and the tract extending in a westerly direction 100 yards from the fence at the end of the golf course fairway."

You question his strategy and he explains: "When the buyer reads that, he will think my client has given in to his demand and that he is getting the land between the Wilson tract and the Woodrow tract, what we call parcel B, and all of what we call parcel E. So, he will sign the contract. But when we actually draw up a plat and convey title, we will convey only parcel D, which lies between the combined parcels A/C, on one side, and parcel E, on the other. One of three things will happen, two of them good: First, the seller may simply accept our interpretation of the contract. Second, the seller may litigate but the court will adopt our interpretation of the contract. Third, the seller may litigate and court will accept his interpretation of the contract—in which case we will, of course, sell him parcels B and E. But we win in two out of three of the scenarios. Pretty clever, eh?"

6. Attorney Francis drafted a complex franchise agreement that her client, Texas Tom's Tacos, Inc., uses with all its franchisees. It took her thirty hours, which she billed at $85 an hour. Several months later, she sent the same documents (with only names and minor details being changed) to Caroline's Bar–B–Q, Inc., for use with its franchisees. She also billed this client for 30 hours at $85 and hour. Caroline's legal department thought the bill was excessive and protested to your firm's Managing Partner, who sent it to you for review. You discover that Francis actually only spent 45 minutes reviewing Texas Tom's franchise agreement and revising it slightly for Caroline's use. What should the firm do?

7. Attorney George, who is Of Counsel to the firm, is the retired CEO of major textile company. Until he joined the firm, he had never actively practiced law. Even now, he

operates mainly as a *rain maker* for the firm, using his extensive business contacts to bring in legal work for the other attorneys in the firm.

Several months ago, he was consulted by his friend Sam Rayon, Vice President of Pine Tree Fabrics, concerning a proposed merger between Pine Tree and Wateree River Textiles. George was sent a copy of the proposed merger agreement and asked to review its terms. He did so and was concerned over a provision under which Pine Tree would be obligated to sell its shares in a wholly owned subsidiary, Finch Thread and Needle Company. To better understand how this sale would impact on the merged company, with Rayon's consent George called Carol Swanson, Director of Sales with Finch, and asked for certain information about market shares, Finch's expansion plans, and other information. Swanson sent him the information in writing. Reassured that the sale would not impact negatively on the new company and that indeed it was a very wise thing to do (Finch was in serious difficulty), George told Rayon that he thought they ought to go ahead with the merger, since "it makes good business sense." The merger was accomplished and Finch was sold to Carlton Canvas, Inc.

Several months later, Carlton Canvas brought a conspiracy to defraud action against Rayon and other officers of the two corporations. George has been served with a subpoena for all documents in his possession involving the sale of Finch Thread and Needle Company. The information he received from Swanson, when viewed in light of certain other facts, strongly implicates the defendants. George does not want to provide the data. He has come to you for advice.

8.   The firm publishes something it calls a *Client News Letter* and a *Client Alert*, containing general information about legal matters, reports about recent case decisions, simple articles on how to avoid legal difficulty, and the like. The mailing list for the *Letter* and *Alert* contains virtually anyone the firm has ever represented, plus various public officials, trade associations, and law professors.

Ten years ago attorney Hannah drafted a franchise agreement that New York Hot Dogs, Inc., has used with all its franchisees. New York Hot Dogs is the largest hot dog chain in the country, with thousands of franchises. The franchise agreement that Hannah drafted heavily favors the corporation over the franchise owners. Neither she nor anyone else in the firm has represented New York Hot Dogs since then, but the company is on the mailing list of the *Letter* and *Alert*.

Recently, the franchise owners formed the NYHD Franchise Owner's Association. They have asked Hannah to draft a franchise agreement on their behalf that will be more favorable to them than the current one is and to represent them in negotiations with New York Hot Dogs.

New York Hot Dogs has found out about this and is protesting Hannah's involvement.

Chapter 6

AN OVERVIEW

Some think of legal drafting principally in terms of writing the document. Although this is an important part of drafting, putting the words to paper is neither the beginning nor the end of the drafting process. It is merely an intermediate part of a larger, more complex endeavor.

Although the process can be broken down into a number of discrete steps, that characterization is somewhat misleading since it suggests a rigid, linear progress. Drafting is more circular than linear. A step once taken may have to be repeated as the drafted document evolves. This chapter will identify and briefly describe these steps, which will then be discussed in more detail in subsequent chapters.

A. DETERMINE THE CLIENT'S OBJECTIVES

This is truly the most important part of the drafting process. It will affect everything that follows. The objective of all drafted documents is to achieve some good or avoid some harm. But it is the client's specific good to be achieved or harm to be avoided that counts, not some good or harm in an abstract sense. Until the drafter knows why the client wants the document, what purpose it is supposed to serve, and what problems it is expected to resolve or prevent, the drafter cannot even begin to serve the client's needs.

Sometimes, the client's objectives are obvious and relatively simple: to sell a house, to form a partnership, or to empower someone to act on the client's behalf. The drafter can usually accomplish these objectives without much prob-

112

ing into motives. Other times, the drafter must look beneath the veneer of a stated objective and discover what impels the client to want this. A client may want to establish a trust for her son. If the client desires this because the son is a spendthrift, the drafter might set up the trust in one way. But if the son is mentally disabled, a different kind of document might be appropriate. Whatever the objective, it will affect the structure and substance of the trust agreement.

Discovering the legislative client's underlying purpose is even more important—and also sometimes more difficult. Legislators tend to think in terms of specific instances and will assume that prohibition or requirement is always the most appropriate solution. Legislation drafted from that superficial predicate is usually ineffective in the long run. The drafter's function is to help the legislator think more broadly in terms of the harm to be prevented or the good to be achieved and also to consider approaches other than prohibition or requirement. A statute banning minors from driving personal watercraft or jet boats might be an appropriate response to a constituent's specific problem involving the annoying teenager across the lake. But if the underlying concern of the legislative client is really boating safety, then the drafter should suggest a more comprehensive statute. The stated objective might also be better met with mandatory training and licensing. The drafter must know what the ultimate objective is before the drafter can intelligently address the problem.

Exploring objectives with the client is discussed in more detail in Chapter 7, section A.

B. IDENTIFY THE AUDIENCE

The primary audience of a document is always the client. First and foremost, the drafter's responsibility is to that client. This is the bedrock on which drafting ethics is based. If the document must be drafted with careful attention to many technical details, then the drafter must have the knowledge and skill to do that. But the drafter must also have the ability to explain what all of it means to a client who may lack any experience in this type of transaction.

The drafter, however, must recognize that other people will also use the document, in a variety of different ways. Unless the drafter knows this audience, anticipates their sometimes conflicting uses, and protects the client as necessary, the drafting venture will be a failure. A simple contract for the sale of a house, for example, may well satisfy the desires of the seller-client and also those of the buyer. Yet, the closing attorney, who more-or-less represents the mortgage company, may find some of its provisions totally unacceptable. Audience identification is discussed further in Chapter 7, section B.

C. EXPLORE THE BROADER LEGAL AND FACTUAL CONTEXT OF THE DOCUMENT

Drafters cannot be myopic. They must have a bird's-eye view of the entire legal and factual landscape that will surround the document to be drafted. This vision influences both the form and the content of the document and will also prevent the document from having unintended consequences.

For example, the legal context of a heavily regulated industry, such as a public utility, is radically different from that of a mom-and-pop grocery store. A long-term supply contract that might be perfectly adequate for one could prove disastrous for the other. A general practitioner with no knowledge of labor law who attempts to draft an employment manual will be entering a minefield wearing snowshoes, with inevitably disastrous consequences. The drafter need not be an expert in every area of the law. But the drafter should have a wide exposure to as much substantive law as possible, enough to at least recognize potential problems and pitfalls, and the ability to then master whatever substantive details are necessary to integrate the drafted document into that legal landscape without creating conflicts and unintended consequences.

Legal context is also important to the legislative drafter. The drafter of a new criminal provision must understand how the prohibition fits into the broader scheme of criminal law and procedure within both that jurisdiction and cognate jurisdictions. Statutory drafters must also know the existing law on the subject being legislated and draft within that context. If legislation on the same subject already exists, the drafter must determine if it needs to be repealed, amended, or reconciled with the legislation being drafted. Consider the example of a state legislator, who, upon receiving many complaints about the number of defamation suits brought against employers as a result of unfavorable employment references, drafted some legislation creating a limited immunity for this. The immunity was broader in some respects and narrower in others than the immunity already available at common law. The legislation, however, did not indicate whether it supplanted or merely supplemented the common law. The legislator reportedly admitted later that he had forgotten the common law already recognized an immunity. This unfamiliarity with the existing law created a totally confusing body of employment-related defamation law in that state.

Similarly, the drafter must discover and fully understand the factual context of the transaction. One cannot draft a construction contract without knowing something about the construction business, accepted practices within that industry, and the tacit assumptions that guide the enterprise. Certain areas of the law have become specialty areas, with lawyers often limiting their practice to that area, not only because the law is extremely complex, but also because practice in that area requires an extra-legal knowledge of the factual context within which these laws operate. Only the specialist can hope to master both the substantive law and become sufficiently familiar with the facts to practice in this area effectively.

Legislative drafters must also fully understand the totality of the complex web of behavior the statute is going to regulate. Absent that understanding, the statute is apt to have unforeseen and sometimes unintended consequences. A securities regulation that is drafted by someone who does not fully understand the securities market, the arcane vocabulary of securities brokers, and the history and reasons for a practice that is now being subjected to regulation will inevitably produce something that is inadequate to the task at hand and either fails to promote the good or prevent the harm intended. Determining the legal and factual context of a document is discussed further in Chapter 7, section C.

D. RESEARCH THE LAW

Eventually, the drafter's focus must shift from the general legal landscape, discussed earlier, to the law that is going to bear directly on the document being drafted. Private documents like employment contracts, corporate charters, and wills are heavily impacted by substantive law. A particular provision may be required, prohibited, or merely authorized. Or, the law may require that a particular provision appear in a particular format. The law also determines the meaning of the words that are used and the legal consequences of the substantive provisions. The drafter must know all of this and draft accordingly. Technique and style count for nothing if the content is substantively deficient.

The law of law-making, which applies to legislative drafting, is more limited, and usually consists of constitutional provisions that dictate both the form and the substantive contents of legislation. It is not uncommon, for example, for state constitutions to require that titles contain particular information, to prescribe the exact wording of enacting clauses, and to limit each bill to a single topic. The legislative drafter must know these things. At the local level, state law may affirmatively prohibit certain kinds of ordinances. Drafters of state and local law must also be aware of the federal law of preemption.

At the substantive level, both the federal and state constitutions are full of limits on what the legislature may do. The legislative drafter, thus, needs to be familiar with the prohibition against ex post facto laws and bills of attainder, with the requirements of due process, with the equal protection notions of over-and under-inclusion in the creation of regulated classes or categories, with the ever changing scope of the First Amendment, and with a host of other constitutional provisions. How the law impacts directly on the drafting process is discussed in Chapter 8.

E.　DETERMINE SUBSTANCE

What does a drafter need to include in a contract for the sale of a house or an ordinance establishing a teenage curfew? The answer to that question lies in a blend of the drafter's legal knowledge and experience, plus the client's desires. The contract drafter will know that some provisions are essential for the document to be valid, while others are extremely important in protecting the client's interests. Conversely, some provisions may be affirmatively illegal. Beyond that, substance is determined mainly by what the client wants. The client, however, may be unaware of the possibilities, thus shifting the responsibility back onto the drafter to educate the client. Checklists, of both the commercial and the drafter-prepared variety, play an invaluable role here.

Similarly, in drafting legislation, the drafter will know that some provisions would be unconstitutional or inconsistent with a law emanating from a higher authority. The drafter's experience may also suggest that a particular provision would be unenforceable or ineffective for some other reason. Beyond that, however, substance is again something for the client to determine.

General principles regarding the substance of both private-and public-law documents are discussed in Chapter 9. The substantive content of specific types of documents is beyond the scope of this text.

F.　GET THE FACTS

Once the drafter and the client agree generally on what will go into the document, the drafter must then get down to the specifics. In a contract of sale, the identity of the goods and the price are easy to determine. But providing the specifics of a plant manager's duties under an employment contract may be something else altogether.

Similarly, the legislative drafter must address all the troublesome details of the statute. Who will be subject to the statute? Who will enforce it? What are the penalties? Where does a person file the application for an exception? These matters are important but sometimes hard to elicit from legislative clients, who are often content to let the drafter decide.

G.   IDENTIFY THE PROPER LEGAL AND FACTUAL CONCEPTS

The drafting process has thus far moved from the general to the specific. The process has been one of analysis—breaking the whole down into its component parts, both legally and factually. The conceptualization stage reverses that process. It involves a process of synthesis—building the components back up in a different form. This synthesis is accomplished principally through the use of concepts.

First, in moving toward the realization of the client's objectives, the drafter must choose from potentially competing legal concepts. Will the client's purposes be better served if the other contracting party is conceptualized as an independent contractor or an employee? Should the conduct that legislation is going to prohibit be conceptualized as a crime or merely a civil wrong? Those legal concepts have different legal consequences.

Second, the drafter must conceptualize the facts in a manner consonant with the client's objectives. Here, the drafter has three sets of choices:

- **General versus specific.** Will the document address a broad category, "domesticated animals," or something more specific, "dogs"?

- **Vague versus precise.** Will the document require that something be done within a "reasonable time," or within "10 days"?

- **Abstract versus concrete.** Will the document focus on an abstract result, "the inducement of fear of physical injury," or something more concrete, "a threat to hit another over the head with a lead pipe"?

These conceptual alternatives are discussed in Chapter 10.

H.   DEVELOP AN ORGANIZATION

Most well-drafted contracts follow a standard organizational format. The same is true of statutes. Other documents—like wills, corporate charters, and partnership agreements—also have fairly standard formats. Within these broad parameters, the drafter still has considerable discretion about how to organize the substance of the contract or statute. Making the correct organizational choice involves the process of division, classification, and sequence.

Division involves splitting the subject matter of the document up into subcategories. A rational division follows three rules: (1) the subcategories must be mutually exclusive; (2) when combined, the subcategories must equal the whole; and (3) the division must be based on one consistently applied principle. Dividing the student body of a law school into 1st year, 2nd year, and 3rd year students is a rational division. Dividing it into 1st year students, women, and people over 5'7" tall violates all three rules.

Classification involves putting each provision in its proper subcategory. This sometimes involves a difficult choice. A provision dealing with the return of the security deposit could go in the section dealing with rent or in the section dealing with the termination of the lease. The secret is to group similar provisions together and to put specific provisions where a reader would most likely expect to find them.

Sequence involves the order in which the subcategories are presented. This can range from an essentially chronological sequence to one based on the relative importance of the subcategory. These principles of organization are discussed in Chapter 11.

I. WRITE THE DOCUMENT

This is probably the easiest part of the drafting process. From a linguistic perspective, the drafter is concerned with the following matters:

1. Ambiguities

Ambiguity is the cardinal sin of drafting. Ambiguity exists when a provision is capable of two or more mutually inconsistent meanings. Unlike vagueness, which merely involves some uncertainty at the margin, ambiguity is without justification. Indeed, the drafter who deliberately uses ambiguity to deceive or mislead the other contracting party is engaging in shady, if not outright unethical, conduct that may ultimately harm rather than help the client, since courts generally construe ambiguities against the party that created them.

Ambiguity comes in three forms. Contextual ambiguity exists when one provision says one thing and another provision says the contrary. Semantic ambiguity arises out the use of words with multiple meanings. Syntactic ambiguity arises out of the order in which the words are used and how they are punctuated. These three forms of ambiguity are discussed in Chapter 12.

2. Rules of Style and Usage

The drafter's rules of style and usage are designed not only to avoid ambiguity, but also to promote consistency, brevity, clarity, simplicity, and professional tone. Although all legal writing shares those objectives, they are the essentials of good drafting. These rules are discussed in Chapter 13.

In some areas of the law, a document must use a specific term of art to accomplish the intended result. This is true, for example, with respect to will drafting and conveyances of real property. Apart from that, there are very few magic words that must always be used in drafted documents, regardless of the type—with the possible exception of the language that is, or should be, used for creating definitions and specific legal consequences.

3. Definitions

Definitions are powerful tools, capable of making the drafter the master of the language rather than being constrained by it. Definitions also promote both clarity and brevity. The drafter, however, must construct definitions with care. The linguistic difference between "means," "includes," and "does not include" is enormous, and the choice of one term over another can radically alter the substance of a document. Definitions are discussed in Chapter 14.

4. Terms Creating Legal Consequences

Drafted documents create rights, duties, privileges, immunities, conditions, authority to act, and other legal relationships. Different words are used to create each of these legal relationships. They include "shall," "shall not," "will," "may," "must," "is entitled to," "is," "warrants," and others. The difficulty is not matching the right word with the intended consequence. The difficulty, rather, is in deciding which legal consequence to create. Would it be better to make something a "right" or a "privilege"? The two are significantly different. Or should something be made a mere condition rather than a duty? Again, each has very different legal consequences. These terms are discussed in Chapter 15.

5. Format

The physical arrangement and appearance of a drafted document is more important than one might think. Look into a United States Statutes-at-Large volume from the late 1800s or resurrect from a firm's client files a contract drafted in the 1920s. What you may see is a gray mass of page after page of sparsely paragraphed, dense prose without any bolded headings or subheadings. These documents are a nightmare to read. They should not be. A drafted document should be easy to read, easy to use as a reference, and easy to understand. Ample white space, numbered lists and enumerations, leader dots, tabbing and indentation, and numbered and captioned headings and subheadings all promote these objectives. These and other formatting techniques are discussed in Chapter 16.

J. REVIEW THE DOCUMENT FOR SUBSTANCE AND STYLE

Following the drafting process just discussed will produce a document that is still perhaps only 90% of what it should be. At this point, it will certainly look final and complete, but that appearance is deceiving. The document must still endure a top-to-bottom, left-to-right review and revision. The drafter must ensure that the document includes everything the client wants, in addition to anything that the law requires. The document must be tested to determine if it will meet the client's objectives. Deficiencies of structure and style must be identified and cured. Typographical errors must be purged and the revised version proofread yet another time. Then, perhaps, the document is ready to be submitted to the client. The process of document review is discussed in Chapter 17.

K. POST–EXECUTION MONITORING

As long as a drafted document has operative effect, the drafter is responsible for it to some extent. Changes in the law and in the client's situation often require changes in the document. The drafter should monitor the document during its lifetime and, within the limits of professional ethics discussed in Chapter 5, advise the client if changes are necessary.

Exercise 3

You recently received the following letter from your old college roommate, Charles Black:

Dear Roomie,

I hope things are going well with you and the practice of law. I continue to enjoy working for Metropolitan Life. I may drive up to visit you when the family gathers at Thanksgiving.

Frankly, I am not looking forward to it—again! Specifically, the mandatory touch football game. As you know, tradition requires that I do the kickoff. Tradition also requires that my cousin Lucinda hold the football for me. Unfortunately, **she** thinks tradition also requires that she pull the ball away (at least on the initial kickoff and sometimes also during the game)—causing me to fall on my butt, to the great hilarity of the rest of the family.

I have asked her to stop, but she just laughs at me and once said, "So sue me, already." Right! Lucinda has a law firm on full-time retainer and thinks litigation is the great American indoor sport. And with the money she inherited from Harry after he died three years ago, she can afford it.

Last year, she actually promised not to pull the ball away on purpose. She did anyway, and claimed she has a muscle spasm. And, she said, "An oral promise is as good as the paper it is written on."

Is there anything you would suggest? Anyway, I will give you a call and perhaps we can get together.

Your friend,

Charlie

What a sad story. Think about it from a drafter's perspective.

Part II

PREPARATION AND PLANNING

Chapter 7

GETTING STARTED

The first three steps of the drafting process involve understanding the client's objectives, knowing the audience, and appreciating the legal and factual context in which the document will operate. These three steps are closely related, as they provide the foundation on which everything else is built.

A. DETERMINE CLIENT OBJECTIVES

A drafted document is not an end unto itself; it is merely a means to an end. Documents of the same general type—wills, for example—may have radically different objectives, depending on the client. The cookie-cutter drafter who does not appreciate this potential for difference among clients is not likely to produce a document that fully meets the client's needs.

Contracts, good contracts, are not solely the product of legal knowledge and skill. They are also the product of business and practical knowledge—*do not leave your common sense at the door to the law school or the law firm!* This business and practical knowledge will be used to interpret the contracts especially in jurisdictions where a weak form of the parol evidence rule is in force; as a result, this knowledge is needed in order to initially draft a good contract. As a result, it is critical that counsel understand the client's business, its goals, and the forces that drive the enterprise. This will enable the drafter to produce practical, precise documentation that will properly allocate risk between the parties, provide a legal mechanism for exchange and redress for shortfalls in performance, and stand up to interpretation and enforcement in the litigation when everything has broken down.

1. The Basic Questions

The questions the drafter needs to ask of every client can be expressed in several different ways. All of them relate to the client's objectives, motivation, and purpose.

- **Why** do you want to give your son a general power of attorney? **Why** do you want to make it illegal for a person to keep or own more than three dogs within the city limits?

- What **purpose** is this exclusive dealership agreement supposed to serve? What is the **purpose** of requiring residents to remove their trash cans from the street within six hours after pick-up?

- By establishing a trust for your granddaughter, what **good** are you trying to provide for her and what **harm** do you want to protect her from? By making it illegal to operate car washes on Sunday, what **good** do you intend to promote and what **harm** do you intend to prevent?

- What **experiences** have you had with this particular type of transaction? Did it go smoothly? What made it work? What went wrong? What **experiences** have you had with this particular problem? What are the desirable aspects of the activity that the legislation should either encourage or leave alone? What exactly were the undesirable aspects that should be corrected or prohibited?

2. How the Information Is Used

The information these questions elicit will dictate both the form and content of the drafted document. Knowing the client's objectives, the drafter can move toward them in the most direct and efficient manner and not clutter the document with provisions irrelevant to that objective.

Suppose that a member of county council says to the part-time county attorney, "A strip-joint has opened up out on Highway 647 and I want you to draft an ordinance dealing with this problem." Wait a minute! What exactly is *the problem*? What is the ultimate objective? Consider the possible alternatives and how they affect the drafter's response to the request.

- **Suppression of immoral conduct.** If this is the objective, then the drafter's job is to define the prohibited conduct in a constitutionally sufficient manner and prohibit it.

- **Impact on neighboring residential property values.** If the location of this type of establishment rather than the intrinsic nature of the enterprise is the problem, then the drafter should probably approach it from a zoning perspective.

- **Connection with alcohol.** The county council member may feel that sex and alcohol are a bad combination. If so, the drafter would want to address the problem from a liquor-licensing perspective.

- **Noise, lights, traffic, and parking concerns.** If this is the problem, the drafter may want to avoid the constitutional problems entirely by broadening the regulation to include establishments other than those engaged in "expressive conduct."

- **Competitive or economic pressure.** The county council member may be under pressure from less controversial drinking establishments to eliminate this form of competition. If so, the drafting would want to approach the problem from an economic perspective.

Sometimes the specific document the client requests is not the document the clients needs at all. A client may ask a lawyer to draft a living will when what this person really needs is durable power of attorney. The drafter cannot know that without making the basic inquiries. Likewise, a legislator's objectives may already be the focus of another statute, with the problem being one of inadequate enforcement rather than the lack of a basic prohibition. If so, the drafter needs to suggest an appropriate solution, such as increased funding for enforcement.

3. Objectives From a Variety of Perspectives

In addition to asking these questions directly, the drafter can also address the client objective inquiry from a variety of other perspectives.

a. Other Parties to the Transaction. Although the drafter typically drafts on behalf of one of the parties to a contract, with that client's objectives being preeminent, the drafter must also keep the other party's objectives in mind. After all, the client's threshold objective is to obtain this other party's assent to the contract or legislation. The client's ultimate objectives are often limited accordingly. Put differently, the client's relevant objectives are the attainable objectives. The drafter must make the client understand that.

In counseling the client in this regard, the drafter may discover that the client really has no desire to contract at all. The proposed contract, rather, will serve some ulterior purpose. For example, a person who is under a duty to bargain with another person but who has absolutely no desire to contract with that person may propose a contract whose terms are patently unacceptable. Or a legislator may want to propose legislation, not in anticipation of it being passed, but rather to serve as political window dressing. The preparation of such documents is game-playing, not drafting in the true sense of the word.

b. Scope of Anticipated Use. The client's intended use of the document is also important. If the document will be used between two named parties and the objective is limited to regulating the transaction between them, then the focus can be limited accordingly. But if the client's objective is to use the document in many transactions, with different parties, each having slightly different circumstances, then the focus must be broader to cover all the possibilities. The drafter of a standard lease agreement that will be used in a large apartment complex must anticipate and deal with all the rental issues that might arise from renting to a wide variety of tenants (differing in occupation, age, marital status, children, pets, and the like). The garage apartment lease agreement between Aunt Maude and her nephew Calvin will have a more limited and focused objective.

Similarly, legislation that is intended to affect a limited and discrete class of persons or transactions will be drafted with a different set of considerations in mind than legislation with a wider anticipated impact.

c. Multiple–Client Objectives.

Determining client objectives is more complicated when the client consists of more than one person or entity. A three-person partnership may decide that it wants to subcontract some of its operations. Partner A may want to save on production costs, Partner B believes a subcontractor can do the work better, and Partner C is looking at the tax advantages. Before the drafter can hope to produce a suitable contract, the drafter must tell the partners that their objectives differ and may even conflict. If the drafter can accommodate all three objectives, and everyone understands why the document might contain provisions totally irrelevant to their particular interest, fine. But if a conflict develops—for example, the higher quality that Partner B seeks is going to conflict with the lower cost objective of Partner A—then the drafter must simply tell the client to work it out.

A similar problem exists when drafting on behalf of a corporation. Accounting may have one objective, Sales another, and Research and Development another. For some purposes, husband and wife are also treated as a single legal entity. Again, however, the individual components of these collective entities may have differing objectives. But until the client becomes of one mind about its objectives, by either consensus or resort to higher authority, the drafter cannot proceed any further.

Finally, the most difficult multiple-client problem arises when two persons purport to share a common objective, but actually have conflicting interests they do not fully realize. Between buyer and seller, the common objective might relate to the sale of a car at a certain price. Between a tortfeasor and an injured person, it is an amicable settlement. But beyond generally shared objective, the specific interests of the parties are apt to differ appreciably.

Legislative drafters face equally difficult multiple-client problems. The drafter who works for a legislative drafting service usually drafts statutes at the request of an individual legislator, who is the client. But the legislative drafter may also be on the staff of a committee, with each member having a slightly different agenda. A consensus may exist over the need for a statute creating liability for sales of alcohol to already intoxicated patrons, but the legislator who is an active member of Mothers Against Drunk Driving may have one objective in mind, while another who is beholden to the Tavern Keepers Association may have another. Whose objective does the drafter attempt to serve? An attorney in private practice drafting proposed legislation on behalf of a consortium of business interests may face similar dilemmas.

4. Evaluating Client Objectives

The drafter's role in evaluating the client's objectives is limited. The general rule is that the client's objectives are the client's business; the drafter's business is to accomplish them. This rule is subject to three exceptions.

First, if the client's objective is illegal or fraudulent, then the drafter clearly cannot produce a document accomplishing that result. However, this rule is easier to state than it is to apply. A contract for murder is one thing; the merger of two companies, possibly resulting in the creation of an illegal monopoly, is quite another.

Second, the drafter has an obligation to point out the other legal ramifications that achieving a particular objective might have. For example, the client's immediate objective might be to obtain total operational control over a particular business entity. Even if that particular transaction is not itself illegal, on a cumulative basis it may pose an antitrust problem for the client in the future.

Third, depending on the nature of the relationship, the drafter should be sensitive to and warn the client of objectives that, when achieved, would frustrate other, more important client objectives. A stringently drafted company policy on taking sick leave might serve the narrow objective of correcting sick leave abuse, but it might be inconsistent with a broader objective of creating good employer-employee relationships. If appropriate, the drafter should advise the client of this. Similarly, it is not unheard of in legislative politics for opposing factions to reach a truce of sorts, under which both sides tacitly agree not to introduce legislation on a particular matter. If the drafter prepares and the legislator introduces legislation in violation of this truce, the result may be retaliatory legislation that is definitely not consistent with the legislator's objectives. The savvy legislative drafter will advise the legislator of this.

In sum, the drafter is more than a thorough planner, investigator, and writer. The drafter is also a counselor to the client, in the highest sense of the word.

B. KNOW THE AUDIENCE

The client is the primary user of the drafted document. But drafted documents are nearly always read and used by a wide variety of people, often for different purposes. This is the audience of a document. The drafter should identify each member of this audience and draft with their varying uses in mind.

1. Identity of the Audience

Assume, for example, that the owner of a piece of commercial property wants to have an office building constructed on the site. The owner asks a lawyer to draft a construction contract. The client's purposes and those of the other potential users of this document can be summarized as follows:

- The **owner** will first use the contract, with attached plans and specifications, to solicit bids from contractors. Later, the owner will use it to monitor the contractor's performance and determine the owner's duty of payment.

- The **mortgage company** will use the contract in evaluating whether to make a construction loan.

- The **zoning or building commissioner** will use it in determining whether to grant a building permit.

- The **potential contractors** will use it in formulating their bids.

- The **winning contractor** will also use it to determine exactly what must be done—when, where, and how.

- Potential and actual **subcontractors** will also use it in making bids and performing their portion of the work.

- **Assignees of rights** and **delegatees of duties** will use it to determine the scope of their rights and duties.

- The **bank** will use it to determine when and whether to issue progress payments.

- The **architect** will use it to determine whether to issue a certificate of completion.

- If litigation ensues, **opposing counsel** will use it to prove or disprove breach.

- The **judge** or **jury** hearing the case will use it to determine liability and damages.

2.   Characteristics of the Audience

The drafter must not only consider the identity and purposes of each potential user of the document, the drafter must also consider the personal characteristics, dispositions, and attitude of each user. The tone, style, terminology, and layout of a document may radically differ, depending on whether it will be used primarily by unsophisticated consumers lacking an opportunity to bargain over the terms or by the lawyers and officers of two large corporations.

The drafter must also take into account whether the various users are going to be friendly or hostile to the interests of the client. For example, although the beneficiary of a will is usually friendly, the disinherited son certainly will not be. Thus, the disinheritance provision should be drafted with special care. Drafters also need to keep the "reader in bad faith" in mind. A contract might be perfectly adequate for regulating the relationship between two parties who are dealing with each other on a good faith basis. But if the drafter suspects that the other party might later discover a strong economic incentive for getting out of the contract, then the drafter should go over the document with a fine-toothed comb, looking for vagueness, anything that is even remotely ambiguous, substantive terms that are left to implication, and other possible loopholes.

The drafter must also recognize that some important users of legal documents, the courts, are particularly hostile to some kinds of contracts and contracting parties. Contracts of adhesion may not be enforced at all; contracts are construed against the party who drafted them; insurance companies, banks, large corporations, merchants, and employers are also the frequent targets of hostile contract interpretation. The courts also scrutinize some types of statutes very closely, such as those purporting to deprive the court of jurisdiction.

3. Accommodating the Various Audiences

Accommodating multiple audiences and purposes is often a difficult task for the drafter. What the lawyer-audience wants and needs in the way of precise legal language, the lay-user audience finds stuffy and incomprehensible. A subject matter that must be quite detailed to satisfy the needs of one audience may need to be more general to satisfy the needs of another. The dilemma is not easily resolved. All the drafter can do is exercise sound discretion, always keeping the client's interest foremost in mind.

Occasionally, a drafter may conclude that the document is intended to have too many people within its audience, each with divergent characteristics and inclinations that cannot be accommodated. Thus, rather than a tri-partite contract between Able, Baker, and Carol, the drafter may decide to create two bilateral contracts—one between Able and Baker, efficiently using terms of art and working from a prior history of business dealings, and another between

Baker and Carol, now avoiding trade jargon and the existence of a shared set of assumptions about what each party is going to do.

C. DETERMINE THE CONTEXT OF THE DOCUMENT

Drafted documents do not exist in a legal vacuum. The drafter cannot simply research only the law that impacts directly on the drafted document or obtain from the client only the specific facts that will be incorporated into the terms of the document. The drafter must fully appreciate the broader legal and factual environment in which the document is going to function.

1. Legal Context

Basic contract law aside, the broader legal context will vary appreciably from contract to contract. One drafting a contract in the heavily regulated securities industry must keep in mind that, while a particular document may be perfectly legal and effective when viewed in isolation, when it is put in the context of other legal requirements and constraints on the conduct to the parties, it simply will not accomplish the desired objective. Contracts involving performance in a foreign jurisdiction often fail their purpose simply because the drafter did not fully understand the broader legal context in which the document was to operate.

Similarly, if the case law evidences a growing hostility toward a particular type of governmental action—regulatory takings, for example, under the Fifth and Fourteenth Amendments—and the legislative drafter does not appreciate this legal environment, then the legislation may ultimately fail, even though at the time of its enactment it apparently met all the controlling tests. A drafter more sensitive to the trend might have drafted the legislation, accomplishing essentially the same objective, in a slightly different manner.

Another kind of legal context that the drafter must accommodate relates to the other contracts the client may have with either the other contracting party or third parties.

The new contract must mesh with the existing framework, or the existing framework may need to be revised.

For example, an employer should not enter into an employment contract with an individual who is subject to a covenant-not-to-compete with this individual's former employer. Doing so may subject the new employer to a suit for inducement of breach of contract. It may never occur to the employer-client to inquire about this, but the drafter should. And if the prospective employee is not forthcoming with the information or seems duplicitous, particularly in an industry where such covenants are standard, then the drafter should inquire of the former employer (with the client's consent). And if this employer is not cooperative in providing that information, then the drafter should consider including a warranty and indemnity clause in the contract, where the employee warrants no existing legal impediments to the contract and agrees to compensate the employer for any losses as a result of a breach of the warranty.

Similarly, a drafter preparing an exclusive dealing contract for a client should make sure that this client does not have an exclusive dealing clause buried in a contract with another party. Clients are often totally ignorant of what they have agreed to in various contracts.

One of the problems with American legislation is that it usually does not follow the code format of civil law countries. The "codes" of federal and state law are nothing more than individual statutes that legislative councils and codifiers have attempted to put together into something resembling a coherent form. In American law, thus, one often finds several different statutes, enacted at different times by different legislators, dealing with the same broad topic. There are, for example, over 50 separate federal statutes that deal with some aspect of the employer-employee relationship. Many of these statutes were apparently enacted in total disregard of the existing fabric of federal employment law. The result is an enormously complex and litigation-ridden set of statutes.

To avoid this, the legislative drafter should first attain a bird's eye view of the entire corpus of relevant law—the statutes themselves and the cases construing them—dealing directly or tangentially with the subject matter at hand. This will then provide the legal backdrop against which the new statute can be drafted. First, an understanding of the full legal context will enable the drafter to avoid duplicate legislation. The Equal Pay Act and the Civil Rights Act of 1964 suffer from this deficiency, since they both prohibit wage discrimination on the basis of sex. Second, new legislation should mesh with existing legislation like the wheels of a clock. This is possible only if the drafter is aware of what the existing wheels look like and how they function.

2. Factual Context

Documents regulating business, commercial, and significant social transactions are predicated on a number of often unstated assumptions and usages of trade. For example, in the field of commercial real estate, rents are quoted in annual rent per square foot of space. Thus, "$12/ft" is really $1/ft per month. Someone outside the industry with experience only in residential leases as a tenant may not know the convention, which the parties assume everyone knows, and could mistakenly draft the lease with rent twelve times higher than the parties intend. The drafter must be familiar with the prior practices between the parties, the usages of the trade in general, and the whole factual context in which the regulated activity is going to occur. This enables the drafter to know generally what should be included in the document.

It would be difficult, for example, to draft a contract between a movie producer and director based solely on information elicited directly from either or both the parties. At the minimum, such an undertaking would require knowledge of how movies are made, the traditions of the producer-director relationship, the tacit assumptions of producers and directors about their duties and responsibilities, and the expectations of each. Similarly, the lawyer who does not understand the complex traditions of the construction business is ill-equipped to draft a document regulating that process. The standard practice of incorporating various trade-association-approved provisions, which are notoriously ill-drafted, is itself enough to drive the neophyte drafter to distraction—because they are based on factual assumptions about trade practices that the drafter is unfamiliar with.

Drafters inexperienced in a particular field are at a distinct disadvantage. This is not the kind of information that can be acquired from a book. The beginning drafter, however, can do one of three things. First, the drafter may have to decline the representation, on grounds of lack of competency to draft the requested document. Second, the drafter may choose to associate with a more experienced attorney and write it off as a learning experience. Third, if the factual context is not too arcane, the drafter may be able to learn enough by asking the client to provide a tour of the plant or business, to explain what is happening and why, and perhaps to discuss the business in general. Most clients are flattered by this interest in their affairs and attention to detail, provided the lawyer does not bill excessively for it.

Legislative drafters are usually more aware of the need to become immersed in factual details than are drafters of private law documents. This, ostensibly at least, is the purpose of the interminable hearings that Congress and the state legislatures hold on pending legislation. Legislation at the city and county level, however, often suffers from a lack of factual understanding by both the drafter and the public officials. This may be due to a lack of resources, political pressure to do something quickly, or an ignorance of the need for such information. The conscientious local legislative drafter should, however, do whatever is practicable to find out exactly what the facts are before drafting ordinances involving them.

Exercise 4

1. Assume that a client has asked you to draft the following documents. You have scheduled a meeting to discuss the matter. The first thing you will want to know, of course, is why the client wants this document. Consider all of the possible objectives the client might have and how each of these objectives would affect the substance of the document.

    a.   A state statute regulating personal watercraft or *jet boats*.

    b.   A provision prohibiting *moonlighting* that will be incorporated into an employee handbook. [Since a handbook is likely to be construed as having contractual significance, its provisions must be drafted with the same care that would be used when drafting any other contract.]

2. Now evaluate these possible objectives from the perspective of other parties to the transaction, prior transactions between these parties, the scope of the anticipated use, and the possibility of conflict if the client is a multiple entity.

3. Identify everyone, other than the immediate parties, who might have to deal with these documents and consider how their characteristics might effect the drafting process.

4. Concisely describe what you would look for when exploring the legal and factual context within which these documents will operate.

Chapter 8

DRAFTING WITHIN THE LAW

The law has an enormous effect on both the form and substance of drafted documents. Constitutions, treaties, executive orders, statutes, court rules, ordinances, administrative regulations, common law rules, and case law form a maze through which the drafter must pass to reach the desired client objective. Some paths lead to a dead end. Some paths are shorter than others. Some paths are blocked by gates, which can be opened only with the right key. The drafter cannot afford to get through the maze by trial and error. Rather, the drafter must see the maze from above, plot the path in advance, and obtain the necessary keys. In other words, the drafter must know the law.

A. FORM

In 1977, the New York General Assembly passed a law requiring that certain consumer contracts be "written in a clear and coherent manner using words with common everyday meanings" and that the document also be "appropriately divided and captioned by its various sections." This marked the beginning of what has come to be known as "Plain English" legislation. Other states followed suit, as did Congress. Today, a plethora of statutes and regulations require, in a variety of ways, that consumer contracts be readily understandable by the average person. The requirements of the law in this area are complex, overlapping, and sometimes contradictory. However, many of them mandate satisfaction with a numerical readability index. One of the more common readability indexes is discussed and illustrated in Chapter 17.

Plain English requirements, however, are not limited to consumer contracts. President Carter once issued an ironically obtuse Executive Order requiring that federal regulations be written in understandable form. Department of Defense regulations also require that equipment manuals written by government contractors satisfy a certain readability formula.

Other laws affect the form of drafted documents in more specific ways. For example, UCC § 2–316 requires that a disclaimer of the warranty of merchantability be conspicuous. To determine what this means, however, the drafter must consult the case law. Some state statutes prescribe the exact wording and typeface for living wills; the slightest deviation may result in the document being declared void. The Federal Trade Commission "Holder in Due Course Rule" mandates that a specific notice appear on all consumer credit contracts.

Compliance with these statutes can be tricky. For example, the Uniform Arbitration Act requires that "[n]otice that a contract is subject to arbitration pursuant to this chapter shall be typed in underlined capital letters, or rubber-stamped prominently, on the first page of the contract...." That seems straight-forward enough. However, one state court of appeals held that the requirement was satisfied by a notice that was typed in all-capital, boldface letters, in a font somewhat larger than that used for the text of the contract, but not underlined. The court held that the purpose of the requirement was to make the notice prominent and that this notice satisfied that purpose. The court rejected a bright-line, literal interpretation of the statute, noting that the following notice would not satisfy the statute if it were construed in that fashion:

This Contract Is Subject To Arbitration Pursuant To § 15–48–10 of the South Carolina Code of Laws (1976).

That notice would fail because it has no line drawn under it and is not in all-capital letters. On the other hand, the court suggested that while the following would satisfy the literal requirements of the statute, it would not serve the intended purpose and might, thus, also be ineffective because of the size of the type.

THIS CONTRACT IS SUBJECT TO ARBITRATION PURSUANT TO § 15–48–10 OF THE SOUTH CAROLINA CODE OF LAWS (1976).

The court rejected a literal interpretation that would disallow the first notice but allow the second one. While the court's approach is reasonable, it flies in the face of express statutory language—which is what a drafter should be entitled to rely on, but in this instance obviously could not.

B.   MEANING

Bridging the gap between form and substance, and partaking a little of both, are the words that the law requires a drafter to use to achieve a particular legal result. Some of these are true terms of art. A word can qualify as a legal term of art in three ways:

First, some specific words must be used to accomplish a particular result; no synonym will do. For example, to be negotiable under UCC § 3–104, a note must be payable to "order" or "bearer." "Merchantability" is also a term of art since that specific word must be used when disclaiming it under UCC § 2–316.

Second, some words are terms of art in the sense that they serve as an abbreviation for a complex legal concept that would take many words to describe fully. In estate law, *"per stirpes"* is such a term. Similarly, the term "Rule of 78" refers to a formula for computing the portion of a finance charge that has been earned at different times during the life of a bank loan. One statutory version of this rule is a confusing 185 words long. But people in the industry know exactly what it means and it can even be used in consumer documents.

Third, some words are terms of art in the sense that the legal meaning is materially different from the conventional meaning. For example, "criminal conversation" has nothing to do with a telephone call between two gangsters. Similarly, "insane" has a legal meaning that is considerably narrower than its colloquial meaning.

The drafter must be aware of all three forms of terms of art and use them appropriately.

The drafter must also be aware of the legal meaning of other words, even though they are not terms of art. For example, a drafter in a particular jurisdiction might discover that the courts have construed the word "street" as not including alleys, but that "public way" covers both. The drafter would then choose the word that matches the intent of the client.

Occasionally, a statute will impose a meaning on words that are used in certain types of documents. A New York statute, for example, dictates the meaning of a real estate mortgage acceleration clause that is worded in a certain way.

In determining a word's legal meaning, a drafter should consult not only a standard legal dictionary, but also the multi-volume *Words and Phrases*. This invaluable set of books contains a comprehensive collection of cases construing every conceivable word that a drafter might be tempted to use. *Words and Phrases* is one of the drafter's most valuable assets.

C. SUBSTANCE

The law also affects the substance of drafted documents.

1. Prohibition

Laws frequently prohibit certain contract provisions. Some prohibitions are express. The UCC, for example, prohibits a contract provision that limits consequential damages for personal injuries resulting from defective consumer goods. Other prohibitions are implied. For example, a person cannot effectively contract away statutory rights if the statute serves a broader public good or if the purpose was to limit this exercise of freedom of contract. An employee cannot contract away the minimum wage and maximum hour protections of the federal Fair Labor Standards Act.

The effect of a prohibition may be nothing more than the nullification of an inconsistent provision. The law thus prohibits, by rendering them unenforceable, employment termination agreements releasing the employer from possible violations of the Age Discrimination in Employment Act unless the agreement contains certain specific provisions. Contracts that are unconscionable or contrary to public policy are similarly prohibited, in the sense that the courts will not enforce them.

In some cases, however, a violation of the prohibition may result in civil or criminal liability. The Uniform Residential Landlord and Tenant Act prohibits certain provisions and imposes a penalty of three months' rent on landlords who knowingly include these provisions in lease agreements. Wage Payment statutes frequently provide treble damages for violations.

Private law documents can also operate by way of prohibition on other private law documents. For example, a contract may effectively prohibit the delegation of duties or assignment of rights under that contract. The drafter needs to know this before attempting to draft a document purporting to do either.

2. Requirement

Some laws affirmatively require that certain things be done or that they be done in a certain manner. The Statute of Frauds requires several types of contracts to be evidenced by a signed writing. State laws frequently require that wills be witnessed by a designated number of persons. UCC § 6–107 requires that bulk transfer notices contain certain specified terms.

Failure to satisfy these requirements usually makes the document no more than unenforceable. A drafter's failure to adhere to some legal requirements, however, will also result in civil or criminal liability for the client. For example, under some state laws, the failure to include a notice of latent defects in a contract for the sale of a house will subject the seller to liability.

3. Permission and Authorization

Some laws merely permit or authorize things to be done or allow them to be done in a certain manner. The National Labor Relations Act allows employers and unions to include in collective bargaining agreements a provision that requires employees to become union members as a condition of employment—a requirement that would otherwise be illegal.

Another provision of the statute, however, also authorizes states to outlaw these provisions—a power they would not otherwise have.

Often, the permission is subject to a condition. Living will statutes create the authority for a person to order the cessation of life support systems, but only if certain rather stringent conditions are satisfied.

4. Denial of Permission or Authorization

Some laws limit the power or authority of certain persons or entities. A not-for-profit corporation, for example, lacks the authority to engage in certain activities. The drafter of a not-for-profit corporate charter needs to have those limits well in mind. Similarly, the law generally limits the power or authority of minors to contract.

5. Other Consequences

The law may establish other consequences that the drafter must be aware of. For example, conflicts law determines which state's substantive law controls the interpretation and enforcement of a contract made between individuals living in different states. The drafter needs to know which state's law will control under these conflicts rules and what that law provides, in contrast to the law of the other state. The drafter may then want to alter the result through a choice-of-law provision in the contract. Drafting estate documents is also heavily influenced by the tax consequences of distributing the assets of the estate one way rather than another.

6. Implied Terms

The drafter needs to know what terms the law will imply if a document is silent on a particular point. Statutes frequently contain "unless otherwise agreed" provisions that supply omitted terms for certain types of contracts. UCC Article 2, for example, contains innumerable gap fillers, terms that will be read into a contract for the sale of goods if the contract is silent. Even in the absence of a statute, if a court determines that the parties intended to create a contract, the court may imply a term simply to keep the transaction from failing. For example, if a contract is silent on the time for performance, the courts will often hold that performance must be within a reasonable time rather than find an absence of assent over what is usually regarded as a critical contract term. Likewise, under both the common law and the UCC, custom and usage are implied terms of many contracts. The courts will also imply a covenant of good faith and fair dealing in certain types of contracts.

A drafter should never deliberately rely on implied terms to fill gaps in a document. Although the drafter may know that these terms will be implied, the parties may not. That may come as an unpleasant surprise later, when the client angrily tells the drafter that this is not what was intended. And even if the implied term is consistent with the client's desires, the better practice is to make it express.

D. CREATING LEGAL CHECKLISTS

A drafter cannot count on remembering everything that the law prohibits, requires, permits, denies authority for, attaches meaning to, or implies. Thus, the drafter's knowledge must be systematized. A legal checklist is an indispensable drafting tool.

Unlike the factual checklist that draws information primarily from the client, a legal checklist draws from the drafter's knowledge of the law. Often, the legal checklist and the factual checklist will be consolidated, for the drafter's benefit, into a single document. The legal aspect of the checklist, however, should cover all the categories of substantive law discussed above. The drafter should create this checklist during the research step of the drafting process. If the drafter anticipates doing this type of document on a recurring basis, then the checklist should be retained in an active file and kept current as the statutory and case law changes.

E. DRAFTING WITH STATUTORY LANGUAGE IN MIND

Tracking specific statutory language is sometimes necessary to achieve a desired result. For example, a merger clause is designed to trigger the operation of the parol evidence rule, by stating that what is written represents the final and exclusive terms of the agreement between the parties. An effective merger clause can be drafted in a variety of ways. However, in a contract for the sale of goods, a drafter would be well advised to follow the language of UCC § 2–202, which is a statutory form of the parol evidence rule, as follows:

§ 2–202. Final Written Expression: Parol or Extrinsic Evidence (emphasis added)

Terms with respect to which the confirmatory memoranda of the parties agree or which are otherwise set forth in a writing **intended** by the parties as a **final expression of their agreement** with respect to such terms as are included therein [achieving *partial integration*] may not be contradicted by evidence of any prior agreement or of a contemporaneous oral agreement but may be explained or supplemented

(a) by course of dealing or usage of trade (Section 1–205) or by course of performance (Section 2–208); and

(b) by evidence of consistent additional terms unless the court finds the writing to have been intended also as a **complete and exclusive statement of the terms of the agreement** [achieving *full integration*].

The purpose of a contractual merger clause is to make the parties' intent express. The parties may intend to do one or all of three things: (1) to indicate that the writing is the final expression of the terms stated, thus achieving a partial integration; (2) to also indicate that these are the only terms the parties have agreed to, thus achieving a full integration; and (3) to indicate that no other agreements of any kind exist with respect to the subject matter of this transaction or, alternatively, to indicate that they do.

The merger clause below incorporates the critical language of the statute (in bold print), as follows:

The parties **intend** for the terms contained in this written contract to be the **final expression of their agreement** with respect to these terms [achieving *partial integration*]. The parties also **intend** for this written contract to be the **complete and exclusive statement of the terms of this agreement** [achieving *full integration*]. No other agreements of any kind exist between the parties [excluding even contracts that might otherwise be deemed *collateral* and thus not subject to the parol evidence rule].

Alternatively, if the parties do not intend to deny the existence of other contracts, then the drafter would replace the last sentence with the following:

> This contract is not **intended** to supercede or negate the existence of a separate contract of this date giving Buyer an option to purchase additional Widgets on the terms and conditions stated in that contract.

Sometimes, precisely tracking the statutory language in this manner will get the drafter into trouble. For example, federal law permits employers and unions to include in collective bargaining agreements provisions that "require as a condition of employment **membership** [in the union] on or after the thirtieth day following the beginning of such employment or the effective date of such agreement, whichever is the later. . . ." A contract provision worded in just that fashion would, however, be illegal. This is because the courts have construed the term "membership" as meaning nothing more than the payment of a pro rata share of the union's expenses as the bargaining representative—a meaning that is vastly at odds with the literal and colloquial meaning of the term. The courts have also held that a union commits an unfair labor practice if it fails to inform employees about the limited nature of their obligation to the union. A union security provision that merely tracks the statutory language would not provide the necessary information, since an employee would normally construe the term "membership" as requiring actual membership.

Exercise 5

A client wants you to draft a waiver of age discrimination claims that departing employees will be asked to sign. These waivers are regulated by the Older Workers Benefit Protection Act, 29 U.S.C. § 626(f), amending the Age Discrimination in Employment Act, 29 U.S.C. §§ 621–634. Prepare a legal checklist based on the provisions of this statute, the EEOC Regulations, and some relevant cases.

A.   29 U.S.C. § 626(f):

(1) An individual may not waive any right or claim under this Act unless the waiver is knowing and voluntary. Except as provided in paragraph (2), a waiver may not be considered knowing and voluntary unless at a minimum—

(A) the waiver is part of an agreement between the individual and the employer that is written in a manner calculated to be understood by such individual, or by the average individual eligible to participate;

(B) the waiver specifically refers to rights or claims arising under this Act;

(C) the individual does not waive rights or claims that may arise after the date the waiver is executed;

(D) the individual waives rights or claims only in exchange for consideration in addition to anything of value to which the individual already is entitled;

(E) the individual is advised in writing to consult with an attorney prior to executing the agreement;

(F) (i) the individual is given a period of at least 21 days within which to consider the agreement; or

    (ii) if a waiver is requested in connection with an exit incentive or other employment termination program offered to a group or class of employees, the individual is given a period of at least 45 days within which to consider the agreement;

(G) the agreement provides that for a period of at least 7 days following the execution if such agreement, the individual may revoke the agreement, and the agreement shall not become effective or enforceable until the revocation period has expired;

(H) if a waiver is requested in connection with an exit incentive or other employment termination program offered to a group or class of employees, the employer (at the commencement of the period specified in subparagraph (F)) informs the individual in writing in a manner calculated to be understood by the average individual eligible to participate, as to—

(i) any class, unit, or group of individuals covered by such program, any eligibility factors for such program, and any time limits applicable to such program; and

(ii) the job titles and ages of all individuals eligible or selected for the program, and the ages of all individuals in the same job classification or organizational unit who are not eligible or selected for the program.

(2) A waiver in settlement of a charge filed with the Equal Employment Opportunity Commission, or an action filed in court by the individual or the individual's representative, alleging age discrimination or a kind prohibited under section 4 or 15 may not be considered knowing and voluntary unless at a minimum—

(A) subparagraphs (A) through (E) of paragraph (1) have been met; and

(B) the individual is given a reasonable period of time within which to consider the settlement agreement.

B. Equal Employment Opportunity Commission, 29 C.F.R. § 1625.22:

. . . .

(b) Wording of Waiver Agreements

. . . .

(3) Waiver agreements must be drafted in plain language geared to the level of understanding of the individual party to the agreement of individuals eligible to participate. Employers should take into account such factors as the level of comprehension and education of typical participants. Consideration of these factors usually will require the limitation or elimination of technical jargon and of long, complex sentences.

. . . .

(6) [T]he waiver agreement must refer to the Age Discrimination in Employment Act (ADEA) by name in connection with the waiver.

. . . .

(e) Time Periods.

. . . .

(5) The 7 day revocation period cannot be shortened by the parties, by agreement or otherwise.

(6) An employee may sign a release prior to the end of the 21 or 45 day time period, thereby commencing the mandatory 7 day revocation period. This is permissible as long as the employee's decision to accept such shortening of time is knowing and voluntary and is not induced by the employer through fraud, misrepresentation, a threat to withdraw or alter the offeror prior to the expiration of the 21 or 45 day time period, or by providing different terms to employees who sign the release prior to the expiration of such time period.

C. *Griffin v. Kraft General Foods, Inc.,* 62 F.2d 368 (11th Cir. 1995):

. . . .

2. Nonstatutory Factors Showing That the Waiver Was Not "Knowing and Voluntary"

The employees contend that the district court should have considered the "totality of the circumstances," in addition to the explicit OWBPA requirements, to determine if their waiver of ADEA rights was "knowing and voluntary." Prior to the OWBPA's enactment, a federal common-law rule based on the ADEA had emerged permitting ADEA waivers only if they were knowing and voluntary, as determined by an open-ended list of factors . . . . . The OWBPA's language and legislative history strongly support the plaintiff's contention that the nonstatutory circumstances considered in these cases survive the enactment of the OWBPA. . . .

D. *Pierce v. Atchison, Topeka & Santa Fe Ry. Co.,* 65 F.3d 562 (7th Cir. 1995):

. . . .

Like the other circuits that currently employ the federal totality approach, a court should look to a number of factors to assess the validity of a particular release, including, but not limited to: (1) the employee's education and business experience; (2) the employee's input in negotiating the terms of the settlement; (3) the clarity of the agreement; (4) the amount of time the employee had for deliberation before signing the release; (5) whether the employee actually read the release and considered its terms before signing it; (6) whether the employee was represented by counsel or consulted with an attorney; (7) whether the consideration given in exchange for the waiver exceeded the benefits to which the employee was already entitled by contract law; and (8) whether the employee's release was induced by improper conduct on the defendant's part. . . .

E. *Wamsley v. Champlin Ref. & Chem., Inc.,* 11 F.3d 534 (5th Cir. 1993):

. . . .

In November and December, Champlin informed Appellants that they were among the employees who were going to be "let go." Champlin provided them with a "Notice Pertaining to Release of Claims" document and a "Release of Claims" agreement. The notice included the following provision:

> Although you may execute the Release of Claims as soon as you wish, you also may take up to 45 days from your receipt of the Release of Claims to consider it. Your decision to execute the Release of Claims and accept benefits under the Termination Pay Plan will be revocable for seven days after execution, and no payment of termination pay will be made until that period has expired. Therefore, to be able to provide your termination pay to you not later than five business days after the termination of your employment, the Company must receive your executed Release of Claims at least seven days before that payment date.

The release provided for Appellants' waiver of any action or claim against Champlin and "its successors, assigns, [and] affiliates," "relating to our arising out of [their] employment with [Champlin] . . . or the termination of such employment, including but not limited to, claims for . . . age discrimination under . . . the Age Discrimination in Employment Act of 1967." The release made clear that the benefits to be paid under the Plan constituted the consideration for the release.

. . . .

Appellants responded to Champlin's motion and proof by tendering affidavits in which each swore to facts surrounding their termination and execution of the release. Appellants claimed to have been told by certain individuals in the Champlin organization that they had to sign and return the release by their termination date, less than 45 days after receiving the notice, in order to receive benefits under the Plan.

. . . .

DISCUSSION

Knowing and Voluntary Waiver

Congress, through enactment of the OWBPA, has determined that employers must afford their employees the right to consider for 45 days whether they should waive any rights or claims *vis à vis* the ADEA in exchange for benefits under a group termination program. 29 U.S.C. § 626(f)(1)(F)(ii). Appellants contend, *inter alia*, that Champlin denied them this right. Champlin responds by arguing that it complied with the 45–day requirement and pointing to the "Notice Pertaining to Release of Claims" document as proof. Appellants counter by swearing that the information contained therein was orally countermanded by certain persons at Champlin. Champlin, of course, denies that Appellants were told anything of the sort.

Which version accurately describes Champlin's dealings with Appellants is an issue that cannot be resolved by the court through summary judgment. . . . We are unable to conclude, therefore, that Appellants' releases were "knowing and voluntary" under the OWBPA. . . .

Chapter 9

DETERMINING SUBSTANCE

The substantive content of a drafted document is subject-matter specific. A residential lease, a contract for the sale of an airplane, and a statute prohibiting extortion would probably contain few, if any, identical substantive provisions. Yet, the content of all drafted documents is similar at a very high level of generality. Content derives from two sources: the law and the exigencies of the transaction. The types of provisions that are discussed below all derive from one or both of those sources.

A. TYPES OF PROVISIONS

The substantive provisions one finds in both private law and legislative documents are of four types.

1. Required by Law

Statutes frequently require that certain provisions be included in documents relating to a particular regulated transaction. The absence of a necessary provision will often deprive the document of its legal efficacy. For example, a waiver of possible age discrimination claims must inform the employee of the right to consult with an attorney before signing. The waiver is otherwise legally ineffective. State constitutions often require that certain prefatory language be included in all statutes. Without that language, the attempted legislation has no legal status. The purpose of legal checklists, discussed in the prior chapter, is to ensure that all the required provisions are included in the document.

2. Going to the Essence of the Transaction

Although not affirmatively required by law, some provisions are inherently necessary to the legal efficacy of the document. A criminal statute that contains no sanction, express or implied, is a nullity. Similarly, an alleged contract for the sale of unidentified and unidentifiable goods suffers from a fatal indefiniteness that makes it unenforceable. Indeed, unless the parties have expressly agreed to what the courts regard as all the essential terms of that type of contract, a court is likely to conclude that no enforceable agreement yet exists. The courts disagree over what is truly an essential term, and modern courts will go out of their way to supply them by implication. For example, under UCC Article 2, the only essential elements to a contract for the sale of goods are the identity of the parties, the identity of the goods, and the quantity. Everything else can be supplied by the Code's gap fillers—including price, delivery terms, payment terms, warranties, and other seemingly fundamental provisions.

The drafter, however, needs to know what the essential provisions are and ensure that the document contains them.

3. Extremely Important

Beyond knowing what is mandatory or intrinsically essential, the drafter must also rely heavily on prior experience and judgment in assessing what else should be included in a drafted document. One drafter, for example, might believe that a buyer's interests are better protected by a termite clause in the form of a warranty by the seller, rather than a clause that merely makes a satisfactory inspection report a condition of the duty to buy. Another drafter might believe otherwise. Similarly, one experienced legislative drafter might feel strongly that administrative enforcement of a particular type of statute will be more effective than enforcement through civil or criminal litigation, while another equally experienced drafter might think that private-party enforcement is best.

The extremely important provisions of a document will usually become readily apparent if the drafter uses the process described in Chapter 7 (Preparation and Planning: Getting Started). Major contingencies that must be dealt with will be smoked out with the proper "what if?" questions. In addition, however, the drafter must be alert to the friction points of the transaction and deal with them clearly and concisely, thereby eliminating them as sources of controversy later on. This information can then be put into the form of a substantive term checklist, discussed below.

4. Optional

Beyond what is required, essential, or strongly recommended, the substantive content of the document is mostly up to the client. The drafter's function is to make the client aware of all the possibilities. An employer desiring to have an employment contract drafted may have never considered whether, in addition to the usual terms, the contract should contain a prohibition against releasing confidential information to competitors. The legislative drafter should likewise review similar legislation in other states for ideas about what might be included in a statute of the type being drafted.

In either case, the drafter's responsibility is to cover all the possibilities, to determine the client's wishes, and to incorporate those desires into the drafted document.

B. SUBSTANTIVE TERM CHECKLISTS

Even the most inexperienced drafter can research the law to determine what terms are mandatory or essential—and reduce this information to a legal checklist, as discussed in the prior chapter. New drafters, however, frequently feel inept at identifying the extremely important provisions or covering the full range of optional provisions. Substantive term checklists provide the necessary help.

1. Commercially Prepared

Formbooks frequently contain annotated drafting checklists that not only identify possible substantive provisions, they also discuss the legal and practical significance of these provisions. A good checklist will also indicate, with respect to each possible provision, the specific facts the drafter should elicit from the client. These checklists are often the most valuable aspect of these books. The model forms themselves are often poorly drafted, at least by contemporary standards.

The legislative drafter can obtain similar checklist-type assistance by looking at legislation in other jurisdictions and model acts, such as those prepared by the National Conference of Commissioners on Uniform State Laws, the American Law Institute, and the Council of State Governments.

2.　Drafter Prepared

The conscientious drafter will use a formbook checklist only as a point of departure and will add to and refine this base as experience dictates. Indeed, a technique exists that even the most inexperienced drafter may use to generate a drafting checklist that should prove adequate for most situations.

Although the specific content of a checklist will depend on the nature of the document, all checklists focus on the same general categories of information. In developing a base or generic checklist covering these areas, the drafter should begin with the "who," "what," "when," "where," and "how" questions that journalists are instructed to ask when investigating a story. From the answers to these questions, the drafter can then determine what provisions should be in the document and what specific information the drafter needs from the client.

The most commonly drafted documents fall into several categories: contracts, estate planning, business organization, and legislation. Since contracts and legislation are the broadest of the four categories, covering a multitude of substantive matters, examples of the journalistic technique for creating checklists will be drawn from those areas rather than from the other two more specialized, substance-specific areas. The same basic principles, however, apply there as well.

Who. The primary "who's" to a contract are the parties. Ensure that names and addresses are correct. If one of the parties is a business entity, use the full legal name, "Wateree Properties, A Limited Partnership," rather than the name the business usually goes by, "Wateree Lake Properties." In addition, determine the legal status of the parties.

- Is either party a minor? If so, it may be better to select an adult, say a parent or guardian, to contract on behalf of the minor. In some states, court approval of contracts for non-necessaries is a prerequisite to enforcement. In some states, the minor's representation that he or she has attained the age of majority will estop them from later seeking to avoid the contract due to minority.

- Do both parties have the mental capacity to contract? This can be a sensitive matter, but if one of the parties is hospitalized or in a nursing home, then the issue needs to be resolved clearly. If in doubt, obtain a doctor's certificate or use witnesses—even if the document does not otherwise require them.

- Is either party operating as an agent? If so, identify the principal and ensure that the agent is acting within the scope of the delegated authority.

- If one of the parties is a business entity, ensure that it is properly formed and has the capacity to sue and be sued in its own name.

- Ensure that the person negotiating or signing on behalf of the business entity has the authority to do so. Indeed, this information should be obtained even before negotiations begin. It is pointless to negotiate an agreement with a person who lacks the capacity to bind the entity. Drafters should also be particularly careful when the client is a domestic corporation that is negotiating a contract on behalf of a foreign subsidiary; the subsidiary may be immune from suit in this country. This is, at least, something the drafter needs to determine in advance.

A collateral "who" relates to the persons the other contracting party may have contracted with in the past. A lawyer drafting a contract between a movie-producer client and the author of a book should inquire about the author's contract with the publisher, to determine if the movie rights have already been contracted away.

The "who's" of legislative drafting are also important. Here, the basic question relates to the appropriate level of generality. Should the protected class be limited to persons classified as "employees"? Or, should it include anyone with a contractual relationship, which would cover "independent contractors"? Should the subject of a prohibition against odometer tampering be universal? Or, should it be limited to persons who are in the business of selling automobiles?

Sometimes, the intended "who" of a statute has no known prior referents. Through the processes of conceptualization and definition, the drafter creates a new category of "who's." Some stalking statutes, for example, carve out a definition of an offender that has no precedent.

What. This goes to the essence of the document. In drafting a contract, the critical "what's" are as follows:

- Determine the subject matter of the contract. If it is a contract of sale, obtain a description of the goods or realty. If it is a contract for services, find out exactly what is to be done.

- Since most contracts involve an exchange of money, determine the amount and method of payment. In some contracts, the payment provisions are very complicated. Find out exactly who is going to pay for what.

- Inquire about possession and delivery.

- Identify exactly what else each party will be obligated to do under the contract. Walk through the transaction with the client, identifying every occurrence or non-occurrence that is necessary to bring the transaction to a successful conclusion.

- Inquire about external events the client assumes will or will not happen. If necessary, protect the client by making the occurrence or nonoccurrence of the assumed events conditions precedent or subsequent. This is where the drafter must play a relentless game of "what if?" What if that brand of pipe is unavailable? What if the builder inadvertently uses a different brand? The drafter needs to resolve these "what if" questions and incorporate the client's desires into the document. The client may want to designate an alternative brand or declare that the contract is voided. Or, the client may want a provision declaring even an inadvertent use of a different brand a material breach, thus justifying termination of the contract.

- Find out what the client would like to do in the event of breach. This will affect the remedies section of the contract.

The "what" of legislative drafting requires a thorough, probing examination of the harm that is to be corrected or the good that is to be promoted. In 1935 Congress believed that certain forms of employer opposition to unionization were causing strikes, which were detrimental to the economy. But figuring out exactly what to prohibit or require involved a closer examination of the problem. Eventually, in the National Labor Relations Act, Congress decided to prohibit employer interference with union activities, company-sponsored unions, discrimination against union members, and a refusal to recognize and bargain with a majority union. Those are the "what's" of that legislation, designed to prevent a particular harm. In 1948 Congress determined that certain union conduct also contributed to the harm the NLRA was trying to prevent, so the statute was amended accordingly. The point is that the relevant harm or good is always the progenitor of the more specific "what" provisions of a statute.

The legislative drafter with experience in a particular field can be an enormous asset to the legislator who perceives a harm to be corrected or a good to be achieved, but who is either indifferent to or ignorant of the various ways of accomplishing that objective.

When. All contracts, expressly or implicitly, contain some time element.

- Find out how important time is to the client. If it is very important, include a "time is of the essence" clause or word the time requirement so that it is both a promise (the breach of which results in damages) and an express condition (the failure of which excuses further performance by your client). If time is important but not critical, find out what the client will accept as excusable delay and consider the possibility of reasonable liquidated damages for other delay.

- Generally speaking, the law is that time is *not* of the essence, and delayed performance will be found to constitute substantial performance rather than material breach unless the parties make time for performance an express condition. Thus the inclusion of the venerable "time is of essence" clause, is often buried in the boilerplate section of the contract. Those "magic words" seem to fix the problem, right? No. Cases are legion in which the courts have found that they are "mere boilerplate" and are contradicted by other words in the contract or the party's actions. So, what is to be done? The solution lies in making it clear that the parties agreed that time of performance was material to their deal. To this end, reference to the time of performance, and perhaps the reason for its importance belong in the recitals of the contract. A covenant of timely performance also belongs in the consideration section along with all the important economic terms. Finally, an argued consequence of untimely performance such as notice, an opportunity to cure (or not), and a remedy should be provided. One cannot handcuff a determined judge or jury, but one can make it harder for them to dismiss a boilerplate five-word statement of such an important condition.

- Even if the contract involves only a one-time exchange, find out when performance is to occur. Do not rely on the "reasonable time" gap filler. Some contracts, like construction contracts and complicated real estate transactions, will contain many time periods within which certain things must be done. Review the duties of each party and determine if performance should be subject to a specific time limit.

- Time-of-payment should be dealt with expressly. Often a contract will identify the goods and the sale price, but leave the timing of the exchange unclear. It then becomes a question of who must make the first move and whether a formal tender is necessary. Resolve all these uncertainties.

- Duration is an important term in transactional and long-term contracts. It could be measured by a date certain, the occurrence of an event, or notice by one or either party.

Time periods are also important in statutes. Perhaps the most critical time relates to when the statute goes into effect. Indicating the effective date of the legislation is not enough. This only tells the courts when they must consider the effect of the legislation; it does not tell them what the effect is intended to be. The effect can vary.

For example, substantive legislation that prohibits, allows, or requires certain conduct could apply either to pre- or post-effective date conduct. Whether such retroactive legislation is constitutional is another matter. Similarly, legislation that changes procedures or available remedies could apply to all causes of action, whether a lawsuit has yet been filed or not; only to cases filed as of the effective date or later; only to cases filed after the effective date; or only to causes of action arising after the effective date. Other permutations of effective date, operative events, and procedural posture are also possible. The courts are notoriously inconsistent in how they deal with these reference points when trying to resolve effective date issues. The legislative drafter should think about these matters and provide for them expressly rather than leaving them up to time-consuming and expensive judicial determination.

Another important "when" involves the limitations period under a statute. The omission of limitations periods in statutes has caused an enormous amount of unnecessary litigation. The courts are forced to imply one. For example, a federal law without a statute of limitations is said to borrow the appropriate state-law statute of limitations, raising the question of which statute of limitations that might be.

Statutes that require a person to do something within a specific time period should indicate whether compliance is jurisdictional or whether it is subject to waiver, estoppel, or tolling.

Where. In drafting contracts, find out where the agreed performance will occur. Is delivery to be at the seller's or the buyer's place of business? Location is extremely important in construction, service, and employment contracts. It will often affect the scope and nature of the duties to be performed. For example, a contractor who agrees to provide service and maintenance on "all Acme Company trucks" would be dismayed to discover later that some of them are at a facility 3,000 miles away. Incorrectly identifying the geographic coverage of an exclusive dealership agreement could result in liability to the dealer already awarded that territory.

Most statutes cover the entire geographical jurisdiction of the enacting entity. But some statutes are location-specific. State hunting regulations may vary from county to county, depending on the nature and size of the game population.

How. Many clients think only in terms of the end result. The client wants an office building built. The drafter, however, must force the client to think about how the client wants to accomplish this. Does the client intend to be its own general contractor and hire subcontractors? Or will the client hire a general contractor? What construction methods will be used?

The drafter should play an active role in helping the client resolve the "how" questions. This is where the drafter's experience, knowledge of the law, imagination, and ingenuity come into play. The client, for example, may be planning to get into the business of acquiring, developing, and managing mobile home parks. The drafter needs to consider, and discuss with the client, all the various ways the business entity might be set up. Would it be better to do this under the umbrella of a single corporation? Or, for tax and liability purposes, should the land acquisition and ownership be done by one corporation and the management by another? Or would some other form of business organization serve the client's needs best, such as a limited partnership?

The "how" of legislative drafting is chiefly a matter of policy, and this is one type of policy where the drafter's input and active involvement is appropriate. The legislative client may know what harm needs to be addressed or what good should be promoted. But, prohibiting or requiring the relevant conduct is not the only or even necessarily the best option. Doing it by prohibition might not work, since that could drive the activity underground. A requirement might be unenforceable. Rather, the more appropriate "how" might consist of the creation of alternatives, incentives, or collateral disadvantages. Discovering and exploiting these possibilities is the drafter's responsibility.

The drafter can create either a generic or a document-specific checklist by focusing on who the document covers, what the regulated conduct is, when various things will happen, where they will happen, and how the ultimate objective is to be achieved. If the document contains substantive provisions dealing with all these matters, then it is likely to be complete.

C. THE ELEMENTS OF A LEGAL RULE

Drafted documents, whether of the private or public law variety, can be conceptualized as a collection of rules. This is helpful because legal philosophers have identified the critical elements of an effective rule, and these can be used to ensure that the drafted documents cover everything that it should, at least a broad sense. The five elements of a rule are as follows:

1. The Person

A rule must identify the person to whom the rule applies. The subject may be universal (everyone) or nearly so (everyone within a broad class).

- No person [universal] shall park within 15 feet of a fire hydrant.
- All subcontractors [universal within the class] are subject to the arbitration-of-disputes provision, ¶ 56(a).

Or a rule may be selective with respect to whom it applies.

- Only the Vice–President of Finance may authorize payments in excess of $10,000.

2. The Conduct

A rule must identify the conduct that is being prohibited, required, or permitted. In the above examples, parking and using the arbitration-of-disputes provision are the relevant conduct.

3. The Object of the Action

A rule usually identifies an object of the action. This may be universal, in which case no further identification is necessary, or it may be limited.

- A person shall not destroy or damage the property of another [universal].

- The Fire Marshall shall investigate all reports of arson of a church [limited] within 24 hours.

4. The Circumstances

A rule often identifies the circumstances of the action. This may consist of when or where the command is operative.

- In Class II cities, the mayor may appoint the city attorney.

- After 10 days, Buyer may terminate the contract and recover fees paid.

Those rules limit the operative place or time. Or the circumstances may consist of a condition that must be satisfied before the command is operative.

- If the Joint Appendix is more than 300 pages long, it must be printed on both sides of the page.

- If Landlord provides 24–hour notice, Landlord may enter the premises for the purpose of showing it to prospective tenants.

Circumstances may also consist of an exception to the rule.

- Retail stores shall not sell alcohol on Sunday, except in counties that have approved these sales through a referendum.

5. Consequences

A legislative rule prohibiting conduct must identify the consequences of noncompliance. This is sometimes called the "sanction." The consequences may be criminal liability, civil liability, forfeiture of goods, invalidity of a document, or simple ineligibility to obtain something.

- A person violating this section is guilty of a misdemeanor and shall be fined $100.

- Documents not bearing the notarized signature of two witnesses are void.

If the consequences of satisfying a requirement are eligibility for benefits, then the rule must identify specifically what they are.

- A person who is 65 years of age or older is entitled to enroll in Medical Plan C.

Legal consequences in private law documents are usually implicit in the term that was used to create the consequence. If something is intended to create a right, then the legal consequence is that the right-holder may use the coercive power of the state to compel the person with the correlative duty to perform or to pay for the damages caused by non-performance. Sometimes, however, the drafter may want to make a legal consequence express.

- Because the vintage automobile that is the subject of this contract of sale is unique and no substitute is available on the market, if Seller fails to deliver or otherwise breaches, Buyer is entitled to a decree of specific performance.

- Contractor shall use only Reading brand pipe. Contractor's use of any other brand of pipe is a material breach. Owner may immediately terminate the contract and Contractor forfeits his or her right to payment.

In sum, if the rules in a drafted document identify the persons to whom the rule applies; the permitted, required, or prohibited acts; the object of those acts; the circumstances of the action; and the consequences of action or non-action, then the document will usually be substantively complete.

D. SUBSTANTIVE GAPS

A document that does not adequately deal with the who, what, when, where, how, and why of the transaction, or that does not contain the all the necessary elements of a rule will nearly always contain substantive gaps. But substantive gaps can also emerge as a result of bad writing.

For example, drafted provisions are often worded in "if ... then" terms—as in "if X then Y." This conditional form of sentence has a fixed meaning in formal logic. It means that if the condition (X) is satisfied, then the consequence

(Y) always follows. In other words, X is a sufficient condition of Y. But that is all the sentence means. X is not a necessary condition of Y. Thus, it does not mean that the absence of X dictates the absence of Y. Concluding otherwise is what logicians call the fallacy of denying the antecedent. Rules of logic to the contrary notwithstanding, this is sometimes what people (including drafters) intend when they use an "if ... then" sentence. Rather, they intend "if" to mean "if and only if."

This can create two related difficulties, resulting in either a substantive gap or an ambiguity. In the "if ... then" sentence, the contract or statute has dealt with what happens if the condition is satisfied. But what happens if it is not? Suppose the contract says, "If Buyer requests it, Seller will ship by United Parcel." What happens if Buyer does not request that mode of shipment? Clearly, Seller is not obligated to use United Parcel. But does this mean that Seller has an affirmative duty not to ship by that mode unless Buyer requests it? Under the rules of logic, the answer is no. But construing the "if" to mean "if and only if" leads to the opposite conclusion—that mode of shipment is prohibited in the absence of a request.

The substantive gap created by "if ... then" logical constructs is one of the major flaws in UCC § 2–207— although the provisions are not literally worded in those terms. For example, paragraph (1) introduces the possibility of an acceptance containing terms "additional to or different from" those contained in the offer. And paragraph (2) tells us what the legal consequence is when an offer contains additional terms. Translating that into an "if ... then" sentence, it says: If an acceptance contains additional terms, they are to be construed a proposal to modify the contract and between merchants become part of the contract un-less.... But UCC § 2–207 does not specify the legal consequence flowing from an acceptance that contains different terms. Do they also become mere proposals to modify the contract, requiring express assent by the offeror? Or do the two inconsistent terms cancel each other out (the "knock-out" rule), with the missing term now being filled with a UCC gap-filler? There is enormous disagreement over that. And the section contains other flaws of that nature.

In sum, whether worded literally in "if ... then" terms or not, if a contract or statute deals with what will happen in a particular situation or upon the occurrence of something else, the drafter should also make sure to deal with what happens in the absence of that situation or occurrence.

Another kind of substantive gap can arise when a contract or statute contains a list of ranges of time, price, or some other numerical element. Consider, for example, this statute:

A person violating the speed limits established by this section is guilty of a misdemeanor and, upon conviction for a first offense, shall be fined or imprisoned as follows:

(1) in excess of the above posted limit but less than 10 miles an hour by a fine of not less than $15 nor more than $25;

(2) in excess of 10 miles an hour but less than 15 miles an hour above the posted limit by a fine of not less than $25 nor more than $50 dollars;

(3) in excess of 15 miles an hour but less than 25 miles an hour above the posted limit by a fine of not less than $50 nor more than $75; and

(4) in excess of 25 miles and hour above the posted limit by a fine of not less then $75 nor more than $200 or imprisoned for not more than 30 days.

This statute covers speeds at 1–9, 11–14, 16–24, and 26+ over the posted limit. Although the statute prohibits driving at any speed over the posted limit, it does not provide sanctions when the driver is going exactly 10, 15, or 25 miles over the posted limit. That is the equivalent of not prohibiting driving at those speeds altogether. That is, in other words, a substantive gap.

One technique for discovering substantive gaps is through the creation of a flow chart of the document, once it is in initial draft stage. Creating a flow chart is discussed in Chapter 17.

Exercise 6

1. A client that owns a small industrial company wants to hire a new office manager and needs an employment

contract. You are to meet with her tomorrow to discuss the matter. Prepare a substantive checklist.

    2.   Your client has recently purchased a small apartment complex (10 apartments) near the University. It is currently being renovated but will be ready for occupancy soon. He has asked you to prepare a lease agreement that he can use. It will be a form agreement, with blank spaces for the tenant's name, the apartment number, and the dates. Prepare a substantive checklist.

Chapter 10

CHOOSING THE RIGHT CONCEPT

At this point, the drafter has some idea of what the client desires the drafted document to accomplish, understands what the law requires or prohibits in this regard, and has determined the substantive content. Translating all of this into written form requires the drafter to engage in the further process of conceptualization. ` ` `   ` ` ` `

A. DEFINITION

A concept is the idea of something formed by mentally combining all its characteristics or particulars. Concepts exist only in the mind. They may be so narrowly conceived that they encompass only one known referent, something that can also be perceived by the senses, as in "the object upon which I am sitting at this moment." On the other hand, the broader concept of a chair encompasses something with four legs supporting a flat surface, with a back and often with arms, which people sit on. This concept thus encompasses an infinite number of referents, many of which may differ radically in their particulars. A chair designed by Salvador Dali, for example, would differ significantly from one fashioned by an Amish carpenter. Any individual chair is capable of being perceived by the senses, but the concept of "chair" is not.

B. THE IMPORTANCE OF CONCEPTS IN DRAFTING

Satisfying client objectives is the fundamental goal of drafting. The drafter's ability to think conceptually and to choose and express the correct concept determines how well that goal is met. Assume that the owner of a small, sophisticated, performing arts theater wants a contract for the purchase of seating. The drafter words the contract in such a way that the supplier can, without breach, supply the seating in the form of an eclectic mixture of beanbag chairs, benches, and bar stools. That drafter either failed to match the appropriate concept with the client's objectives or lacked the ability to express that concept in appropriate words. However impeccable the contract might be in form, organization, and style, the result is a total failure.

C. TYPES OF CONCEPTS

Concepts come in two types, legal and factual.

1. Legal Concepts

The drafter can draw from many well-established legal concepts. "Just cause for termination," "negligence," "*per stirpes*," "consideration," "goods," "employee," "fraudulently," "agent," "corporation," and others all have established meanings. These concepts are often complex. Sometimes they are vague. But once the drafter fully understands the client's objectives, the drafter may be able to match those objectives with one of these legal concepts. The client, for example, may want to retain the services of someone to perform a specific task; this person will supply his or her own tools and will work without the need for client supervision. Here, the client's objectives match up with the legal concept of "independent contractor" rather than the concept of "employee."

Serving the client's objectives may sometimes require the drafter to consolidate several existing legal concepts into a new one. Thus, a drafter addressing the recent phenomenon known colloquially as "stalking" may decide to define it in terms of a combination of the existing legal concepts of "threat," "invasion of privacy," and "assault." The resulting amalgam will eventually take on a conceptual identity of its own. But in the meantime, because it draws upon three well fleshed-out and understood doctrines, it should avoid constitutional vagueness problems.

Sometimes, however, the operative legal concept has no prior name or definition and one cannot be cobbled together out of existing concepts. For example, federal disability law defines a "handicapped individual" as a person who "has a physical or mental impairment *which substantially limits one or more of such person's major life activities.*" That represented the creation of an entirely new legal concept, the meaning of which is still evolving.

Some new legal concepts are defined with a fair degree of precision—either by the legislature or, as is increasingly the case, by the administrative agency charged with enforcing the statute. Other times, however, a legislature may choose to characterize a new legal concept in deliberately vague or open-ended terms, leaving it to the courts to work out the details. The Sherman Antitrust Act of 1890, for example, simply prohibits "unreasonable restraints on trade," and the courts have spent the last 113 years giving meaning to the concept.

Private law documents may similarly require the use of old legal concepts in new ways or the creation of new legal concepts. A condominium developer, for example, may want to structure the relationship between the various owners in a way that is unconventional. The drafter will thus carefully define that relationship and give it a name.

2.   Factual Concepts

The difference between the concept "objects that can be sat upon" and the concept "theater-style seating" is a critical one. Drafted documents deal with four kinds of facts: people, things, conduct, and events. In choosing or creating the factual concept that will best effectuate the client's intent, the drafter is faced with three sets of decisions with respect to those four types of facts: (1) determining the proper degree of generality/specificity; (2) determining the proper degree of vagueness/precision; and (3) determining the proper degree of abstraction/concreteness. In all three instances, what is proper depends on the client's objectives.

a. General versus Specific. Words or word combinations are like boxes into which any number of specific referents can be fit. "Nemo, a Boxer–Labrador mix owned by Squire Haggard" is a very small box into which only one referent will fit. "Dogs owned by Squire Haggard" is a larger box into which Gus, Fritz, and many others would also fit. "Dogs" is a larger category yet, as are "domesticated animals" and "animals." Put differently, going from Nemo to animals involves moving from the specific to increasing levels of factual generality.

Determining what level of specificity/generality to use requires a keen and thorough understanding of the good to be achieved or the harm to be avoided. If the good or harm consists of more than one referent, then the drafter must know what all of them are. If all of these referents will fit into a recognized category or box, and if nothing else will fit into that box, then this is the level of generality at which the document should be drafted.

For example, the drafter of an animal control ordinance must decide what category of animals to include in the regulation. Although the county council member who requested the ordinance may be acting in response to a constituent's complaint about a particular dog, Nemo, getting into her trash, an ordinance drafted at that level of specificity/generality would probably be inadequate. Nemo is probably only one of many referents causing the type of harm the council member wants to prevent; and that harm may not even be limited to the trashing of trash cans. So, the category of "dogs" might not be the proper level of generality and the offensive conduct might also need to be expanded. For example, what about cats who spray and make smelly deposits in a neighbor's flower bed? Or pet rabbits who get into Mr. McGregor's carrot patch? If the activities of these animals are also part of the harm to be prevented, then the drafter will want to try to move to a higher level of generality. However, "domesticated animals" is too broad because it encompasses horses, cows, pigs, and many other animals that do not cause the kind of harm the statute is expected to prevent. And, unless the ordinance is intended to be a leash law, "running loose" might be too broad as the prohibited conduct.

Frequently, the specific referents the client has in mind (and, probably, similar specific referents that the client has not thought of but might like to include) have no previously recognized conceptual label—dogs, cats, and rabbits, for example. Here, the drafter is required to create a new factual concept and give it a name. This is usually accomplished with a definition, a drafting technique discussed in Chapter 14.

As that example suggests, finding the proper level of generality is usually more of an issue in legislative drafting than in private-law document drafting. Legislation, by definition, deals with broad classes of persons and things. The matter also has constitutional significance. Unless the legislated category is a fairly close match with the harm to be avoided or the good to be achieved, the statute may be over- or under-inclusive, and thus violate the Equal Protection Clause.

Private law documents, on the other hand, are usually more specific in their focus. A particular car is being sold or a specific individual is being hired. This is not always so, however. The contract duties of an individual, rather than being specifically listed, might fit nicely into a recognized category or higher level of generality, like "prepare and package the goods for shipment"—which, under the customs of the industry, means doing it in a particular way. Likewise, an employment policy that is intended to provide a particular benefit may specifically identify the individuals who are eligible for the benefit or, as more likely will be the case, it may identify them in increasing broad categories or levels of generality—managers and supervisors, first shift employees, or all employees.

Instead of drafting in terms of the appropriate generality, some drafters instead try to draft in terms of all the specifics that encompass the generality. This is bad drafting for two reasons.

First, the drafter may overlook something. In Dick Francis' novel *Banker*, the owner of a breeding stallion had, in a long list of specifics, insured the horse against almost every conceivable contingency capable of diminishing the horse's value as a stud. No one even imagined that the horse might produce deformed foals. But it apparently did, no one was willing to use it for breeding, and it was not insured against this total loss in value. As the owner aptly put it, "The policy had been too specific. They should have been content with something like 'any factor resulting in the horse not being considered fit for stud purposes.'"

Some drafters who are prone toward listing specifics try to avoid this kind of unintentional exclusion by adding a catch-phrase at the end, such as "and other similar ...," counting on the *ejusdem generis* rule of interpretation to take up the slack. This, however, only adds one bad drafting technique to another. It gives the courts, rather than the client, the power to determine inclusion or exclusion.

Second, drafting in terms of the appropriate generality is the more efficient way to do it. Referring to "elected city officials" is shorter than listing them all, even if the list is complete. The following National Park Service regulation is a classic example of wordy over-specificity:

§ 50.10 Trees, shrubs, plants, grass, and other vegetation.

(a) General injury. No person shall prune, cut, carry away, pull up, dig, fell, bore, chop, saw, chip, pick, move, sever, climb, molest, take, break, deface, destroy, set fire to, burn, scorch, carve, paint, mark, or in any manner interfere with, tamper, mutilate, misuse, disturb or damage any tree, shrub, plant, grass, flower, or part thereof, nor shall any person permit any chemical, whether solid, fluid, or gaseous, to seep, drip, drain or be emptied, sprayed, dusted or injected upon, about or into any tree, shrub, plant, grass, flower, or part thereof, except when specifically authorized by competent authority; nor shall any person build fires, or station, or use any tar kettle, heater, road roller or other engine within an area covered by this part in such a manner that the vapor, fumes, or heat therefrom may injury any tree or other vegetation.

In other words, "Do not harm the plants."

b. Vague versus Precise. A term is vague when its definitional lines are uncertain. Thus, it may be difficult to determine whether a specific referent is within the category in question. As any painting contractor can tell you, the term "red" is extremely vague. A particular color may seem red to one person, orange to another, and maroon to yet a third. The term "reasonable" is commonly used in commercial contracts, such as where one party is required to do something within a "reasonable time." The term, however, is also vague. Whether a specific unit of time is reasonable depends on the nature of the transaction, the context, the prevailing commercial practice, the past practice of the parties, and many other variables. A precise term, on the other hand, has fixed and easily identified definitional boundaries. "Red #567" (from the printing industry's standardized color chart) describes the color with precision, as does "twenty-four hours" with respect to a unit of time.

Vagueness should not be confused with generality. "Dangerous pit bull terriers kept within city limits" is vague (because of the terms "dangerous" and "kept"), but it is fairly narrow or specific with respect to the size of the class it covers (excluding non-dangerous dogs of this breed, other breeds, and dogs outside of the city limits). Conversely, "persons with a Texas driver's license" covers a large number of persons and is a high level generality, but it is also very precise. A term can be both vague and general. A standing-to-sue provision covering anyone "adversely affected" by an administrative regulation is both vague and general. Note too, however, that once the vagueness is resolved and some meaning is given to the term by the courts, this will also serve to delimit the size of the class or the generality of the term.

Vagueness should also not be confused with ambiguity, which refers to a term with mutually inconsistent or contradictory meanings. As will be discussed in Chapter 12, ambiguity is an unmitigated evil in drafting. Vagueness, on the other hand, may have certain advantages.

First, using a vague term is sometimes the only alternative. If a right, duty, or condition is dependent on particular circumstances, infinite in number, variety, and combination, no human drafter possesses the prescience to anticipate all of them. One, for example, would be guilty of over-precision by attempting to define a term like material misrepresentation with the same degree of specificity that one might use in defining a term like "regulated industry."

Second, even if further particularization were possible, a vague term may still be the preferred approach. Using vague terms cuts down on transaction costs. It would take a lot of thought, and thus drafting time and cost, to reduce the vague term, "the reasonable value of the goods and services provided," to a precise list of prices, particularly if the identity of the goods and services that are going to be provided is itself somewhat open-ended and the market value of these goods and services will vary over the term of the contract. It may thus be more efficient to assume that the parties in good faith will be able to agree on this later, as the need arises. Alternatively, the parties may want to agree in advance to a mechanism for resolving the vagueness, such as a neutral third party or a price index.

Indeed, at some point, the transaction cost of drafting with precision may be so high that the transaction simply does not occur. At the contract negotiation stage, the parties have a semi-adversarial relationship and are apt to bargain hard to achieve even the most minute of advantages. The greater the number of specific details that the parties must bargain over, the more likely it is that they will be unable to reach an agreement. Stubborn disagreement over the precise content of some relatively inconsequential term or over how to resolve a contingency that may never even arise may become a deal buster. The greater economic advantage of the transaction, to both parties, is thus lost.

The third advantage of vagueness is that in private law documents, it provides the flexibility that is necessary to make the transaction work. A "reasonable time for performance" provision recognizes that different situations may call for different time periods. But once the hard bargaining is over and the contract is agreed to, a subtle shift often occurs in the relationship between the parties. It goes from being semi-adversarial to being collaborative. Consummating the transaction is now the objective of both parties, and they are not likely to let it be frustrated by minor disagreements over vague terms. Good faith and a little give-and-take by both parties can avoid that.

Fourth, in the statutory context, vagueness is often used deliberately to produce an evolving, almost experimental approach to the resolution of a problem. The legislature is content to paint with a broad brush, using intentionally vague terms and leaving it to the courts to determine on a case-by-case basis whether the facts fit within the coverage of the statute or not. This is unremarkable because the meaning of similarly vague common law rules is determined in an identical fashion.

Vagueness, however, is not without its shortcomings as a drafting technique. Most of the disadvantages are simply the down side of the advantages. First, there is greater possibility for disagreement over the meaning of vague terms than precise terms. Despite the professed flexibility and good faith of the parties, sometimes these disagreements cannot be resolved short of litigation. Similarly, a legislature would be ill-advised to use vague terms when drafting legislation which is likely to be vigorously resisted by a significant segment of the population. Labor legislation, for example, is frequently drafted in enormously vague terms. But the question of what is or is not within the scope of the legislation can have a profound financial impact on a business enterprise, which provides a great incentive to litigation. Consequently, for the last 40 years, state and federal courts have been clogged with an enormous amount of employment-related litigation, most of it relating to the fundamental meaning of the vague terms used in the statute.

Second, the legal drafter has a responsibility to protect and advance the interests of the client, whether that client is a single individual who desires a contract or legislator acting on behalf of the public. This responsibility carries with it the concomitant power to control the content and meaning of the document. This is not a responsibility and power that should be casually regarded. Whatever affirmative justification the drafter has for drafting with vague terms, this comes at the cost of surrendering the responsibility and power to determine document content and meaning.

In contracts, this is fine as long as the parties are willing to engage in on-going good faith negotiations over the administration of the contract. But if they are unable to do that, then the responsibility and power falls upon the courts or a neutral arbitrator—and the drafter's ability to protect the client's interests now turns on litigation rather than drafting skills. Similarly, the legislative drafter who insists upon vaguely worded statutes must be made to understand that these words will be construed by judges who may be hostile to the objectives of the legislation. Conversely, an overly zealous administrative agency may be impervious to the implicit compromises and tacit agreements as to the intended meaning of the legislation among groups with an interest in the legislation. In either event, the drafter and the drafter's client have lost control over the document and what they created may be a far cry from what they intended to create.

What emerges from this consideration of the pros and cons is that vagueness should be used only with conscious deliberation. The drafter should be sure that the advantages of using a vague term outweigh the dangers. Thoughtless or inadvertent vagueness, on the other hand, is a form of drafting sloppiness that is without excuse.

Although a high percentage of English words possess some degree of vagueness, those that are used most often in drafting—often legitimately, but sometimes not—are as follows:

adequate	available
approximately	best efforts
comparable	convenient
discretion	due care or diligence
excessive	good faith
immediately	material
necessaries	neighborhood
practicable	prejudicial
promptly	proper
reasonable	regular
remote	safe
satisfactory	serious
substantial	sufficient
suitable	temporary
undue	valuable

c. Abstract versus Concrete. An abstract term is one that deals with a quality or result, while a concrete term relates to something that causes or manifests that quality or result. "Hard" is abstract; "steel" is a concrete counterpart.

A drafter should use abstractions cautiously, because they are more difficult for people to grasp. When encountering a word, people try to form a visual image of a tangible reality. "Washington Monument" evokes a mental picture of that specific structure. "Car" likewise easily evokes a mental picture of one of those tangible realities, although that image may vary from individual to individual. But the mind fuzzes over when it encounters "an object capable of being held in the hand that is often used to drive something that is straight, thin, and inflexible through or into two other hard objects for the purpose of holding them together." Eventually, the mind will figure out that this refers to a "framing hammer." Moreover, although "car" is capable of producing different mental images, everyone sees about the same thing, this is not true of abstractions. When one person sees the word "soft," that person may think of a pillow. Another person's visual image, however, may be of a piece of sponge cake. And neither image may have the slightest thing to do with whatever the drafting provision containing the word "soft" really addresses. Second, since abstractions are often also fairly high level generalities, they are subject to the danger of over- and under-inclusion. In addition, since abstractions are also often vague, they are subject to all the drawbacks associated with that drafting approach as well.

Factual abstractions are, however, sometimes the best way to conceptualize and present the substance of a document. Two situations come to mind.

First, an abstraction can be used when this is the only way the client has identified the object of the document or provision—the good to be accomplished or the harm to be prevented. For example, a buyer's only concern might be that the seller package and ship the goods in a manner that ensures their safe and prompt delivery. The buyer does not care if they are packed in stout cardboard boxes, cushioned with foam pellets, and sent UPS; or wrapped in plastic bubbles, put in barrels, and shipped air freight. Rather, the buyer will be content to have the seller's duty stated abstractly: "Seller shall pack and ship the goods in such a manner as to ensure that they arrive at the place of delivery promptly and undamaged."

Second, an abstraction can be used when the specific, concrete referents are numerous, infinite in variety, and thus incapable of being listed with precision or completeness. The courts, for example, have taken the abstract approach to the problem of "hostile environment sexual harassment." Roughly speaking, they define it as any kind of conduct that a reasonable person of the plaintiff's sex would find offensive because of that person's sex. In other words, the offense is defined in terms of the abstract effect of the conduct rather than in terms of the conduct itself. A drafter attempting to codify this form of discrimination would likely adopt a similar approach.

D. CHOOSING THE RIGHT WORD TO REFLECT THE CONCEPT

Once the drafter has the concept in mind, the next task is to choose the right word to communicate this concept to the reader. This aspect of the drafting process is fraught with difficulty. The English language is notoriously slippery, and words often have multiple meanings. For example, the operative concept may be that of a small child or baby, so the drafter uses the term "infant." A court, however, may construe the term as referring to any minor. Similarly, to someone brought up on a ranch, a "large animal" would probably mean something like a horse or cow; but to a resident of Manhattan, it might include a Labrador retriever.

To ensure that the word matches the concept, the drafter should consult three sources: an unabridged English dictionary, a legal dictionary, and *Words and Phrases*. However, in addition to the lexical and legal meaning of words, the drafter must also consider their conventional meanings. The Supreme Court once determined what it means to "use" a firearm in connection with a drug offense by relying on a linguistic study of how people actually use the word.

Exercise 7

Use a legal dictionary or *Words and Phrases* to answer these questions:

1. Senator Lawrence Arthur Wentworth, who is in his dotage and is getting forgetful, recently went into the Capital City Café, carefully hung his umbrella on the coat rack, ate a hearty breakfast, and then left—leaving the umbrella on the coat rack. He visited the newsstand, the barbershop, and the bank. He roamed around the Capital Building for a while, and then went to his office. Later in the day, as he was about to leave the Capital, it started to rain. The Senator looked around his office for his umbrella, but was unable to locate it. He figured he had left it somewhere in his morning travels, but he could not remember where. He was very disturbed, because his late wife had given the umbrella to him. *Senator L.A.W.* was engraved on the handle.

Around mid-morning of that same day, William "Slick Willie" Malone had been in the Capital City Café. He was the only patron at the time. As he paid his bill, he noticed the umbrella on the coat rack. Since no one else was in the Café, he figured he could just take it. When he took it down from the coat rack, the owner of the Café objected, but Willie said "Losers weepers, finders keepers" and ran out of the Café. Willie noticed the engraving, but made no effort to locate the owner.

A week later, the Senator saw Willie with the umbrella and had him arrested for theft. The District Attorney, however, refused to prosecute, saying that Willie's conduct did not exactly fit under any of the existing criminal statutes.

You work in the Capital's Legislative Drafting Service. At the Senator's request, a bill has been drafted. In essence, it says that in a situation like that described above, the owner of the premises has the sole right to retain possession of the property pending a search for the true owner and that anyone else who takes the property is guilty of theft.

What is the most appropriate property law term/concept to use when creating a criminal statute dealing with the possession of property under the described circumstances— *Abandoned Property, Lost Property,* or *Mislaid Property?*

2.   The State Liquor Commission is required to hold hearings on all applications for a liquor license. The old statute allowed anyone who might be "adversely affected" by the grant or denial of a license to intervene. The facts in these matters are rarely in dispute. The question is always whether under the undisputed facts the "adversely affected" standard was satisfied. The Commission had adopted an extraordinarily narrow approach to the question of who was "adversely affected," while the courts in the state had adopted an extremely expansive definition. The result was a lot of unnecessary litigation.

The House Health & Welfare Committee proposed an amendment that lists the criteria the Commission should consider in deciding whether to allow someone to intervene in a hearing. The Committee, however, wants to curtail judicial "second guessing" of the Commission's decisions. As Representative Sarah Repeal puts it, "The Commission decision should stand unless it is arbitrary, capricious, unfair, or totally inconsistent with the facts and relevant criteria."

You have been asked to draft the provision dealing with judicial review of the Commission's decisions. Which standard of judicial review would best match Representative Repeal's description: *substantial evidence, clearly erroneous, preponderance of the evidence, abuse of discretion, clear and convincing evidence,* or *beyond a reasonable doubt?*

3.   Think of some kind of problem that might arise within the context of your University that relates to student status. This is the *harm* to be corrected or prevented. The most immediate manifestation of this problem is in Johnny Walker, a 2nd year law student who sits on the second row in this drafting class. The problem may be limited to him, or it may encompass the entire student body of the University—or it may fall somewhere in between. Starting with Johnny Walker, creating an increasing broad series of categories leading up to the broadest possible category, the entire student body. Within that range, what would be the proper level of generalization, given the nature of the problem that you have in mind?

4.   Assume the following levels of specificity/generality:

I.   Employers

A. Public employers [same subdivision as in I.B., below]
B. Private employers
    1. Less than 15 employees [subdivisions as below]
    2. 15–100 employees [subdivisions as below]
    3. 101 and more employees
        a. Engaged in manufacturing [subdivisions as below]
        b. Engaged in transportation
            (1) Air transportation [subdivisions as below]
            (2) Land transportation
                (a) Carrying passengers only [subdivisions as below]
                (b) Carrying goods only
                    (i) Intra-state [subdivisions as below]
                    (ii) Interstate
                        [A] Carrying non-toxic materials
                        [B] Carrying toxic materials
                            [1] Carrying non-radioactive materials
                            [2] Carrying radioactive materials

What would be the proper level of specificity/generality if the client's objective was:

    a. To enact a regulation requiring drivers working for large trucking companies to wear radioactive monitoring badges?
    b. To enact a statute making terminations in violation of the 5th or 14th Amendments an actionable tort?
    c. To provide an exemption from certain tax rules for operators of small commercial planes?

    5. What appears to be the lowest common denominator linking each of the following sets of entities? What would be an appropriate term to describe that concept?

    a. Larry who is in law school; Mary who is in medical school; Victoria who is in veterinary school; and Donna who is in dental school.

Would Martin Luther, who is enrolled in Theology School, be a similar entity? What about Terry Turner, who is enrolled at Bevo Technical College, studying Technical Writing?

> b. The book *The Red Badge of Courage*, the movie *Hunt For Red October*, the comic strip *Beetle Bailey*, and a "Joe Camel [dressed in Army fatigues] Supports Operation Iraqi Freedom" billboard advertisement.

What if you add an audiotape of the book *General Custer at Little Big Horn* to the list?

> c. A Ford Ranger pickup truck, a Mack Truck gravel hauler, a Norfolk Southern coal car, and a Mississippi River garbage barge.

What if you add a riding lawn mower? What if a double-decker bus manufactured in England is specifically excluded? What if an electric golf cart is also specifically excluded?

6. Provide a precise substitute for the following vague terms (use a legal dictionary or *Words and Phrases* if necessary):

> a. within a reasonable time
>
> b. necessaries (in relation to what a non-custodial parent must provide for his or her children)
>
> c. net profits
>
> d. fixtures
>
> e. regular (in relation to when maintenance must be done on a machine)
>
> f. serious misconduct (in relation to grounds for termination from employment)
>
> g. clean and neat condition (in relation to a furnished apartment that is being rented)
>
> h. intoxicated

7. Provide a vague term to replace the following precise terms:

> a. within 24 hours after actual receipt of the notice of defect (in regard to when repair or replacement must occur)

b. assault and battery with intent to kill, attempted murder, bribery of a public official, carnal knowledge of a female child, perjury, soliciting for prostitution, embezzlement, extortion, fraudulent conversion, and larceny (in regard to the types of crimes for which a lawyer can be permanently disbarred)

c. 20 feet, plus or minus 3.5 inches (in regard to how close to the property line a home owner wants the nursery to plant a line of trees)

d. a personal contact if the person is in town; a certified letter if the person is out of town; a newspaper advertisement if the location of the person is unknown (regarding the efforts a creditor must make to contact the debtor before filing a lien on the property)

e. defects that will cost less than $2.00 to correct or repair (regarding what is not grounds for revoking acceptance of the goods)

Chapter 11

ORGANIZATION

The drafter has determined the client's objectives, identified the full audience, mastered the legal and factual context in which the document will operate, decided with the client what to include in the document, and chosen or created the appropriate legal and factual concepts. The drafter now has a mass of data and insights that must be assembled into some kind of order. Organization consists of division, classification, and sequence.

A. DIVISION

Division involves creating the hierarchical categories into which the data is to be placed. In the document, they will appear as numbered and headed sections. Rational division is based on three rules: (1) mutual exclusivity, (2) total coverage, and (3) singularity of the principle of division. To illustrate these rules, assume a division that separates the class of "motor vehicles" into two subclasses, "Ford cars" and "red cars." Consider how that division violates all three rules.

Rule One—Mutual Exclusivity. The categories must be mutually exclusive, meaning no datum can fall into two or more categories. If the categories are mutually exclusive, then a particular provision can go in only one place. Where, however, would one put a red Ford Mustang?

Rule Two—Total Coverage. The categories together must equal the entire class; there must be nothing left over. Everything that the drafter wants to put into the document must have a place. But where in the motor vehicles classification scheme suggested above would one place a green Toyota Tundra? The drafter who cannot find a place in the divisional scheme for a particular provision often creates a new category, "miscellaneous," that ends up being full of minor, unrelated, substantive provisions. This is the sign of a bad divisional scheme.

Rule Three—Singularity of the Principle of Division. The division should be based on one consistently applied principle. Red cars and Fords are divisions based on two principles—color and make. This division would totally confuse a user of the document.

Within each category, the drafter should create as many levels of sub-categories as is needed—moving from the general down to each specific provision. Each sub-category should also follow the rules of division. For example, within the "cars" category, a drafter might create the following sub-category levels in descending order:

III. Cars

    A. Manufacturer

        1. Make

            a. Model

                (1) Year

                    (a) Color

                        (i) Vehicle Identification Number

As in that example, the main category and every sub-category should have an appropriate letter or number designation for easy identification and a descriptive heading—although that is sometimes omitted at the lowest level of division. For statutes and ordinances, the drafter must follow the rules or conventions of the jurisdiction in this regard. But the private law drafter has total discretion and should exercise it in the direction of more rather than fewer sub-categories. The drafter must also follow the conventional rules of outlining.

If a category is going to have sub-categories, it must have at least two. Although often violated, this is not just an arbitrary rule. Its logical justification derives from the fact that a category is the sum of its parts. The category heading is simply a more generalized way of expressing what the various parts add up to. A well organized outline provides information and insight about both the individual components, indicating what they represent as a whole, and the whole, indicating what it consists of. On the other hand, the following is a meaningless distinction or division:

I. *Compensation*

    A. *Salary*

II. *Etc.*

If the remuneration under the contract is a salary of $70,000 a year and that is the whole of it, simultaneously giving it a broad designation, "compensation," and a more specific designation, "salary," is pointless. Call it one thing or the other and make a single category of it.

Headings should be carefully worded. The designation must accurately identify what is contained in that category. If each provision has been properly classified and put within a particular category, then these provisions will have a common denominator. Determine what it is and word the heading accordingly. The common denominator of base salary, commissions, incentive pay, and bonuses is that they are the compensation the employee will receive. Give the category that heading, rather than something unenlightening like "Employee Rights"—which also suffers from over-inclusion, since the employee will also have other non-compensation rights under the contract.

A correct description is important for two reasons. First, a reader looking for a particular provision in the contract will be able to scan the bolded headings and find the relevant provision quickly. If it is buried under a non-descriptive heading, finding it will be difficult and time consuming. Second, the wording of the heading may have legal significance. A court will probably refuse to enforce a disclaimer of warranties that is contained in a section entitled "SELLER'S WARRANTIES." And if a category is headed "Employee's Duties," this may make it difficult for the employer to later claim that the document created an independent contractor relationship rather than one of employer/employee.

Some state statutes that dictate the form and content of legislation contain a provision stating that "headings are not part of the statute." This is designed to prevent the wording of a heading from having any legal significance regarding the interpretation of the statute. The legislative drafter, however, should still not be indifferent to the wording of headings, since the average citizen may rely on them in trying to determine what the statute means, whether the courts do or not. Unfortunately, disclaimers of this kind also sometimes appear in private law documents. This should be regarded as an open admission that the drafter is either too lazy to find the proper words to describe a collection of provisions or lacks the linguistic competence to do so.

B. CLASSIFICATION

Classification involves putting each bit of information into its proper category and sub-category. If the drafter of a lease has created a category entitled "Limits on Occupancy," then a specific provision dealing with overnight guests should be included under that heading, not under one dealing with "Alteration of the Premises." Conversely, a provision prohibiting the replacement of ceiling fixtures should not be put in the "Limits" category.

The classification decision is more difficult if the drafter has fudged a bit in complying with the rules of division, especially the one requiring the sub-classes to be mutually exclusive. Indeed, no division can be completely airtight, and some items can usually fit into more than one category. For example, a prohibition against smoking at the worksite could go in an employment policy's Safety section or in its Employee Rules of Conduct section, depending perhaps on the purpose of the rule. In making classification decisions, the drafter must always keep the user in mind. If a user wanted to find a provision dealing with a specific topic, where would that person look first? That is where the provision should go.

In practice, division and classification are not two separate intellectual processes. Although a rough divisional scheme usually comes first, the process of classification will often reveal defects and may even suggest an entirely different scheme. Moreover, these division and classification rules reflect the ideal. Sometimes it is not practicable to follow them rigorously, especially when dealing with subsections. After all of the provisions of the document have been classified, the drafter may find an odd one that does not seem to fit anywhere. Rather than completely redo the division scheme and force it to a level of abstraction that is more confusing than useful, the drafter should include this provision in whatever section it is most relevant to. This, certainly, is preferable to putting it in a "Miscellaneous" category.

C. SEQUENCE

The sequence of the major components of a contract is discussed in Chapter 2 and that of a statute in Chapter 3. However, within the substantive component itself—as distinguished from the definitions, recitals, preambles, housekeeping provisions, and formalities—several sequences are possible. The overall document may follow one general sequence, but the major sections may have their own internal logical sequence of a different variety. Whatever sequence the drafter adopts, the measure of its validity is the extent to which it helps readers use the document in the regulation of their affairs. The major sequential possibilities are as follows:

1. Chronological

If the document will regulate a relationship extending over several phases, then the drafter can deal with the events in the order in which they are going to occur. The sequence of a construction contract, for example, could parallel the construction process itself. Similarly, the major divisions of a lease can be presented in roughly chronological order, as follows:

- **Pre-occupancy:** identity of the parties, identity of the premises, duration, rent, and other fundamentals.

- **Occupancy:** limits on use of the premises, landlord's right to enter for maintenance and repairs, noise abatement, and other matters relevant to when the tenant is in possession.

- **Termination:** condition of the premises, return of security, and other post-occupancy matters.

The headings of a chronologically-divided document should indicate what is happening in this order. Unsophisticated readers, like many of those involved in consumer transactions, can better understand a complex document if it is organized by reference to the sequential actions of the various parties rather than to abstract legal classifications. Thus, rather than referring to "Revocation Rights," which is a legal concept, title it "Revoking the Contract," which puts the emphasis on the action.

2. Importance

Within a category of related rules, a drafter might choose to present the most important ones first. For example, in an employment contract, salary is a very important term, while the employee's choice of make and color of company car probably is not. Unscrupulous drafters will sometimes put an extremely important provision that strongly favors their client at the end of a long document, often following or included among a series of trivial provisions. In extreme cases of deception, usually involving consumer transactions, the courts have declined to enforce these provisions.

3. Frequency of Occurrence

Provisions dealing with events that are likely to occur frequently during the transaction can precede those dealing with rare or episodic events. In a construction contract, change orders are a frequent occurrence; discovery of historical artifacts is not. That should dictate the order in which these matters are dealt with.

4. Familiar Before Unfamiliar

Some transactions are built around a familiar set of facts or events, with the rights and duties of the parties being fairly commonplace. A particular transaction, however, may move off into previously uncharted territory. To give the parties a shared point of departure, the drafter may choose to deal with the familiar provisions first and then move into the more novel aspects of the undertaking.

5. Rules Before Exceptions

State generally what a requirement or prohibition applies to first. Then identify any exceptions. For example, a section of a harbor regulation might contain a long list of things that a vessel under way is required to do. This could then be followed with a list of situations where the general rules do not apply, such as in an emergency. Putting the exceptions before the general rule would only confuse the reader.

6. What Before How

A description of what the parties to a document must do should generally come before a description of how they are required to do it. For example, a contract for the sale of goods would normally indicate what is being sold, by and to whom, and for how much; it would then cover how delivery and payment are to be made.

7. Substance Before Procedure

Regardless of the nature of the document, the substantive provisions should normally come before the procedural or enforcement provisions. For example, an employer's sexual harassment policy would first identify what is being prohibited; it would then describe the procedures that the employer will follow in enforcing the policy.

Exercise 8

1. List the possible divisional criteria the following could be subject to:

6   b 8 t <u>13</u> # 12 r v <u>s</u> 5

o 2 W $\geq$ <u>c</u> y s k x <u>q</u> 3

x B j j & 7 p <u>9</u> u u 8

2. Assume that you have tentatively decided to organize (divide) an apartment lease into the following categories:

    A.   The Parties

    B.   Description of Leased Premises

    C.   Security Deposit

D. Rent

E. Duration

F. Landlord's Rights and Duties

G. Tenant's Rights and Duties

H. Termination

I. Miscellaneous

Into which category would you then place the following bits of information (only a partial list of what might ultimately go into the lease):

a. At the termination of the lease, the Landlord may withhold from the security deposit any money owed for back rent, for damage to the apartment, or for other losses caused by Tenant's breach of the lease.

b. *An oral modification* clause.

c. The Landlord is Cornell Apartments.

d. The Landlord is entitled to and the Tenant is obligated to allow the Landlord to enter the apartment to perform routine maintenance, to show the apartment to other prospective tenants during the last month of the lease, and to inspect for damage prior to Tenant's departure from the premises.

e. Except in cases of emergency, the Landlord will give and the Tenant is entitled to have at least 24 hours advance notice prior to the Landlord's entry into the apartment to perform routine maintenance, to show the apartment to other prospective tenants, or to inspect for damage.

f. The common areas that all Tenants may use include the parking lot, the volleyball court, the tennis court, the swimming pool, and clubhouse, and the washer/dryer room.

g. Rent is due on or before the first day of the month.

h. At the end of the initial term of the lease, the lease will automatically renew on a month-to-month basis unless either party gives at least one month's notice of intent to terminate the lease or unless the lease automatically terminates because of nonpayment of rent or other substantial breach of the lease terms.

3. Assume that you have drafted a set of Law School Honor Code Regulations, consisting of the following provisions. In what order would you arrange these provisions? Why? What subheadings would be appropriate?

a. Appeal from Honor Council decision to the Faculty.

b. Sanctions.

c. Students duty to report violations (with failure itself being an Honor Code violation).

d. Composition of Honor Council.

e. Definition of the prohibited classes of conduct.

f. Accused's right to written notice of charge.

g. Report of alleged violation to the Dean.

h. Time and place of hearing before Honor Council.

i. The Dean's investigation of alleged violation.

j. Statement of why an Honor Code is important in a law school.

k. Disposition of matter by the Dean on admission of guilt.

l. Accused's right to submit evidence to the Dean during the Dean's investigation of the charge.

m. The Dean's submission of unresolved charge to Honor Council.

n. Effective date.

o. Miscellaneous procedural matters relating to the hearing before Honor Council.

p. Appeal from the Faculty to the University Disciplinary Committee.

q. Authority of Honor Council to enforce Honor Code.

r. Accused student's right to confront accusers, to cross examine witnesses, to introduce evidence, and to be represented by counsel.

s. Violation of Honor Code is based on a preponderance of the evidence standard.

t. Responsibility of the Student Prosecutor.

u. Dismissal of charge by the Dean.

v. Report of Honor Council.

Part III

DRAFTING TECHNIQUES

Chapter 12

AVOIDING AMBIGUITIES

The *Oxford American Writer's Thesaurus* provides a number of synonyms for the word "ambiguous" reflecting how this word is often used colloquially. These include "open to debate/arguable," "abstruse," "dubious," and others. In drafting, however, the term is used in its formal, logical sense. That is what this chapter is about.

A. DEFINITION

"Ambiguity" means capable of having two or more distinct and mutually inconsistent meanings. An ambiguous term can either mean one thing or it can mean another thing, but it cannot mean both.

Although the two terms are often used interchangeably, ambiguity is distinct from vagueness, which merely means that the term in question has indistinct borders. A "reasonable time" is vague, because the two points that bracket a "reasonable" time (with "unreasonably" short on one side and "unreasonably" long on the other) are both uncertain and will have to be determined by the particular circumstances. But it unambiguously refers to times somewhere between the uncertain lower and upper limits of what is "reasonable"; it does not refer to any times beyond them.

B. THE CONSEQUENCES OF AMBIGUITY

Ambiguity is the greatest cause of litigation over drafted documents and litigation is always expensive, whether one wins or loses. The results of ambiguity-based litigation are always bad for someone. An ambiguity could be fatal to the efficacy of the document, rendering a contract or statute void and totally frustrating the objectives of the contracting parties or a legislative body. Or, the court might construe the ambiguity against the drafter, causing the client serious disadvantage and opening the door to a malpractice action. If the ambiguity was a deliberate contrivance to deceive, the drafter may also be guilty of an ethical violation. Ambiguity is fundamentally inconsistent with the central mission of drafting, which is to avoid problems without the need for expensive and often unsuccessful litigation.

Consider two possible litigation scenarios involving an ambiguous term. The contract is for the sale of goods to arrive on the ship *Peerless* from Bombay. Clearly, the parties have in mind one particular ship. But, unbeknownst to either party, two ships named *Peerless* are scheduled to sail from Bombay at different times. The term *Peerless* has two mutually inconsistent meanings and is, thus, ambiguous. The buyer, moreover, knows only of the October *Peerless*, and the seller knows only of the December *Peerless*. The ambiguity, combined with the different meanings that the parties attached to the term, would defeat the existence of a contract based upon the doctrine of mutual mistake. The drafter's fault, although perhaps understandable, consists of a failure to investigate sufficiently the facts surrounding the transaction and to identify which ship *Peerless* was meant, perhaps by specifying its sailing date.

But suppose the buyer knows that two ships *Peerless* exist. The buyer still intends the October *Peerless* and knows or has reason to know that the seller thinks only one ship *Peerless* exists, the one sailing in December. The buyer's attorney, aware of all this, nevertheless drafts the contract in terms of the ship *Peerless*, without qualification. Although the ambiguity still exists, in this instance it will probably be resolved under the doctrine of unilateral mistake against the buyer, who will be bound to a contract for the goods arriving on the December *Peerless*.

C. TYPES OF AMBIGUITY

There are three types of ambiguity that may infect a document: contextual ambiguity, semantic ambiguity, and syntactic ambiguity.

1. Contextual Ambiguity

Contextual ambiguity exists when one allegedly controlling provision is inconsistent with another allegedly controlling provision. An internal contextual ambiguity exists when the inconsistency is within the contract or statute itself. Consider the two following provisions in a lease:

3. **Security Deposit:** Within 30 days after the termination or expiration of the lease, landlord will return the security deposit, less any amount owed for damage to the premises caused by tenant.

28. **Unpaid Rent:** At the termination of the lease period, landlord may apply the security deposit to any rent then owed by tenant.

A reasonable interpretation of the security deposit provision would be that, subject to the landlord being entitled to withhold only any amount that is due for damages to the premises, the entire amount must be returned. That interpretation, however, is negated by the unpaid rent provision, which allows the landlord to also use the security deposit to cover rent still owed.

Faulty definitions are another common source of internal contextual ambiguity. An insurance policy that defines both "building" and "business personal property" as including machinery and equipment is ambiguous if the two classifications have different and mutually inconsistent legal consequences, such as deductibles or limits of liability, with respect to the items that are included.

Some contextual inconsistencies, however, are more subtle and are often the result of poor conceptualization. The Civil Rights Act of 1964 contains the following definition:

The terms "because of sex" or "on the basis of sex" include, but are not limited to, [1] because of or on the basis of pregnancy, childbirth, or related medical conditions, and [2] women affected by pregnancy, childbirth, or related medical conditions shall be treated the same for all employment-related purposes, including receipt of benefits under fringe benefit programs, as other persons not so affected but similar in their ability or inability to work, ... (Bracketed numbers added)

Congress apparently did not have a clear idea of what it intended to prohibit. Phrase [1] imposes an unequivocal prohibition against discrimination because of pregnancy, but phrase [2] requires only equal treatment. Those are not equivalents and are, indeed, potentially inconsistent. Suppose an employer has a policy of not hiring persons who will need significant leave time during the first year of their employment. Under this policy, the employer has declined to hire persons who anticipate having major surgery during the first year. When the employer declines to hire a pregnant woman under this policy, that decision is clearly because of her pregnancy, but it is also equal treatment. Which prevails? The Supreme Court ultimately resolved the ambiguity in favor of the second phrase. But that expensive litigation could have been avoided if the drafter had conceptualized the prohibited conduct better and characterized it in a single, unambiguous way.

References to other documents can also create a form of contextual ambiguity. A general contractor agrees to remedy "all the itemized defects per owner's punch list of 9/2/06." If two lists of that date exist, containing a materially different itemization of defects, this creates an ambiguity. To avoid this ambiguity, the referenced document should be physically attached to the agreement. Even if only one other document exists, physical attachment will prevent this other document from getting lost, creating not an ambiguity but a void.

Statutes that incorporate by reference portions of other statutes run a high risk of contextual ambiguity. First, since the incorporated material was probably not intended to focus on the specific problem now being legislated, a perfect fit between the incorporating and the incorporated materials is highly unlikely. Conflicting implications frequently arise. Second, when the material incorporated by reference is later repealed or amended, the effect of this on the incorporating legislation is unclear. A statute in the Virgin Islands poses a similar problem. In 1921, the legislature adopted as the common law "the restatements of the law prepared and approved by the American Law Institute." The reference in 1921 was implicitly to the first Restatement, with a contextual ambiguity arising when the Restatement (Second) came out.

An external contextual ambiguity arises when the inconsistency is between what one contract or statute says and what another contract or statute says. For example, a client asks the drafter to prepare a contract for the purchase of a house and specifies the terms and conditions. The drafter fails to discover that the client already has a lease on the house and that it contains an option to buy, albeit on different terms. Which document controls? Similarly, the legislative drafter who does inadequate research may draft a statute that appears to require what another statute prohibits, creating an ambiguity.

2. Semantic Ambiguity

Semantic ambiguity arises out of the use of specific words and phrases. The following categories of words are among the most troublesome.

a. Homonyms. Words that are spelled the same but have different meanings can sometimes cause confusion in drafted documents. The word "bar," for example, could refer to a place where drinks are served, a device to secure a door, something used to pry objects loose, something every lawyer must pass, what lawyers practice before, or a measure of music. Usually, the context will inform the reader of the intended meaning of a homonym, as in that example. But some words with multiple and mutually inconsistent meanings cannot be resolved by context. The drafter should be especially aware of the following words and expressions:

- **Doctor.** This could refer to a Ph.D., an M.D., a D.M.D., a D.V.M., or an LL.D. The difference could be rather important if the document is identifying the qualifications of persons eligible to hold a particular position.

- **Public.** When used in reference to a place, this may mean a facility that is governmentally owned, a place that is accessible without restriction, or a place that can be readily seen by other persons. A reference to a public parking lot or a prohibition against doing something in a public place may be ambiguous.

- **Residence.** This could refer to one's legal domicile (for voting or tax purposes) or one's place of abode at any given time.

- **Sanction.** This can mean either an approval or a penalty. To refer to "conduct sanctioned by the legislature" is thus ambiguous.

- **Since.** This word can be used both to express a causal relation and to indicate the passage of time. A recital in a contract might state, "Since the seller defaulted on the prior contract, buyer has begun manufacturing its own bolts." This could indicate when the buyer began to manufacture its own bolts or it could indicate why. To avoid this ambiguity, some drafters limit "since" to its temporal connotation and use "because" to indicate causation.

- **While.** Similarly, the word "while" can be used to express a time period or to mean although. Assume that a contract modification stipulates as follows: "While the delivery date of June 19, 2004, is suspended due to the Canadian embargo, buyer shall not attempt to obtain goods from another source." The "while" could either mean "during the time that" or "although." Because of this potential for ambiguity, the preferred usage of "while" is in its temporal sense. And the drafter should also make sure that this is clear from the context.

b. **"And."** This word can mean either jointly or severally. For example, if a contract says, "Executor shall distribute $1,000 to Bill and Mary," this could mean that they must share the $1,000 jointly. Or it could mean that each of them separately gets $1,000. The drafter should choose between the following, depending on the testator's intent:

Executor shall distribute $1,000 to Bill and Mary, to be shared jointly.

Executor shall distribute $1,000 each to Bill and Mary.

The use of "and" following a preposition can also cause significant problems. Suppose Bill and Mary were once married and had children; they have since divorced and remarried and both have children by the second marriage. What does "To the children of Bill and Mary mean?" It could refer only to the children of their union. Or it could also include the children of their second marriages.

Ambiguity may arise when the reader cannot determine from context whether the "and" is intended to identify several different entities or to identify the traits of a single entity. This is especially true when the "and" phrase includes modifiers. The classic example comes from a will litigated in 1799, where the testator bequeathed to a particular individual, "All my black and white horses." He died leaving six white horses, six black horses, and six horses with both black and white colors. Which horses should the beneficiary inherit?

Similarly, a document might refer to "charitable and educational institutions." Does this mean to institutions that are both charitable and educational? Or does it refer to two entities, charitable institutions and educational institutions? The drafter can avoid this ambiguity by referring to "institutions that are both charitable and educational," to "institutions that are either charitable or educational," or to "institutions that are charitable, educational, or both."

An ordinance might provide that "Every owner and operator of a taxicab shall report annually." Does the ordinance apply to a single entity, namely someone possessing both the trait of being an owner and the trait of being an operator? Or does it apply to two classes of entities, persons who are owners and persons who are operators? Or does it apply to three classes of entities, owners, operators, and persons who are both an owner and an operator? Depending on what is meant, the ambiguity could thus be resolved as follows:

*A person who is **both the owner and operator** of a taxicab shall report annually.*

*A person who is the **owner** of a taxicab and a person who is the **operator** of a taxicab shall report annually.*

> *A person who is the **owner** of a taxicab, a person who is the **operator** of a taxicab, or person who is **both the owner and operator** of a taxicab shall report annually.*

Sometimes drafters intend to use "and" in the disjunctive rather than the conjunctive sense, although this can only be determined from the context, which thus makes it ambiguous.

> *Bill and Mary are entitled to exercise the option to repurchase the land.*

Obviously, Bill and Mary cannot each separately exercise the option. But the sentence could mean that they must do it jointly or it could mean, construing "and" to mean "or," that either one of them can do it—presumably, whoever acts first. Depending on what the client intends, the drafter could draft it in one of the two following ways:

> *Bill and Mary are entitled to exercise the option jointly.*

> *Either Bill or Mary is entitled to exercise the option.*

    c. "Or." The word "or" can have an exclusive connotation, meaning "A or B, but not both." It can also be used in an inclusive sense, meaning "A or B, or both." Suppose a criminal statute imposes a penalty of "a $500 fine or ten days in jail." Does this mean that the judge can impose the fine or the term in jail, but not both? Or can the judge impose both? Or suppose a will states, "The Executor is authorized to sell my jade collection in New York or Chicago." Does this mean that the executor must choose between the two cities? Or may the executor sell parts of the collection in both cities?

    Although a simple "or" is usually construed in its inclusive sense, the drafter should make this clear. Say "$500 or ten days in jail, or both." If the disjunctive is intended, say "either $500 or ten days in jail, but not both."

    Drafters sometimes intend to use "or" in its substitutionary sense, creating further uncertainties. If a will provides, "To Bill or his heirs," an executor or court would construe this as meaning that the bequest goes to Bill's heirs, but only if Bill is not alive, since Bill cannot have heirs until he is dead. Here, the substitutionary sense of "or" can be determined from the factual context. But what if the will provides, "To a non-profit corporation devoted to the restoration of 18th Century homesteads, if one exists, or to the Texas Historical Foundation." Is this "or" being used substitutionally or alternatively? When "or" is used in its substitutionary rather than alternative sense, make this clear.

> *To Bill, or if Bill is not alive at the time of my death, to his children.*

A related ambiguity exists when "or" is used to connect classes of entities from which a selection is to be made. For example, a contract might provide, "Seller shall ship 1,000 red or blue widgets." If it is important to the buyer that all the widgets come from the same color class, then the contract should make that express by requiring the seller to ship "either 1,000 red widgets or 1,000 blue widgets." Otherwise, the seller might feel free to ship 500 of each color.

d. "And/Or." "And" is generally inclusive. To draw on tort language, it is joint and several. "And" can mean A and B, together (jointly), and each separate and apart (severally). But there are times when "and" needs to be restricted to its joint sense (when "A and B" means only both together). "Or" can be exclusive (A or B but not both) or inclusive. *See Am. Surety Co. v. Marotta*, 287 U.S. 513, 53 S.Ct. 260, 77 L.Ed. 466 (1933) (holding that "or" includes "and"); 11 U.S.C. § 102(5) (accord). Since both "and" and "or" are potentially ambiguous, combining them into one term only multiplies the ambiguity. Because of this, "and/or" has been the subject of considerable judicial hostility. One judge expressed it this way:

> It is manifest that we are confronted with the task of construing "and/or," that befuddling, nameless thing, that Janus-faced monstrosity, neither word nor phrase, the child of a brain of someone too lazy or too dull to express his precise meaning, or too dull to know what he did mean, now commonly used by lawyers in drafting legal documents, through carelessness or ignorance or as a cunning device to conceal rather than express meaning with view to furthering the interests of their clients.

Judges have also called "and/or" (1) "a mongrel expression," (2) "a meaningless symbol," (3) "a weasel phrase," (4) "a verbal monstrosity," (5) "one of those inexcusable barbarisms which was sired by indolence and damned by indifference," (6) "an abominable invention," (7) "as devoid of meaning as it is incapable of classification by the rules of grammar and syntax," and (8) "a hybrid, contradictory combination, frequently as bewildering, mystifying, and perplexing as Poe's raven—or was it fiend? on the 'night's Plutonian shore.'"

The outrage is fully warranted. Suppose a contract provides a sales commission for "transactions originating and/or consummated within the Columbia city limits." Construed inclusively, the "or" component suggests that the commission is due if the transaction originated in Columbia, was consummated in Columbia, or both originated and was consummated in Columbia. If the "and" is construed as referring to two entities with separate characteristics, that reaches almost the same result—although to be fully consistent it would have to also be construed as encompassing a third entity possessing the characteristic of both being originated and consummated in Columbia. On the other hand, if the "or" is construed in its disjunctive sense and the "and" is construed as referring to a single entity with two characteristics, then the result mandated by the "or" is inconsistent with the result mandated by the "and."

The same ambiguity exists in a statute that says, "Any person found guilty of operating a motor vehicle while in an intoxicated condition and/or who shall cause injury to person or property shall be guilty of a felony." The "and" component suggests that this is a single offense consisting of two elements, intoxication and causing injury. The "or" suggests that the statute defines two possible offenses, intoxication and causing an injury.

The dwindling remnant of drafters who defend the use of "and/or" contend that it is a concise way of saying "A or B or both." Certainly, that is one way that it can be construed. But since there are also other ways it can be construed, the phrase remains fatally ambiguous despite their protestations. Moreover, in most cases where an "and/or" is used, a simple "or" would suffice since it is usually construed in its inclusive sense. A reference to a person who is "a citizen at or over the age of 21" would not be construed as excluding a citizen over the age of 21.

Often, drafters will fail to indicate whether the items in an enumeration or list are cumulative or alternative.

An employee may be allowed up to 30 days unpaid personal leave each calendar year if—

> *(a) The employee requests the leave in writing at least 7 days in advance;*

> *(b) The reason for the leave could not have been anticipated at the time the employee took his or her regularly scheduled vacation.*

The provision implies "and/or," making it just as ambiguous as if the term were express. Does this impose two requirements? Or does (b) operate as an exception or alternative to (a)? The implied, or silent, "and/or" in an enumeration should be changed to "and" or "or," depending on what the client intends.

A partial solution may be the use of "and" only jointly, "or" only severally, and "and/or" to indicate joint and several relationships. This could be accomplished by use of a provision defining the terms. This would require one to carefully and consistently use the defined terms appropriately. Because 100% consistency is the exception rather than the rule, this may be unworkable in the rigors of actual practice. One can also use constructions such as "A or B or both," "A or B but not both," or "A and B together but not separately" and the like. Confront this issue, adopt a workable solution, and apply it uniformly to your drafting.

e. Specific Dates. Drafters use a variety of expressions in reference to specific dates. Some are clear. But some have been construed in different ways. Others have a legal meaning that is inconsistent with the conventional meaning.

● **"Between ... and ..."**

*Buyer may exercise the option **between** July 1, 2009, **and** July 29, 2009.*

The courts generally construe this literally. Thus, the option could not be exercised on either of those two dates, only in the period between them. However, that construction is inconsistent with how many lay persons would construe the language, namely including the two dates and the period between the dates.

- **"By . . ."**

  *Buyer must exercise the option **by** July 29, 2009.*

Most courts hold that the option may be exercised on that date, but the matter might be worth litigating if a great deal of money was at stake.

- **"From . . . to . . ."**

  *Buyer may exercise the option **from** July 1, 2009, **to** July 29, 2009.*

Some courts hold that the option can be exercised on neither date. Some courts hold that the "from" date is excluded but the "to" date is included. Some courts hold that both dates are included.

- **"Until . . ."**

  *Buyer's option is open **until** July 29, 2009.*

Most would hold that the option can be exercised on that date.

Because all of these date-related phrases have been variously construed and are thus ambiguous, the drafter should avoid them. Usually, they can be replaced with a set of terms that are generally regarded as not being ambiguous, whether they are used together or individually, as follows:

- **"After . . . before . . ."**

  *Buyer may exercise the option **after** July 1, 2009, and **before** July 29, 2009.*

  *Buyer must exercise the option **after** July 1, 2009.*

  *Buyer must exercise the option **before** July 29, 2009.*

Courts hold that the option may not be exercised on either date. Many, however, find it counter-intuitive to specify in a document a date that is not included in the allowed time period. To accommodate both legal and conventional understandings, many drafters use "on or after" and "on or before" terminology.

*Buyer may exercise the option **on or after** July 2, 2009, and **on or before** July 28, 2009.*

Indeed, since "on" is fairly consistently construed to include the full day referenced, many drafters are content to use it in lieu of any "after . . . before" expression.

*Buyer's option begins **on** July 1, 2009, and ends **on** July 29, 2009.*

Drafters exercising extreme caution would also include the times, at "12:01 a.m." and "at 11:59 p.m."—or some other times, if desired.

f.   Time Spans. Drafted documents often refer to time spans rather than specific dates. Precisely measuring the beginning or end of the time span can sometimes be difficult.

- **"Within**. . . .**"** If a document requires that something be done "within 30 days," an immediate question arises, "Within 30 days of what?" Often, the intent is that it be done within 30 days of the signing of the contract. But if the contract requires Able to do something and then Betty to do something "within 30 days," does the 30 days still refer to the date of the contract or does it refer to the date of Able's act?

- **"After** . . .**"**

  *The option lapses 7 days **after** the Landlord receives Tenant's notice of non-renewal.*

As is true with respect to specific dates, courts consistently hold that the day of the triggering event is not included and that the reference is to full days. Thus, if the landlord received the notice on July 5th, July 6th would be the first of the seven days and the option would lapse at the end of the day on July 12th. The careless use of the word "time" in this kind of provision can cause possibly unintended consequences, however.

*The option lapses 7 days **after the time when** the Landlord receives Tenant's notice of non-renewal.*

If the landlord received the notice at 2:00 p.m. on July 5th, then the option is likely to lapse at 2:00 p.m. on July 12th, even though that might well not be the intent of the parties.

- **"Before** . . .**"**

Alternatively, the option provision could be expressed as follows:

*Tenant must exercise this option **before** 11:59 p.m. of the seventh day after the day on which the Landlord receives Tenant's notice of non-renewal.*

Although "before" and "after" are fairly safe to use in identifying time spans, the drafter must be careful not to create unintended substantive gaps.

Penalties for late filing are as follows:

1. *10 days and before the 20th day—$45.*
2. *After 20 days and before the 30th day—$100.*
3. *After 30 days—$500.*

What is the penalty for the person who files on the 20th or the 30th day? Using "on or before" would cure that problem.

- **"Within . . ."**

  *A Tenant who files a notice of non-renewal must then exercise the option **within** 7 days.*

Most courts construe this as beginning on the first day after the filing of notice and ending at 11:59 p.m. on the seventh day. Alternatively, some drafters use "before the expiration of" or "before 11:59" of instead of "within." If the "within" is used in reference to a future date certain, as in "within 30 days of June 15," does this refer to the 30 days prior to June 15, the 30 days after June 15, or both?

g. Days, Weeks, Months, and Years. These terms are used in connection with time spans, which present one form of ambiguity, as discussed above. The terms, however, can also be ambiguous in their own right. A document is signed at 2:00 p.m. on Wednesday, July 28, 2009. It provides:

Buyer has two days to arrange financing, one week to secure insurance, three months to make the first payment, and five years to make the final payment.

Does "day" mean calendar days, beginning on the midnight of July 28th, or consecutive 24–hour periods, beginning at 2:00 p.m. on July 28th? Do "days" include weekends and holidays? Or is the intended reference to business days? If the term "business days" is intended or used, does its meaning change depending upon when the parties operate their businesses? In this increasingly 24/7 world, arguably every day is a business day. Similarly, does a "week" mean seven consecutive calendar days? If so, does the week include that Wednesday and thus end on Tuesday? Or does it begin on Thursday and end on the next Wednesday? Or does "week" mean the next unit beginning on Sunday and ending on Saturday? If the document was signed on Monday, is it possible that the reference is to a five-day business week? Similarly, does "months" refer to full calendar months, beginning with August and ending on October 31? Or do the three months run from the time and date of signing, with the three months ending at 2:00 p.m. on October 28? Or perhaps it means the lunar month of 28 days. Similar problems exist with respect to the exact length of and how to mark the beginning and end of a "year."

The usual construction is that "days" includes Saturdays, Sundays, and holidays; that a "week" refers to seven consecutive days; that a "month" covers the period between and including a date-certain in the starting month (July 4) and the day before that date in the next month (August 3); and a "year" covers the period between and including a date-certain in the starting month (July 4, 2009) and the day before that date in the next year (July 3, 2010). But if the context would suggest otherwise, or if the intent is otherwise, then the drafter should not leave matters to chance. If a specific date can be calculated, then reference it in the manner discussed above. Alternatively, express the length in words that leave no room for uncertainty.

> *Each party has 7 days to object to the report, beginning on the day and at the time the report is filed and ending at 5:00 p.m. on the seventh day (excluding weekends and federal holidays) following the day the report is filed.*

If the report was filed at 10:00 a.m. on Monday, October 5, 2009, objections would be due before 5:00 p.m. on Wednesday, October 14, 2009.

In statutes and complex private documents, if days, weeks, months, or years are referred to in several places, then a definition identifying when these periods begin and end would eliminate the awkwardness of the provision suggested above.

"Day" means the next full 24–hour period following the event referenced, beginning at 00:01 a.m., and each consecutively following full 24–hour period, exclusive of Saturdays, Sundays, and federal holidays.

h. "Bimonthly," "biannually," "biennially," "semimonthly," and "semiannually." Bryan Garner's authoritative *A Dictionary of Modern Legal Usage* says that "bimonthly" means every two months and "semimonthly" means twice a month. But he recognizes that "bi-" is also used to mean twice. The *New Oxford American Dictionary* says that bimonthly can mean either twice a month or every two months. Garner says that "biannually" and "semiannually" both mean twice year, while "biennially" means every two years. No further proof of the ambiguity of these terms is needed. They should be avoided altogether and "every two" or "twice a..." used instead, depending on what the drafter intends.

i. Hours. A contract that requires something to be done "by no later than 2 o'clock" is probably intended to refer to 2 p.m., since few people are out and about during the early morning hours. But the context of the contract might suggest otherwise, thus creating an ambiguity. Drafters should always clarify their time references with "a.m." or "p.m."

Even these references can be ambiguous in one instance. Assume that a city ordinance prohibits parking in a certain area "between 8 a.m. and 12 p.m." A person is given a ticket for parking in the area at 1:30 p.m., assuming that the "12 p.m." reference was to noon. The city maintains that "12 p.m." refers to midnight. Although that is how "12 p.m." is normally construed, with "12 a.m." being construed as referring to noon, the term is at least potentially ambiguous. And technically, neither party is correct. According to the Naval Observatory Time Service Division, "p.m." refers to the time from when the sun is directly overhead to when it is directly overhead the directly opposite part of the earth and "a.m." refers to the time from then until the sun is back directly overhead. But neither term can be used to describe when the sun is directly overhead or in the converse position. The Observatory recommends using "noon" or "midnight."

"Noon" may be safe enough, but "midnight" is not. A reference to "midnight on October 23, 2009," could refer to the midnight joining the 23rd with the 24th, which is the generally accepted American usage, or it could refer to the midnight joining the 22nd with the 23rd, which is how it is used in some European countries. The clearer references would be either to "00:00:01 a.m. on October 23, 2004," or to "11:59:59 p.m. on October 23, 2004."

j.   Relational Words. Do not use "now," "currently," or "presently." The danger is that this time reference will be construed literally, when that is not what is intended, thus creating potential for ambiguity. For example:

> *Seller shall not charge a price in excess of that **currently** charged in the Atlanta wholesale cotton seed market.*

What if the allowed price is $1,000 at the time of contracting but when the price is actually charged the Atlanta regulated price has dropped to $900? Which controls? If the contract price is intended to fluctuate, delete "currently" and add "in effect the time of delivery." If the reference is to the price allowed on the date of the contract, delete "currently" and add "as of the date of this contract." Alternatively, simply write in the existing price as of that date.

k.   Ages. Contracts refer to the ages of the parties less often than do statutes and private law documents like wills. These references are often ambiguous.

> *Nephew will not smoke or drink until he is over 21 years of age.*

Can the nephew start smoking and drinking after his 21st birthday? Or must he wait until after his 22nd birthday? Whichever interpretation is intended, it should be stated in just those terms.

> *Nephew will not smoke or drink until after his 21st birthday.*

l.   "Provided that." The word "provided" is ambiguous because it can be used in so many senses. Its only proper use is as a verb.

> *Seller will provide transportation for the goods.*

The "provided that" form of the word traces its origin to the time when the Latin phrase *provistum est* was used to introduce each separate and independent section of a statute. The full English translation was used later. "It is provided that...." This at least gives the sentence a grammatical subject, albeit an expletive, "it," and a verb, "is." Eventually, the "it is" was dropped. What is left defies grammatical analysis. Provisos produce single sentences that are often hundreds of words long. Knowledgeable drafters have railed against them for years.

Apart from being a grammatical abomination, "provided that" is ambiguous because it can be used variously to introduce exceptions, qualifications, conditions, and even new substantive provisions.

> ***C. Cure.*** *Seller may attempt to cure any defects, **provided**, however, **that** notice of intent to cure is given within 10 days of the notification of the defect; and **provided that** buyer does not waive notice; and **provided** further **that** if the attempt at cure is unsuccessful, seller will replace the item and compensate buyer for any losses due to delay.*

The first proviso imposes a condition precedent. The second proviso states an exception. And the third proviso deals with an altogether new substantive provision. These should be dealt with directly, using the terms that create each of these legal consequences, as follows:

> ***C. Cure.*** *(a) Seller is entitled to attempt to cure any defects. (b) If seller elects to attempt to cure, seller must give notice of that intent within 10 days of notification of the defect, unless seller has waived notice. (c) If seller's attempt to cure is unsuccessful, seller will replace the item and compensate buyer for any losses due to delay.*

Implementing this suggested usage is an uphill battle, as the introduction of baskets and materiality thresholds in contracts with "provided, however, that" and "provided further, however, that" is widespread and accepted practice in, among other places, the majority of large transactional law firms.

m. Legalese. Apart from being archaic and unnecessarily wordy, some legalese is also ambiguous because these terms often have multiple referents. Suppose that a sentence in a regulation concludes, "and the benefits provided herein are available to all dependents who file within 30 days of termination of service." Does this apply only to whatever benefits are described in that sentence, to benefits described in that particular section, or to benefits described anywhere in the regulation?

"Hereunder" could also be construed as referring to any of those three possibilities, or it could be construed as referring only to things appearing in the agreement after the word is used. Similarly, a reference to "aforementioned benefits" is ambiguous if the document has earlier referenced several different sets of benefits. Are all of them included, or only the last grouping?

Replace these ambiguous terms with specific references, like "the benefits provided in subsection 304(a)(ii)."

If you are trying to say "in this document," say that—name the document (using a defined term—this Agreement, this Lease, etc.—can be helpful here). If you are trying to say "in this paragraph/section/etc.," just say it.

The same applies to all the here-, there-, and -said words like "hereby," "hereinafter," "therefore," "therein," "aforesaid," and others. Similarly, "same" and "such" should be avoided if at all possible. They are weak substitutes for proper pronouns and good defined terms. They can also create ambiguous references.

n. Shall, May and Will. The key problem here is that "shall" is commonly (mis)used for all three words, causing ambiguity. "May" is permissive—meaning the actor has an *option* of taking an action or receiving a benefit—it expresses a privilege. "Shall," on the other hand, means the actor has no choice; he or she has a duty.

> *At or before the closing, the Seller shall deliver the Purchase Price to the Escrow Agent.*

> *Buyer may waive any of the conditions to Buyer's performance in its sole and absolute discretion.*

The word "shall" is properly used only to create duties that attach to particular persons. When "shall" is used in connection with a non-person in a passive voice sentence, it may be unclear whether this is intended to create merely a condition or to impose a duty on the implied actor. For example:

> *The house **shall** be completely painted before the payment of $400 is due.*

Does this mean that the painter has assumed a duty to paint the house that is also a constructive condition of the owner's duty to pay $400—a bilateral contract? Or is this simply a unilateral offer the acceptance of which, by completely painting the house, triggers the owner's duty to pay—but itself not creating any duty on the painter's part to accept?

"Shall" can also be ambiguous when it is misused in a descriptive sense:

> *The Mayor is empowered to appoint the Chief of Police who **shall** be a resident of the city.*

Does this merely describe the Mayor's pool of eligible appointees, limiting it to persons already living in the city, with the appointment of a non-resident going beyond the scope of his power? Or does it mean that although the eligible pool is unlimited, once appointed the Chief of Police has a duty to become a resident of the city?

Differentiate between rights (entitlements) and duties (obligations). Rights are created by "entitled to" phrases (tenants are entitled to quiet enjoyment of the premises); duties are created by "shall" phrases (tenants shall clean and maintain the area around their front doors in good repair). It is best to use "shall"—which is fairly archaic English—only to refer to duties.

You may be tempted to use "must" in place of "shall". However, this is not standard in United States practice and opposing counsel and colleagues may object. "Must" is appropriate for creating a condition precedent.

"Will" is similar to "shall," as it may refer to a duty. When indicating a duty, it is best to stick to "shall" and eliminate "will" to avoid the implication of different meanings since "will" is also used to refer to events that are to occur after closing. It is essential though that in using "shall" or "will" to create a duty, that the drafter pick one term and use throughout.

If the bill passes as it is, the President will veto it. At the end of this session, the Legislation will adjourn. At that time, Contractor shall begin installation of new carpet in the Assembly Chamber.

The closing will take place at ***[address].***

If the name of a party does not appear before the word "shall" in an apparent shall/duty clause, it is probably incorrect use of the imperative tense. For example, agreements often state that they "shall" be governed by the law of a particular state. This is incorrect. Rather, the agreement should state the choice of law clause as a present tense actual circumstance, using "is."

This agreement is governed by the laws of [state].

If the provision is a declaration of a future fact, use "will" in its predictive sense instead of "shall."

Final approval or disapproval will occur no later than June 1, 2010.

Note, however, that this same phrase, cast in the active voice to identify the actor, becomes a "shall clause":

The Buyer shall approve or disapprove performance no later than June 1, 2010.

And when drafting, include consequences of a failure to perform the duty, either by listing it as an event of default that may trigger a remedy or by specifying that failure to, for example, approve or disapprove performance by June 1, 2008, will not be deemed to be approval.

o. "Among" and "between." The Oxford English Dictionary says to use "between" to express the relation of a thing to other things individually.

*The contest will be **between** the various plant managers.*

But use *"among"* to express the relationship of a thing to other things collectively and vaguely.

*Fund recipients must work **among** the poor.*

The conventional wisdom, however, is that "between" refers to two things and "among" refers to more than two things.

*This is just **between** you and me, but I intend to distribute the reward evenly **among** Ann, Betty, Carol, and Diane.*

Number is not the only distinction between "between" and "among." A contract is made *between* three parties, not *among* them. Essentially, "between" indicates a direct relationship from each party to each party. "Among" is less specific and may connote an arrangement where some parties are directly connected and some are not.

Suppose a will says:

> *The Executor shall divide my estate [**among** or **between**] my son and the two children of my deceased daughter.*

If the choice is "between," then a court adhering to the conventional wisdom would divide the estate into two equal shares, one for the son and the other split into equal amounts for the two children. But if the choice is "among," then the same court would divide the estate into three equal shares. The drafter should not leave such an important matter to the whims of conventional wisdom.

3. Syntactic Ambiguity

Syntactic ambiguities arise principally out of the order in which words appear and how they are punctuated, which affects what other words they modify or refer to. Consider the following notice in the parking garage of a health care facility:

> *All patients must park on the same level as the doctor you are visiting.*

Now you understand why you can never find a parking place when you go to the doctor!

The most common forms of syntactic ambiguity are as follows.

a. Pronoun Reference. The general rule is that a pronoun refers back to the immediately preceding noun. When this construction is inconsistent with the sense of the provision, an ambiguity arises. Which is to prevail, the general rule or the sense? Consider this classic example:

> *Holding up a cookie box for his sister to see, a boy says, "If you can guess what kind of cookie is in this box, I'll give **it** to you."*

"Chocolate chip," she replies.

"Right," he says, as he removes the cookie, eats the cookie, and hands her the now empty box.

Here, the antecedent "it" is ambiguous. The sister reasonably believed the prize was the cookie. The boy, however, can rely on the general rule and assert that the grammatical reference was to the box.

Or suppose a contract provides as follows:

Seller will load a dumpster onto a vehicle provided by Buyer. ***It*** *will be capable of holding three tons.*

Common sense dictates that "it" does not refer to the buyer, although that is what the rules of grammatical construction would suggest. But does it refer to the dumpster or the vehicle?

In addition to being in bad style, using "such" as a demonstrative pronoun often creates ambiguity:

Employees shall not remove any die tap tools from the plant that are not checked out with the Tool Supervisor and each Shift Supervisor shall inventory ***such*** *tools weekly.*

Does the Shift Supervisor have a duty to inventory all die tap tools weekly, to ensure that none are missing? Or does the duty extend only those that are checked out, to determine how many are checked out and where they are?

b. Modifiers. Modifiers are a ready source of ambiguity and come in a variety of forms.

Items in a series. It is unclear in some phrases whether an adjective is intended to modify only the noun that immediately follows or all of the series of nouns that follow. Similarly, it is often unclear whether a trailing clause modifies only the last preceding noun or other parts of the sentence as well. Suppose that a will authorizes the executor to select and give a certain amount of money to "educational institutions and corporations working with the hearing impaired." This could mean at least four different things, depending on what is construed as modifying what. A technique known as tabbing allows the drafter to identify the possibilities inherent in this phrase, as follows:

- educational institutions

  and

  corporations working with the hearing
  impaired

- educational

  institutions

  and

  corporations working with the hearing
  impaired

- educational institutions

  and

  corporations

  working with the hearing impaired

- educational

  institutions

  and

  corporations

  working with the hearing impaired

Each option reflects a different intent. The ambiguity can be easily resolved through the technique of enumeration, discussed in Chapter 16. This simply involves putting those examples in sentence form, using numbers and letters in parentheses to identify the groupings, and perhaps also using the tabbing or indentation convention, as follows:

I direct the Executor to distribute $10,000 to one or more (a) educational institutions or (b) corporations, either of which works with the hearing impaired, with the selection of the recipients and amount given to each recipient to be within the discretion of the Executor.

-or-

I direct the Executor to distribute $10,000 to one or more

    (a) educational institutions or

    (b) corporations

who are working with the hearing impaired, with the selection . . . .

Quality Versus Identity. When an entity is modified by a chain of adjectives, it may be unclear whether the modifiers in combination describe the collective quality of the thing or are suggesting that separate entities are involved, each possessing one of the qualities described.

Distributor shall supply red, white, and blue caps.

Must each cap contain all three colors (quality)? Or may the distributor supply solid red, solid white, and solid blue caps (identity)?

Linkage Problems. Does "working dog owners" refer to persons who own a dog classified within the working breed category—linking "working" and "dog" together? Or does it refer to persons who work and also own dogs— linking "working" and "owners?"

Dangling Modifiers. Another form of ambiguous modifier is one that "dangles." A modifier, usually an introductory phrase, dangles if the reader cannot identify what the modifier refers to in the main clause of the sentence. Consider the following provision in a will:

If alive but incompetent at the time of my death, my son's guardian shall inherit half of my estate for his continued care and keeping.

Suppose the son is dead and the guardian is alive but now incompetent. Does the guardian inherit? Grammatically, the introductory clause applies to the guardian, who should thus be entitled to inherit. This, however, is not the likely intent of the testator. This potentially legally significant dangling modifier can be corrected by making the subject of the introductory phrase express.

If my son is alive but incompetent at the time of my death, his guardian shall inherit half of my estate to provide for my son's continued care and keeping.

Squinting Modifiers. A modifier "squints" if the reader cannot determine whether it modifies the preceding or the following word or phrase.

*If buyer determines the goods are defective **within 20 days** seller shall replace them.*

Is the buyer's determination limited by the 20 days? Or does that relate to the seller's duty of replacement?

Passive voice. The passive voice often contributes to the use of dangling modifiers—which is just another reason to avoid it. Consider this sentence:

> *To prove satisfaction of the notice requirement, a courier service approved by the Department of State under 34 U.S.C. § 89–667 must be used.*

Upon first reading, it would appear that "a courier service" is the entity trying to satisfy the notice requirement. That, obviously is not what is intended, as is finally indicated by the trailing passive voice phrase "must be used." The ambiguity can be resolved by stating the main clause in the active voice.

> *To prove satisfaction of the notice requirement, the parties must use a courier service approved by the Department of State under 34 U.S.C. § 89.667.*

c. Participles. A passive past participle can produce ambiguities of status.

> *Each person who was admitted to the Club **on** January 1, 2009, is eligible.*

Does this include only persons who became members on that particular date? Or does it refer to persons who enjoyed the status of membership on that date? Even an active voice participle can be ambiguous if the noun it modifies is unclear.

> *No person shall accost another wearing a police uniform.*

Does this provide protection to persons wearing police uniforms? Or does it mean that you cannot don a police uniform and accost people?

d. Chain Prepositions. Chains of prepositions create ambiguity because it is unclear what they refer to.

> *Each stockholder **of** a Chapter 9 corporation **in** Georgia is entitled to....*

Does this refer to each Chapter 9 stockholder who resides in Georgia? Or does it refer to each stockholder in a corporation that operates in Georgia?

e. Negative Pregnants. A negative pregnant is a sentence that denies something in particular, but that can also be construed as an implied admission of what is not denied. Because the implication may or may not be read into these sentences, they are necessarily ambiguous. Suppose, for example, the contract is for the sale of widgets, smidgets, and gidgets. A recital states:

> *The parties acknowledge that Seller is not a merchant of widgets.*

Later, an issue arises over seller's status as a merchant of smidgets or gidgets. Is the recital an implied admission that the seller is a merchant of these other items?

f. "If ... Then" Sentences. Many drafters use the "if ... then" construction when dealing with conditions. Usually, this causes no problems. But, as was discussed in Chapter 9, "if ... then" sentences can present substantive gaps. If a gap can be filled in two plausible ways, as is often the case, then an ambiguity exists. Assume that a collective bargaining agreement contains the following provision:

> *If an employee requests an unpaid personal leave in writing at least 10 days in advance and has no unused vacation time, then the shift supervisor shall approve the request.*

The "if" clause imposes three conditions precedent to the shift supervisor's duty to approve the request—in writing, 10 days in advance, and no unused vacation time. If the conditions are satisfied, the duty is activated. That seems clear enough. But what if the shift supervisor approves a request that was submitted only 7 days in advance? The union files a grievance, claiming that this is a breach of the contract and that this shift supervisor is showing favoritism. The question is whether that provision contains a negative inference that the shift supervisor can approve an unpaid personal leave request only under those circumstances. Logically, that is not a valid inference, although that was probably the intent of the parties—hence the ambiguity.

"If ... then" clauses can be ambiguous in another sense. Suppose a contract provides:

> *If delivery is on or before June 30, 2004, **then** purchaser will tender cash.*

This pretty clearly imposes a duty on the purchaser to tender cash when the seller elects to make delivery on that date. But suppose on June 30th the purchaser tenders cash and demands immediate delivery? Is the seller under an affirmative duty to make delivery on that date? As a matter of formal logic, the answer is no. From "If A, then B; B," one cannot infer "A." That is known as the fallacy of affirming the consequent. But the context, circumstances, or prior conduct of the parties may suggest that the tender of cash activates a duty to make delivery on that date. The drafter should determine the intended relationship between the delivery date and the tender of cash and make that relationship express through appropriate language, thus avoiding the ambiguity.

In sum, although the "if … then" configuration is a useful one, it is fraught with potential ambiguities that the drafter should be aware of and avoid.

g. "Because" Clauses. A sentence containing a "because" clause may be ambiguous if the reader is unsure if the clause modifies only the immediately preceding phrase or if it modifies the entire statement.

> *Owner may not deny requests for time extensions **because of** anticipated labor disputes.*

Does this refer to an unacceptable reason for denying a request for a time extension, namely because of an anticipated labor dispute? Or does it refer to a particular type of request for extension that cannot be denied, namely those based on an anticipated labor dispute?

h. "Unless" Clauses. "Unless" is a term of negation. If the conditions of the "unless" clause are satisfied, this negates the concept that it refers to.

> *Unless the ship* Peerless *comes in on Wednesday, Acme will buy the cotton.*

The "unless" clause, if satisfied, negates the promise to buy cotton. That is, if the *Peerless* does come in on Wednesday, Acme is not obligated to buy the cotton. Conversely, if the "unless" clause is not satisfied, then whatever it refers to remains operative. So, if Wednesday passes without the appearance of the *Peerless*, the promise to buy is activated.

An "unless" clause that relates to a clause that is itself already stated in negative terms can cause enormous confusion. Normally, the negation of a negation creates a positive. "It is not the case that the hose was unconnected" logically means that it was connected. In drafted documents this is not always what is intended.

> *Seller will not ship by rail* **unless** *the Teamsters are still on strike on December 10, 2009.*

If the "unless" clause is satisfied and the Teamsters are still on strike, this negates the prior clause. Logically, this means, "It is not the case that Seller will not ship by rail." But what does that mean when translated into conventional English? Does it merely mean the duty to not use that mode of shipment is vacated, still leaving it open to the Seller to use it or other methods of delivery? Or does it mean that Seller now has an affirmative duty to ship by rail, with the two negatives canceling each other out? Although other shipment provisions in the contract might resolve that ambiguity, the careful drafter would not let it arise in the first place.

i. "Only." Technically, the word "only" modifies the word or phrase it immediately precedes. Under this rule of construction, the placement of "only" is very important. Note how the meaning of the sentence changes by the addition and location of "only."

> **Base Sentence:** The buyer shall inspect the goods on the dock.
>
> (1) *Only the buyer shall inspect the goods on the dock.* [This means that no one except the buyer shall inspect.]
>
> (2) *The buyer only shall inspect the goods on the dock.* [This was probably intended to reflect the same idea as sentence (1). Technically, however, it modifies "shall inspect," which means that the activity is limited to inspection, perhaps in distinction to taking possession of them.]
>
> (3) *The buyer shall only inspect the goods on the dock.* [Splitting the compound verb with "only" makes it even

clearer that buyer's dock activity is limited to inspection.]

(4) *The buyer shall inspect **only** the goods on the dock.* [This means that the inspection is limited to the goods on the dock.]

(5) *The buyer shall inspect the goods **only** on the dock.* [This limits the location of the buyer's inspection, although it could also be construed as limiting the goods to be inspected, namely those on the dock.]

(6) *The buyer shall inspect the goods on the dock **only**.* [This violates the rule of construction, since the "only" precedes nothing. It was probably intended to limit the goods to be inspected, although like sentence (5) it might also be construed as limiting the location of the inspection.]

These examples suggest that the careful drafter should probably avoid the use of "only" altogether and express the idea in clearer, less ambiguous terms.

j. Truncated Passive. A normal passive voice sentence might state:

All change orders over $500 must be reported to the bank by the contractor within 10 days.

Apart from its wordiness, nothing is substantively unclear or ambiguous. But in a truncated version of the passive voice, the actor disappears from the sentence altogether.

All change orders must be reported to the bank within 10 days.

Who has the conditional obligation to make that report? Is it the contractor or the owner?

k. "Which" and "that." The choice between which and that is important, but not because the two words themselves have significantly different meanings. The choice is important, rather, because it can affect the syntax, structure, and meaning of the entire sentence. This is true, at least, when these words are used to introduce restrictive and nonrestrictive clauses.

A restrictive clause defines the noun it follows.

*The buyer shall inspect the goods **that are on the loading dock.***

The bolded clause is restrictive because it identifies and narrows the class of goods the buyer has a duty to inspect— namely a sub-class consisting of those that are on the loading dock. Restrictive clauses are not set off by commas.

A nonrestrictive clause, on the other hand, provides additional information about an already defined or identified noun.

*The buyer shall inspect the goods, **which are on the loading dock**.*

Here, the bolded clause is nonrestrictive because it assumes the buyer already knows the identity of the goods to be inspected. The clause merely indicates where they are located. Nonrestrictive clauses are set off with commas.

Old-fashioned grammar purists vigorously insist on using "which" only in nonrestrictive clauses and "that" only in restrictive clauses, as in the above examples. While agreeing that "that" cannot be used to introduce a nonrestrictive clause, many modern style manuals allow the use of either "that" or "which" in restrictive clauses. The better drafting practice adheres to the old-fashioned approach. This is not just a matter of grammatical purity and proper style. In some instances the misuse of "which" and "that" creates ambiguity. Consider this sentence in a stipulation to arbitrate disputes under a construction contract.

The basement wall defects which cost less than $100 to correct shall not be submitted to this arbitration.

Does this constitute an admission that none of the alleged defects in the basement wall will cost more than $100 to correct and that the parties are agreeing not to arbitrate them? If that is what was intended, the clause "which cost less than $100 to correct" should be set off with commas. This indicates that the clause is simply providing additional information about these defects. Under that construction, the owner demanding arbitration of some basement wall defects might be estopped from later claiming that these particular defects will cost more than $100 to repair. Alternatively, the sentence could merely mean that some of the defects in the basement wall (as yet undetermined) are being excluded from this arbitration—those that will cost less than $100 to correct. If that is what was intended, the drafter should have replaced "which" with "that." This provides the identity of the defects that are being excluded from the arbitration.

Finally, if a drafter can eliminate either "which" or "that" without creating an ambiguity, then do so in the interest of brevity. "The house **that** John built" can easily become "The house John built."

1. Plural Nouns. Drafted documents generally use the singular even when more than one entity is subject to the legal consequence being created.

> *An applicant must file an appeal within 10 days after the day on which the application is denied.*

This applies to all applicants. The convention avoids ambiguities that sometimes arise when a drafter uses plurals. For example, consider the following:

> *Employees with children qualifying for coverage must file affidavits of eligibility from persons listed below:....*

Does this apply only to employees with more than one child? Does it require more than one affidavit, presumably from all of the listed persons? These uncertainties can be resolved by using singular nouns and saying:

> *An employee with a child qualifying for coverage must file an affidavit of eligibility from a person listed below:....*

Usually, "a," "an," "the," or nothing at all before a singular noun is sufficient to indicate that the sentence applies to everything within that noun class. However, if a sentence could be construed as allowing a duty to be discharged by applying it to a single member of the class or a right to be exercised by only one member of the class, then use "each," "every," or "all" plus a plural noun. The following sentence is capable of that construction:

> *A student with perfect attendance will be given a grade enhancement.*

Matthew, Mark, and Luke all had perfect attendance, but the professor gave only Matthew a grade enhancement, claiming that the rule required that this be done for "a student," which indeed has been done. To prevent such pedagogical duplicity, the sentence should say:

Every student with perfect attendance will be given a grade enhancement.

m. Commas and Semi–Colons. Courts sometimes assert that punctuation is not a part of the statute. This non-deference to the grammatical implications of punctuation originated back when legislation was introduced orally. The punctuation was later added by clerks, who may or may not have understood either the intent of the legislature or the rules of punctuation. Today, almost all legislation is introduced in printed form. Along with the words that are used, the punctuation is one of the most important indicators of meaning. Drafters who ignore the significance of punctuation do so at their peril. Whether it is in legislation or private law documents, ambiguity can result from the misuse of commas and semi-colons.

Omission of the Serial Comma. The serial comma is the comma that follows the penultimate word or phrase in a series joined by "and" or "or." The comma clearly identifies each unit in the series.

a. In a compound sentence composed of a series of short independent clauses the last two of which are joined by a conjunction, commas should be placed between the clauses and before the conjunction:

The attorney presented his closing argument, the judge instructed the jury, and the jury retired to consider the case.

b. In a series consisting of three or more elements, the elements are separated by commas. When a conjunction joins the last two elements in a series, a comma is used before the conjunction:

Small, Nelson, and Lee attended the conference.

The owner, the agent, and the tenant were having an acrimonious discussion.

Omission of this comma can sometimes cause ambiguity.

> *Dealer will maintain a supply of hats in the following colors: red, blue, orange and black.*

Is the dealer obligated to maintain a supply of, three kinds of hats or four? Putting a comma after "orange" makes it clear that the contract contemplates four kinds of hats, one in each color. To make the three-hat option clear, the drafter might say:

> *Dealer will maintain a supply of red hats, blue hats, and orange and black hats.*

A series connected by more than one "and," but lacking the serial comma, can also be ambiguous with respect to which "and" creates a unit and which "and" links the series of units together. For example:

> *The Committee consists of one delegate chosen from each of the following four municipal areas: Able City, Bakersfield, Clarendon and Dover and Euclid.*

Are Clarendon and Dover a unit? Or Dover and Euclid? A comma in the right place will resolve that ambiguity. The omission of a serial comma can also raise the question of whether it is a list of several units or one unit followed by a descriptive or defining phrase. For example:

> *The screening panel consists of five judges, two Democrats and three Republicans.*

Does the panel consist of five judges, with the political affiliations as indicated? Grammatically, that is probably the most likely construction, although it could be made clearer by saying:

> *The screening panel consists of five judges, two of whom shall be Democrat and three Republican.*

Or does the original sentence contemplate a panel containing 10 people, consisting of (a) five judges, (b) two non-judge Democrats, and (c) three non-judge Republicans? If that is what was intended, it should have been stated in just that form. A simple serial comma after "Democrats" (without the lettered parentheticals) would also support that construction, although less clearly.

The omission of the serial comma can also create ambiguities of modification, as in this example:

Tenant will not allow to remain on the premises over-night any persons not related by blood or marriage, minor children or pets weighing more than 25 pounds.

The omission of the serial comma suggests that the 10 pound infant who screams all night can stay all night! Similarly:

The Health Inspector may close a restaurant because of fire hazards, unclean facilities and rats.

One certainly cannot tolerate dirty rats.

Even in situations where the omission of the serial comma would not create an ambiguity, an omission may nevertheless create confusion and misunderstanding.

The buyer must inspect all incoming rail shipments within 10 days of arrival, promptly notify the seller of any discovered defects or shortages and arrange for transportation away from the rail site.

Here, the omission of the comma after "shortages" does not render the sentence ambiguous in any literal sense. The omission does, however, make the sentence difficult to understand and thus ambiguous in a loose sense, because it obscures the fact that the buyer has three distinct duties.

Finally, even if the omission of a serial comma will not create ambiguity or render the sentence obscure, the comma should always be included for the sake of consistency. Using the last comma will never be wrong, but omitting it may cause confusion. However, if you choose to forego the last comma, be consistent throughout the document and examine your result carefully to ensure your intended meaning is clear and legally precise.

Semi-colons. Although a semi-colon can be used as either a strong comma (separating phrases in a series that are either very long or already contain internal commas) or a weak period (joining independent clauses), in either case in drafted documents each semi-colon unit is expected to have its own independent legal consequence or effect. But when that rule of construction is at odds with the sense of the sentence, an ambiguity results. Suppose that a statute prohibits the sale or use of Class III fireworks, but further provides:

Nothing in this Act is intended to prohibit a resident wholesaler's sale of Class III fireworks for which a permit has been granted by the Department of Public Safety; or the sale of any kind of fireworks for shipment directly out of state; the use of Class III fireworks by railroads; or the use of Class III fireworks as maritime signal flares by boats in distress.

Sam Pyro, a retailer, sold $10 worth of Class III fireworks to Betty Popp who immediately shipped them to her brother out of state. Is Pyro's sale within the exceptions to the prohibition? If the phrases separated by semi-colons have an independent legal consequence or effect, the answer is yes. The first phrase thus applies to wholesalers. The second phrase applies to anyone, including Pyro. The third phrase applies to railroads. And the fourth phrase applies to boaters in distress. But if the harm to be avoided is the possession within the state by actual or potential users of the fireworks covered by the Act, then one would conclude that Pyro is not covered by the exception. Rather, the sense of the statute is that the direct shipment exception was intended to apply only to wholesalers. If that is what was intended, as is likely, then the second phrase should not have been set off from the first phrase with a semi-colon.

In a series consisting of three or more elements that are themselves either clauses or sub-series, use a semi-colon in place of a comma for the highest level of the list. For example, "the available color combinations are red, white, and blue; yellow, green, and tan; and gold, red, and purple."

Exercise 9

Identify all the ambiguities in the following hypothetical provisions. That is, be prepared to state precisely that it could mean *this* or it could mean *that*. Read them from the perspective of the *reader in bad faith*—namely, a person who will exploit every possible loophole to gain even the slightest advantage, even if it is nothing more than a litigation settlement chit. Thus, do not let common sense blind you to the arguments that this person might make—arguments that may well fail, but only after expensive litigation. Some of the examples may contain multiple ambiguities.

    a.   The *Bluebook*, Rule 12.9 at page 87 (17th Edition):

Note that except when referring to the U.S. Code provisions, the word "section" should be spelled out in law review text and footnote text, although the symbol "§" may be used in citations. See **rule 6.2(b).**

The *Bluebook*, Rule 6.2(b) at page 49 (17th Edition):

[S]pell out the words "section" and "paragraph" in the text (whether main text or footnote text) of law review pieces and other documents, except when referring to a provision in the U.S. Code, at state code, or a federal regulation (see **rule 12.9**).

Note that these ambiguities have been eliminated in the eighteenth edition of the *Bluebook, A Uniform System of Citation.*

   b.   The Chair and Vice Chair may nominate up to three candidates for admission.

   c.   This prohibition applies to papers written by students and faculty.

   d.   Students in Legal Writing § 1 and Torts § 3 must attend the Wednesday orientation session.

   e.   The winner will be a student chosen from Professor Hamilton's and Professor Wright's sections.

   f.   Students on Law Review, possessing a 3.4 average, and certified by the Associate Dean are entitled to apply for the exception.

   g.   For this weekend only, employees may apply to work overtime on Saturday or Sunday. Because only a limited number of positions are available, for each of these days the work will be awarded to employees on the basis of seniority.

   h.   With respect to all packaged meat products entering the facility, the delivery dock inspector must certify that the USDA seal was intact at the time of delivery or the Head Cook may conduct bacterial tests, which must be paid for by seller.

   i.   To graduate, a student must take either Advanced Commercial Law (4 credits) or Sales (2 credits) and Commercial Paper (2 credits).

j. To graduate a student must take Drafting and/or Real Estate Transactions.

k. A zoning variance may be obtained upon: (a) proof of a varying use prior to June 1, 2004; (b) proof that the public interest will be served by the variance; (c) written consent of adjoining property owners.

l. To be eligible for the severance package, an employee who is being terminated must sign the ADEA waiver form between October 1, 2004, and October 15, 2005.

m. If a law school applicant has not filed a notice of intent to matriculate by June 1, 2004, that student's acceptance will be automatically revoked.

n. An applicant for public assistance during the 2003–2004 fiscal year has until July 1, 2003, to provide proof of indigency.

o. Subject to the termination-by-notice provision of this contract, Buyer's obligation to purchase all its Carbolic Smoke Balls from Seller continues from October 23, 2003, to October 23, 2004.

p. A terminated employee has until 14 days after the time the notice of termination is given to file a grievance.

q. Measured from the day on which the notice of termination is given, an employee may transfer into another department without penalty before the 20th day; an employee may transfer into another department with loss of seniority after the 20th day and before the 30th day; an employee has no transfer rights after the 30th day.

r. [Offer dated July 1, 2004] You must accept this offer within 14 days.

s. [Notice of intent to terminate credit account, dated Wednesday, July 10, 2004] To avoid a $100 penalty, you must at least pay the accrued interest within 5 days.

t. Landlord agrees to clean the pool bimonthly and have a Department of Health bacteria inspection semiannually.

u. This contest begins at midnight on October 1, 2004, and ends at noon on October 31, 2004.

v. [Order of the Zoning Commission dated July 28, 2004] Whenever the Zoning Commissioner contemplates a change in the zoning category of a piece of residential property, it shall send by registered mail a notice of the proposed change to all persons presently residing within 12 blocks of that property.

w. All persons over the age of 15 must pay full adult fare.

x. Buyer will accept delivery on October 31, 2004, provided, however, that prior to that time Seller provides proof of clear title.

y. 1. Job categories are divided into three groups:

    (a) Group #1: Captain, First Mate, First Engineer, and Cook.

    (b) Group #2: Second Engineer, Assistant Cook, Crew, Net Handlers, and Dock Handlers. All the job categories referenced hereinabove are also subject to Section 6(b) of the Union contract.

    (c) Group #3: Apprentice Seamen, longshoremen, and temporary employees in all categories.

z. The 12 football tickets will be divided between the Dean and members of the Faculty.

aa. Contractor will install a loading dock with a sloped ramp on the side and it will be 18 feet long.

bb. Employees on the second shift will be assigned some of the duties formerly performed by employees on the first shift, and such employees will be entitled to bid for jobs on the carbolic production line.

cc. This leave policy applies to pregnant production department employees, shipping department employees, and R & D employees who have not otherwise exhausted their optional leave time.

dd. This section applies to motorized vehicles, except those used in connection with the business and not licensed for road use.

ee.   Every employee with a spouse working in the Long-town Plant is entitled to participate in the Plan.

ff.   If damaged during shipment between Boston and New York, the standard rail car on which the goods were loaded at Boston will be replaced with a Conrail Supershock rail car for further shipment to Washington, D.C.

gg.   Only persons who were employed within two weeks prior to the effective date of the policy are required to provide the supplemental information listed below.

hh.   Every spouse of an employee with dependents of a prior marriage may opt for full coverage.

ii.   Seller will provide the lumber, pipes, and insulating material, but is not required to deliver the lumber to Buyer's work site.

jj.   If Buyer does not specifically request delivery by rail, Seller is not obligated to ship by that method. [Buyer does request delivery by rail. Is Seller obligated?]

kk.   If Seller is to be obligated to ship by rail, then Buyer must request it. [Buyer does request shipment by rail. Is Seller obligated?]

ll.   Dogs may be prohibited from the premises because of tendencies for barking.

mm.   Employees with less than 10 years seniority are not eligible to hold 1st shift jobs unless the shift supervisor consents in writing. No employee with less than 4 hours of OSHA disaster response training is eligible for 1st shift jobs.

nn.   Subcontractors only are subject to sections 45(a)-(t).

oo.   Owner and contractor agree that authorization by the City Building Code Commissioner will be obtained and the $1,000 fee paid before construction begins.

pp.   All students must take an advanced legal writing course which includes legal drafting.

qq. Applicants for pre-school tuition aid must bring their children to the Department of Social Services for an interview.

rr. An employee who completes the February training session will receive a $10 bonus and a certificate signed by the Plant Manager.

ss. Every student must write a five-page paper on each of the following: Moses, the founding of modern Israel, Jesus and the right to die.

tt. The prohibition against carrying weapons in vehicles on company property does not apply to the vehicles of employees on the first shift (11:00 p.m. to 6:00 a.m.) who park in Lot A; nor does it apply to the storage of weapons in the trunk of a car if that car is parked in lots B, C, or D.

Chapter 13

DRAFTING STYLE AND USAGE

The appropriate style of legal drafting is dictated by its function, which is to establish legal relationships—unambiguously, concisely, clearly, and simply.

A. CONSISTENCY

Emerson said that "a foolish consistency is the hobgoblin of little minds." In legal drafting, however, there is no such thing as a foolish consistency. Ambiguity is the most egregious form of inconsistency. But other forms of inconsistency are the result of bad style. Conversely, good style requires the following:

1. Consistent Terminology

Always use the same term to refer to the same person, thing, entity, or concept; always use different terms to refer to different persons, things, entities, and concepts. That is not saying the same thing twice. One could consistently use "premises" to refer to each individual apartment within the complex, but also use that word in reference to something else, such as the a common areas—adhering to the first component of the rule, but violating the second. Or, one could never use "premises" to refer to anything except the individual apartments, but also refer to the apartments by other names, such as "leasehold"—adhering to the second component, but violating the first. So, follow both aspects of the rule. This is not only necessary to prevent reader confusion, a violation of the rule can also lead to a judicial interpretation that may be different from the intent of the drafter. Although the drafter may have intended for both "premises" and "leasehold" to refer only to an individual apartment, once a court determines that one of these—"premises," for example—clearly refers to the individual apartment, the court is likely to conclude the different term, "leasehold," must necessarily refer to something else, such as all tangible property-related entitlements under the lease, including use of common areas.

This rule of terminological consistency in drafting is contrary to the so-called rule of "elegant variation," which is sometimes taught in English composition classes. This composition rule posits that the same word should rarely be used twice in the same paragraph. An essayist, thus, would be encouraged to refer to the "car" as also the "vehicle," the "automobile," and "Jane's Ford." For the legal drafter, it remains a "car" throughout.

2. Consistent Grammatical Structure

Drafters frequently write sentences containing multiple phrases. Each phrase must have the same—or parallel—grammatical structure. Consider the following regulation:

> *Producers of toxic chemicals have the following options: (1) require purchasers to assume responsibility for subsequent spills, (2) depositing money in a damages escrow fund, (3) termination of production, or (4) a conspicuous disclaimer of liability on every container.*

The phrases in this list are not grammatically parallel. The producer's options are variously described with a verb, "require;" a gerund, "depositing;" a nominalization, "termination;" and a noun, "disclaimer." This is an awkward and confusing regulation. With the four phrases put into parallel grammatical form, the regulation reads as follows:

> *Producers of toxic chemicals have the following options: (1) require purchasers to assume responsibility for subsequent spills; (2) deposit money in a damages escrow fund; (3) terminate production; or (4) post a conspicuous disclaimer of liability on every container.*

Consistency between the items in a series also requires that the introductory word or phrase tie in grammatically with the language of each item in the series. The following provision is defective in that regard.

> *Buyer may accept the goods without inspection, authorize the shipper to hold the goods pending inspection, accept the goods and reserve a right of later inspection, or the provisions of section 6 dealing with acceptance will otherwise control.*

The introductory word, "may," is appropriate for the first three phrases. But it makes no sense to say, "Buyer may . . . the provisions of section. . . ." For the last phrase to be parallel, it should read, "or otherwise proceed under the provisions of section 6 dealing with acceptance."

When the various parts of a multi-phrase sentence are enumerated and tabbed under the introductory phrase, drafters tend to forget that this is still a single sentence. The grammatically consistent structure of the sentence is then destroyed when the drafter attempts to bury another sentence within that structure, as in this example:

> *The recipient of Title IX funds may—*
>
> > *a. use the money to fund day care centers directly,*
> >
> > *b. channel the money to day care centers through a tax-exempt charity.* ***The charity's articles of incorporation must list this as a purpose of the charity.***
> >
> > *c. fund college scholarships for students majoring in pre-school educational and child care programs, or*
> >
> > *d. sponsor funded research into preschool education and child care programs.*

The bolded sentence breaks the larger sentence cleanly in half. The defect could be cured by referring to "a tax-exempt charity whose articles of incorporation list this as a purpose."

3. Consistent Document Structure and Approach

A reader can more easily understand how a statute or contract operates if everything in the document is organized in a consistent or parallel fashion. For example, if the internal sequence of section A is chronological, stay with the chronological approach in the following sections unless the subject matter compels a different sequence.

Internal headings and numeration should likewise be consistent. If section A is,

   A. Heading

      1. Heading

         a. Heading

           (i) Heading,

Organize section B of the same document the same way.

The point is to establish a rhythm that allows the reader to anticipate and more easily understand the logical structure and legal consequence of each provision. Doing the same thing in different ways disrupts that rhythm, promotes reader uncertainty, and may lead to misunderstanding.

B. CONCISION

Next to the avoidance of ambiguity and inconsistency, being concise is the next most important objective of the drafter. Concision can be achieved by eliminating the following.

1. Unnecessary Content

Chapter 9 dealt with the substantive content of a document, breaking it down into what is required by externalities; essential given the nature of the transaction; extremely important given the peculiarities of the transaction; and optional. Anything beyond that is totally unnecessary and its omission will enhance the concision of the document. The problem arises often in complex multi-party contracts where one or more of the players (often an escrow agent or an architect) is really only agreeing to certain provisions. If that is the case, use a separate signature page for that party, indicating what provisions he or she is agreeing to.

2. Cross-references and Section/Paragraph References

Cross-referencing can help cut down on repetitive provisions. It is usually better to cross-reference to articles, sections, and paragraphs rather than pages, since pages change in the drafting process. A good general rule is to use the word "section" to refer to separate provisions of a formal agreement and the word "paragraph" to refer to separate provisions of an informal letter or letter agreement. The key is to be specific and consistent. Remember to proofread cross-references at the very end of the drafting process to make sure they remain accurate. Some drafters prefer to leave the section or paragraph reference blank until the last draft, *e.g.*, "section ___," essentially forcing themselves to proof the cross-references.

3. Repetitious Substance

Avoid repetition; say what needs to be said and say it only once. Consider this lease provision:

Landlord's acceptance of rent payments in arrears does not otherwise affect any right Landlord has under this lease. An acceptance of late rent payments does not constitute a waiver of Landlord's right to insist upon timely rent payment in the future. Landlord's failure to call an immediate lease forfeiture when rent is late does not preclude Landlord from calling such forfeiture at any time before payment is tendered.

That provision says the same thing three times. It could be stated once, as follows:

The non-enforcement of any provision of this contract does not constitute a waiver of the right to enforce the provision in the future.

Similarly, formbook boilerplate often follows a pattern of unnecessary terms, consisting of a word of total inclusiveness, followed by redundant paraphrases and then some examples, as in the following:

During liquidation, the court-appointed trustee shall distribute all [a word of total inclusiveness] of the Petitioner's assets, of any kind or character, tangible or intangible [paraphrasing "all"], whether in the form of cash, real estate, movable property, inventory, equipment, accounts receivable, securities, goodwill, or anything else of value [examples], in strict compliance with the terms of subparagraph 89(b)(16).

In most contexts, a simple reference to "assets" will cover "any and all" of them, regardless of "kind or character," and will include both the "tangible" and the "intangible." The list of examples adds nothing to that, and in some cases these example lists have been construed as words of limitation. It could probably be stated as follows, without any danger of ambiguity or vagueness:

> *During liquidation, the court-appointed trustee shall distribute Petitioner's assets in strict compliance with the terms of subparagraph 89(b)(16).*

Whether this is adequate or the longer version is necessary is a question of law that must be resolved by the drafter before the stylistic aspects are addressed.

4. Redundant Couplets, Triplets, and Other Chain Synonyms

Avoid legal doublets and triplets.

These are those famous repetitious chains of words that are part of the hoary legal chant that has come down through the ages. Examples include: "null and void;" "settlement and compromise;" "swear and affirm;" "right, title and interest;" and others listed below. Ask: do I really need each of these terms? Will fewer do? Will listing these terms leave the provision vulnerable to the doctrine of *expressio unis et exclusio alterius*? (See Chapter 4 for more discussion.) It may be tempting to think that a proper interpretive doctrine or equitable maxim will assist in correcting any ambiguity in documents that you draft. The problem is that for every doctrine or maxim that would favor one interpretation, there is another that will defeat it. These principles are largely ceremonial support for reaching the result that the court has determined is just rather than the reasoning that leads to that determination. If *expressio unis* may be a problem, consider using a more general term that contains within its meaning all desired alternatives.

Further, tucking a general reference such as "etc." or "and the like" at the end of a list to cure the *expressio unis* problem may invoke the dangers of the doctrine of *ejusdem generis* ("Of the same kind").

At one time in English legal history, Norman French, Middle English, and Latin all competed to become the dominant or authoritative language of the law. The same legal concept could be expressed in three different languages. Cautious lawyers used the words from all three languages to ensure that they achieved the desired legal consequence. Even after the words evolved into the English as we know it today, lawyers continued to use these chains—as if they were some religious talisman that would guard them against a claim of malpractice. It is interesting to note that early document drafters, called "scriveners," were paid by the word.

The most common couplet and triplet phrases are totally unnecessary. The drafter should pick the simplest word of the group and drop the others. A partial list of these traditional phrases is as follows:

acknowledge and confess	act and deed
adjust, compromise, and settle	advice, opinion, and direction
agree and covenant	aid and abet
all and every	all and singular
alter or change	annul and set aside
any and all	assign, transfer, and set over
assumes and agrees	attorney and counselor at law
authorize, direct, and empower	bear, sustain, or suffer
bind and obligate	build, erect, or construct
business, enterprise, or undertaking	by and with
cancel, annul, and set aside	cancel and terminate
cease and desist	cease and come to an end
cease and terminate	chargeable or accountable
changes, variations, and modifications	confessed and acknowledged
conjecture and surmise	consolidation, amalgamation, or merger
contract, agreement, covenant, and understanding	convey, transfer, and set over
costs, charges, and expenses	covenant and agree
cover, embrace, and include	deem and consider
do, execute, and perform	documents, instruments, and writings
due and owing	due and payable
each and all	each and every
engage, hire, and employ	entirely and completely
evidencing or relating to	excess and unnecessary
fair and equitable	fair and reasonable
false and fraudulent	final and conclusive
finish and complete	fit and proper

fit and suitable

for and in consideration of

force and effect

free and clear

free and without consideration

full and complete

furnish and supply

give, devise, and bequeath

good and sufficient

heed and care

if and when

in and to

in truth and in fact

initiate, institute, or commence

keep and maintain

kind and nature

lands, tenements, and hereditaments

legal, valid, and binding

levies and assessments

loans or advances

lot, tract, or parcel

made and provided

make, declare, and publish

meet and just

mentioned or referred to

modified and changed

nominate, constitute, and appoint

obligation and liability

observe, perform, and carry out

ordain and establish

order, adjudged, and decreed

pardon and forgive

pay, satisfy, and discharge

perform and discharge

place, install, or affix

power and authority

relieve and discharge

represents, warrants, and covenants

rest, resident, and remainder

right, title, and interest

rules, requirements, and regulations

seized and possessed

shun and avoid

situate, lying, and being in

stipulate and agree

suit, claim, or demand

term or covenant

for and during

for and on behalf of

fraud and deceit

free and unfettered

from and after

full force and effect

give and grant

goods, chattels, and effects

have, hold, and possess

hold and keep

in and for

in my stead and place

indebtedness and liabilities

just and reasonable

kind and character

known and described as

last will and testament

let or hindrance

lien, charge, or encumbrance

loss or damage

made and entered into

made, ordained, constituted, and appointed

maintenance and upkeep

mend, maintain, and repair

mind and memory

nature or description

null, void, and of no force and effect

obey, observe, and comply with

of and concerning

order and direct

over, above, and in addition to

part and parcel

peace and quiet

performance or observance

possession, custody, and control

release and discharge

remise, release, and quitclaim

representations, understandings, and agreements

revoked and annulled

rights and remedies

save and except

sell, transfer, alienate, and dispose of

signed, published, and declared

sole and exclusive

suffer or permit

supersede and displace

terminate, cancel, or revoke

then and in that event
truth and veracity
understood and agreed
vacate, surrender, and deliver
    possession
void and of no force
within and under the terms of

true and correct
type and kind
unless and until
void and of no effect

void and of no value

Examine lists of synonymous terms and rank them in a hierarchy. Are they all of the same rank? If not, this is an indicator that *expressio unis* and *ejusdem generis* problems may be lurking in the list. Consider eliminating lower rank words and using fewer words of a higher rank. Consider the list "carrots, peas, and other vegetables." Why not replace all three words with one, "vegetables." Similarly, the list "tigers, lions, and other animals" can be reduced to "animals." Legal terms can be similarly arranged and the term or terms at the correct hierarchical level can be chosen.

On the other hand, do not indiscriminately delete pairs or triplets. They may exist for a reason and not simply as a list of synonyms. For example, in a real property sale agreement, the seller should be under a duty to "execute *and* deliver" the deed to the property. Execution without delivery (and vice versa) is ineffective to transfer title.

5.   Other Redundant Expressions

The statements made in this section are general ones, and you must evaluate in each instance whether the general advice should be followed. In drafting agreements, concentrate especially on whether your chosen word has the correct level of specificity. Underlying these rules is the belief that overdressing one's writing makes it harder to read and does not demonstrate education or sophistication. Rather, education and sophistication are shown by drafting that makes its meaning clear with little effort on the reader's part. Still, reasonable minds can differ on matters of word choice. Use the following suggestions as a guide, but, as with most legal drafting, it is best for you to make up your own mind as to what is appropriate under the particular circumstances.

Avoid compound prepositions:

Avoid	Use Instead
the question as to whether	whether (the question whether)
all of the issues	all the issues

Avoid	Use Instead
at that point in time	then
in the nature of	like

Avoid overly showy words:

Avoid	Use Instead
additionally	also
adequate number of	enough, sufficient
adjacent	next to (specify distance?)
aforesaid	previous, prior
any and all	any
at the time	when
approximately	about
at [the] present [time]	now
by means of	by
cease and desist	stop, cease
circumstances in which	when, where
commence	begin
contained in	in
contiguous	next to
due [to the fact that]	because
eventuates	occurs, happens
facilitate	help, assist
has a negative impact	harms
including but not limited to	including
inquire	ask
null and void	void
notify	tell, inform
permit	let, allow
penultimate	second to last
request	ask
retain	keep
ultimate	last
utilize	use

Some things are implicit in certain words, making it unnecessary to state them expressly. Implicit in "three hours" is the notion of a time period. The expression for a "time period of three hours" is redundant. In the following examples, the bracketed portion is implicit in the remaining term and can be deleted.

[a distance of] two miles	[a period of] a week
all [of the] materials	alongside [of]
appreciate [in value]	ascend [up]
[as to] whether	[at a] later [date]
[close] scrutiny	combine [together]
[completely] destroyed	depreciate [in value]
descend [down]	[different] kinds
during [the course of]	during [the month of] July

each [and every]
[empty] space
few [in number]
join [together]
[local] residents
never [at any time]
postponed [until later]
recur [again]
regress [back]
[separate] entities

each [separate] provision
eradicate [completely]
[foreign] imports
[general] public
merged [together]
off [of]
[rate of] speed
refer [back]
revert [back]
5 p.m. [in the afternoon]

6. Legalese

A lay person might erroneously think that the chains of words discussed above are necessary, and thus admire their lawyer's attention to detail. Still, even the most unlearned lay person knows that the "wherein's," "aforesaid's," and "hereinafter's" are unnecessary. Indeed, nothing has contributed more to the bad reputation of legal writing than these archaic terms. Do not use them, or, if you must, use them sparingly. A partial list of legalese:

above-mentioned
aforesaid
behooved
forthwith
hereafter
hereby
hereinabove
hereinbefore
hereinunder
heretofore
hereunto
hitherto
insofar
nowise
thence
thereabout
thereat
therefore
therein
thereon
theretofore
thereunto
to wit
unto
whatsoever
whensoever
whereby
wherein
whereon

aforegranted
before-mentioned
foregoing
henceforth
herebefore
herein
hereinafter
hereinto
hereof
hereunder
herewith
inasmuch
notwithstanding
saith
thenceforth
thereafter
thereby
therefrom
thereof
thereto
thereunder
therewith
under-mentioned
whatever
whence
whereas
wherefore
whereof
wheresoever

whereupon   whosoever
whilst   within-named

Another form of legalese consists of antique phrases like the following:

Being first duly sworn, Sam Jones deposes and says:

Further affiant [or deponent] sayeth not.

In witness whereof I have hereunto set my hand and caused my seal to be affixed.

Know All Men By These Presents:

To All To Whom These Presents Come, Greeting:

WITNESSETH:

All of these phrases can be eliminated. Use common English in their place.

The words "said," "same," and "such" are another form of objectionable legalese, even if the usage is grammatically correct. Never use "said" as an adjective. Delete it or replace it with "the," "that," "this," or an appropriate pronoun.

> *Director shall grant or deny said application within 10 days,*

becomes

> *Director shall grant or deny the application within 10 days.*

Never use "such" as an adjective before a singular noun; replace it with "the," "that," or "this." However, "such" may be used as an adjective before plural nouns, without running afoul the rule against the use of legalisms, to mean "of this kind, nature, or degree," as in "such acts of misconduct will not be tolerated."

Never use "same" or "such" as a pronoun.

> *Director shall review the application within 10 days and grant or deny same [or such]*

becomes

> *Director shall review the application within 10 days and grant or deny it.*

Or consider this even more barbaric use of "such" as a pronoun:

> *While on duty, employees shall not drink alcoholic beverages, take illegal drugs, or smoke controlled substances. Such [replace with "these actions"] are grounds for immediate termination.*

7. Compound Prepositions and Prepositional Phrases

A preposition is a word or phrase that expresses the relationship of one word with another. In "payment is due **after** delivery," the word "after" expresses the temporal relationship between "payment" and "delivery." Compound prepositions (also called prepositional phrases and complex prepositions) consist of two or more words that function as a single-word preposition would. Henry Fowler has said that compound prepositions "are almost the worst element in modern English, stuffing up what is written with a compost of nouny abstractions." Most compound prepositions can be replaced with a single word that is clearer and more direct. Lawyers probably use more compound prepositions than any class of writers in the English-speaking world, especially in drafted documents. They should be avoided.

The more common compound prepositions, together with their replacements, are as follows:

Compound Preposition	Replacement
along the lines of	like
as a consequence of	because of
as to	about
at that point in time	then
as the present time	now
at the time at which	when
at this point in time	now
be of help to	help
by means of	by
by reason of	because of
by virtue of	by, under
during such times as	when
during the course of	during
during the time that	while
for the duration of	during
for the purpose of	for, under
for the reason that	because
from the point of view of	for

Compound Preposition	Replacement
inasmuch as	because
in a manner similar to	like
in all probability	probably
in addition to	besides
in accordance with	by, under
in association with	with
in back of	behind
in case of	if
in close proximity	near
in connection with	by, from, about, at
in excess of	more than, over
in favor of	for
in lieu of	instead of
in order to	to
in receipt of	received
in regard to	about, concerning
in spite of the fact that	although
in terms of	at, in, for, by, with
in the absence of	without
in the case of	if
in the course of	during
in the event that	if
in the midst of	amid
in the nature of	like
in the immediate vicinity of	near
in view of the fact	because, considering, that
notwithstanding the fact that	although
on account of	because
on the basis of	by, from
on the grounds of	because of
on the part of	by, among
prior to	before
similar to	like
subsequent to	after
the manner in which	how
under the provisions of	under
until such time as	until
with a view to	to
with reference to	about, concerning
with regard to	about, concerning
with respect to	about, with, on, concerning, for, in
with the exception of	except
with the object of	to
with the result that	so that

8. "The fact that"

This wordy idiom usually appears in dependent clauses. A dependent clause is a group of words that contains a verb but does not qualify as a complete sentence. Dependent clauses are often used to fill the slot in a sentence that calls for a noun. A dependent clause containing "the fact that" can function as any of the following:

(1) **A subject:** "The fact that the buyer fails to inspect constitutes waiver."

(2) **A direct object:** "Upon delivery, the shipper must note on the invoice the fact that the buyer failed to inspect."

(3) **An indirect object:** "The consequences of the fact that the buyer fails to inspect are that buyer waives all defects."

(4) **An object of a preposition:** Under paragraph (c), the buyer may recover for defects that were not discovered because of the fact that the seller made timely inspection impossible.

The drafter can avoid these obtuse constructions by replacing the dependent clause with a true noun or noun clause, as in the following revisions to the above sentences:

(1) "The buyer's failure to object constitutes waiver."

(2) "Upon delivery, the shipper must note on the invoice the buyer's failure to object."

(3) "The consequences of the buyer's failure to object are that buyer waives all defects."

(4) "Under paragraph (c), the buyer may recover for defects that were not discovered because the seller made timely inspection impossible."

9. Rhetorical and Transitional Words and Phrases

Certain transitional words and phrases common in a brief or memorandum serve no purpose and should be omitted in a drafted document. These words and phrases include the following:

admittedly	again
also	although
accordingly	as a result
because	besides
but	consequently
despite	even if
even though	for example

for instance	furthermore
granted that	hence
however	in addition
instead	likewise
moreover	nevertheless
next	nonetheless
on the other hand	similarly
still	so
therefore	too
to the contrary	thus

The relationship between the various components of a drafted document should be evident from the organizational scheme of the document and the numbered/lettered heading that it contains.

Their use, however, is arguably appropriate in two situations. First, the Recitals (or Background) in a contract and Findings (or Preamble) in a statute are usually expository in form and transitory words enhance the readability of these portions of the document. Second, if a document is intended minimize the harsh legalities of a relationship—an employment manual, for example—then transitory words will contribute to that tone of informality.

10.   "Of the . . ." Phrases

This phrase can be either deleted or made into a possessive with an apostrophe. So, instead of saying,

> All *of the* applicants must attach a current photograph to the visa application,

say,

> All applicants must attach a current photograph to the visa application.

Instead of saying,

> Children *of a* resident alien must be listed on line 4 of Form 459,

say

> A resident alien's children must be listed on line 4 of Form 459.

11.   Unnecessary   "who's,"   "which's,"   and "that's"

Eliminating these words will often make the sentence leaner and more efficient. Instead of saying,

> *Voters **who** are registering to vote absentee must file within 30 days,*

say,

> *Voters registering to vote absentee must file within 30 days.*

Instead of saying,

> *The goods, **which** are sold only in bulk, are warranted against insect infestation,*

say,

> *The goods, sold only in bulk, are warranted against insect infestation.*

Instead of saying,

> *The inspection **that** the buyer conducts is subject to section 3(a),*

say,

> *The inspection the buyer conducts is subject to section 3(a).*

Do not delete these words for style's sake, however, if this will create an ambiguity. For example, in the sentence "The buyer will inspect the goods on the loading dock," it is unclear whether the location relates to the identity of the goods to be inspected or indicates where the inspection will take place. If it relates to identity, then "the goods **that are** on . . ." would make that clear. If it relates to the location of the inspection, convert it into a dependent clause—"goods, which are on the loading dock." Alternatively, this might be an appropriate place for the passive voice, "The buyer's inspection of the goods will be conducted on the loading dock."

12.　Redundant Numeration

Lawyers commonly present numbers in both the Arabic and written form.

> *This section is subject to the four (4) exceptions contained in section 8.c.*

> *One-half (1/2) of the payment is due on delivery.*

> *Seller will deliver thirty (30) crates.*

It is common practice that numbers used in legal agreements are both spelled and represented in numerals to avoid confusion and make later alteration more difficult. For example, "the sum of five-thousand, five hundred dollars ($5,500) will be paid at closing." This is wordy and serves no rational purpose other than making later document alteration difficult (say, with a check or other negotiable instrument). The reader knows what "thirty" means, knows what "30" means, and knows that they mean the same thing. It is not necessary to say it twice unless one is concerned with the possibility of later document alteration as in the case of the key amounts specified in negotiable instruments.

Leading commentators on modern formal use of English disfavor writing out numbers in words. Unless concerns about alteration of the document are strong, drop the double form of expression and use numerals exclusively. Alternatively, write out the numbers one through ten in words and use numerals for 11 and up. Either system makes documents easier to proofread and prevents the opportunity for words to conflict with numerals, eliminating another source of ambiguity.

A combination of the numerical and the written version of a number should, however, be used when dealing with figures in the million range that end with a triplet of zeros. Rather than saying "$25,000,000" or "$25,400,000," say "$25 million" or "$25.4 million."

13. Expletives

In the grammatical sense, an expletive is a word without substantive content; it is a surrogate noun that is being used merely to satisfy the grammatical requirement that the sentence have a subject. For example, in "There are six residential units in each pod," the grammatical subject of the sentence is "there." The word refers to nothing, however, and serves no function other than to provide the proper syntax for the sentence. The intended subject of the sentence is "residential units." With the expletive deleted, the sentence reads, "Six residential units are in each pod." The most common expletives found in drafted documents are "it is," "there is," and "there are."

Notice how much clearer and less wordy the non-expletive version is in comparison with the expletive version.

Expletive:

(1) It is the intent of Congress for this Act to prohibit all forms of obscenity.

(2) There is included in every lease subject to this Act an implied covenant of good faith and fair dealing.

(3) There are 6 requirements for the job.

Expletive Deleted:

(1) Congress intends for this Act to prohibit all forms of obscenity.

(2) Every lease subject to this Act contains an implied covenant of good faith and fair dealing.

(3) The job has 6 requirements.

14. Nominalizations

Unbury verbs. Nominalizations contribute enormously to the wordiness and generally constipated tone of most drafted documents. Nominalization is simply a fancy term for turning an ordinary five-and-dime verb into a country-club noun, and then tacking on another verb to satisfy syntactical requirements. The simple "pending" becomes "during the pendency of." Nominalizations in a drafted document should nearly always be converted back into their simpler verb form.

The most common nominalizations and their verb replacements are as follows:

Nominalization	Verb
draw a conclusion	conclude
file a complaint	complain
give consideration to	consider
give recognition to	recognize
has pertinence	pertains
have knowledge of	know
have need of	need
in agreement with	agree
in collision with	collide with
in the determination of	to determine
is applicable	applies

Nominalization	Verb
is dependent on	depends on
is in attendance at	attends
make a contribution	contribute
make an appointment	to appoint
make application	apply
make payment	pay
make provision for	provide
render a decision	decide
submit a payment	pay
suggestive of	suggests
take action	act

As these examples show, nominalizations can often be identified by their endings, such as: -al, -ancy, -ant, -ence, -ent, -ion, -ity, -ive, -ment.

15. Passive Voice

In an active voice sentence, the subject acts upon the object in some fashion, as in "The Seller [subject] warrants [verb, indicating what action the subject is performing] the goods [object]." Contract clauses should be drafted in the active voice whenever possible. Test your sentence by looking for a subject-verb-object structure (SVO), specifying *who* is doing *what* to *whom* (or *what*).

In a passive voice sentence, on the other hand, the subject of the sentence is being acted upon by something else, as in "The goods [subject] are warranted [verb, indicating an action upon the subject] by the Seller." To spot a passive voice construction, first look for an actual "by" prepositional phrase following the verb, as in that example. In the truncated passive, however, this "by" phrase is merely implied, as in "All change orders must be reported to the bank [read *by owner* or *by contractor* and it could be either, hence the ambiguity], as the case may be within 10 days."

In addition to the ambiguity of the truncated passive discussed in Chapter 12, wordiness is the other principal defect of the passive voice. An active voice sentence is nearly always more concise than its passive voice counterpart.

The passive voice, however, does have some legitimate uses in drafted documents. For example, it can be used if the intent is to put the emphasis on what must be done rather than on who must do it. This is accomplished more effectively with "Applications must be filed by each candidate before

July 12'' than with ''Each candidate must file an application before July 12.'' Although other techniques are also available, the passive voice can be used to avoid gender-specific pronouns. Instead of saying, ''An attorney must file his personal affidavit as an attachment to the motion,'' one might say, ''An attorney's personal affidavit must be filed as an attachment to the motion.''

16. ''To be'' Verb Forms

The forms of ''to be'' that one often encounters in drafted documents are ''was,'' ''is,'' ''are,'' ''were,'' and ''been.'' Unless it is a part of an auxiliary verb, as in ''Johnson is acting as Seller's agent,'' a ''to be'' verb should be used only to define or identify, as in ''the seller is a resident of Texas.'' When a ''to be'' form of the verb is used in any other sense, the resulting prose is both dull and wordy. If the drafter replaces the ''to be'' verb with an active verb, the sentence will be more lively and shorter. Consider this ''to be'' verb-laden paragraph.

> *If a subcontractor **is** in breach of the agreement, then the security bond **is** voided. If there **are** any suppliers of goods or materials who **were** in expectation of receiving payment, then the general contractor **is** expected to reimburse them out of the escrow funds which **are** held by the owner. [51 words.]*

If the ''to be'' verbs are replaced with active verbs, it would read as follows:

> *If a subcontractor breaches the agreement, this voids the security bond. If any suppliers of goods or materials expected to receive payment, the general contractor must reimburse them out of the escrow funds held by the owner. [38 words.]*

''To be'' verb forms often occur in connection with expletives, nominalizations, and the passive voice—as well as in sentences when the drafter has not used the proper word to create a particular legal consequence. Eliminating the errant ''to be'' verb is an indirect way of correcting these other mistakes. The ''to be'' verb phrases that drafters tend to use most often, and their replacements, are:

To be verb	Replacement
is able to	can
is authorized to	may
is binding upon	binds
is empowered to	may
is unable to	cannot
is directed to	shall
is required to	shall
it is the duty to	shall

C. CLARITY AND SIMPLICITY

A document free of ambiguity, inconsistency, and excessive wordiness is a clearer and simpler document. Lists, enumerations, and tabbing, which are discussed in Chapter 16, also promote clarity. In addition, these objectives are served by the following rules of style:

1. Short Sentences

An average sentence length of 26 words is an admirable objective for a drafted document. The closer the drafter comes to that objective, the clearer the document will be. Look for places to divide longer sentences into two or more.

2. Simple Sentence Structure

Draft the way people think:

Someone [noun] does something [verb] to something [direct object].

The normal, active voice word order in English is *subject, verb,* and *object*. If you wish to change this order for emphasis, remember that the strongest places in the sentence are the beginning and the end. Generally, stick to subject, verb, object (SVO) order. The best contract clauses follow this order; they tell the reader *who* is to do *what* to *whom, when,* and *what will happen* if they do not do so.

Try not to separate the noun from the verb or the verb from the direct object with dependent clauses, ideas buried between parentheses, or other intrusive asides. These are called "gaps." A single sentence can carry only so much substance. Let several sentences share the load. In the following provision, the bolded portions show verb/noun and noun/object gaps that make the sentence convoluted and confusing.

Buyer, **upon receipt and inspection of the goods,** *will,* **provided they are found to be in compliance with the contract and otherwise as warranted,** *immediately notify,* **per section 6 of this contract,** *the seller of acceptance.*

Consider this alternative:

Upon receipt of the goods, buyer will inspect them. If buyer finds that the goods comply with the contract and are as warranted, buyer will immediately notify seller of acceptance. Seller's notification must satisfy the requirements of section 6 of this contract.

Avoid inserting clauses between the subject and the verb, particularly if the clause can be transferred to the beginning or end of the sentence.

Avoid	Use
The borrower, in its notice of borrowing, should specify the method for computing interest.	*The borrower should specify the method for computing interest in its notice of borrowing.*

Keep modifiers next to the word they modify.

Avoid	Use
The weak lawyer's contract.	*The lawyer's weak contract.*

This, of course, assumes that "weak" is intended to modify "contract," not "lawyer."

Do not insert adverbs between the component parts of verbs unless done for emphasis. This is particularly true for infinitives ("to clearly write"). The "unless done for emphasis" exception to this rule is more widely accepted now than in the past, but take care to know what your audience prefers. Split infinitives tend to *really* bother traditionalists.

Keep objects close to verbs.

Avoid	Use
The local court has repeatedly interpreted incorrectly that line of cases.	*The local court has misinterpreted that line of cases repeatedly.*

The overuse of dependent clauses set off by commas, parentheses, and dashes can be confusing and often indicates that a single sentence is being employed to do too many things. Instead, use separate sentences:

Tenant (unless Landlord has agreed in writing in advance) shall not keep or allow the presence of pets (including dogs, cats, rabbits, birds, hamsters, gerbils, or reptiles of any kind) in the Leased Premises (as defined in paragraph 6(b)(7)), and any violation of this provision is a material breach (justifying immediate termination of the lease).

versus

Tenant shall not keep or allow the presence of pets in the Leased Premises. Landlord may waive this provision in advance in a signed writing. For the purpose of this provision, "pets" includes dogs, cats, rabbits, birds, hamsters, gerbils, and reptiles of any kind. A violation of this provision is a material breach of the lease, justifying immediate termination.

3. Present Tense

Draft in the present tense. A contract or statute is said to be constantly "speaking." Drafted documents assume that whatever they are dealing with is currently happening, not that it happened yesterday or is going to happen tomorrow. The use of past tense, present tense, and future tense in the same document promotes confusion.

If seller's inability to deliver on time **is** *[not* **was** *or* **has been**] *caused by circumstances beyond seller's control, buyer* **is** *not [not* **will not be**] *entitled to cancel.*

4. Simple, Ordinary Words

Do not use the fancy version of a word, or collection of words, when the simple, ordinary counterpart is more readily understood by the average reader.

Word	Replace With
accommodate	adapt, fit, suit
accomplish	perform, do
accorded	given
accumulate	collect, gather
acknowledge	recognize, admit
acquire	obtain, or buy
adequate number of	enough
adjacent	next to, near
admit of	allow
advantageous	good

Word	**Replace With**
afforded	given
allocate	divide
alternative	choice, option
appropriate (verb)	take
approximately	about
ascertain	determine
assist, assistance	help
attempt	try
cease	stop
commence	begin, start
complete	finish
conceal	hide
consequence	result
contiguous	next, adjoining
determine	decide, find
donate	give
duplicate	copy
during such time as	while
during the course of	during
effectuate	carry out, cause
eliminate	remove
employ	use
endeavor	try
eradicate	remove, erase
erroneous	false
evince	show
execute	sign
exceptional	rare, unique
expedite	hasten
expeditiously	immediately
expend	spend
expiration	end
feasible	possible
finalize	complete
forthwith	immediately
frequently	often
fundamental	basic
furnish	give
heterogeneous	mixed, unlike
homogeneous	same, alike
horizontal	level, flat
immaculate	clean
immovable	fixed
impact on	influence
in arrears	late
indebtedness	debt
indicate	show
inform	tell, report
infrequent	rare
initiate	begin
inquire	ask
institute	establish, begin, start
intelligible	clear

Word	Replace With
interrogate	question
locality	place
locate	find
magnitude	size
manner	way
maximum	most, largest, greatest
minimum	least, smallest, fewest
modify	change
necessitate	require
obliterate	erase
obtain	get
occasion (verb)	cause
peruse	read, review
portion	part
possess	have
preserve	keep
prior	earlier
prior to	before
proceed	go
procure	obtain, buy, get
proficient	skilled
promulgated	issue, publish
proximity	nearness
purchase	buy
purchaser	buyer
recompense	reward, compensate
redundant	extra, unneeded
remainder	rest
remuneration	salary, compensation, pay
render	make, give
request	ask
require	need
retain	keep
specified	named
state	tell, give
subsequent	after, later
suffer	permit
sufficient	enough
summon	call, send for
terminate	end, finish
transmit	send
transparent	clear
unavailability	lack
utilize	use
verify	prove

5. Terms of Art

As discussed in Chapter 8, a word or phrase may qualify as a term of art because the law requires that it be used to achieve a particular result; because it is a defined term expression for a complex legal concept; or because its legal meaning is different from its conventional meaning. Terms of art may facilitate communication among lawyers, but they are a total mystery to lay readers of drafted documents. Thus, terms of art defeat a primary objective of drafting, to be clear to everyone within the intended audience.

Yet, many lawyers resist giving up the use of terms of art, asserting this will cause confusion and precipitate needless litigation. This fear is largely without foundation. First, most terms of art are not as precise and fixed in legal meaning as their defenders contend. Consider, for example, the multiple meanings that the courts have given to "appurtenances," "fixtures," and "tenantable"—words that real estate lawyers consider sacrosanct terms of art, but that have proved not to be. Second, some terms of art have a fixed meaning, but one that is so general it is virtually worthless in a drafted document. For example, all lawyers know that a "right of first refusal" creates an option and regard that as a term of art. Certainly, that is its fixed, generalized meaning. But for an option to be enforceable, it must specify the details of the transaction. The option is an option to buy what, at what price, and subject to what payment, delivery, and other terms? That is what an actual contract must focus on, and a glib "Jones has a right of first refusal" is insufficient, even if that is an esteemed term of art. Third, specific words or phrases that absolutely must be used to achieve a particular legal result are relatively rare. Most terms of art can be expressed in other words—words that are both more familiar to the lay reader and that provide the precision and specificity required.

6. Technical and Trade Terms

The drafter should also take care when using technical, scientific, commercial, and other terms with specialized meanings. If the context suggests that a word is being used in a specialized sense, the courts will construe it accordingly. If the specialized meaning is not what is intended, then the drafter must select a different word. For example, although a tomato is scientifically a fruit in the produce world, among consumers it is regarded as a vegetable. Defining the term can eliminate the ambiguity.

7. Foreign Words and Phrases

Unless it is a true term of art, like *"per stirpes,"* avoid foreign words and phrases. These are usually Latin or French. Even commonly recognized words like *"bona fide"* can be replaced by their English counterpart, like "good faith." The most commonly abused foreign words and phrases, often found in old formbooks and file documents, and their more suitable replacements are as follows:

Foreign Word or Phrase	Replacement
ad infinitumin	indefinitely
causa mortis	approaching death
cum copula	sexual intercourse
exempli gratia (e.g.)	for example
femme sole	unmarried female
fructus fundi	produce of the land
id est (i.e.)	that is
inter alia	among others
inter se	among themselves
lex loci	law of the, jurisdiction
mutatis mutandis	with the necessary, changes in detail
non compos mentis	not of sound mind
per annum	a year
pro rata	proportionately
pari passu	of the same priority
seriatim	separately
vis-a-vis	in relation to
viva voca	orally

8. Words Ending in "-ee" and "-or"

Even lawyers sometimes get confused over the identity of the lessor and the lessee, the mortgagor and the mortgagee, and the vendor and the vendee. When describing the parties, use dissimilar, plain English terms, like "landlord" and "tenant," "borrower" and "lender," and "seller" and "buyer."

9. Compound Adjectives and Noun Phrases

Limit your use of hyphens. Generally, hyphens should be used to form compound adjectives:

The short-term loan agreement contained a cross-default clause.

A compound adjective is two adjectives, with the first adjective modifying the second adjective and the two adjectives combined then modifying the following noun, thus creating a noun phrase. Use a hyphen to signal to the reader that the adjectives function as a unit: "one-owner vehicle." Hyphenation is even more important if the phrase contains three adjectives: "a year-round container supply." No amount of hyphenation will save extensive noun chains, however. Do not refer to a Research-and-Development-Department-approved rotor-wheel-abrasion-removal device. Refer to it as a device for the removal of abrasions on rotor wheels that has been approved by the Research and Development Department.

There are, however, exceptions. Nonpayment, intercompany, and *pro rata* should all be written without hyphens. Even if omitting a hyphen results in a double letter, a hyphen should generally not be used to attach a prefix to a word. However, if the result would cause confusion or mispronunciation (such as in the case of co-op or re-lease), a hyphen is justified. When in doubt as to the use of a hyphen, write the word as one unit. To be accurate, consult the most current unabridged or legal dictionary available to ascertain the preferred modern usage for your requirements.

In some cases hyphens are helpful in distinguishing use of a word as a verb (no-hyphen) or a noun (hyphen). Verb: "... *the bank is entitled to set off any deposit* ..." Noun: "... *the bank is entitled to a set-off in the event* ..." But the same effect can be generated with the use of an article to indicate the noun, as is also done in this example with the indefinite article "a."

10. Unconventional Capitalization

Eighteenth Century drafters often capitalized important nouns, a practice probably derived from German. Unfortunately, this quaint practice is still followed in certain types of contracts. It would not be unusual, for example, to find something like this in a construction contract:

> *All Bills of Lading will be kept on file at the Construction Site.... Change Orders must be approved in writing.... The anticipated Completion Date of Construction is....*

This is unnecessary and distracting. Capitalize only proper nouns, including defined terms.

11. Positive Versus Negative Expression

If something can be said either positively or negatively, say it positively. This is clearer because people think this way. Instead of saying,

> *The curfew does not apply before midnight,*

say,

> *The curfew applies only after midnight.*

Double negatives are especially confusing. Instead of saying,

> *This section does not apply to applicants with no dependent children,*

say,

> *This section applies only to applicants with dependent children.*

12. Exceptions

Try not to draft in terms of a larger class from which certain members are then excepted; draft in terms of the targeted subclass directly. Instead of saying,

> *All applicants **except** those who are 40 years old or older must complete Form 647,*

say,

> *All applicants who are less than 40 years old must complete Form 647.*

On the other hand, when drafting directly in terms of the excepted subclass would leave a substantive void with respect to what happens to the larger class, then the exception approach is necessary. For example, "Charleston, Richland, and Greenville Counties are not entitled to emergency relief funding" fails to create a positive entitlement by the other counties to receive the funding. Thus, one should use the exception approach, saying, "All counties, except Charleston, Richland, and Greenville, are entitled to receive emergency relief funding."

13. Personal Pronouns

One of the objectives of the plain English movement was to make documents readily understandable by lay readers, especially consumers. Drafters were thus encouraged to use personal pronouns like "you," "I," and "we," on the theory that this made the document less formidable and more comprehensible. Drafters also sometimes use these pronouns to establish a tone of informality in documents like employee handbooks and application instructions. Although these pronouns serve a useful purpose in a limited class of documents, they should never be used at the expense of clarity and precision.

The principal dangers are as follows. First, the reader may misunderstand who is "I," who is "you," and who is "we." Second, the danger is compounded if the transaction involves multiple documents and they are not all written from the same point of view. The consumer may be "I" in one document, but "you" in another. Third, using personal pronouns can be more confusing than helpful in transactions involving more than two parties.

Pronouns are not the precise drafter's friend. As a general rule, identify the parties by name, title, or status and a defined term—not with a personal pronoun.

D. SOME BASIC RULES OF GRAMMAR RELEVANT TO DRAFTING

1. Forming the possessive

a. Form the possessive singular of nouns by adding " 's"

The judge's ruling. James's case.

The possessive is *not* used when specifying a time period, such as a notice period. For example, it is "20–days notice" (compound adjective form) rather than "20 days' notice" or, worse, "20 day's notice" (incorrect possessive forms).

An apostrophe followed by an "s" is often used to form the plural of letters, single-digit numbers, and symbols. While this form looks like possessive form, it is merely plural. It is incorrect to pluralize names with an apostrophe followed by "s". For example, "the Brown's" is the incorrect plural form. The correct plural form is "the Browns" with no apostrophe.

b. Form the possessive plural by adding an apostrophe

The lawyers' presentations.

c. Its, it's, his, and hers

"Its" is the possessive form of "it."

"It's" is a contraction for "it is."

"His" and "hers" are possessive and take no apostrophe.

2. Use of the Semicolon vs. the colon

a. The Semicolon

When joining two or more grammatically complete (independent) clauses without a conjunction, use a semicolon. Think of its use in this fashion as representing a weak period.

The attorney's argument was compelling; he persuaded the jury.

Apart from being used to separate items in a list that are themselves long or compound, this punctuation mark has limited relevance to contracts and transactional documents. If you find that you are using semi-colons in transactional documents other than as part of a list, examine your use carefully.

b. The Colon

A colon directs the reader to what follows. It usually follows an independent clause and can be used to introduce a variety of related statements: a list of particulars, a quotation, an appositive, an illustration, or an amplification. Even two independent clauses can be joined with a colon if the second interprets or amplifies the first.

A list can have only one item.

It is not necessary to use a colon every time a list is introduced. For example, "The model you like is available in red, blue, white, and ochre" takes no colon. Overuse of a colon with lists is cumbersome.

Commentators are split on whether the first letter of the word that follows a colon is capitalized. Most agree, however, that if that word is the first in a list of multiple items, each item begins with a lower case letter.

3. Slashes

The slash should not be used in legal writing because of the ambiguity involved. The slash could indicate "and" (conjunctive) or "or" (disjunctive), thus creating unnecessary ambiguity. The only acceptable use for a slash in legal writing is for dates (03/13/10) and fractions (½).

4. Subject and Verb Agreement

Subject and verb must agree in number.

a. The number of the subject determines the number of the verb. This is true even if other nouns are connected to it by "with" or "no less than."

The statute, as well as the regulation, favors a strict construction.

The statutes favor a strict construction.

b. Plural vs. Singular nouns.

A. When "none" means "no one" or "not one" use a singular verb. If "none" suggests more than one thing or person, use a plural verb.

B. Remember—forum, memorandum, datum, and criterion are singular; fora, memoranda, data, and criteria are plural.

C. Singular verbs should be used with "either" and "any" and, in its usual form, "neither . . . nor."

5. Parentheses

A sentence containing a parenthetical expression is punctuated outside the parenthesis exactly as if the parenthetical expression were absent. The parenthetical expression itself is punctuated as if it stood by itself, except that the final or "terminal" punctuation mark is omitted unless it is a question mark or an exclamation point:

Payments of interest should be made quarterly (on the first business day of each quarter), but will be compounded daily.

The defendant protested (and why should we doubt his word?) that he had delivered the goods as specified.

(When a wholly detached statement is contained in parentheses, the final punctuation comes before the closing of the parenthesis, as here.) If the point is to make the statement stand out (rather than be concealed) a pair of dashes is probably the better tool.

6. Quotation Marks

The placement of quotation marks in relation to other punctuation marks (commas, periods, colons, semi-colons, question marks, and exclamation marks) is a matter of some disagreement in the English speaking world. The British practice differs in significant respects from the American practice. But just as British spelling is not favored in documents drafted in this country, neither is the British practice with respect to quotation marks. The American practice is as follows:

- Always put commas and periods within the quotation marks.

Unless referring to a specific individual, author will not use any gender specific terms in the text, including "he," "she," "him," "his," or "her."

- Always put colons and semi-colons outside the quotation marks.

When shipping packages containing hazardous materials, seller shall clearly mark them as "hazardous materials"; all of the materials listed in section 302–b are considered "hazardous."

- Put exclamation and question marks inside the quotation marks if they are actually part of the quoted material; if they are the drafter's own addition, place them outside the quotation marks. Although exclamation and question marks are rarely used in drafted documents, the drafter may need to use them in correspondence relating to a drafted document.

Allow me to say this in response to your question, "Why does the contract not contain a liquidated damages provision?" [Also note the absence of a terminal period.]

Were you serious when you suggested that we change the reference in the statute from "bars" to "jook joints"?

The legal drafter, however, should deviate from these conventions when drafting amendments. Periods and commas should be outside the quotation marks unless they are intended to be a part of what is being amended. Colons and semi-colons should be inside the quotation marks if they are intended to be a part of the amended language.

- *Section 7. Section 499(c)(4) is amended by striking the word "children" and inserting "dependent minors".* [In the original, the word "children" was in the middle of a sentence and had no punctuation following it; the amended term must also be devoid of punctuation, thus requiring the terminal period to come after the quotation mark.]

- *Paragraph 64 is amended by inserting "territory already assigned to another agent;" after "Agent may not solicit sales in any of the following areas:"* [Insert is added at the beginning of a list that is separated by semi-colons.]

7. Spacing After Sentences

The traditional rule is that two spaces are used between a sentence's terminal punctuation and the first word of the next sentence. This aids the reader when skimming or speed-reading the document by providing the eye with a double space to identify the beginning of the next sentence. This rule has eroded in recent years, apparently due to the rise of word processing and proportional spacing.

E. MISUSED AND ABUSED WORDS AND EXPRESSIONS

Effect/Affect. "Effect" as a noun means "result" or "appearance." As a verb it means "to bring about" or "to accomplish." "Affect," a verb, means "to influence" or "to simulate."

Farther and Further. Use "farther" when distance is involved and "further" when referring to time or quantities. My dog chases balls "farther" than other dogs. Attorneys often pursue a subject "further" than others.

Fortuitous. This word refers to something that happens by chance. It is not limited to fortunate or lucky happenings.

In regard to. It is incorrect to use "in regards to." "As regards" is correct, and means the same thing. "Regarding" is preferred.

Irregardless. Use "regardless" rather than "irregardless."

Fewer/Less. "Fewer" refers to number; "less" refers to quantity. *I have less trouble in my practice than Mary because I have fewer clients.*

Like. Often incorrectly used for the conjunction "as." "Like" is a preposition that compares nouns and pronouns; "as" is a conjunction used to introduce subordinate clauses (which generally contain a verb). This distinction has seen some erosion in recent years but is still drawn by purists.

Wrong	Right
He addressed the jury like an expert.	*He addressed the jury as an expert would.*

Loan. "Loan" is a noun. "Lend" is the verb, as in "I shall lend you $50."

Nor. Use "or" after negative expressions rather than "nor" to avoid unintentionally communicating a double negative.

Principle and Principal.

    a. "Principal" is an *adjective* meaning the most important or the base amount of an investment (the "principal sum, plus interest"). It is also *a noun* meaning "one with controlling authority."

    b. "Principle" is a *noun*, meaning a fundamental law, doctrine or assumption upon which all things are based or which guides conduct.

Secondly, Thirdly, Etc. Consistency would lead one to begin with "firstly." It is preferred to use "first," "second," "third," etc. If you choose to use "secondly," "thirdly," and the like, begin with "initially" to avoid the awkwardness of "firstly."

F. GENDER–SPECIFIC LANGUAGE

A drafted document that offends, annoys, or even distracts a member of the intended audience is a less effective document. For a time, no issue more bitterly divided the legal writing community than the issue of gender-specific language. This refers to the androgynous use of male pronouns and terms ending with a male designation—"his," "he," and "him," "chairman," "draftsman," and "fireman."

The traditionalists argued that the pronouns have always been understood as including persons of both sexes when the reference is masculine. They further argued that the term chair refers to a thing and should not be confused with a reference to a person. And they made great sport of some of the ridiculous substitutions that were being proffered, e.g., person-hole cover. To them, this was a linguistic and not a political issue. And they believed that traditional usage need not be sacrificed to the otherwise worthy goal of social and political equality of the sexes.

The traditionalists' counterparts were those who saw latent sexism lurking in every word, sentence, and paragraph. To them, a clear link existed between linguistics and politics. To achieve the goal of political and social equality, the language must be purged. The opponents of gender specific language were not unimaginative in coming up with substitutes—"(s)he," "s/he," "her/his," indiscriminate or alternative generic use of both male and female pronouns, and some absurd non-words like "shero."

Between the two extremes sat the hapless writer and drafter, intent on making an important and complex substantive point, but now distracted by the need to avoid offending either faction. Ultimately, a middle position prevailed. Drafters discovered that many writing devices exist for avoiding gender specific words without being conspicuous. These techniques are as follows:

Eliminate Unnecessary Pronouns. An agency regulation might read:

> *An employee of the Department of Health may elect to file under section 327 and **he** may obtain the proper form for doing this from Payroll.*

The "he" is totally unnecessary and can be deleted.

Reword. A provision in an insurance policy might read:

If he fails to report the injury within 10 days, the Insured forfeits coverage.

This could be rewritten as follows:

The Insured must report the injury within 10 days or forfeit coverage.

Repeat the Noun. Instead of using a noun and then a gender-specific pronoun, simply repeat the noun. This alternative is more palatable in drafted documents than in briefs or memoranda, where fluidity is important.

*If a distributor fails to . . . . That distributor [rather than **he**] must then . . . .*

Use a Shortened Form of the Noun or a Synonym.

*The Director of the Department of Health must certify that all imported poultry is parasite free. The Director [rather than **he**] has the discretion to either refuse entry to poultry that contains parasites or order it destroyed.*

Some drafters might also use a synonym here—"This official," for example. Although this violates the rule about using the same word to refer to the same person, entity, or concept, it is safe enough if no ambiguity would result.

Change the Pronoun to "the," "a," or "this."

*If Buyer exercises the [rather than **his**] right of first refusal, ...*

Use "It."

*If any animal in the zoo escapes from its [rather than **his**] cage, all personnel shall immediately . . . .*

Use "One."

*If one [rather than **he**] elects to file under section 335, ...*

Use "You." Subject to the constraints on the use of personal pronouns discussed earlier, in some cases using the second person you may be a viable alternative to a male pronoun. In a set of course instructions, instead of saying:

*A student must supply **his** own computer,*

say,

You must supply your own computer.

Use the Imperative Mood. In a set of work rules directed at employees, instead of saying,

> *Each employee shall stay at **his** work station until relieved by an employee on the next shift,*

say,

> *Stay at your work station until you are relieved by an employee on the next shift.*

Replace "he" with "he or she." Because it is so wordy, the "he or she" phrase is not a particularly desirable alternative. However, it is better than the totally impermissible alternatives of "he/she," "s/he," using "he" and "she" alternatively, or other linguistic abominations. Although consistently putting the "he" first may seem sexist, most people find alternating it with "she or he" to be extremely distracting.

Use Plural Subjects. In discursive writing, lawyers often avoid gender-specific pronouns by using a plural subject and referring back to it with "they," "them," or "their." Since drafted documents normally use singular subjects, this option may not be available often. It can, however, be used occasionally. Instead of saying,

> *A candidate for county council must pay a $500 filing fee. **He** must also provide a list of contributors,*

say,

> *Candidates for county council must pay a $500 filing fee. They must also provide a list of contributors.*

In an attempt to have the best of both worlds, some drafters use the singular noun and the plural pronoun, as in "An investor must notify their broker within 10 days." Although a few will contend that historical and literary precedent exists for some forms of this noun/pronoun disagreement, it is grammatically wrong, logically incoherent, and an unnecessary elevation of gender sensitivity over the canons of good style and usage.

Use the Passive Voice. This is also an option of last resort. But, instead of saying,

*When an applicant files Form 207, **he** must attach a photograph,*

say,

A photograph must be attached when an applicant files Form 207.

Use Gender–Neutral Descriptive Terms. Many words ending in "man" can be replaced with gender-neutral terms. For example:

councilman becomes council member

crewman becomes crew member

draftsman becomes drafter

fireman becomes fire fighter

longshoreman becomes stevedore

meterman (or -maid) becomes meter reader

policeman becomes police officer

salesman becomes sales clerk

watchman becomes guard

Drop the "-man" or Replace It With "-person." "Chair" instead of "chairman" and "anchor" instead of "anchorman" have become acceptable usage. But for other terms, the convention is to replace the "-man" with either "-er" or "-person." "Spokesman" has, thankfully, become "spokesperson," rather than "spoker." But, again thankfully, "draftsman" has become "drafter" rather than "draftsperson." Some "-man" terms, however, have become terms of art, like "journeyman" in collective bargaining agreements, and their usage still persists to some extent.

Exercise 10

Identify what is stylistically wrong with and edit the following provisions. More than one thing may be wrong with several of them.

    a.   Cleanup, Inc., will sell, subject to the following terms, industrial solvent to the Needsitmucho Company: ..... Seller warrants that.... but buyer agrees to use the solvent only.... Supplier further warrants that ..., subject to user's compliance with EPA Regulation 445–8–c-(33)q.

b.   Contractor will: (a) install a lawn sprinkling system; (b) allowing the system to be tested and approved by a certified IQEW inspector; (c) restoration of disturbed sod; and (d) signs warning persons when the system will come on automatically.

c.   A.   This section is intended to provide preliminary information about the parties, the coverage of the contract, and other general matters that will assist in the interpretation of this contract.

      1.   Parties. The parties to this contract are Clean-up, Inc., and the Needsitmucho Company.

      2.   Site Covered. The chemical cleanants covered by the terms of this contract will be used exclusively at the Needsitmucho Company's commercial laundry facility located at 666 Danger Road, Cesspool, Yourstate, 46321.

. . . .

R.   CHEMICALS/COMPOUNDS NOT COVERED: The following chemicals and chemical compounds are not covered by this contract:

(a) Dimerriamwebsterchronocyclamate.

(b) Collegiatedictionarious-hydrogenated.

(c) Fiberfaced-pollygrinus secretions.

. . . .

W.   Exceptions—The provisions of this contract do not apply to:

§ W.1—Any cleaning that is conducted in connection with laundry from the U.S. Navy Nuclear Testing Facility at Port Kall.

§ W.13: Any cleaning that is conducted in connection with laundry certified as Class B by the State Health Department.

d.   Manager is an at-will employee and Company may terminate Manager at any time and for any reason or no reason at all. Manager is an at-will employee and may resign at any time and for any reason or no reason at all. As an at-will employee, Manager has no right to be terminated only "for cause."

e. Whereas, in consideration and exchange for $10,000 and other good and sufficient consideration, the aforementioned being over, above, and in addition to whatever compensation, pay, or consideration is otherwise hereinbefore or hereinafter due and owing to John Jones (hereinafter referred to as "Manager") in connection with the termination, end, and cessation of his employment, in hand paid, said Manager agrees, covenants, and contracts to provide a full and complete release and discharge of the sundial Company (hereinafter referred to as "Company") for each, all, and every claim, charge, and cause of action of every kind and nature arising out of or relating to Manager's employment. Any, all, and every contract[s], covenant[s], agreement[s] or understanding[s] between Manager and Company that are to the contrary or inconsistent with, or contradict, the terms, provisions, conditions, and promises contained herein are null, void, and of no force and effect.

Manager further agrees that all private, secret, and confidential papers in Manager's possession will be returned to Company or completely destroyed, that for the period of time of one year Manager will not be employed by any competitor of Company located within a distance of 100 miles of said Company's facility, located in the City of Columbia, County of Richland, State of South Carolina, United States of America.

f. In order to file a claim with respect to injuries that have occurred in the course of the work day, an employee must have medical costs that are in excess of $100. In the event that the employee claims the injuries will cause a permanent disability with the result that the employee can no longer work, the claim will be held in abeyance until such time as this can be determined.

g. Buyer will pay $10,000 for the goods. Next, Buyer will accept delivery of the goods at the Galveston rail terminal, although Seller will provide at least 10 days notice of the delivery date. In addition, Seller will obtain for the Buyer a pass into the terminal. On the other hand, Buyer will use a bonded common carrier to transport the goods from the terminal to the Buyer's facility.

h. This subsection applies to all of the dependents of an applicant who are listed in section 3(a). An applicant who is submitting documentary evidence of dependency must comply with the Guidelines of the Commissioner, which were promulgated on June 3, 1996. The documents that an applicant submits must be verified. Applicants have twenty (20) days to complete the file.

i. Section 1. It is the public policy of the State of California to promote a pollution-free environment. Public policy, however, also gives recognition to the need for a healthy economy. It is the purpose of this Act to provide an accommodation for those two goals.

. . . .

Section 7. There are 10 factors that the Department of Health and Environmental Control shall give consideration to when deciding whether to grant approval of a wetlands dredging operation.

j. An application for a visa extension must be filed by a resident alien on or before June 1, 2004. An extension may be granted if the work area has been certified as Class 4 by the Department of Labor.

k. If the parties are in agreement, the contractor is under an obligation to then proceed with installation. If the parties are unable to agree, the dispute is to be submitted to an arbitration that is binding.

l. After Owner and Contractor have agreed on a construction schedule, they will, unless the Surety requires it earlier, file that schedule by no later than 10 days before construction begins, and they will periodically update the schedule as construction proceeds, to reflect delays as they occur.

m. If inclement weather caused a delay, the contractor's duty will be excused. But if the contractor could have avoided the delay by rescheduling the order in which work proceeds, then contractor had a duty to do that.

n. At the expiration of the comment period, the Director shall forthwith promulgate regulations requiring owners of properties contiguous to the site to procure hazardous waste insurance and to execute a release waiving all rights to remuneration for damage caused by the government.

o. (1) An employer who engages in a corporate employee-component reduction exercise must give the employees 30 days advance notice.

(2) Applicants may obtain their pre-existing medical condition disclosure forms from the Director of Health.

p. (1) The vehicle is not safe.

(2) The exception does not apply to persons with more than 3 children.

(3) Under Rule 36, a defendant who does not plead not guilty is not entitled to representation by the Public Defender.

q. All law students at the University of Texas, except those whose legal residence is in Texas, must complete Form 765–3.

r. (1) An applicant whose file has not been acted upon within 60 days is entitled to begin receiving benefits and he may also file a notice of noncompliance with the Commissioner.

(2) Unless a contractor complies with this provision, he will be personally liable for providing workers' compensation insurance.

(3) The Director of the Agency shall make the termination decision. If he decides to terminate, the decision is final.

(4) A member of the Supreme Court or the Court of Appeals must certify the appeal. He must then file a motion for self-disqualification.

(5) If a defendant does not assert his privilege against self-incrimination in a timely fashion, it will be considered waived.

(6) Section 3 applies to a dog that is over 100 pounds. If he is one of the breeds listed in Section 6, then Section 4 also applies.

(7) He who elects to proceed under Rule 6 must complete Form 334–9.

(8) [In an employment manual] Each employee must supply his own steel-toed shoes.

(9) [In a student handbook] A student must be punctual in getting to his 8:00 a.m. classes.

(10) Each applicant must provide his Social Security number.

(11) When a contractor subcontracts, he must notify the owner within 10 days.

(12) An employee must file his application for lease at least 10 days in advance.

Chapter 14

DEFINITIONS

Legal drafters must define the terms used in statutes and contracts. Sometimes, this can be difficult. A county in Florida—apparently concerned over skimpy bikinis, thongs, lingerie fashion shows, and the costumes worn in bars—wanted legislation prohibiting the display of "the buttocks." The drafter finally managed to define this portion of the body as follows:

> *The area at the rear of the human body which lies between two imaginary lines running parallel to the ground, when a person is standing. The first or top of such line drawn at the top of the cleavage of the nates (i.e. the prominence formed by the muscles running from the back of the hip to the back of the leg) and the second or bottom line drawn at the lowest visible point of this cleavage or the lowest point of the curvature of the fleshy protuberance, whichever is lower. And between two imaginary lines on each side of the body, which lines are perpendicular to the ground and to the horizontal lines described above, and which perpendicular lines are drawn through the point at which each nate meets the outer side of each leg.*

The definition may not be artful, but it is at least precise.

A.   GENERAL PRINCIPLES OF USAGE

Definitions tell the reader what a particular word or phrase means. Well drafted definitions promote clarity, brevity, and consistency. Definitions are properly used:

- To give a defined-term identity to terms and concepts that have no previously established lexical (dictionary) meaning; essentially, one is creating a proper noun.

- To resolve an ambiguity in terms that have more than one possible meaning.

- To clarify terms that have a lexical meaning, but an impossibly vague one.

- To add to or subtract from a lexical meaning.

Definitions are powerful medicine, and drafters should use them sparingly and with care. A badly drafted definition will infect every portion of the document where the term is used. The drafter should keep the following considerations in mind when creating definitions.

Overly broad or narrow definitions can inadvertently introduce ambiguity or reallocate benefits and burdens. Defined terms can also be used to intentionally cloud meaning. The less-than-careful reader will often assume that a term has its ordinary, lay meaning and will not refer to a definitions section for clarification. Consider a contract that provides that refund claims submitted to a local company "will be Paid In Full within 90 days of Receipt." The initial-capped terms are defined, many pages away, as meaning "compensated in lawful money of [name of non-domestic country or state], calculated at the then prevalent exchange rate" and "when received by the Claims Processor [itself defined as a company in China]," respectively.

But be careful—if you define a term, it must *only* be used in the defined sense in the document. If not, ambiguity crops up. This is closely related to the practice of elegant variation from English composition classes. Those courses often encourage the use of different words for the same concept to avoid repetitive prose. The rule is different in legal drafting. *Use the same words for the same meanings every time.*

To protect against inadvertent use of defined terms that may create ambiguity, many drafters adopt a standard form of defined term that varies the normal rules of format, capitalization, and the like. Examples include: Initial Caps, ALL CAPS, *italics*, **boldface**, or <u>underlining</u>. The predominant form appears to be Initial Caps, further analogizing a defined term to a proper noun.

Initial capitalization drapes the defined term in the mantle of a proper noun. This is appropriate because, within the document, the term essentially becomes a proper noun. This book places the defined term in parentheses and quotes when it is initially defined, *e.g.*:

> ...June 7, 2005 ("Due Date").

When the defined term is later used, it is in initial capitals (also known as "Initial Caps"), but without quotes, *e.g.*

> "...on the Due Date, the Payer shall..."

This is not a perfect solution, as it really changes the problem from using the defined term in its defined sense every time to ensuring that defined terms are initial capped every time they are used. It is, however, the dominant solution in practice.

Finally, take care to make the definition either inclusive or exclusive. Consider, for example, whether trade secrets constitute Intellectual Property under each of the following definitions:

> Inclusive: *"Intellectual Property" means intellectual property as that term is generally used and includes all patents, copyrights, and trademarks. (Yes).*

> Exclusive: *"Intellectual Property" means patents, copyrights, and trademarks. (No).*

> Ambiguous: *"Intellectual Property" means and includes patents, copyrights, and trademarks. (Maybe?).*

Party definitions can be tricky. For example, if "Big Financial Co." is defined in a mutual settlement and release agreement to be "Big Financial Co., Inc.," and all of its subsidiaries, parent corporation, officers, directors, employees, attorneys, and accountants, so as to give these Big Financial Co. related individuals the benefit of the release of all claims granted by the other side, does it follow that Big Financial's release of the other party includes a release by all those defined as part of Big Financial? That appears impossible in most cases. Think it through.

1. Terms With Established Meanings

Do not define a term that already has a perfectly adequate dictionary meaning. Consider, for example, a totally unnecessary definition found in a federal regulation:

"Form" means a piece of paper containing blank spaces, boxes, or lines for the entry of dates, names, descriptive details, or other items.

Before defining a term, check an unabridged dictionary, a legal dictionary or book on legal usage, and *Words and Phrases*. The drafter can determine from these sources whether it is necessary to create a new definition.

2. Terms of Art and Technical Terms

Although legal terms of art and other technical terms have established meanings, the drafter may choose to repeat those definitions. This is especially true if the intended audience of the document includes persons who might not know what these terms mean or suspect that they have a special meaning. Documents used in consumer transactions often include this type of definition. A loan agreement, for example, might appropriately contain the following definition.

"Mortgage" means a charge or lien on real or personal property owned by Borrower to secure repayment of the loaned amount.

3. Humpty–Dumpty Definitions

Do not define a term in a way that is totally at odds with its commonly accepted or dictionary meaning. This is called a "Humpty–Dumpty definition," in honor of the Lewis Carroll character who opined as follows:

"When *I* use a word," Humpty Dumpty said, in rather a scornful tone, "it means just what I choose it to mean—neither more not less."

"The question is," said Alice, "whether you *can* make words mean so many different things."

"The question is," said Humpty Dumpty, "which is to be master—that's all."

Humpty Dumpty was technically correct. The drafter has absolute liberty here. Were he or she so inclined, the drafter could create a whole new language:

"uittithiday" means a buyer in good faith.

"flibberdejibbit" means not subject to third party defenses that could have been raised against the original seller.

"huh?" means "is" or any other appropriate form of the verb "to be."

Hence, the drafted document would provide, "Uttithiday huh? flibberdejibbit."

That is ridiculous. But consider the following definition taken from a federal statute:

"September 16, 1940" means "June 27, 1950."

The federal government may be master of what September 16, 1940, means, but in this case, it is a silly master indeed.

More is involved than mere foolishness, however. First, the drafter who has defined "up" to mean "toward the center of the earth" may later forget this counter-intuitive definition and use "up" in its more conventional sense later in the document, thus creating a contextual ambiguity.

Second, the ordinary reader is even more likely to forget this weird definition and thus be misled by the contract. Indeed, when the defined meaning of a term is so at odds with its conventional or dictionary meaning, and when the defined meaning would work to the significant disadvantage of the party who did not draft the contract, a court might refuse to enforce the contract, on grounds of unconscionability.

Third, Humpty–Dumpty definitions deprive the appropriated term of its conventional meaning, thus leaving the concept without a handy referent. If the word "up" has been defined to mean what we normally think of in terms of down, how is one to refer to the concept of moving from the center of the earth toward the sky? Perhaps the perverse drafter of "up" would then define the word "down" to refer to what we normally think of in terms of up.

Finally, consider the ethical implications of using defined terms to obfuscate or mislead. Does it matter that the contract is a form, once prepared by a team of lawyers, distributed by non-lawyers to commercial clients? To consumers? Beyond ethics, what about the morality of that conduct? Is there a standard to judge when elegant, persuasive drafting of a contract crosses a line and is criminal, tortious, unethical, or immoral? There are no firm answers.

4. Circular Definitions

A definition should never define the term by reference to itself. This is a circular definition:

> *"Harass" means a course of conduct directed at a specific person which seriously alarms, annoys, or harasses the person.*

Some drafters recognize an exception to this rule when a compound expression is consistently used to refer to the operative concept and only one word in the expression requires definition. A statute, for example, might repeatedly refer to an "underinsured motorist," with only "underinsured" requiring substantive clarification. To maintain the unity of the concept, some drafters thus define the entire phrase as a subclass of the broader category of motorist.

> *"Underinsured motorist" means a motorist whose personal liability coverage is under $25,000 per individual per accident.*

Other drafters would adhere to the rule and provide only a definition of "underinsured."

> *"Underinsured" means having personal liability coverage under $25,000 per individual per accident.*

5. One–Shot Definitions

Definitions are useful primarily because they avoid the necessity of having to repeat a lengthy chain of words every time a concept is referenced in the document. The definition provides a defined-term way of expressing that concept. If the corporate buyer's authorized agents consist of ten named individuals, it would be cumbersome and wordy to repeat their names every time the concept of an authorized agent arises. Defining authorized agents in terms of these ten individuals and then using that term achieves an economy of words.

On the other hand, a definition that is referenced only once in the document does not achieve an economy of words.

A corporate officer shall annually disclose to the Board of Directors any stock ownership of or financial dealings with any business in direct competition with Acme Industrials. For the purpose of this provision, "corporate officer" means the President, Vice President, Secretary, and Treasurer of Acme Industrials, but does not include the General Counsel. [53 words]

versus

The President, Vice President, Secretary, and Treasurer of Acme Industrials shall annually disclose to the Board of Directors any stock ownership of or financial dealings with any business in direct competition with Acme Industrials. [34 words]

However, a one-shot definition may be justified when the concept being defined is complex and when incorporating it into the substantive provision would create a sentence of unwarranted length.

An employee may be immediately terminated for theft of company property valued at $50 or more, driving a company vehicle or fork lift while under the influence of alcohol or drugs that impair reaction time, or engaging in any conduct involving unwelcome touching, patting, pinching, caressing, intentional and unnecessary brushing against another's person's body, other sexually suggestive physical contact, explicit sexual propositions, suggestive comments, sexually oriented kidding or teaching, practical jokes involving sex or excretory functions, sexually oriented jokes, comments and questions about sexual attributes or activities, foul or obscene language or gestures, display of foul or obscene pictures or printed material, indecent exposure, and attempts to invade the sexual privacy of another person.

The substantive prohibition would be better worded in terms of sexual harassment, followed immediately by a definition of that term in a separate sentence. Moreover, this would allow the use of the defined term (rather than its full explication) in other documents, such as a supervisor's disciplinary report.

6. Definitional Mazes

When a definition uses a term that itself is the subject of a definition—with that definition also including a term that is subject to a further definition, and so on—the reader enters a maze that may be abandoned before completed. This totally frustrates the communication function of the document. Consider the following definitions section of a statute, with emphasis added to illustrate the maze:

> *(1)* ***"Underinsured motorist"*** *means an* ***owner,*** *operator, passenger, lessor, or person with the right to direct the control of a motor vehicle who....*
>
> . . . .
>
> *(6)* ***"Owner"*** *includes the person in whose name title is held, a lessee, a bailee for hire, and* ***a holder of a security interest*** *in a motor vehicle.*
>
> . . . .
>
> *(9)* ***"Holder of a security interest"*** *means a* ***"lienholder"*** *as defined in Code Section 14B:167–3(a).*

The reader then goes to the cross-referenced statute and discovers:

> *3(a)* ***"Lienholder"*** *includes ..., and any other person with a non-possessory* ***property interest*** *in the goods.*
>
> . . . .
>
> *3(q)* ***"Property interest"*** *includes ... an* ***equitable interest*** *in the goods.*

B. SUBSTANTIVE MATTERS

Definitions give meaning to words; they should not serve as vehicles for substance. Burying a substantive provision in a definition can have devastating consequences or be used to intentionally cloud meaning. The drafter might forget that it is there and later draft an inconsistent provision in the main body of the document, creating a contextual ambiguity. The parties, who often think it is unnecessary to read definitions carefully, may inadvertently act in an inconsistent manner and incur significant liability. Conversely, courts sometimes treat substantive provisions that are incorporated into definitions as being without significance. This is because these provisions rarely use the proper terms to create rights, duties, and the like. Is the substance permissive or mandatory? Is it a duty or a condition? Whom is it addressed to? And what are the consequences of noncompliance? Definitions containing substance rarely answer any of these questions.

Definitions containing substantive terms are not, however, uncommon. For example, the Civil Rights Act of 1964 defines "religion" as follows:

> *The term "religion" includes all aspects of religious observance and practice, as well as belief, unless an employer demonstrates that he is unable to reasonably accommodate to an employee's or prospective employee's religious observance or practice without undue hardship on the conduct of the employer's business.*

In other words, if it cannot be reasonably accommodated, then it is not religion. The "unless" clause provides an exception to the substantive prohibition against religious discrimination and should be included in that portion of the statute, not buried within a definition of "religion" itself. Similarly, this Act includes pregnancy within the meaning of the term "sex," but then makes discrimination on that basis illegal only if similarly situated non-pregnant employees are treated differently. Again, that is a substantive limitation on the scope of the prohibited discrimination. It should not have been buried in a definition. It is perhaps not entirely coincidental that the meaning of these substantive provisions, which are artlessly buried in the definitions section of the statute, are among the most heavily litigated with respect to what they mean.

Substantive terms sometimes creep into contract definitions as well.

> *"Place of delivery" means seller's warehouse, where appropriate loading equipment will be made available and used to avoid damage to the goods.*

The "where" clause apparently imposes a duty on the seller and should be in the substantive portion of the contract. If a loading dock confrontation occurs and the parties refer to their contract to resolve the dispute, neither of them may ever think of looking in the definitions section. And even if they did, the passive voice construction leaves it unclear who has the duty of providing the equipment.

Finally, substantive requirements in definitions sometimes create unintended gaps in coverage:

"Vendor" means a person, licensed by the Director of the Department of Parks, who offers for sale food, drinks, souvenirs, or other merchandise.

The intent, apparently, is to require that vendors be licensed, which is a substantive provision. Assume that another section of the regulation then prohibits vendors from operating in certain areas of the park. Sally, who has not been licensed, is selling hot dogs in one of the identified areas. However, because she is not licensed, she also does not fit within the definition of a vendor. Consequently, she is not violating the regulation.

C. DEFINITIONS INCORPORATED BY REFERENCE

Legislative drafters sometimes borrow definitions from other statutes and incorporate them by reference into a new statute. This is bad practice. First, the borrowed definition may have been drafted with a particular problem in mind. The new statute may involve an entirely unrelated set of legislative circumstances, for which the former definition ultimately proves inadequate. For example, one might define a "healthcare facility" one way in a statute dealing with certification and another way in a statute creating tax exemptions.

Second, the courts may later interpret the definition in the first statute in a way that is totally appropriate for the first statute but inappropriate for the one that incorporates it by reference. If the interpretation follows the incorporation, as is often the case, chaos may result.

Third, the first statute may be amended or repealed, with the legislature not realizing the effect of this on the statute that incorporates the definition by reference. Does the definition still have the force of law for the purposes of the second statute? Even if it does, when a new edition of the code or compiled statutes appears, the incorporated definition may be virtually undiscoverable, except in the superseded-volumes section of a major law library.

Fourth, when the text of a definition is buried in another statute, it is apt to be forgotten. The drafter may then draft something elsewhere in the document that is inconsistent with that definition. Similarly, persons affected by the new statute may ignore it altogether, to their disadvantage.

Private-law documents that incorporate a statutory definition are subject to the same problems. Drafters of these documents should incorporate statutory definitions only when the law requires that the term have the same meaning in the document as it does in the statute to which the reference is made. Articles of incorporation and by-laws are sometimes subject to this requirement. The better practice is to repeat the statutory definition verbatim rather than incorporate it by reference, on the theory that the reader of the document should not be forced to go to another source to find out what critical terms mean.

D. TYPES OF DEFINITIONS AND TERMINOLOGY

1. Defined Terms

If the document is a short one, if definitions are not numerous, or if it makes sense for some other reason, definitions can be introduced in the first place they occur, including in the preamble, introductory paragraph or the recitals. For example:

> This ASSET PURCHASE AGREEMENT AND ESCROW INSTRUCTIONS (the "Agreement") is entered into and effective as of March 10, 2007, at Seattle, Washington, by and between _____ ("Seller"), and _____ ("Buyer"), on the basis of the following facts and constitutes (i) a contract of purchase and sale between the parties and (ii) escrow instructions to _____("Escrow Agent"), the consent of whom appears at the end of the Agreement.

Defined terms used in only one section may be defined when used. If defined when used and a definitions section is included, the term should be included in the definition section as well, stating "defined as stated in section ___" for its definition. The idea is to ensure that, if the definition is changed, the change will ripple through the document automatically to avoid ambiguity that could be caused by revising one appearance of the definition and not another.

This is the most common form of definition and is used in all forms of legal writing. A "vest pocket definition" provides the defined term that the document will subsequently use to refer to a party or concept. For example:

> *James Madison ("Seller") and Alexander Hamilton ("Buyer") enter into this contract for the sale of Blackacre Estates of Dinwiddie ("Property").*

Do not lapse into legalese and say, "Hereinafter referred to as 'Seller.'" Some drafters prefer to delete the quotation marks, on the grounds that they tend to clutter up the page with "bird tracks." Some drafters prefer to put the defined term definition in all capital letters and sometimes also in bold face type. They will then use that same typographical convention whenever the term is used in text. Other drafters, however, view this as unnecessary and distracting, particularly the capitalization.

Give a person, entity, or concept only one defined term definition, not two. Do not say, "This is a contract between Jim Beam ("Buyer" or "Beam") and . . . ." Once a term has a defined-term definition, use that abbreviation consistently in the remainder of the document. Do not start using the full term again. Moreover, do not create a defined term definition unless the defined term is actually used again later in the document. "Commencement Date" and "Termination Date" sometimes fall into this category.

2. Full Definitions

When an agreement's definitions are numerous or complicated, the terms should be defined, and should be set out alphabetically in a separate section located near the beginning or end of the agreement.

This is the first of the more conventional forms of "defined terms." A full definition—also sometimes referred to as a "stipulative definition"—provides the complete and exclusive meaning of the term. It has fixed boundaries and the courts are bound to construe it literally, thus disallowing the addition or deletion of referents by implication. Since a full definition is both complete and exclusive, it must be drafted carefully and with all the possibilities in mind. The word "means" signifies a full definition.

"Vehicle" means an automobile, bus, trolley, tram, or electrically driven cart.

Under this definition, a horse-drawn carriage would not be included. This might be a significant omission if the drafter were drafting an ordinance dealing with traffic congestion around Central Park in New York City.

Although two unrelated words should never be given the same full definition, this is not true of a word and its derivative forms. For example, a document may use both "writing" and "written." If the drafter intends for them to mean the same thing, then this form of definition would be appropriate:

"Writing" means the recording of words on paper, and "written" has a corresponding meaning.

A full definition is appropriate in a variety of contexts. For example, a document may use a term that has no dictionary definition.

"Oceanside condominium property" means . . . [whatever the referents are going to be].

Similarly, the drafter may want to use a term that has a useful connotation but whose lexical meaning is too vague to be used safely.

"Industry standards" means the product standards promulgated by the National Association of Widget Manufactures as of the date of this contract, which are attached as Exhibit A.

Note that, although that is an incorporation by reference, it overcomes the defects of that type of definition because the definition is attached to the contract.

Full definitions are also used to limit or provide new meaning to, and thus replace, the lexical definition.

"Apartment" means unit number 6–B of the Fairview Apartment complex, 6216 Wilson Road, Sandy Beach, South Carolina.

Finally, full definitions are often a by-product of the conceptualization process discussed in Chapter 10. For example, an attorney for a school district might be asked to draft a rule prohibiting students from possessing weapons on the school grounds. Upon further inquiry, the drafter determines that the weapons in question definitely include knives, sword canes, straight razors, guns, stun guns, mace, blackjacks, brass knuckles, and the other common paraphernalia of urban warfare. The drafter considers conceptualizing the problem and wording the prohibition in those terms, with an appropriate "and other" clause tacked on at the end. However, the drafter also discovers that students have used a sock containing a billiard ball, hot pepper juice in a squirt gun, and a knotted rope in assaulting each other, teachers, and administrators. The drafter worries whether those objects would be covered by the "and other" clause. In addition, the drafter discovers that students have used staplers, scissors, ball point pens, compasses, and rulers with a sharpened metal edge—objects one hardly thinks of as weapons, but objects the school superintendent wants the rule to deal with anyway. These items seem to have little in common, but after much thought, the drafter finally conceptualizes the intended objective of the prohibition in terms of an abstraction and defines the word accordingly—"things that are capable of causing injury to others and that are in the possession of a student who intends to use them in that capacity." Or, the drafter may come up with some other complex and novel conceptualization of the problem. Whatever the resulting concept, the drafter will incorporate it into a definition.

3. Partial Definitions

A partial definition takes the lexical meaning of a word as the point of departure and clarifies its boundaries, by inclusion or exclusion of specific referents.

a. Enlarging Definitions. To ensure that a particular concept is included within the meaning of a term with a conventional dictionary definition or to add to that definition something the term would not otherwise encompass, drafters use the term "includes." Although "but is not limited to" is unnecessary, many drafters add the phrase to ensure that the list is not construed as being exclusive. Consider the following examples:

> *"Employee" includes, but is not limited to, persons working on a part-time or temporary basis. [Ensuring inclusion.]*

"Apartment" includes, but is not limited to, the hallway, stairways, and other common areas. [Adding something probably not within the conventional meaning.]

The drafter of enlarging definitions must also take care not to be like Humpty Dumpty. Consider the definition contained in an old English statute:

"Cows" includes horses, mules, asses, sheep, and goats.

b. Limiting Definitions. The term "does not include" is used to ensure that something that might be within the conventional definition is excluded or to exclude something that otherwise would clearly be included. For example:

"Automobiles" does not include taxicabs.

The drafter, however, should take care not to exclude something that goes to the core of the conventional meaning, as in:

"Potable liquid" does not include water.

Water is the very essence of a potable liquid.

Often, a drafter could use either a limiting or a full definition to accomplish the same objective.

"Employee" does not include persons performing services for the company for less than 40–hours a week.

versus

"Employee" means persons providing services to the company for 40–hours a week or more.

The drafter should think about the purpose of defining "employee" before deciding which approach to take. Although drafting in terms of exceptions is generally not favored, if the purpose is clearly to exclude part-timers, then the "does not include" approach would be best. But if the purpose is to include within the definition of "employee" persons who might otherwise be considered independent contractors or leased employees, then the "means" approach would be best.

4. Combining Full and Partial Definitions

A partial definition may both include and exclude.

"Lake front property" includes property separated from the water only by a publicly-owned road, but does not include property any portion of which fronts water that, for at least 50% of the shoreline, is less than one foot deep.

Similarly, a full definition can be further clarified by a partial definition, through either inclusion, exclusion, or both.

"Headquarters personnel" means persons employed at the corporate offices in Chicago and includes persons working there for more than 30 days on temporary duty from another office, but does not include persons working as guards under contract with Strongarm Protective Agency.

The terms "includes" and "does not include" must always, however, have a prior reference—either a lexical or a stipulated meaning. A term cannot simultaneously mean and include the same thing:

"Corporate officers" means and includes the president, vice president, secretary, and treasurer.

The "includes" assumes "corporate officers" has a dictionary meaning and purports to ensure that it covers the named officers; the "means," however, replaces that lexical definition with what follows, making the whole thing redundant and circular.

5. Examples

Definitions containing examples are similar to the list of included items in an enlarging definition. The purpose, however, is slightly different. The purpose of an "includes" list is to clarify either a lexical or stipulative definition that is fuzzy at the edges, and to ensure that the items listed are included. Inclusion on the list trumps whatever vagueness is inherent in the concept.

This is not true of examples. Here, the elements of the full or stipulative definition still totally control. Whether a particular act that is generally encompassed by the example falls within the definition may depend on the specific circumstances under which the act occurred. This would have to be determined by reference to the definition; the example language would not be dispositive. In other words, the list of examples merely gives the reader an idea of what the definition might mean in more concrete terms.

Thus, a school regulation might contain a stipulative definition of "cheating." The definition, however, may be both complex and somewhat vague. A list of examples of conduct that will usually satisfy that definition—such as tearing pages out of a library book—assists the reader in understanding what is being prohibited. The administration, however, could not punish a student for simply tearing the pages out of a library book; rather, it would have to prove that this particular tearing incident fell within the elements of the definition of cheating.

Drafters should use examples sparingly, because they are apt to be construed as being more definitive than intended. Use of an example is a technique of last resort. The better approach is to craft the definition in such a way as to make examples unnecessary.

E. METHODOLOGY

Various methods exist for creating definitions.

1. Use More Familiar Terms

Although the term "commons" has meaning to property lawyers, it is a term that most lay persons are unfamiliar with. It could be defined in more familiar terms, as follows:

"Commons areas" means the condominium property open for use by all Owners and includes the grounds, driveways, the parking lot, the tennis court, the swimming pool, and the recreation center.

2. Use More Precise Terms

Vague concepts can sometimes be clarified with scientific precision.

"Dangerously hot" means a heat index of 100 degrees or above.

3. Identify Components

An "automobile" could be defined by reference to the sum of its parts. Although that would not be feasible because of the large number of parts, sometimes this approach works very nicely.

"Mix #3" means a mixture in equal parts of gravel pebbles, 1/2 inch crushed granite, and sand.

4. Identify Specific Referents

A term can also be defined by listing the term's intended referents. Indeed, this is probably the most common form of definition. For example:

"Appliances" means the refrigerator, stove, microwave, disposal, window unit air conditioners, washing machine, and dryer.

The danger is that of omitting something crucial. If the landlord also intended to include the central vacuum cleaner system in the list of items that the tenant is responsible for repairing, this definition will not accomplish it. Adding "and other similar items" would probably cure that oversight, but the better practice is to force the client to think about these details and deal with them expressly.

5. Indicate Relationship to a Larger Unit

Often, the meaning of a term hinges on its inclusion in an existing class of entities. The definition builds on that class membership and creates a subclass.

"Tax-exempt recreational personal property" means an item exempt from taxation under state, county, or municipal tax law that is used exclusively for non-income producing purposes.

The existing class is "items exempted from taxation under other laws." The defined subclass refers to items used for a particular purpose. Similarly, definitions often focus on sub-classes whose identity relates primarily to what they are not, in relation to the larger classification.

"Fair share members" means unit employees who are not full or affiliational members of the Union.

F. LOCATION

Statutes and complex private law documents usually contain a separate section dealing only with definitions. This section may include vest pocket definitions, although most drafters prefer to create these whenever the term is first used in the text. For reader convenience, this section is usually placed at the beginning of the document and the defined terms are listed in alphabetical order.

That sounds like a sensible approach to the location problem, and usually it is. But there are drawbacks. In a lengthy document with many defined terms, the reader is constantly forced to refer back to the definitions section to obtain a full understanding of what is being read—and when this proves to be too troublesome, the reader plows ahead and often ends up with an inadequate grasp of the substance.

To help avoid this, if a term is used in only one section of the document, the drafter should define the term in that section itself. This certainly makes the document a less formidable reading assignment. This is especially important in consumer-related documents, since the average lay person probably will not read a separate definitions section and may not even refer back to it when the term is encountered in the document.

G. WHEN TO DRAFT DEFINITIONS

The conventional wisdom is that drafters should do definitions last. The theory is that the drafter does not know what needs to be defined until the document is otherwise complete. That, however, reflects an inadequate understanding of the integrated nature of the drafting process. Definitions can be, and usually are, drafted before, during, and after the substantive provisions have been reduced to writing.

First, the drafter may know from the onset that certain terms must be defined. If the intended legislation will apply only to business entities with 50 or more employees, then the drafter can write a definition of "employer" in those terms right at the beginning of the process.

Second, the need for definitions will most often occur to the drafter during the critical conceptualization stage. If the drafter is creating a new or hybrid concept, then the drafter will nearly always need to use a definition to capture the essence of that concept.

Third, during the post-drafting review of the document, the drafter may discover that a concept is fully stated several times in the document. The drafter would then decide to define the concept and use the defined term instead of its full explication whenever the concept appears in the document.

In sum, drafting definitions is an interactive process, not something that is always done at the same time.

H. TESTING DEFINITIONS

The drafter can test a document's definitions in several ways. First, the drafter should go through the document and highlight every use of the defined term or, if working on a computer, use the word processor's "find" function to locate each instance of the term. This may reveal several things. The drafter may discover, for example, that the term is not used at all in the document or that it is used only once. More importantly, the drafter may discover that the term is occasionally used in its conventional, rather than its defined sense. Finally, the drafter may discover that when the full definition replaces the defined term in the text, the result is linguistic and logical incoherence. Assume that a definition provides, " 'Representative' means being party to a written agency agreement with the Company." The substantive provision of the contract then provides, "Representatives shall report all sales monthly." If the term is replaced with its definition, we have this monstrosity: "Being party to a written agency agreement with the Company shall report all sales monthly." Representative should be redefined in terms of a person who has a written agency agreement with the Company.

The second way to test definitions is to look not for the use of the term itself, but for the defined and closely related concepts. For example, if "recreational activity" means hunting, fishing, and camping, then that term should always replace those combined concepts in the text. If nothing else, this will ensure that the defined term is being used consistently to replace the full description.

Exercise 11

1. What is wrong with the following definitions?

a. "Pencil" means an implement for writing, drawing, or marking consisting of or containing a slender cylinder or strip of solid marking substance surrounded by a wood, metal, or plastic sheath.

b. "Pencil" includes a paint brush, a spray can, a ball point pen, a fountain pen, and a felt-tip marker.

c. "Felony" means murder, assault with intent to kill, armed robbery, arson, kidnapping, rape, first degree sexual assault, lynching, child molestation, and other felonies.

d. As used in these regulations, "new animal drug" means any form of medicine for animals that has been developed since January 1, 1996, except that the Secretary of Agriculture may exempt such drug from regulation if the Secretary finds that the drug is safe, effective, and pure.

e. "Tax exempt bonds" means and includes bonds issued under Section 347 of the Securities Act of 1937.

2. Create:

a. A full or stipulative definition for some areas that might be regarded as common areas (shared by all tenants) in a large apartment complex.

b. A full or stipulative definition for a class of entities consisting of cows, horses, mules, pigs, goats, sheep, and chickens.

c. An enlarging definition that will ensure that part-time students, transient students, and persons who are auditing a course are subject to a school rule that affects "students."

d. A limiting definition that ensures that teaching assistants, adjuncts, visiting professors, retired professors, and nonacademic deans are not subject to a rule that affect "faculty."

e. A limiting definition that ensures that a typewritten name does not satisfy the requirement for a "signed writing."

f. A full or stipulative definition that ensures that only a handwritten signature satisfies the requirement for a "signed writing."

Chapter 15

TERMS CREATING LEGAL
CONSEQUENCES

This chapter is about terms creating legal consequences. Few words that drafters use have any true magic to them. Usually, the drafter can choose from among a wide variety of words to produce identical results. Terms of art, document-defined terms, and terms creating specific legal consequences are, however, exceptions to the general rule.

A. THE IMPORTANCE OF THESE TERMS

The primary function of a drafted document is to create legal consequences. The legal consequence of a contract for the sale of the sloop *El Verde Gallo* is that the current owner of the boat, the seller, is now obligated to transfer title and possession to the buyer, who is entitled to invoke the power of the sovereign, acting through its courts and law enforcement officials, to compel the seller to do this. In other words, the contract imposes a duty on the seller and creates a corresponding right for the buyer.

Most of the words in a drafted document relate to the substance of the legal consequence—the identity of the boat, the price, delivery, warranties as to fitness, and the like. But how is the reader to know that the contract created a duty and a right, rather than mere discretionary authority to sell and buy? These legal consequences are significantly different. The words that create these different legal consequences, though few in comparison with the words of substance, are of critical importance.

B.   IDENTIFYING AND CREATING THE APPROPRIATE LEGAL CONSEQUENCES

Providing the proper legal consequences in a drafted document is a three-step procedure. First, the drafter must fully understand the client's specific desires and broader objectives. Second, the drafter must then match those desires and objectives with the appropriate legal consequences. Third, the drafter must choose the appropriate words to express those consequences.

For example, at the initial interview, the drafter may discover that the client wants a contract to purchase certain goods but that the client probably wants these goods only if they can be delivered on or before June 1, 2010. After that date, the client may be able to obtain the goods from another source and will want to have the option of canceling the contract. The drafter would recognize that delivery on or before June 1, 2010, should be a condition of the client's duty to accept and pay for the goods. But the drafter would also recognize that the legal consequence that should flow from the failure of this condition is that the client will have the power or authority to cancel the contract. The drafter would then draft a provision expressing these client desires, as follows:

> *If Seller fails to deliver on or before June 1, 2010, Buyer **may** cancel the contract.*

In sum, the drafter has ascertained what the client wants, has translated that into a recognized legal consequence, and has used the proper words ("if" and "may") to create those legal consequences, thus meeting the client's desires. This is what drafting is all about.

C.   THE LACK OF UNIFORMITY

Despite the importance of legal consequences and the significance of the differences between them, the courts and legal drafting authorities enjoy considerable disagreement over exactly what words should be used to create them.

For example, the style manual of the Office of the Federal Register states, "Use of 'shall' as an auxiliary verb is the most forceful way of indicating an obligation to act."

But one study located over 1,100 cases litigating the meaning of this term. "Shall" has been construed as meaning "may," as meaning "must," and as meaning something in between. Many drafters thus shun the term altogether.

Another widely respected statutory drafting organization states one of its rules as follows:

(a) A duty, obligation, requirement, or condition precedent is best expressed by "shall" or "must":

(1) Use "shall" if the verb it qualifies is in the active voice. Example: "The aggrieved party 'shall file' (active verb in active voice) the application."

(2) Use "must" if the verb it qualifies is an inactive verb or an active verb in the passive voice. Examples: "The applicant 'must be' (inactive verb) an adult." "Any prior convictions 'must be set forth' (active verb in passive voice) in the application."

One is troubled by the intellectual confusion evidenced by this rule. "Duty" and "condition" represent radically different legal consequences, yet this rule says they are governed by the same linguistic convention. Moreover, "obligation" and "requirement" are loose, colloquial terms that could represent an intent to impose a duty or an intent to impose a condition—which makes them both ambiguous and redundant of the other terms used in the rule. Moreover, judging from the substance of what is being said, all three of the examples, involve conditions, not duties. And in this regard, the "shall" example could create enormous confusion if the same document later uses the term where the intent was probably to create a duty. For example, "The Parole Board shall approve or deny the application within 10 days." Is the applicant whose application has not been acted on within that period entitled to a writ of mandamus because this is a breached duty? Or is a timely resolution merely a condition of an efficacious order, giving the applicant grounds for getting the order set aside if the application is denied?

Similar problems exist with respect to "may." Often, the same court will find it to be permissive in one statute, but mandatory in another. As with "shall" and "must," the organization referred to above also has a confusing and intellectually obscure rule about the use of "may not" and "must not" in expressing what it calls "prohibitions," which, judging from the examples given, could refer either to a denial of discretionary authority to act or the imposition of a negative condition.

Legislative drafters also use several approaches in writing criminal statutes, which generally involve duties to refrain from acting in particular ways. These include:

No person shall . . . .

A person shall not . . . .

A person who . . . is guilty of . . . .

It is unlawful to . . . .

A person may not . . . .

In the face of this diversity, the legal drafter should choose terms that are both lexicographically sound and enjoy the widest usage. The dean of American legal drafting, the late Reed Dickerson, developed and vigorously defended a set of conventions meeting those criteria. An expanded version, also dealing with legal consequences he did not specifically address, follows.

D. THE SUGGESTED CONVENTIONS

1. Duties

A duty consists of a legally enforceable obligation to do or refrain from doing certain things. The breach of a statutory duty subjects the breaching party to some kind of sanction—a fine, incarceration, disqualification, a cease and desist order, or something else. The nonperformance of a contractual duty makes the breaching party liable in damages to the other party or, alternatively, subject to a decree of specific performance; it may also excuse the other party's performance, temporarily or permanently.

a. Statutory Duties. "Shall" and "shall not" are the operative words of civil obligation and should be used in legislation to create duties to act or refrain from acting. These words express what legal positivists call the "command of the sovereign."

Sec. 34 (a). The owner of an animal classified as "dangerous" **shall** *keep that animal in a wire mesh enclosure* *as defined in subsection 34(q) and **shall not** allow that animal outside its enclosure unless it is on a leash capable of restraining it or is being transported in a secure cage.*

This is the proper use of "shall" and "shall not."

Unfortunately, one of the reasons "shall" is in such disrepute is that drafters use it for too many other purposes. When "shall" is used other than to issue a command, it is called a "false imperative." For example, definitions often provide:

*"Vehicle" **shall** mean....*

The drafter, however, is not commanding that the term be defined in that fashion. The intent, rather, is to give the word that meaning. Definitions involve their own set of conventions, discussed in Chapter 14. Similarly, contracts often provide:

*This option **shall** expire at noon on March 1, 2004.*

Again, the drafter is not commanding the option to expire on that date. Rather, the drafter's intent is to create that legal consequence directly. Words other than "shall" are appropriate for doing that.

Contracts and statutes also often use the duty-creating word "shall" erroneously to create rights, other duties, or discretionary authority to act.

*The tenant **shall** have the right to immediate occupancy of the premises.*

*Buyer **shall** have the duty to make payment within 10 days of delivery.*

*The union **shall** have the authority to initiate grievances in its own name.*

Since the term "shall" means "has a duty," then these provisions say that the tenant has a duty to have the right, that the Buyer has a duty to have the duty, and the union has a duty to have the authority.

Despite Reed Dickerson's influential endorsement of "shall" as the proper term for creating duties, a minority of drafters still favor "must," exclusively or in combination with "shall," depending on the syntax of the sentence, as in the rule discussed earlier. The primary drawback of this convention is that it disqualifies the word "must" from being used to create conditions, thus forcing drafters to find yet another word or phrase to accomplish that legal consequence.

b.   Privately Created Duties. Although "shall" and "shall not" are used most often in legislative drafting, drafters also use them frequently in private law documents when one entity is essentially commanding another entity to do or refrain from doing something. A party creating a trust, for example, is imposing duties on the trustee.

> *Trustee **shall** distribute the earned income from the trust in the manner provided in section 8(d).*

Private law documents also use "will" to create duties. The term "shall" is preferable because "will" is also used to refer to events that will occur "in the future"—after execution of the contract or other private law document. What is essential however, is that the drafter pick one term, "shall" or "will," to create a duty and use it consistently throughout.

2.   Negation of Duties

If the existing legal relationship between the parties involves an express or implied duty on the part of one of them, then another drafted document might operate to negate that duty. The legal consequence, in other words, is to eliminate a pre-existing legal consequence. Use "is not required to" to negate the existence of a duty, of either the statutory or contractual variety. For example, if a statute imposes a general reporting duty and the administrative agency is also given authority to waive that requirement, an agency regulation might read as follows:

> *A source **is not required to** file annual discharge reports under section 8–009.1(b) of the Clean Water Act if the amount of pollutant discharge is less than ...*

Or suppose that a general common law rule requires employees to perform reasonable overtime work when requested. An employment contract might negate or limit that duty, as follows:

> *Employee **is not required to** perform any overtime work on that employee's day of religious observance (such as*

Saturday or Sunday) unless Employer is unable to use other employees without these religious convictions to do the work on those days.

Similarly, a statute or contract may first create a broad duty and then immediately limit its scope.

*Landlord shall maintain the premises in a habitable condition, but Landlord **is not required to** bear the expense of correcting habitability defects that have been created by Tenant's own use or abuse of the premises.*

This states the general duty and then a limitation on the scope of that duty.

The negation of a duty can also be expressed in terms of an exception, discussed below, although that approach is not favored for stylistic reasons.

3. Rights

Rights are the converse of duties. A rights-possessor is the party to whom the duty is owed. The right entitles that party to invoke the power of the state in the enforcement of the duty, whether the duty is of a statutory or contractual nature, and the state may often invoke the right on behalf of the rights-holder. Use "is entitled to" to create a right to do something or refrain from doing something.

*The prevailing party in litigation under this contract **is entitled to** recover attorney's fees and expenses from the other party [and also implicitly creating a duty to pay].*

*A registered voter **is entitled to** review the County Election Board's roster of eligible voters [and also implicitly creating a duty to make the roster available].*

The legal consequence of those two examples could also be created by imposing the duty directly, thus making the right implicit. Many times, conceptualizing the consequence in terms of a duty makes more sense than conceptualizing it in terms of a right. It would be counterintuitive, for example, to conceptualize payment of the sales price in terms of the buyer's right to receive the payment.

Finally, what many drafters attempt to treat as a right is often better conceptualized in terms of a privilege or the creation of a discretionary authority to act. Examples of this are given in the discussion of privileges, below. This distinction may be fading and many drafters take the position that one may use either "may" or "is entitled to" to create both rights and privileges. If one adopts that view, one should choose one formulation and use it consistently throughout the document.

4. Negation of Rights

A legal relationship between the parties may involve the possession of a right by one of the parties, created by the common law, a statute, a prior private law document, or even the existing document. A later document or provision might then operate to limit or extinguish that right. Use "is not entitled to" to limit or negate the preexisting right. Suppose, for example, that the state's landlord-tenant statute generally requires reasonable notice before eviction, but allows a lease to abrogate that right in some situations. A provision in the lease might read as follows:

> *In case of an eviction under the terms of this paragraph, Tenant **is not entitled to** any prior notice.*

Similarly, a document may create a broad right and then immediately limit or qualify it.

> *Buyer **is entitled to** [creating the right] require Seller to open for inspection and reseal shipping cartons when they arrive at the Port Authority, but Buyer **is not entitled to** [qualifying that right] require Seller to open any cartons that have been shipped under seal from the Port of Canton.*

Alternatively, this could be conceptualized and expressed in terms of an exception to the general duty, "... all cartons ... except ...."

5. Surrendering Rights or Causes of Action— Waiver and Releases

A statute may create a right, but also provide for the forfeiture of that right in some situations. A person may have a statutory or contractual right, but be willing to give it up for some reason. Or, the law may have created a duty that has been breached; a right has been violated and a cause of action now exists, but the parties want to settle. These arrangements involve extremely important legal consequences to both parties and they must be worded with care.

When dealing with the forfeiture of rights, the operative term is nearly always "waives."

By requesting an administrative review of the claim, an aggrieved party **waives** *the right to seek immediate judicial review.*

In consideration of Buyer's payment of an additional $10,000, Seller **waives** *its right to charge a retail sale origination fee for goods sold in California.*

When litigation is threatened or in progress, the parties often enter into a settlement agreement. The wording of these agreements varies. One approach focuses on the asserted claim the potential plaintiff is giving up, an approach that shields the potential defendant of any implication of an admission of wrongdoing. This approach favors the word "waives." Another approach shifts the focus onto the putative wrongdoer, by emphasizing that the liability this person is avoiding is through the beneficence of the would-be plaintiff. This approach favors the word "releases." Obviously, the defense bar prefers the first approach and the plaintiff's bar prefers the second. The difference, however, is more cosmetic than real, and some settlement agreements use both words to accomplish this legal consequence.

In return for $1,000, Jane Smith **waives** *her rights under the Workplace Safety Act and* **releases** *the Blunder Corporation from any liability that it might have for existing violations of the Act.*

6. Privileges

A privilege creates a discretionary authority to act. Use "may" to create a privilege.

A privilege differs from a right in that the other party has no corresponding duty other than honoring or accepting the choice made—shipping by rail or terminating the lease. Even if the effect on someone else is merely to refrain from interfering with the act or from imposing some detriment on the actor, that should be expressed in terms of "right" or "duty." For example, the privilege against self-incrimination is more properly thought of as a right we have, with the government having a duty not to beat confessions out of us and to not treat silence as an admission of guilt.

On the other hand, the only effect that the existence of a privilege has on others is that they are legally bound to accept or be bound by the actor's choice.

> *Seller **may** ship by air, truck, or rail.*

This simply means that if the seller ships by one of these methods, the buyer's duty to pay for the goods, which has been created separately, comes into play. The buyer is bound by the seller's choice in this regard.

A contract or statute may also give an individual the discretionary authority to create, unilaterally, a direct legal consequence.

> *Either party **may** cancel this contract by giving notice in advance by certified mail.*

If either party does that, then the contract comes to an end, whether the other party likes it or not. In other words, the exercise of this privilege cancels or terminates the other party's rights under the contract, which is why the converse of a privilege is said to be a "no-right." If the seller cancels, the buyer has no right to continue to insist on performance under the contract.

Those are the only legitimate uses of privilege. Something may be both a right and a privilege.

> *Tenant **will** pay $550 rent on the first of every month [creating a Tenant duty to pay and an implied landlord right to obtain payment, the breach of which would give rise to an action for damages] and Landlord **may** immediately terminate the lease upon non-payment within 10 days after a payment is due [also giving Landlord discretionary authority to create that legal consequence].*

7. Negation of Privileges

If a privilege would otherwise exist, a legal consequence of a particular provision might be to negate that privilege. Use "may not" to deny or limit the existence of a pre-existing discretionary authority to act. Assume that under the law of agency a landlord's resident manager would have the presumed authority to alter the terms of the lease and the effect would be that the landlord is bound by the modification. To negate that privilege, the lease might provide:

*Landlord's resident manager **may not** alter the terms of this agreement without the express written approval of Landlord.*

8. Immunity

An immunity exempts the immunity-bearer from liabilities that would otherwise attach. To create an immunity, either use the term "immune" (more commonly done in statutes) or express the legal consequence directly (the usual contract approach).

*Officers acting under the provisions of this Act are **immune** from criminal prosecution and civil liability.*

*Tenant **is not responsible for** any damage to the premises caused by third-party invitees of the Landlord.*

9. Conditions

a. Definition and Types. A condition is something that must be satisfied before some other legal consequence attaches. Express conditions are the mechanisms that control how a transaction progresses. Non-satisfaction of a condition simply means that the legal consequence does not come to pass. A condition thus differs from a duty, in that the party charged with satisfying a condition is not liable in damages for a failure to do so. A constructive condition has both promissory and conditional aspects, as in:

*Buyer **will** [or shall] pay for the goods prior to delivery.*

What this means is that Buyer has an express duty to pay, the breach of which will result in liability. But payment also appears to be a constructive condition of the seller's duty to make delivery.

Similarly, something may be both an express condition and a duty.

*Builder **will** [or shall] install plumbing pipes of the Reading brand [creating a duty]. If Builder fails to install Reading Pipes, Owner's obligations under this contract, including the obligation to pay, are suspended until the defect is cured and if they are not cured within a reasonable time, Owner may terminate the contract and is relieved of all duty, express or implied, to compensate Builder [also making this an express condition].*

There are several types of conditions. A condition may relate to the conduct of the parties. A seller, for example, may have no duty to ship the goods until the buyer has paid in full. Or a condition may relate to external events. These events are sometimes referred to as "contingencies." Thus, a seller may have no duty to ship until an embargo ends.

In most contract negotiations, one party will seek to include many conditions, especially conditions to closing or another event when they must part with consideration, and the other only a few. For example, in a purchase and sale agreement, the seller will try to limit the conditions to closing to as few *objective* conditions as possible, such as any needed third party approvals and the lack of any prohibitory injunction or other adverse ruling by governing bodies. By doing so, the seller is seeking to lock the buyer into the deal.

The buyer, on the other hand, will want to build in as many conditions, and to keep these conditions as *subjective*, and dependent upon the buyer's own judgment, as possible. By doing so, the buyer can more easily walk away if due diligence reveals that things are other than as expected, or enjoy the opportunity to later renegotiate terms in exchange for a waiver of the condition. For example, buyers may seek to include as a condition that its due diligence will conclude with satisfactory results (as judged by the buyer in its sole discretion). This sort of condition can also be framed as "lack of material adverse change" condition to closing. Pay careful attention to what "lack of material adverse change" means, and who determines whether the condition has been met. Buyers, keep it as subjective as possible and attempt to maintain control over the determination that the condition has been met. Sellers, keep it as objective as possible. Also consider including a materiality threshold to define a material adverse change.

Conditions must be carefully drafted and integrated into the rest of the contract. First, you must take care to draft the condition so its terms are clear. Conditions generally trigger duties ("shall" clauses) or privileges ("may" clauses). The reader must be able to determine when the condition is satisfied and, if not, what consequences follow. Word choice is key.

Another common condition is that of one party obtaining financing and final written approval by all internal and external entities with any jurisdiction over the transaction. Again, the buyer is motivated by two desires: (a) the ability to back out of the deal if it is no longer interested in proceeding for whatever reason, and (b) the ability to threaten to back out in order to gain more favorable terms.

Consider the benefits of linking your client's material duties to the condition that the other party use its best reasonable efforts to perform either all or an enumerated list of duties under the contract. This is especially worthwhile in the case of parties with unequal economic or bargaining power in which the weaker party's success is dependent upon the other party's performance. In those circumstances, a best reasonable efforts clause is to the weaker party's advantage. Examples include construction agreements, distribution agreements, and intellectual property agreements.

A duty to use "best efforts" in contract cases usually arises in one of three ways. First, the contract itself may specifically require that the promisor put forth his or her "best efforts." Second, the contract language might specify a result, and this may be interpreted as imposing a duty of best efforts. Finally, a court may impose a duty of best efforts based simply on the facts and circumstances surrounding a contract.

There appears to be no firm rule as to what constitutes adequate or sufficient best efforts. In general, each case turns on its particular facts. Some cases suggest that best efforts requires the same amount of effort under a contract as that expended under other, similar contracts where the quality of effort has not been questioned. Others imply that the promisor should merely avoid manifestly harmful conduct. The duty to act "reasonably", like a duty to employ "best efforts", or to act in "good faith," is not to reducible to a fixed formula—unless the contract itself provides the formula or an objective measure.

A duty of best efforts is separate and distinct from the duty of good faith. Good faith is a standard with a moral component that has honesty and fairness at its core, and that is imposed on every party to a contract. The best efforts standard focuses on diligence in performance or attempted performance.

Case law demonstrates that inclusion of a "best efforts" clause may give rise to an almost fiduciary level duty on the part of the burdened party. Even without a best efforts provision, one may be implied into an agreement like an exclusive license. Inclusion of a "best efforts" clause should cause some concern unless the contract defines "best efforts" and provides an objective measure (such as dollars or time spent) for when the standard is met. The prudent approach is to include a standard for performance (e.g., best efforts) and then define the standard, including any limitations intended (e.g., contractor shall only be required to expend $50,000 in attempt to . . .).

Conditions can be either subsequent or precedent. A condition precedent must be satisfied for the legal consequence to arise. The legal consequence is often the creation of a duty, as in the above examples. The party to whom the duty is owed, the right-holder, generally has the burden of proving a condition precedent. A condition subsequent operates to terminate an existing legal consequence, again usually a duty. The party possessing the duty generally has the burden of proving a condition subsequent. Most conditions can be expressed as either precedent or subsequent. But given the difference in the allocation of the burden of proof, the difference can be significant. A provision favoring the buyer could be worded as follows:

> *Buyer will purchase the cotton contained on the ship Lady Adams, but **only if** this ship arrives at Nantucket Roads on or before July 14, 2009. Otherwise,. . . .*

A provision favoring the seller could be worded as follows:

> *Buyer will purchase the cotton contained on the ship Lady Adams unless this ship arrives at Nantucket Roads on or after July 15, 2009.*

If the arrival time of the *Lady Adams* cannot be proved conclusively either way, then the buyer wins under the first provision and the seller wins under the second.

You must confront the fact that parties and courts often ignore or waive conditions. Contracts are often full of clauses providing that a party's failure to act or enforce a right shall not be deemed to be a waiver of that right, and that any waiver of a current right shall not be a waiver of any other right or a future incidence of the same right. The litany of the non-waivable continues: time is of the essence; non-severability; no amendment or waiver by conduct; All amendments and waivers must be in writing; recitations that both parties have been represented by counsel, or at least had the opportunity to consult with counsel, have read the agreement and understand it.

All these provisions are attempts by the parties to avoid having a court later refuse to enforce a condition by finding that it was waived by conduct, was unconscionable, would otherwise lead to a forfeiture, and the like. A determined court can often find some way to excuse a failed condition should it choose to do so, and can usually do so in a ruling that is so fact-based that it is largely immune on appeal. (Why are fact-based decisions more immune on appeal than purely legal determinations? Consider the applicable standard of review, generally clearly erroneous (factual findings) or *de novo* (legal conclusions)). The drafter can best guard against this result by (a) drafting the consequences of failure of a condition into the condition, not just leaving it to the default and remedy provisions of the agreement; (b) employing good boilerplate to document the parties' intention that all the terms of the document be strictly construed; (c) explicitly stating the reason that the condition was included; and (d) that the condition was a fundamental inducement for one or more of the parties to enter into the transaction.

b.   Terminology. Conditions must be carefully drafted and integrated into the rest of the contract. First, you must take care to draft the condition so its terms are clear. Conditions generally trigger duties ("shall" clauses) or rights ("is entitled to" clauses). The reader must be able to determine when the condition is satisfied and, if not, what consequences follow. Word choice is key. If the condition is in the form of someone's conduct, use "must" or "if." Use "must" when satisfaction or non-satisfaction of the condition affects the actor's entitlement to something.

> *Buyer* **must** *give notice of intent to cancel by no later than the 30th day prior to the anniversary date of this contract.*

Use "if" when satisfaction or non-satisfaction of the condition triggers a duty on the other party.

If Buyer discovers and reports defects in the goods within 10 days after delivery, Seller will immediately replace the goods.

When a condition requires the occurrence of an external event to trigger the duties of one or more of the parties, use "if," "when," or "after."

If the United States lifts the trade embargo with Japan before December 7, 2004, Seller will deliver six carloads of . . . .

Use "when" or "after" if the occurrence is relatively certain, but the timing is not.

When the bank submits its credit report, Seller will immediately arrange for . . . .

After receiving the EEOC notice of a right to sue, the charging party must . . . .

Term	Use
Shall	Use "shall" to create a duty.
Will	"Will" may be used to create a duty but "shall" is preferable.
Must	Use "must" to create a condition precedent.
May	Use "may" to create a privilege or an option. Use "may not" to negate a privilege.
Entitled	Use "is entitled to" to create a right. Use "is not entitled to" to negate a right.
Waive	Use "waive" to indicate a forfeiture of a right.
If	Use "if" when satisfaction or non-satisfaction of a condition triggers a duty.

E. REPRESENTATIONS, WARRANTIES, RELEAS-
ES, GUARANTIES, AND INDEMNITIES

Contracts frequently use representations, warranties, guaranties, and indemnities. Each is a different type of provision, and it is important to select the proper type to generate the proper legal effect. Perhaps more than any other set of provisions, those described in this chapter highlight the litigation or default planning aspects of transactional practice and contract drafting. Each of these provisions gives rise to a particular set of causes of action in the event of breach or error.

In particular, representations, warranties, guaranties, and indemnities are interrelated and reinforce each other. A represented fact will induce a party to enter into negotiation and documentation of a transaction. If it is false, a misrepresentation action will support recession or damages. That representation will likely be converted into a warranty as to that fact that may survive closing. The surviving warranty provides a breach of warranty action that can support an award of damages. Finally, to the extent that the non-warranting party has been damaged by the breached or incorrect warranty, an indemnity or a guaranty creates a route for damage recovery.

Unlike the way you were probably taught to analyze a set of facts for tort, contract, or property claims (element by element with damages or other remedies last), when thinking about these sorts of clauses as a drafter, you should approach the problem from the desired *remedy* first. For example, if certain facts are misstated, what remedy do you wish to seek? Possibilities include rescission pre-closing, rescission post-closing, or consequential or liquidated damages from the other party or from a credit-worthy third party. Then select the type of provisions that will produce a cause of action for your client that is ripe when needed, lies against the appropriate defendant, and provides the desired remedy.

1. General Rules and Techniques: Typical Representations and Warranties

Each of the general rules regarding representations and warranties can be altered by language of the contract itself, so none can be drafted or interpreted in a vacuum.

Typical representations and warranties include (i) the party is duly organized, in good standing, and authorized to enter in the transaction, (ii) the transaction is not a breach of any other agreement and does not violate the law, (iii) a seller or lessor has good title to all assets being sold or leased, and those assets are free of liens and encumbrances, and (iv) all material facts have been disclosed. Each is often phrased as "except as disclosed on schedule X to this agreement, [representation or warranty]"—an example of a "carveout." As noted above, this structure makes the provision more than just a representation or warranty—it becomes a due diligence tool that shifts the burden of finding and discussing exceptions to the statement to the representing and warranting party. Representations and warranties of this type are often combined with a covenant to defend against claims that are adverse to any of the representations and warranties, and an indemnification (see next section) against losses caused by inaccurate representations or warranties.

2. The UCC Approach

In a sale of goods contract covered by the Uniform Commercial Code, however, any "affirmation of fact or promise made by the seller to the buyer which relates to the goods and becomes part of the basis of the bargain creates an express warranty that the goods shall conform to the affirmation or promise." U.C.C. § 2–313. This approach blurs the distinction between classic definitions and distinctions between representations, warranties, covenants, and even conditions.

An important method of reducing the scope of a representation or warranty, and any covenant or indemnity linked to it, is a knowledge limitation. In light of the prior paragraph, it bears revisiting. For example, "the representations and warranties of section X below are limited to facts of which a, b, or c [people] have actual knowledge on the date of this agreement." This is a fair limitation, as long as the appropriate persons are specified: those who would naturally have the knowledge sought. Do not stop at the senior executive level—as knowledge there is generalized—but delve down to cover the knowledge of middle management and even the operations level of a business, as appropriate. Carveouts, e.g., "except as listed on schedule 2.4," and materiality thresholds—also called "baskets"—e.g., "except that Seller may dispose of inventory in the ordinary course of its business consistent with past practice," can also be used to limit the scope of a provision.

3. Representations

Classically, a representation is a statement of presently existing facts that is intended to induce reliance and action by a party, such as entering into a contract. An incorrect representation will support an action for rescission or damages sounding in contract (and tort, if fraud is present).

Unless otherwise specified, the representation speaks as of the execution of the document in which it is contained. The cause of action is, therefore, generally ripe as of that time, which may be pre-closing. Pre-closing representations may terminate at closing by operation of law unless the contract specifies that they survive the closing. Check governing law in your jurisdiction on this point and address the matter specifically in the contract with a survival or cancellation clause.

Representations are meant to give one party some reassurance that the other party's statements of fact are true. In this sense, they shift the risk that a stated fact is untrue to the representing party. Typical subjects for representations include the accuracy of financial statements; due formation and compliance with laws; and the existence of adverse claims, breached or defaulted contracts, liens, encumbrances, and legal actions.

Representations are also used to shift the burden and cost of investigation and disclosure in the due diligence process. For example, assume that your client wishes to purchase a business but wants to know if there are any claims or lawsuits against the business. You and your client could search relevant court records, perhaps nationwide. You could also dig through all of the business records looking for evidence of claims. These are burdensome and expensive activities. Alternatively, you could insert a representation into the purchase agreement in which the seller states that, except as disclosed on an attached schedule, no claims or lawsuits have been asserted against the company. This sort of blanket statement is known as a flat or unqualified representation. It shifts the burden of investigation and disclosure back to where it belongs, on the seller, which is the entity that is in the position of the least cost, the provider of the information.

Typically, the seller's counsel would respond with the suggestion that the representation be qualified, often by narrowing it to relate to claims or lawsuits of a certain type or over a certain size (a "materiality threshold") or known to certain specific individuals (a "knowledge limitation"). Depending on the circumstances, this may be acceptable to your client. If so, make sure that either limitation is not overbroad. Materiality thresholds should be set at levels that sound appropriate alarms, but filter out the noise generated by immaterial claims. Knowledge limitations should specify persons who are likely to know the *details* involved; rarely will it be sufficient to limit knowledge to that of the uppermost tier of management. In this way, the burden of necessary investigation and disclosure can appropriately be shifted to the sellers.

The inclusion of a knowledge qualifier has the effect of shifting the representations from those of the facts themselves to *awareness* of the facts. A party may justify its need to include a knowledge qualifier by arguing that it should not be required to make an assertion that it does not know to be the truth. If a party has incomplete knowledge, or if the truth of a fact is fairly immaterial and difficult or costly to obtain, a knowledge qualifier may be appropriate. On the other hand, if the fact is based upon something within the party's control or is one that the other party wishes to rely upon in deciding whether to proceed with the transaction, a knowledge limitation is inappropriate.

Representations are generally drafted in the form:

[Buyer, Seller, other defined term] represents [representation carefully stated as to scope and substance].

Representations should almost always be drafted in the present or past tense, not the future tense, to prevent them from being interpreted as covenants.

A representation is often combined with a warranty, in which case the form is:

[Buyer, Seller, other defined term] represents and warrants [representation and warranty carefully stated as to scope and substance].

This combination ensures that a cause of action will lie post-closing if the representation has terminated as of closing but the warranty survives or as part of an overall "belt and suspenders" approach.

4. Warranties

Classically, a warranty is a statement made about certain facts whereby the warrantor promises to ensure that those facts are as stated. A breached or incorrect warranty will support an action for damages sounding in contract, and the cause of action is ripe as of the closing of the transaction and survives closing unless the contract provides otherwise or, in the case of traditional real estate law, it is not reflected in the deed as well as the purchase agreement. Since the law is not uniform with regard to survival, the best practice is for the contract to explicitly address the issue.

Warranties are generally drafted in the form:

[Buyer, Seller, other defined term] warrants that as of [date or dates, certain or referent] [warranted facts carefully stated as to scope and substance].

Like representations, they should almost always be drafted in the present or past tense, not the future tense, to prevent them from being interpreted as covenants.

5. Guaranties and Indemnities

A guarantor is one who promises that, if another party does not perform a duty, the guarantor will.

The word "guarantee," when used in the colloquial sense of a warranty (on your microwave oven, for example) has one spelling, and "guaranty," when used in its formal legal meaning (a promise to perform a third party's obligation) has a different spelling. *There should be no double-e guaranties in your contracts!*

Remember that a guaranty is only as good as the guarantor.

6. Indemnities

An indemnity is a collateral contractual obligation where one party, the indemnitor, engages to hold another, the indemnitee, harmless from losses to third parties. A common indemnity is one that covers any losses from a breach or inaccuracy of any representation or warranty in the agreement. The indemnitor need not be the other party to the contract. Like guaranties, indemnities are only as good as the indemnitor.

The basic issues that arise with indemnities are related to scope. Scope of indemnification is defined or limited by (i) the time period during which claims can be asserted, (ii) the time period during which the event underlying the claim occurred, (iii) the minimum and maximum amount of any claim or of all claims in the aggregate, or over a particular period of time, (iv) the damages covered (actual pecuniary loss to third parties, consequential damages, punitive damages, liquidated damages), and (v) the mechanism for presenting claims and solving disputed claims.

7. Releases

A release of a right, claim, or privilege is a cancellation of the right to assert a right, claim, or privilege. A similar result may be achieved by assignment of the claim, which can have other different effects that are useful in creatively structuring a transaction, such as maintaining the subordinate priority of other claims or one party's judgment-proof status.

8. Conclusion—Cautionary Procedures

At the outset, consider including a master provision that eliminates or disclaims as far as legally possible, all express or implied representations, warranties, indemnities, and releases except as expressly provided in the contract. This is an attempt to wipe the slate clean of common law and statutory implied provisions such as the UCC's warranty of

merchantability or fitness for intended use. *But see* U.C.C.
§§ 2–316(1) (disclaimers of express warranties in conflict
with apparent warranty will be inoperative if that construction is unreasonable); 2–316(2), (3) (disclaimer of implied
warranties with specific disclaimers, general disclaimers,
buyer inspections, and course of performance). A disclaimer
of warranties may be subject to different, peculiar drafting
requirements that seem to indicate hostility to overreaching
disclaimers and releases obtained by economically dominant
parties. Include a merger or integration clause to trigger the
parol evidence rule to exclude evidence of any statements
that could be construed as agreements, representations, warranties, covenants, etc., made during negotiations or earlier
rounds of documentation.

The use of the wrong type of provision can result in the
provision working in unintended ways, limiting a party's
rights, or giving rise to unintended consequences. For example, since warranties concern the present existence of facts,
the characterization of a covenant as a representation or
warranty may prevent the covenant from applying to a
future breach of the obligation. Likewise, the characterization of a covenant as a representation or warranty may
create fraud or misrepresentation tort liability, including
potential punitive damages, for the promisor's breach, but
that breach should only be a contract claim (limiting damages to compensatory ones in most jurisdictions), if a true
covenant is used.

Claims of breach or inaccuracy accrue and statutes of
limitations run at different times depending upon the type of
provision used. A claim for misrepresentation can arise at
the time of signing a purchase and sale or other agreement.
A breach of warranty claim generally arises at the time of
the closing or sale. A breach of covenant claim accrues when
the party does not honor the covenant, which may be in the
distant, post-closing future.

Do not confuse a letter of credit with a guaranty. A
letter of credit establishes a separate, direct, primary obligation between the issuer to the beneficiary. A guaranty
creates an obligation secondary to that of the primary obligor. A guarantor has subrogation and reimbursement rights
against the primary obligor, while an issuer of a letter of

credit has only reimbursement rights and whatever security interest it negotiated. The beneficiary of a letter of credit must comply strictly with the terms of the letter of credit, and the issuer has few defenses to payment. This may not be the case with a guaranty and a guarantor.

Failing to recognize a guaranty as a guaranty may lead to failing to include a waiver of the guarantor's suretyship defenses, exoneration rights, notice, presentment, exhaustion of claims against the primary obligor, or unique state law provisions, such as the anti-deficiency or "one form of action" statutes of many Western states. Anti-deficiency statutes typically provide that a lender secured by a lien on real property may only look to that property to satisfy the debt upon default. *See, e.g.* CAL. CIV. PROC. CODE § 580b (anti-deficiency provision applicable to so-called seller-takeback financing for one-to-four unit dwelling occupied by borrower). "One form of Action" or "One Action Rule" laws limit a lender to first proceeding judicially against the collateral in a judicial foreclosure action and then, in that same action, obtaining a deficiency judgment against the borrower *or* electing to waive the result to seek a deficiency judgment by proceeding non-judicially against the collateral, such or by a deed of trust. *See, e.g.,* CAL. CIV. PROC. CODE § 726. Pro-debtor laws of this sort were enacted in many Western states, where land and homes were financed by Eastern banks and financial institutions. Local counsel can be invaluable in identifying issues like this.

If an indemnity is used to cover a warranty claim, the indemnitee may not have a claim if the indemnitor can limit its liability to true indemnitor liability. This includes only reimbursement of the indemnitee for its liabilities to third persons. Self-sustained and remedied damages are not included. This limitation can be drafted around in many jurisdictions by expressly including otherwise excluded damages.

An indemnity against liability becomes collectible immediately when the indemnitee become liable to a third person. An indemnity against anything else (such as claims or damages) becomes collectible only after the indemnitee has paid the third person.

Finally, an indemnity may not be effective if the indemnitee's own negligence contributed to its obligation to a third party. Generally, an indemnitee can recover in these circumstances only if the indemnity expressly provides for recovery under those circumstances. Draft carefully.

F. EXCEPTIONS

Drafted documents often create exceptions to or limitations on the rights, duties, privileges, and immunities that they otherwise create. In the past, these exceptions were often worded in terms of "provided further, that no ...." Modern drafters should attempt to avoid these archaic provisos, although their usage is widespread. Some use "except that" language for simple exceptions.

> *The Executor may disburse the remainder of the estate as her discretion dictates,* **except that** *she may distribute no funds to any political party.*

Although "unless" is a potentially ambiguous term, some drafters use it to express exceptions.

> **Unless** *expressly bequeathed to a specific individual under the terms of this will or a written and attached memorandum, my estate goes to....*

For longer and more complicated exceptions, the approach can be even more direct.

> *This section does not apply to (1)....; (2)....; and (14) ....*

Exceptions can also be conceptualized as and worded in terms of conditions:

> *Seller will continue to deliver buyer's monthly requirements of widgets at $10.00 per ton, but this obligation terminates if the Canadian embargo ends [creating an exception to the duty to deliver].*

> *If the wholesale price of okra goes over $1.50 per pound before the delivery date of June 30, 2010, Buyer will pay an additional.... [creating an exception to the contract duty to pay at another price level].*

G. EVENTS OF DEFAULT AND REMEDIES

In contracts courses, law students study common law rules regarding remedies, from limits on damages to the availability of specific performance and other equitable remedies. As a contract drafter, you need to plan you way into or around these legal rules to allow your client to recover as much as possible in the event of the other party's breach. Good transactional lawyers know the substantive law applicable to their transactions and then plan and structure transactions to take advantage of favorable law (*e.g.*, tax effects, validation of liquidated damages provisions, etc.) and to avoid, or "draft around," unfavorable law.

Default is a broader concept than breach of contract. The default and remedy section of a contract should begin with a listing of what actual events are "events of default." Although the enumerated events of default generally include events that would be a breach of the contract under the common law without a specific default section (for example, non-payment of rent under a real property lease) they can also include many things that would otherwise not be considered a breach, such as changed financial status as measured by financial ratios, a failure to maintain casualty insurance for collateral, and other insecurity provisions. Events of default or a declaration of default under one contract can also be a default or an event of default under another agreement, including an agreement involving a completely separate transaction and completely different parties. This is known as a "cross-default."

Events of default are selected for each transaction. Common events of default include:

- Failure to perform an obligation.
- Failure to pay monies when due.
- Failure to maintain a certain status (membership, financial condition, etc.).
- Breach or inaccuracy of a representation or warranty.
- Bankruptcy and similar insolvency-related conditions and proceedings (although these are generally unen-

forceable if the contacting party is the subject of a bankruptcy case).

- Default under another agreement.
- General insecurity of the other party.

The contract can make the occurrence of an event of default an automatic default under the contract entitling the non-defaulting party to exercise its remedies. It may require the non-defaulting party to give notice that the event of default has occurred and declare a default. The latter form gives the non-defaulting party more flexibility, but also requires more careful monitoring of the other party, especially if non-monetary defaults are involved. As a practical matter, every jurisdiction will require some form of notice of the default prior to exercise of remedy. Remember, a notice of default or termination will generally not be effective if the defaulting party is in bankruptcy before the proper notice is given of an event of default.

Many default provisions include the concept of a right to cure, or fix, the default and avoid application of the remedies provided in the contract. Different cure periods can apply to different events of default, and the contract should specify when the cure period begins to run. In drafting, one of two approaches is used to provide for cure rights. One either drafts a separate provision addressing the right to cure or builds the cure right into each event of default provision.

The provisions that establish a default are generally followed by provisions that specify (i) remedies, (ii) whether those remedies are automatic or elective on the part of the non-defaulting party, (iii) how the election of remedies, if any, is to be made and (iv) whether the remedies are mutually exclusive or cumulative. Consider the legality and enforceability of remedies as well. The most effective ones that you can imagine are often unenforceable or of limited enforceability.

The mutual foreseeability test of *Hadley v. Baxendale*, 9 Exch. 341 (Court of the Exchequer 1854), would limit liability unless the drafter used, among other provisions, a liquidated damage clause and a prevailing party attorneys' fee clause. Alternatively, the drafter could include recitals showing what damages were reasonably foreseeable by all parties.

Similar issues arise in other areas, including provisions for acceleration of payment obligations, post-judgment attorneys' fees, interest, default interest, prepayment fees, or calculation of interest based upon an actual year or a 360–day accounting year. The drafter needs to assess all applicable issues, the limiting or expanding effect of otherwise applicable law, and possible draft-arounds available to serve the client's interests.

A final note about default and remedies: when an event of default has occurred, and it is time to declare the default, the notice of default (generally in the form of a letter) should be *drafted in unequivocal language and should track the language and requirements of the contract exactly*. There is no need to be either overly kind or insulting in tone. A neutral description of the contract, the pertinent provisions, the event of default that has occurred, a declaration of the default, an election of remedies, if needed, and any demand for action will suffice. The notice of default should be transmitted exactly as specified in the contract. Failure to strictly adhere to the contractual requirements will afford the defaulting party a defense to enforcement and may allow additional time to cure and reinstate the agreement.

H.   WHEN NOT TO FOLLOW THESE CONVENTIONS

Although the above conventions enjoy wide usage and the drafting environment would be significantly improved if made universal, the courts do not always follow them when construing documents. If the drafter is in a jurisdiction particularly prone to its own idiosyncratic interpretation of words that create legal consequences, then the drafter will need to defer to the local law. This may involve using alternative terms or simply calling what is intended to be a duty a "duty," a right a "right," and so on.

> Buyer **is obligated to** . . . . *[if that is the preferred usage for creating duties].*
>
> Buyer's **duties** *under this contract are as follows:* . . . . *Seller* **has the right** *to require Buyer to* . . . . *Buyer's duty to pay the contract price on June 30, 2003,* **is expressly conditioned on** *Seller's delivery of the goods on or before that date* . . . . *Buyer* **has the power and**

authority to terminate this contract upon 10 days notice to Seller.... [stating the intended legal consequence
directly].

Tenant **must** give notice of intent to vacate at least one
month in advance. This is an express condition and
failure to give this notice results in forfeiture of the
security deposit. [Using the conventional term but also
stating its intended meaning and legal consequence].

The object is to express the intent of the parties in such
a way that the courts, when construing the document, will
give effect to that intent. Keeping the unique rules of
interpretation of that state well in mind, the drafter should
use whatever words are necessary to do that, regardless of
how artless they may seem.

Exercise 12

1. In a statute, create a duty for a person who has a
   swimming pool on the property to put a fence
   around it.

2. In a construction contract, create a duty for the
   builder complete the project by June 30, 2004.

3. In a city ordinance, create a duty on a police officer
   to not exceed the posted speed limit unless the blue
   light and siren are on.

4. In a partnership agreement, create a duty on each
   partner to not engage in any business that is in
   competition with the business of the partnership.

5. Assume that in a construction contract the builder
   can use substitute materials if the materials called
   for in the specifications are unavailable, but that is
   also customary in the industry to inform the owner
   first. Draft a provision that excuses the contractor
   from that implied duty.

6. Assume that a landlord-tenant statute gives the
   tenant the right to assign the lease, unless the lease
   agreement provides otherwise. Draft a lease provision that negates that statutory right.

7. Assume that a landlord-tenant statute makes the
   assignment of leases invalid, unless the lease agree-

ment provides otherwise. Draft a lease provision that so provides.

8. In a government environmental regulation, draft a provision that requires regulated entities to file a Form 675–r application if they want to request permission to exceed established pollution discharge limits.

9. Assume that in a supply contract the seller has to provide all of the wingdings that the buyer needs, but the parties want to agree to suspend the seller from that obligation whenever the price of carbonmetalic compound goes over $1.50 per pound. Draft a provision to accomplish that.

10. Assume that in a construction contract the parties want to provide that the contractor has a duty to obtain the building inspector's approval of the foundations and only then will the owner have the duty to make the first partial payment. Draft a provision that accomplishes this.

11. The parties want the effective date of the contract to be July 4, 2004. Draft a provision that makes it so.

Chapter 16

DOCUMENT TYPOGRAPHY AND LAYOUT

———————

The objectives of drafting are two-fold: to establish legal relationships and to state those relationships in ways readily understandable by all users of the document. Everything discussed in the previous chapters contributes to those objectives—determining client desires, careful legal and factual investigation, precise conceptualization, impeccable organization, clear and concise expression, and the other aspects of good drafting. All is lost in the end, however, if no one cares to read the document.

A. PHYSICAL APPEARANCE

Lawyers' offices are often decorated with framed 18th Century debenture bonds, written with a fine quill pen, covering from edge to edge a piece of crinkly pale-brown parchment paper of extraordinary dimensions, and authenticated with seal-embossed glob of red wax with ribbon attached. Try reading one sometime. But then look at what that lawyer's printer is spewing out. Apart from the content, the appearance is often the same—solid masses of dull, gray text.

The Plain English movement had its excesses. But one of the movement's more cogent points was that the physical appearance of drafted documents should enhance even the least literate user's understanding of the substantive content of the document. Plain English proponents thus enlisted the aid of experts in the fields of typography and layout design.

Their contribution to good drafting has been significant. The basic principles are as follows.

1. White Space

The readability of the document is enhanced by lots of white space, referring to the spaces on the page where nothing is printed. The drafter should make a conscious effort to avoid producing a document in which every square centimeter is filled with text.

2. Type Size and Font

Text should be no smaller than 12 points. Indeed, some appellate court rules require that briefs be in 14 point type, and contract drafters would be wise to emulate that rule, in at least two situations. First, if the document will be frequently referred to during the term of the agreement (and particularly if it will be used on a construction site or the shop floor), it should not be accessible only by use of a magnifying glass. Conversely, type size is not that important if the document will simply establish a legal relationship and then be filed away, usually being resurrected only if the transaction fails and litigation ensues. Second, an adequate type size is especially important in consumer-oriented documents, where easy readability may be a condition of enforceability. For example, one court held that a portion of an installment sales contract that was printed in 8 point type rather than the required 10 point type violated the Truth in Lending Act. Standard real estate contracts, which in many respects represent drafting at its worst, are often crammed into the seemingly mandatory two-page (front and back of a standard piece of paper), densely packed, tiny print format that defies reading or comprehension.

Choose a typeface that is easy to read, usually a member of the Times family. This book is written in Times New Roman. Avoid—

- Courier, which is a holdover from the days of typewritten legal documents.

- Sans serif typefaces, like Albertus Medium, are modernistic but tiresome in lengthy documents.

- Any kind of script or cursive font, even as the heading to the document, because it is difficult to read.

- Old English type or any of the goofier fonts found in a word processor.

3.   All Capitals and Underlining

Type that is set in upper and lower case is easier to read than type set in all capitals, and underlined text is a strain to the eyes. When most contracts were typewritten, all caps and underlining were the only way to set off the headings and provide emphasis to select portions of the text. Hence, one might see something like this.

T. DISCLAIMER OF WARRANTIES. Except as provided in paragraphs c, q, and r above, <u>THIS PECAN SHELLER IS SOLD WITHOUT ANY WARRANTIES, EXPRESS OR IMPLIED, INCLUDING THE WARRANTY OF MERCHANTABILITY AND OF FITNESS FOR ANY PARTICULAR USE AND ANY PRIOR REPRESENTATIONS BY SELLER, ORAL OR IN WRITING, TO THE CONTRARY ARE VOID.</u>

Today, in the absence of statutory requirements to the contrary, the better practice is to use bolded headings with a font-size two points larger than the rest of the text and bolded phrases for the critical words to satisfy conspicuousness requirements.

> **Another way to satisfy conspicuousness requirements is to put the required language in a text box like this one.**

4.   Line Length

Text designers are not of one mind about this. Some suggest that the most easily read line length is from 39 to 52 characters, while others opt for the 50 to 70 character range. Most legal documents are done on a standard 8 1/2 by 11 inch piece of paper, with one inch margins. The typeface and size affects the number of characters in a line. A line of 14 point New Times Roman text contains approximately 67 characters, while a 12 point line contains 78 characters.

Increasingly, one will see a drafted document—usually of the printed, fill-in-the-blank variety—done in newspaper-type columns. After all, newspapers are the most widely read things in America, and if it is good enough for the *New York Times*, then it is surely good enough for the orange contract between Sam's Market and John Smith. Two or three newspaper sized columns will fit on a standard piece of paper.

A columned newspaper, however, is easy to read only because journalistic paragraphs are rarely more than two or three sentences long. Imagine what a newspaper would look like if it adhered to the conventional rules of paragraphing. They would consist of long, gray, uninviting columns of text. So do most documents formatted in that fashion. On the other hand, a two-columned document on a standard piece of typing paper is less objectionable, and drafters who view line length as a major problem may want to adopt that approach. In addition, columns may be appropriate when the document, like a newspaper, contains many one-or two-sentence sections or paragraphs. These read more easily when they are in three or four short lines, rather than in a single line or two stretching across the page. Even so, columned text requires the reader to go to the bottom of the page, back to the top, and then down to the bottom again—a lot of eye muscle exercise for someone merely scanning the document.

Finally, the shorter the line of text, the shorter the tab should be—no longer than 1/2 an inch for 6 1/2 lines and 1/4 an inch for 4 inch lines.

5. Justification

Some believe that full left and right justification not only makes for a neater looking text, it also makes paragraph breaks more distinct, thus contributing to the comprehensibility of the document. And many experts believe that a fully justified text is easier to read.

Not everyone agrees with that. One source of the disagreement is the Securities and Exchange Commission; drafters of documents with that agency as an audience should take note. Although it is only a recommendation, the SEC and many practicing attorneys believe left-only justified text is easier to read, because fully justified text has uneven spacing between the words. This can be minimized by the use of short words (a desirable trait in drafting), the automatic hyphenation feature of the word processor, and standard rather than column length lines. The jury is still out on this issue. But make justification a conscious choice.

6. Line Spacing

Most typed and printed documents are single-spaced. This is actually more readable than a document that is double-spaced throughout. Some drafters, however, prefer to use a 1.2 or 1.3 spacing between lines believing this will enhance the readability of the text.

Most printed material does not double space between paragraphs. Many drafters also feel this is unnecessary in drafted documents. Others opt for the white space that the extra line between paragraphs provides.

7. Blank Spaces

Standard contracts are often printed with blank spaces for things like the date, the names of the parties, the identity of the property or goods, the price, and other terms and conditions. Unfortunately, the blank spaces are often not nearly large enough, in either length or height, for the information that must be handwritten. Indecipherability and resort to writing vertically in the narrow margins often result. The length problem can be easily dealt with. Just make sure you provide enough. However, a 12–point, single-spaced document still does not allow enough height for the handwriting of most people. And the 8–point or smaller type that is used in many commercially printed documents is simply impossible. The solution is to either use 14 point type or 1.2 spacing between the lines, or both.

B. TEXT

The text of a drafted document can be made more comprehensible in a number of ways.

1. Table of Contents

A lengthy document should contain a table of contents on the cover page. This enables the parties to find what they are looking for quickly. A table of contents may also be appropriate even in short consumer documents. The table of contents should contain all the headings and subheadings of the document, together with the page number on which they appear.

2. Numbered Pages

Even a short document should be page numbered. Usually, a simple "5" or "–5–" at the bottom of the page is sufficient. But some drafters, exercising an excess of caution in important documents and to ensure that no page is later removed, use the "Page 5 of 100 pages" convention. These documents also often provide a space for the initials of the parties on each page. It would be pretentious, however, to use these conventions on an ordinary house painting contract.

3. Numbered or Lettered Paragraph Headings

Numbered or lettered paragraph headings are the visual signposts of the document. They make it easy for the reader to find a particular provision and they give the top-to-bottom reader an indication of what the next provision is about. A document without them provides the reader with a vexatious, frustrating, and tedious reading experience.

The headings and subheadings reflect the organization that the drafter has decided upon. Indeed, an inability to produce the necessary heading and subheadings, using a proper outlining structure with respect to the numbers or letters, is a sure sign of a faulty organization.

Some drafters prefer this type of numbering format:

I. Seller's Obligations

    A. Delivery

        1. Method

        2. Time

        3. Place

    B. Installation

Others prefer to do it this way:

§ 1 Seller's Obligations

    § 1.1 Delivery

        § 1.1.1 Mode

        § 1.1.2 Time

        § 1.1.3 Place

    § 1.2 Installation

The numbers or letters make it easy for the parties to refer to specific sections and allow for clear cross-reference within the document itself. However, after the document is complete, the drafter should double check all cross-references. In an early version of the document, the referenced material may have been in paragraph I.B.3.(a). In the final version of the document the material may appear in I.B.4.(a). Unless the cross-reference is changed, the document will be confusing, at best. Indeed, an erroneous cross-reference could make the document ambiguous or produce totally unintended results. One may minimize the danger of an erroneous numerical cross reference by also including the paragraph heading in the cross reference, in the hope that the referenced subject matter will prevail over the referenced number. That, however, is no substitute for careful proofreading.

The headings must accurately reflect the content of the paragraph. One should not, for example, bury a disclaimer of warranties in a paragraph marked "Warranties." Such a disclaimer may not even be legally effective due to lack of conspicuousness.

Some drafters are inclined to include a provision stating that headings are not part of the contract and should not be used to limit, expand, or interpret the substantive text. This is an admission of sloppy drafting. The better approach is to word the heading so that it is totally coincident with the substantive text that follows. The drafter's inability to do this easily may indicate a fundamental flaw in the conceptualization or organization of the document.

4. Lists

Lists enhance readability and ease of reference when dealing with a number of items. A list consists of an introductory sentence that expresses the nature of the relationship between the items in the list by indicating whether the items are cumulative or alternative. For example, if the sentence is imposing a duty, the sentence should indicate whether the holder of the duty is required to satisfy all of the items on the list or only one. The introductory sentence may end with a colon or a period. Each item in the list begins with a capital letter and ends with a period. The items should be numbered, lettered, or introduced with a bullet or other visual representation. For example:

> **B.   Appliances.** *Landlord will furnish the following appliances and maintain them in good working order:*
>
> 1.   *Refrigerator.*
>
> 2.   *Stove.*
>
> 3.   *Disposal.*
>
> 4.   *Washer.*
>
> 5.   *Dryer.*

> **IV.   Verification.** *An applicant must verify citizenship status by supplying one or more of the following documents.*
>
> **A.**   *Birth certificate.*
>
> **B.**   *Driver's license.*
>
> **C.**   *Social Security Card.*
>
> **D.**   *Department of State certificate.*

5.   Enumerations

Enumerations can also be used when dealing with items in a series. Unlike a list, however, an enumeration retains its single-sentence structure. The introductory clause may have no terminal punctuation at all, although dashes and colons are sometimes used. Each item in the enumeration is terminated with a comma or a semi-colon, except the last one, which takes a period. The nature of the relationship between the items in the series is indicated by an "and" or an "or" following the next to last item. A single "and" or "or" following the penultimate item in the series is sufficient; it is not necessary to put the connective after each item in the series. The enumeration can be accomplished with parenthesized numbers or letters (for ease of reference) or simple bullets. For example:

> *Agent's territory consists of*
>
> - *All of South Carolina, except the counties of Greenville, Richland, Horrey, and Charleston;*
> - *All of Georgia, except the City of Atlanta; and*
> - *North Carolina.*

*Q. **Tenant's Duties Upon Termination of the Lease.** At the termination of the lease, Tenant will*

> *(1) restore the property to the same condition it was in at the beginning of the lease, except for changes caused by reasonable wear and tear;*
>
> *(2) arrange for the disconnection of all utilities for which Tenant is responsible;*
>
> *(3) return all keys to Landlord;*
>
> *(4) remove all furniture and personal belongings; and*
>
> *(5) vacate the premises by no later than 4:00 p.m. on the last day of the lease.*

While that is a 73–word sentence—far too long by conventional standards—the fragmentation of its parts into an enumeration makes it easy to follow. So, whenever a drafted document contains a series of items joined by an *"and"* or *"or,"* the drafter should consider using the enumeration technique.

Moreover, although "and" and "or" have materially different meanings, the drafter can use either one in an enumeration to accomplish the same result. It all depends on the introductory language. Consider the following, which mean the same thing:

> *Eligible employees are those in the*
>
> > *(1) shipping,*
> >
> > *(2) production and maintenance, **and***
> >
> > *(3) research*
>
> *departments at the May Plant.*

or

> *To be eligible, an employee must be in the*
>
> > *(1) shipping,*
> >
> > *(2) production and maintenance, **or***
> >
> > *(3) research*
>
> *department at the May Plant.*

Because an enumeration is one complete sentence, it cannot be broken into in the middle by another complete sentence. Consider the following provision:

> *Upon completion of construction, the prime contractor will*
>
> > *(1) remove all trash, debris, and unused materials from the building site.* ***This includes materials left by subcontractors and suppliers.***
> >
> > *(2) grade the property to fill in all tire ruts, holes, and ditches; and*
> >
> > *(3) remove all temporary utility poles.*

The period after "site" *and the following bolded sentence buried in paragraph (1) leave paragraphs (2) and (3) dangling. The offending sentence can be incorporated into the overall structure of the sentence by making it a parenthetical.

> > *(1) remove all trash, debris, and unused materials from the building site (including materials left by subcontractors and suppliers);*

The introductory phrase of an enumeration must fit, grammatically and substantively, each item in the series. A "bastard enumeration" is one that does not respond to the introductory phrase. In the following clause, (e) is an exception to rather than a portion of what the landlord must provide. It should be stated in a separate provision.

> *Landlord will provide:*
>
> > *(a) gas heat,*
> >
> > *(b) a window air conditioning unit,*
> >
> > *(c) electricity,*
> >
> > *(d) garbage service,*
> >
> > *(e) but Tenant is responsible for obtaining and paying for cable service if desired.*

Enumerations not only make complicated provisions easy to read and understand, but are also extremely useful in resolving ambiguities. If the contract states that "Seller is to provide red caps, jerseys, and pants," does this mean that all three items must be red? Or only the caps? It could be expressed as either

Seller will provide (a) red caps, (b) jerseys, and (c) pants,

or

Seller will provide red (a) caps, (b) jerseys, and (c) pants.

6. Tabbing

Drafters also often use a device called tabbing to avoid ambiguities of modification. Consider the following provision written in conventional paragraph form:

*A person who drives an automobile on a public road recklessly, negligently, or at a speed or in a manner posing a danger to others **considering the condition of the highway and the weather** is guilty of a misdemeanor.*

Does the bolded language only modify the dangerous manner of the driving? Or does it also modify "recklessly," "negligently," and "at a speed?" One court construed the phrase in a similar statute as modifying all four of the preceding expressions. However, this could have been expressed more clearly by the statute itself, through the tabbing device.

A person who drives an automobile on a public road

> *recklessly,*
>
> *negligently,*
>
> *at a speed posing a danger to others, or in a manner posing a danger to others,*

considering the condition of the highway and the weather, is guilty of a misdemeanor.

By bringing the "considering" phrase back over to the margin, the drafter indicates that it modifies all four of the tabbed items.

7. Charts and Graphs

Often, a chart or graph is the clearest way to present complex information. Consider, for example, how the following chart more clearly and easily describes the terms of a maintenance agreement than pure textual sentences would.

Service	Time			
	30 Days	60 Days	180 Days	1 year
Check all fluids	X	X	X	X
Check all belts	X	X	X	X
Change oil filter	X			X
Change air filter	X			X
Replace transducer				X
Rotate bearing drivers		X		X
Test voltage output	X	X	X	X
Test radiation levels		X		X

8.   Computations

Computations can be presented clearly in two ways—by list and by formula. A list details the computation step by step.

To determine the Flesch–Kincaid Readability Index, by grade level:

a.   Divide the number of words by the number of sentences to determine the average sentence length (ASL).

b.   Multiply the ASL by .39.

c.   Divide the number of syllables by the number of words to determine the average syllables per word (ASW).

d.   Multiply the ASW by 11.8.

e.   Add the results of steps b. and d.

f.   Subtract—15.59.

The formula approach simply presents a mathematical formula for the computation.

The Flesch–Kincaid formula for determining the Readability Index, by grade level, is as follows: Grade Level = [.39 × (number of words—number of sentences)] + [11.8 × (number of syllables—number of words)]—15.59.

Consider including an example of any specified formula in use. In other words, provide a step-by-step computation under a hypothetical set of facts.

Exercise 13

Reformat the following document according to the typographical and layout principles discussed in this chapter—plus whatever supplemental preferences your instructor might have when the text suggests several options. Do not otherwise change the wording or substance.

Contract of Sale

Alan Lourie (Seller) and Horatio Nelson (Buyer) enter into this contract for the sale of a boat and other equipment, as described below, and mutually agree to the following terms and conditions:

Seller will sell and Buyer will purchase the 56–foot sloop, Rooster, United States registry number 45499756, equipped with a 750 horsepower Briggs and Stratton diesel motor; auxiliary 90 horsepower Mercury motor; a Raymarine Raychart 620Plus plotter; a Furuno FCV–1100L Color Sounder; a Webco HF/SSB Radiotelephone; a JRC 3800 Series Raster Scan Radar; 2 Avon Ocean Lifecrafts; jib (self-furling); storm jib (self-furling); main sail (roller reefing); spinnaker; anchors; anchor rode; Simpson Lawrence Windlasses for jib and mailsail; Winchester bilge pump; galley refrigerator; gally stove. Sale does not include fenders, life vests, cushions, bathook, tools, galley utensils; binoculars, bedding, or other personal items that may be on the boat when the contract is signed.

At the time and place of delivery, Buyer will pay Seller $1.5 million for the boat, by certified check.

Buyer will deliver and Seller will accept delivery on October 23, 2005, at the Lands End Marina, Edisto Island, South Carolina.

Seller warrants that he has clear title to the boat and equipment listed above; and that there are no unpaid taxes on the boat.

Except as provided above, **SELLER DISCLAIMS ALL WARRANTIES, EXPRESS OR IMPLIED, INCLUDING BUT NOT LIMITED TO A WARRANTY OF MERCHANTABILITY, A WARRANTY OF FITNESS FOR ANY PARTICULAR PURPOSE, AND A WARRANTY BASED ON COURSE OF DEALING OR USAGE OF THE TRADE.** Buyer has had an opportunity to inspect the boat and equipment and agrees that there are no warranties that extend beyond the description of the boat and equipment as above and accepts the boat **AS IS.**

Chapter 17

REVIEWING AND REVISING DRAFTED DOCUMENTS

The final step in the drafting process is to do a comprehensive review of the document and on the basis of that review to do one final revision. This review process also occurs when a drafter is asked to review and revise documents prepared by others, not only to bring these documents into compliance with the more modern conventions of good drafting style, but also to satisfy legal requirements, fill substantive gaps, and cure ambiguities. For example, a law firm may have used essentially the same retainer agreement with its clients for the last 50 years. The document is filled with legalese, wordy constructs, lengthy sentences, and overloaded paragraphs; it also lacks some provisions required or highly recommended as a matter of legal ethics. The firm asks one of its better drafters to prepare a revision. Similarly, although specific substantive changes nearly always provide the impetus for statutory revisions (because of the difficulty and complexity of the amendment process), it is not uncommon for other types of legislation to be periodically reviewed and revised without any substantive changes. For example, as a result of Plain English legislation, an administrative agency may find it necessary to revise their rules and regulations.

In any event, the components of a comprehensive review and revision are about the same, whether it involves a document the reviewer has just prepared or one that was prepared earlier by someone else.

A. PREPARE A FLOWCHART

One technique that may prove helpful is preparation of a flowchart. A flowchart is simply a schematic diagram of a drafted document or portions of it. Doing a flowchart will accomplish four things.

First, if the drafter is reviewing an earlier contract or regulation, a flowchart will enable the drafter to master the substance of the document. Many of the documents needing revision are exceedingly dense. That is, the substance is hidden in a forest of bad drafting, rendering the document incomprehensible to the ordinary reader. The drafter, however, must determine what the substance is before attempting to present that substance in a more palatable form. Doing a flowchart will accomplish that.

Second, the rules of flowcharting impose a discipline that will force the drafter to identify and deal with substantive gaps, those created by "if . . . then" constructions, for example. The flowchart will illustrate (or show the lack of) not only the consequence when the "if" clause is identified, but also what happens when it is not satisfied. The infamous UCC § 2–207, which was supposed to resolve the battle of the forms, does not always do that. A flowchart of that section is not only enormously complicated, it also reveals that the framers did not think the process through thoroughly or provide answers to all the questions that can arise in deciding whether a contract exists and on what terms. A flowchart filling the statutory gaps with the official comments, caselaw, and the authors own policy preferences can be found in Thomas R. Haggard, *U.C.C. 2–207: A Suggested Analysis*, 10 J. Law & Commerce 257 (1991).

Third, if the drafter discovers that passage through the flowchart could arguably lead in two different directions (two "yes" exit doors from the same block, for example), then this means that the provision in question is ambiguous and needs to be revised.

Fourth, if the logical analysis of a provision, as reflected in the flowchart, suggests that it should start at one point and the document, as written, starts somewhere else, then this will suggest a sequence problem that needs to be corrected.

The steps for creating a flowchart are:

- Reduce the document to its individual, component parts. This could consist of an action to be performed, a criterion to be applied, an element to be satisfied, or a procedure to be exhausted. Each component becomes a separate block in the chart.

- Express the component in the form of a question. "Has claimant filed form 285?"

- Identify the various ways in which each question can be answered. Usually, the choices are "yes" and "no." Sometimes, however, several answers are possible. For example, the question might be, "Which section is claimant filing under?"—for which there might be three possible answers, "§ 258," "§ 259," and "§ 260."

- Make each possible answer an exit gate from the block, with a path down which the analysis will flow.

- At the end of each path, identify the consequences of taking that path. Often, the consequence is that another component must be dealt with. In other words, the path will usually lead to another block, containing another question, and another set of exit gates and paths.

- Continue the chart until it reaches the ultimate conclusions. This could be something like, "Claimant qualifies for the benefit" and "Claimant does not qualify for the benefit." Or, other alternatives might exist, like "Claimant is required to file supplemental information within 30 days."

Consider UCC § 2–205, which deals with firm offers. It provides as follows:

An offer by a merchant to buy or sell goods in a signed writing which by its terms gives assurance that it will be held open is not revocable, for lack of consideration, during the time stated or if no time is stated for a reasonable time, but in no event may such period of irrevocability exceed three months; but any such term of assurance on a form supplied by the offeree must be separately signed by the offeror.

Section 2–205 is not overly complex or confusing, it is free of ambiguities and substantive gaps, and one can easily see how its components fit together in the following flow-chart:

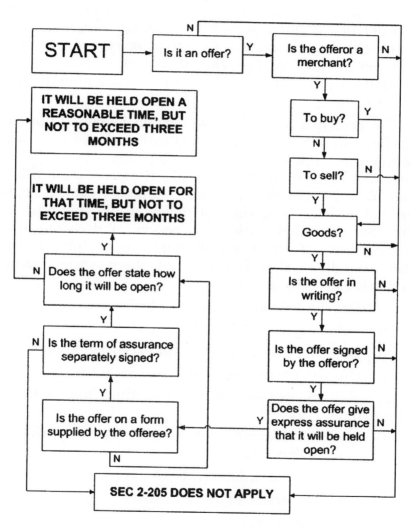

A person trying to determine if a particular offer is firm can track through the flowchart, answer each question in sequence, and come out with the correct answer. On the other hand, consider this mythical tax statute provisions:

RIGHT TO REVIEW

To obtain an administrative hearing of a Commission tax ruling, a person who has filed under section 12(b) or section 115 unless the tax-deferred credit exception applies must notify the Director of intent to appeal, provide documentation of the claim within 15 days thereafter, and if so requested in writing by the Director or by order of the administrative law judge assigned to hear the case sign a release for all bank records; to obtain direct review by the Director, such person must in addition place one-half of the contested amount in an escrow fund.

The principal ambiguity, which the following flowchart identifies through the use of dotted rather than solid lines, is whether the "unless" clause modifies only "§ 115 filings," or whether it also modifies "§ 12(b) filings." If the filing is under neither section or if the "unless" clause applies, presumably there is no right of review under this provision. If another provision deals with review of decisions under other sections of the Code, it might be helpful for this section to indicate that. In any event, the provision could be flowcharted as follows:

[1] Did the person file under § 12(b)?

[2] Did the person file under § 15?

[3] Does the tax-deferred credit exception apply?

[4] Has the person given notice of intent to appeal?

[5] Has the person documented the claim within 15 days?

[6] Has the Director requested in writing that the person sign a release?

[7] Has the ALJ ordered the person to sign a release?

[8] Has the person signed a release?

[9] Has the person requested direct review by the Director?

[10] Has the person placed one-half the contested amount in an escrow fund?

[11] Uncertain consequences.

[12] Direct review by the Director.

[13]   Review in an administrative hearing.

[14]   Person is not entitled to a hearing under this section.

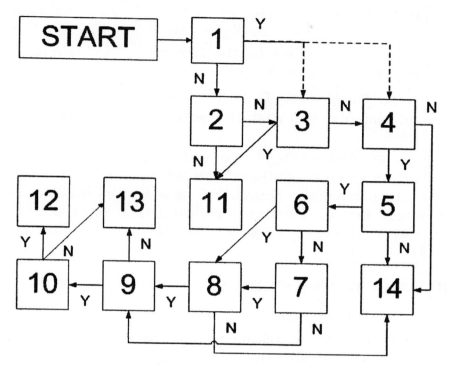

Resolving the ambiguity in favor of having the credit exception apply only to § 115 and giving the reader a reference to the other review provision in the statute, the statute might possibly be revised, as follows:

Section 44–56–299—Right of Review

A. Review of Section 12(b) and Certain Section 115 Commission Tax Rulings. Persons who file under

  (i) Section 12(b) or

  (ii) Section 115 and provided the tax-deferred credit exception does not apply

must do the following to obtain review of a Commission tax ruling:

1. Administrative hearing. To obtain an administrative hearing, a person must:

(a) notify the Director of an intent to appeal;

(b) document the claim with 15 days after filing the notice of appeal; and

(c) if the Director requests it in writing or the administrative law judge assigned to hear the case orders it, sign a release for all bank records.

2. Direct Review by the Director. To obtain direct review by the Director, a person must:

(a) satisfy the requirements of subsection 1, above; and

(b) place one-half of the contested amount in an escrow fund.

B. Review of Other Commission Tax Rulings. To obtain a review of other Commission tax rulings, including rulings under Section 115 to which the tax-deferred credit exception applies, a person must follow the procedures provided in Section 44–56–1087(a)-(t) of this statute.

B. DOCUMENT REVIEW

1. Review by the Drafter

Once the initial writing is over, the thinking process begins anew. Basically, the drafter must ask, "Is this document going to work?" That is, will it serve the client's objectives effectively, efficiently, and without the need to resort to litigation? The drafter should review the document several times, each from a different perspective.

- Substantively, does it cover everything that it needs to cover?

- Does it satisfy all the legal requirements?

- Does it contain fatal ambiguities?

- Does it contain potential loopholes that a hostile reader could exploit?

- Is it internally consistent?

- Are the rights, duties, and other legal consequences clearly and unequivocally stated?

- Are the objectives of the document properly conceptualized?

Some of the items on this review list involve what is called "vertical review," requiring the drafter to look in depth at each provision in turn for hidden ambiguities and stylistic flaws. Other items on the list involve what is called "horizontal review," requiring the drafter to compare how a particular topic is handled in different provisions throughout the document. The drafter's search for inconsistency, for example, may require the drafter to track through multiple provisions to ensure that the person who is renting the property is always referred to as the "tenant."

a. Review for Content—A Ten Point Checklist

When reviewing documents drafted by others, and when critically examining your own drafting, use the following questions to focus your review:

● **Parties, Dates, Dollar Amounts, and Interest Rates.**

Does the document identify the correct parties in their proper capacities? Are the dates correct? Are all currency amounts and interest rates correct and complete? Never assume that any factual statement is correct. Trust, but verify.

● **Appropriate Structure.**

Does the document and the overall structure of the transaction suit your client's needs? Do you understand the deal that is at issue? Is there an alternative structure that is more desirable for your client, perhaps for reasons outside the immediate transaction, such as accounting and tax treatment? Does the document match your client's expectations? Does it match your client's earlier description of the deal to you?

● **Clear Expression of Duties, Rights, and Privileges.**

Does the document contain clear mandatory duty provisions regarding all performances by other parties? Are mandatory duties specified using the words "shall" or "must?" Are rights or privileges expressed in terms of "is entitled to" and privileges in terms of "may"? Do these provisions clearly state who does what to or for whom or what, when? Timing of performance is essential; do not neglect to specify the "when."

● **Representations and Warranties.**

Does the document contain representations and warranties running in favor of your client regarding all facts, statements, and assurances upon which your client is relying? Are any qualifiers (knowledge, material, thresholds, etc.) appropriate? If these representations and warranties prove false, is there a mechanism (perhaps a covenant coupled with an indemnity, an event of default coupled with a remedy, or a covenant and third party guaranty) for recovering from a credit-worthy entity, for rescinding, or for otherwise modifying the transaction? Does the document require your client to make broad or unnecessary representations and warranties? Can these be estimated, narrowed, or limited in temporal or geographic scope? Can a materiality threshold limiting the representation to things over a certain amount (*e.g.,* claims in excess of $25,000) be added to limit the breadth of the statement? Can a knowledge limitation be inserted so that a representation, especially as to the lack of something, is limited to the knowledge of a specific individual at a specific time? Are those representations and warranties that your client is making factually correct? How about those of the other side? Are there any that you know to be false?

• Internal and External Consistency.

Does the document fit the desired structure? Is it complete and consistent, internally and with any other documents involved in the transaction? Defined terms and boilerplate should be consistent across all documents in a transaction to avoid confusion and potential ambiguity. Do all the documents contain a non-severability clause? Are they governed by the same integration, merger, choice of law, choice of forum, and alternative dispute resolution provisions?

• Substantive Understanding.

Do you understand each provision of the document? Review each of them until you understand it completely and its interaction with the other sections of the document and related documents.

• Hypothesize Performance.

Think through the life of the transaction and the document under various fact patterns. What will happen, moment by moment, if the parties comply with all the terms in a timely manner? Sometimes it is useful to think this life cycle through in reverse to determine if the final product is supported in all respects by the agreement's provisions. Are performances required in the proper order?

• Hypothesize Non–Performance and Default.

What if one or both parties fail to perform all or part of the agreement? Are the consequences of failure of conditions or failure to perform stated and closely linked to the performance required? Are there clear events of default and associated remedies? Does the document address other issues and problems that are likely to arise in the course of performance? Resolve issues and problems now, at the drafting stage, rather than waiting for the parties to reach the problem. It is likely that the parties will never be more amenable to working out details than they are at the inception of the deal. Capitalize on the opportunity to prevent trouble before it occurs.

• Address Bankruptcy Risk.

Analyze what will happen if one of the parties files a bankruptcy petition or becomes subject to a receivership. Will property or rights that are important to the other party become "property of the estate" under 11 U.S.C. § 541? Will performance be stayed or affected by the automatic stay of 11 U.S.C. § 362? Will the document be considered an "executory contract" subject to assumption or rejection under 11 U.S.C. § 365? If so, will this assumption or rejection be possible independently from assumption or rejection of the other documents in the deal? If so, is there a way to structure the transaction so that this property or these rights are held by a third party that is unlikely or unable to be the subject of a bankruptcy case? Can the document incorporate, or be incorporated into, other documents from which it should not be divisible? Do the recitals in the contract make clear what performances and property rights are important to each of the parties and what injury and damage they may suffer if they are deprived of them? Can you provide for a lien, security interest, or third party credit support, such as a guaranty or letter of credit, to secure the opposing party's payment and performance obligations?

• Consider the Worst Case Scenario.

Assume that the document is executed and the parties become openly hostile, seeking to undermine each other at every opportunity. Will the document provide sufficient guidance to govern the relationship? Will it provide sufficient guidance to a court interpreting the document or imposing remedies if the parties are locked in mortal combat with no thought to the opportunity or litigation costs involved? Although this may be a worst-case scenario, that is the appropriate test for a well-drafted transactional document.

b. Review for Style and Usage

It is probably best that the drafter of the document not perform this function. We all become blind to our own writing weaknesses and deficiencies, and this task is best performed by *another* competent drafter. Take this person's criticisms and suggestions to heart. In particular, if a reasonable reader thinks a provision is unclear, then that provision is, by definition, unclear. Do not argue. Revise it. If, however, another person is not available, then the drafter must make a conscious mental effort to change from a drafting persona to an editing persona.

In addition, the solo drafter should always use the style and grammar checkers that come with most word processing systems. They will identify many writing deficiencies and make valuable suggestions for improvement. The drafter, however, should only consider these suggestions and not follow them if good reasons exist for not doing so. The drafter, for example, may have consciously decided to split an infinitive, use the passive voice, or enumerate a series of items in a sentence that is longer than the computer thinks appropriate. The computer may also suggest simplified substitutes for words that are terms of art or have special legal meaning. One should not, for example, follow the advice to replace "affirmative action" with "yes action."

A particularly valuable feature of style and spelling checkers is the document readability index it creates. Many of the techniques for achieving brevity, clarity, and simplicity discussed elsewhere in this text have been incorporated into these indexes. There are several of them. The Flesch–

Kincaid index, which the United States Department of Defense uses for contractors producing manuals for the armed services, is very popular. The insurance industry relies on the Flesch index, and some states even require that insurance policies meet a certain readability standard. The Fog index is used mainly in education.

Linguists and lawyers have debated the reliability and utility of readability indexes since they were first devised back in the 1920s. Most drafters regard them as useful tools, but also recognize their shortcomings. If a document has a poor readability index, it should probably be revised. An apartment lease need not have an index suggesting that it is comprehensible only to someone with a Ph.D. degree. On the other hand, a good readability index does not necessarily guarantee that the document is comprehensible. Factors other than sentence length, number of syllables in each word, and the commonness of the words are also relevant. For example, readability indexes do not measure whether the substance of the sentence makes sense. To borrow from a famous linguistic example: "Colorless green ideas sleep sharply" scores just as well on a readability formula as "Beautiful white houses sell quickly." Readability indexes also do not measure whether the document follows a logical sequence, nor do they take into account the grammatical structure of the sentence—both of which affect comprehensibility tremendously.

However, consider the following bit of statutory drafting prose:

> *Notwithstanding any other provisions of this title, it shall not be an unlawful employment practice for an employer to apply different standards of compensation, or different terms, conditions, or privileges of employment pursuant to a bona fide seniority or merit system, or a system which measures earnings by quantity or quality of production or to employees who work in different locations, provided that such differences are not the result of an intention to discriminate because of race, color, religion, gender or national origin; nor shall it be an unlawful employment practice for an employer to give and act upon the results of any professionally developed ability test provided that such test, its administration or*

action upon the results is not designed, intended, or used to discriminate because of race, color, religion, sex, or national origin. It shall not be an unlawful employment practice under this title for any employer to differentiate upon the basis of sex in determining the amount of the wages or compensation paid to employees of such employer if such differentiation is authorized by the provisions of Section 6(d) of the Fair Labor Standards Act.

This has a Flesch–Kincaid index of 16, which means that one would need 16 years of education or a college degree to understand the document. Even though this statute is directed primarily at lawyers, that is too high for even this audience.

But consider this provision from a form lease, which would presumably be read and used by lay landlords and tenants as the basic charter of their relationship:

If the leased premises, or the building of which they form a part, are partially damaged by fire or other casualty, not occurring through fault of Tenant, its agents, servants, or employees, and such damage can be repaired within one-hundred and twenty (120) days of the date of such occurrence, this lease shall remain in full force and effect, and the Landlord shall promptly repair such damage at its expense, and in that event there shall be a proportionate abatement of rent for so much of the leased premises as may be untenatable during the period of repair or restoration. If in the opinion of a registered Architect or Engineer appointed by the Landlord the leased premises are damaged by fire or other casualty, as aforesaid, to such an extent as to make them wholly untenantable for a period of sixty (60) days or more from the date of such occurrence and such damages cannot be repaired or the premises restored within said time, this lease shall terminate at the option of Landlord upon the written notice given within thirty (30) days after such occurrence. If twenty-five percent (25%) or more of the leased premises or the building of which they form a part, are damaged by fire or other casualty, as aforesaid, to such an extent that the same cannot be repaired or restored within sixty (60) days of the date of such occurrence, this lease may be canceled at the option of the

Landlord upon thirty (30) days written notice from the date of such occurrence, even though the premises occupied by the Tenant have not become untenantable, and there shall be an adjustment of the rent to said date of termination. In addition, there shall be no obligation upon the part of Landlord to repair or rebuild during the last three (3) lease years of the term of this lease agreement unless Tenant shall, within fifteen (15) days after such occurrence, exercise any option to extend the term of this lease agreement that may be afforded to Tenant under the terms hereof. Landlord's obligation to repair or rebuild pursuant to this paragraph shall be limited to a basic building and the replacement of any interior work which may have originally been installed at Landlord's cost.

This example of drafting malfeasance also has a Flesch–Kincaid index of 16.

c. Prepare a Summary

This is not necessary or practical for all documents, but the practice is especially helpful for legislation and complex private law documents. Summarize the document provision-by-provision. This will accomplish several things.

First, if the drafter finds it difficult to summarize the content of the document, this suggests that the document will be even more incomprehensible to a reader who is not already familiar with it. The problem may be one of inadequate conceptualization, poor organization, artless expression, or all three. In any case, this is a serious problem indicating that major revision is necessary.

Second, after preparing a summary and comparing it against the document, the drafter or another reader may discover discrepancies. The summary usually reflects what the drafter intended to say and also what the drafter thought he or she said. If this is not the case, then the document must be revised.

Third, after preparing the summary, the drafter may discover that its language is superior to the language of the document itself. The drafter should opt for the better language.

Fourth, after all the necessary revisions are made, the summary will give the drafter something to use at the next step in the process.

2. Review by Other People

Drafting by committee is a fruitless, frustrating, and pointless exercise. In its initial stages, drafting must be an individual endeavor. Substantively, however, the individual drafter is error prone, particularly if the document is subject to extensive legal requirements. It is too easy to omit a critical substantive term. This sometimes occurs with respect to a term that has not been the focus of the negotiations, such as a piece of critically important boilerplate, that will cause the transaction to flounder if omitted. Another person, well versed in these substantive requirements, should be asked to review the document with a critical eye. Similarly, this reader may be able to suggest alternative ways of dealing with the problem.

When someone reviews your work and proceeds to mark it up or otherwise make comments, this is not a sign of failure. In fact, to the extent that the reviewer, be it client, supervising attorney, or opposing counsel, makes any comments at all, this expresses interest in the document and shows that you have the reviewer's attention. When given a document to review, most lawyers reach for a pen, knowing that they will use it. Receiving comments and mark-ups of your work is par for the course. You should get used to it as soon as possible to avoid unnecessary pain and anguish.

There are different considerations for each type of reviewer and review.

a. Your Colleagues and Supervisors

Especially when starting out, the first group to review your documents will probably be your colleagues and supervisors. These comments will be designed to improve the documents and your client's position. As such, you should receive them as what they are: constructive commentary from a different perspective, produced with the benefit of different experiences and knowledge that are meant to improve the final work product. They are *not* a personal indictment of your failure to grasp what needs to be done.

First, make any suggested changes that improve the document, then make the other ones that do not harm the document (this is much easier than explaining why you think they are unnecessary). Disregard, *with* explanation, the ones that harm the document. Even if you are in the unfortunate position of receiving comments that appear designed to undermine your confidence and sense of self-worth (which does happen from time to time), you should look for the constructive, beneficial points hidden within what may appear to be venom. Even comments that seem minor or purely stylistic are important. They should be internalized so that the next project involving that commentator incorporates the feedback from the last project in its first draft. Do not incorporate these changes into all your projects in the future, unless (a) you like them or (b) you are working with another client, or colleague, with similar style.

An effective technique to minimize your reviewer's time and effort and to focus attention on the areas that most require review is to use "black lining," also known in modern parlance as "track changes." In a black-lined document, revisions are indicated by using text to indicate deletions from a prior draft and underlining to indicate additions. The beauty of black lining is that, when reviewing successive generations of drafts, the reviewer knows exactly what is new and needs to be reviewed, the other material presumably having been approved earlier. Black lining may even be appropriate at the first draft stage if you are basing the document on an exemplar, especially one prepared by your reviewing attorney.

If you use black lining it must be accurate and complete. Inaccurate black lining will establish your reputation as sloppy within your firm and with your client. With opposing counsel it is likely to create distrust and concerns about your ethics.

It is also valuable to communicate to the reviewer what you need reviewed, when you need it back, and other contextual matters. Find out how they like to get this information, what information they like to get, and the best method for getting it to them.

To minimize comments about your work that may impact negatively upon your reputation, take great care to make your document as good as you can be *before* turning it over for review. Attorneys and clients are busy people for whom time and effort are valuable resources. Skilled practitioners can spot a misspelled or misused word, a grammatical mistake, or even an extra space from a mile away. These distractions impede their review of the substance of your prose—they feel compelled to scratch in a correction with their pen.

Learn the rules of your supervising attorney and follow them before turning in work for review. Although most supervising attorneys will clean up your grammatical and typographical mistakes, this is not their job. Forcing them to do so is not good for your career. Develop your eye for detail as early as possible.

Finally, especially for new attorneys, it is easy to find yourself in a cycle of endless revisions that are rather pointless. After a certain point, polishing results in no further material increase in quality. If you bill your client for the time spent on these rounds of revisions, your work product will be overpriced. If you do not bill for the time, you will be working without compensation. If you find yourself making endless rounds of non-substantial changes, such as changing all instances of "Seller's" to "of the Seller" or vice versa, and are making no meaningful changes. Stop.

b. Review by the Client

No complex document should be submitted to the client on a "Here it is, sign on the dotted line" basis. Much may have been lost in the translation—from the client's desires, to the client's expression of those desires, to the drafter's understanding of those desires, to the specific words that are used to express those desires. The conscientious drafter will sit down with the client and review the document provision-by-provision, explaining what each provision means and ensuring that the document reflects the client's wishes. The summary merely serves as a written form of this review. In legislative drafting, the summary may also become a part of the legislative history.

The degree of depth of this client review depends upon your client representative's level of interest and training. Inside counsel and accountants can be expected to give the document a relatively thorough reading and rarely require much in the way of explanatory cover letters. For those without such detail-intensive backgrounds, you may want to enclose a cover letter highlighting the most important points in the documents or this round of revisions to ensure that the client is "on notice" of these items and will pay attention to them during the review.

Some clients will not want to review the documents at all, or will be happy to review them at the same time that the other side reviews them. In such a case, the documents should be transmitted with a cover letter to opposing counsel stating that the documents have not yet been reviewed by your client and are therefore subject to modification. It is a good idea to make sure that your client reviews the documents at least once prior to the final draft. You should take note of their comments and modify the documents accordingly. This ensures that you really do understand the directions your client has given to you.

Remember, clients rarely care if you fail to incorporate comments from the other side. They *do* mind when their comments—however minor, inconsequential, or wrongheaded they may seem to you—are not incorporated or at least discussed with them and discarded after that discussion.

c. Review by Opposing Counsel

You have transmitted the documents to the opposing counsel—is your review over? *No.* Take a break, so that your next review of the document will be conducted with fresh eyes. Then, without waiting for opposing counsel to get back to you, review the document one more time and note any corrections that appear. Things will be readily apparent to you at this stage that you could not see earlier. You will then be prepared to raise them in your first conversation with opposing counsel, thus avoiding protests based on notions of waiver, closure, or re-opening negotiations. Your changes will also provide you with a selection of trading points to use as consideration for changes requested by opposing counsel.

Encourage opposing counsel to provide you with a marked-up copy of the document showing specific line-edits that are desired, not vague comments like "we need an indemnity here" or "this won't work." It is usually a waste of time for this mark-up to be accompanied by lengthy commentary in the cover letter explaining and justifying each change, and those letters are costly. They should be generated only when it is important to make a detailed record of the negotiations beyond what marked-up drafts would show. This may be the case in extremely large multi-party transactions where one attorney is collecting and synthesizing the comments of many lawyers; in situations when negotiations are going badly and may fall apart, perhaps precipitating lawsuits; or when they are required by clients who wish to receive this sort of costly narration and entertainment.

Comments from opposing counsel fall into one of four categories and should be responded to as follows:

Category of Comment	Response
Beneficial to all parties or to the document and the deal.	Make the changes, perhaps thanking opposing counsel for insight and contribution in the cover letter.
Matters of style of opposing counsel and that do no harm to the documents or your client's position.	Consider making the changes. It is less expensive than trying to negotiate out opposing counsel's pet peeves. But also consider how acquiescence across the board can affect the way you are viewed by opposing counsel and your colleagues. Acquiescence can be perceived as a sign of weakness. Sometimes you have to put your foot down and say "no" to a change that would not really matter to maintain your authority and credibility.
Harmful to either your client's position or the smooth operation of the document.	Reject the changes, with an explanation of the problem that they cause. If the effect that opposing counsel was aiming for is evident, and you believe the effect may be desirable or merely neutral, consider suggesting an alternative method of reaching the same end without doing violence to your client's interests or the document.

Category of Comment	Response
Valid points for future negotiation.	Consider what, if anything, you would request in exchange for the change. You could also be tentative about making the change, perhaps inserting the requested change into the document as an alternative to the original provision, which is also retained. Make reference to the trade off, if any, or to keeping the issue open in your cover letter. *Do not acquiesce without receiving something in return unless you and your client have run out of points, issues, and comments. Once you give something away it is difficult or impossible to come back and try to charge for it.*

For each comment you receive from opposing counsel, or anyone else, think: What is the point of this comment? What substantive effect are they trying for? Then determine if that effect is acceptable to your client. This may require checking with your client and gaining authority for the change. If acceptable, ask yourself, "Is this the best way to gain this effect?" If it is not, respond with an alternative change that has the same effect, pointing out that it addresses the same issue, but is better because it is more elegant, will take less time to institute, will not affect other issues, is less costly, etc.

For example, a landlord's counsel may demand a large cash security deposit from a start-up tenant with little or no track record. This may be unacceptable or impossible for your client, but your client may be able to obtain a letter of credit from a reputable bank or provide a guaranty from a well-heeled shareholder. Either of the alternatives should satisfy the landlord's legitimate desire for some form of credit support. But, unlike the security deposit, they do not require your client to part with its cash at the present time. If the effect is unacceptable, you will have to respond by rejecting the comment or change and, if necessary, explaining why it is unacceptable.

After you have made the changes you and your client are willing to make in response to the opposing counsel's comments, go over the document one more time, looking for conforming changes. If the same language that was changed appears in other locations and it is appropriate to make the changes there as well, do so.

C. PROOFREAD THE DOCUMENT

After all the corrections and revisions have been made as a result of the review process outlined above and the document has been printed, it is still not final until it has been proofread one final time. Again, this is best done by someone other than the drafter. But it must be done by someone, because many mistakes occur in the very process of correction and revision. And a simple typographical error is capable of making the drafter, despite all the effort and expertise that went into the document, nevertheless appear incompetent and unprofessional.

Exercise 14

1. You are staff counsel to the Senate Agriculture Committee. A member of the committee has drafted a bill dealing with the classification of agricultural land. He has asked you to review it for substantive gaps and ambiguities. The material in brackets is not part of the statute. Prepare a flowchart of the statute as written and then revise it, resolving any ambiguities in whatever manner you deem appropriate (but presumably reflecting the intent of the Committee).

(a) This section applies only to land that is outside the boundaries of a city incorporated pursuant to Section 7–17–37. [Assume that under state law "cities" are not the only legally recognized form of municipal government and the cities may be incorporated under several sections.]

(b) If such land is more than one mile outside the boundaries of any such city, is used for raising cattle or sheep in herds of 100 or more, has been so used for more than five years, and is also used as the principal residence of the owner or a tenant, it shall be classified as Agricultural Use A.

(c) If such land satisfies the requirements of subsection (b), above, but is not used as the principal residence of the owner or a tenant, it shall be classified as Agricultural Use B, unless the county in which said land exists has zoned the land for non-residential use only, in which case it shall be classified as Agricultural Use C.

(d) All other such land shall be classified as Agricultural Use D; provided, however, that the Secretary of Agriculture may designate such land for Agricultural Use E after notice to the landowner and an opportunity for a hearing.

2. Revise the employment statute quoted in paragraph B.1.b. above.

3. Revise the lease provision quoted in paragraph B.1.b. above.

Part IV

Additional Exercises

Exercise 15: Surety Agreement

Background: On a construction job, the contract between the owner and the contractor/builder usually requires the contractor/builder to post surety or performance bond. This bond is in the form of a contract between the contractor/builder and the surety (usually an insurance company). The contractor/builder is referred to as the "Principal" and the owner is referred to as the "Obligee" (since this is who the surety company owes the obligation to, as a third party beneficiary of the contract).

This particular provision of the typical surety agreement is intended to describe the circumstances under which the obligation of the surety company terminates. It reads as follows:

> *Now, THEREFORE, the condition of this obligation [the surety's obligation to pay the Obligee] is such that if the Principal shall faithfully perform the work on his part to be performed, and shall fully indemnify and save harmless the Obligee from all claims and demands incurred by the Principal in the performance of said contract [the construction contract between the owner/Obligee and the builder/contractor/Principal]; and from all loss or damage which may arise to the Obligee by reason of any default on the part of the Principal, then this obligation shall be null and void; otherwise it shall remain in full force and effect.*

a. Be prepared to critique this provision in class. Look for excessive wordiness, lack of clarity, potential ambiguities, defective grammar and punctuation, and the like.

b. Try to figure out what this provision is really trying to say. Once you have done so, then draft a simplified version of it. However, retain the basic approach by identifying the circumstances under which the surety's obligation is discharged.

Exercise 16: Contract Boilerplate

Your firm does a fair amount of contract drafting work. Each member of the firm uses his or her own version of the common *boilerplate* terms—or use several different versions, borrowing indiscriminately from prior contracts, form books, or other sources. Some of these are good. Others are not. You have been asked to draft a set of boilerplate terms that will be exemplars of the drafting art and can be used by everyone in the firm. Include the following:

- A severability clause.
- A non-severability clause.
- A choice of law provision.
- A no oral modification clause.
- A no waiver clause.
- A provision disallowing assignment and delegation.
- A provision allowing assignment and delegation.
- A survivability clause.
- A non-survivability clause.

Exercise 17: Contract for the Sale of a Car

Sally Celler and Bill Beyer have asked you to draft a contract for them. Celler owns a 1948 two-door, black Chevrolet, VIN5–6670p2vvfkd76709. It has special California "classic car" license plates, TRH 1939. Celler has agreed to sell it to Beyer for $4,000. Beyer will give her a $1,000 down payment and $150 a month for the next 20 months. The tags will be assigned with the car. Beyer will pay the fee to transfer title and tags. Celler will retain a lien on the car until the car is paid for.

The old '48 Chevy had something called a "vacuum shift." It was supposed to make shifting easier, but it frequently did not work and caused other transmission problems. For example, the second gear on this car does not work and Celler has advised Beyer of this. Celler, however, thinks everything else is fine but she does not warrant anything about the condition of the car. [See UCC 2–316.]

Beyer also knows that Mike Mecanichek worked on the car recently. Celler says that Mecanichek has been paid in full for his work, but Beyer wants Sally to warrant the car is being delivered free of any rightful claims (mechanic's or other liens) by Mecanichek or other third parties and that she has good title herself. She has agreed to do this. [This would be an implied warranty if Celler were a merchant, which she is not. See UCC 2–312].

Beyer will take delivery of the car when he pays the down payment, at Celler's home, 647 Rivershore Drive, Longtown, South Carolina. They have agreed that the sale will take place two weeks from the date of the contract. During this time, however, Bill wants to be able to take the car to a mechanic of his choice and to rescind the contract if the mechanical condition of the car is found not to be to Beyer's satisfaction.

Celler has informed you that Beyer's payments must be in cash, since she plans on not reporting this as income to the IRS.

a. Is there anything you should do, ethically, before you draft the contract? Or is there anything that might keep you from drafting the contract altogether? Be prepared to explain briefly in class.

b. As you draft the contract, you decide that before you deliver it to the parties you are going to offer Celler $4,500 for the car, cash payment in full at the time of delivery. Is there anything unethical about that? Suppose you were representing only Celler? Be prepared to explain briefly in class.

c. Draft the contract.

Exercise 18: Public Drinking Ordinance

City Council Member Carrie Nations is concerned about what she calls *public drinking* and wants you to draft an ordinance to prohibit it. Upon further inquiry, you discover that her concern includes derelicts who sit in doorways and on sidewalks guzzling cheap wine, sports fans who bring and consume beer at the city baseball stadium (inside the stadium and in the parking lot), kids who congregate at night for drinking parties in remote corners of shopping mall parking lots (despite efforts of mall security to evict them), and the denizens of abandoned houses and weedy vacant lots who are dealing in drugs ("this will give the police an alternative reason for arresting these scumbags," she says).

"What about the concession stand at the Mellon Center for the Performing Arts?" you ask. "They sell wine. Do you want to prohibit that?" "Of course not," she snaps. "They have a license to sell liquor."

"What about the Dessau Motor Speedway?" you ask. "They drink in the stands and parking lot there all the time." "That is private property," she replies. "If Charlie Dessau doesn't care, I don't care."

"Will the police actually have to witness a person drinking the alcohol?" you ask. She thinks about that for a moment and replies, "No, that would make proof too hard. Make possession enough. Or just figure out something, for the love of Pete! Isn't that what we pay you for?"

Prepare the requested ordinance.

Exercise 19: Age Discrimination Waiver

John Barleycorn is the Yard Superintendent at the Birmingham rail yards of the Somerset & Dorset Railway Company. Barleycorn has a high school degree. As Yard Superintendent, Barleycorn has had considerable responsibility for the business, employment, and other contractual affairs of the Company. Barleycorn has always been a good employee.

However, the Company has decided to computerize the rail car switching operations at its Birmingham facility. Barleycorn is not familiar with the computer technology that will be used and has indicated no willingness to try to learn it.

The Company has thus decided that it must terminate Barleycorn. Since Barleycorn is not being terminated *for cause*, he will be entitled to severance pay in the amount of one month's salary.

The man who will replace Barleycorn is 37 years old. He has the necessary expertise to supervise a computerized operation.

Although the Company believes that it has a legitimate and nondiscriminatory reason for replacing Barleycorn, it is fearful that Barleycorn will bring an age discrimination law suit. It has thus asked you to draft a waiver. The company is willing to pay Barleycorn an extra two week's pay (in addition to the regular severance pay) in return for this waiver.

Using the substantive checklist you developed in Exercise 5, prepare the necessary waiver.

Exercise 20: Employment Contract

Barbara Halmark Webster, owner of Webster Wire & Cable Company, Inc., recently terminated her office manager. It had been an unsatisfactory relationship, because they were in constant disagreement over job duties, what benefits the manager was entitled to, and the scope of her authority. Before Webster hires a new manager, she wants to have an employment contract prepared that will forestall these problems. She has asked you to draft one.

You met with her, went through the checklist you prepared in Exercise 3.1, and took the following notes.

———

Webster Wire & Cable Company, Inc., PPB = 8867 Airport Blvd., Austin, Texas 79703. Family owned, closed corporation (Texas). Barbara Halmark Webster, President.

Manufacturers and fabricates various grades of industrial wire, some by special order. Has clients in Texas, Okla, and La. Production mgr—in charge of production, 27 employees. Sales mgr—supervises 6 sales persons. Head of shipping—handles all shipments and supervises 2 loading-dock workers. Maintenance chief—with crew of 3, repairs and maintains machinery. These department heads have contracts. Everyone else is at-will.

Job title—office manager.

Job duties—hire/fire/supervise 1 receptionist/secretary, 2 clerical employees, and a bookkeeper. Must have computer skills (various word processing, spreadsheet, and data base software programs—find out specifics, Webster doesn't have a clue as to what they use). Arrange for office cleaning and maintenance (currently using a service). Be in charge of all office equipment and supplies; keep personnel and payroll records—tax withholding, social sec., and medicare withholding. Arrange for computer support services (currently use Mike Roe Soft Computer Consultants & Technicians, Inc.). Handle advertising and public relations (currently limited to sponsoring a girls softball team). Act as personal secretary to Webster. Assist production mgr, sales mgr., and shipping in handling various paperwork, as needed. Otherwise serve as "girl Friday" (advise client not to use that term). Reserve right to modify duties, as needed.

Full time.

$42,000 per year, payable in semimonthly payments.

Vacation—3 weeks each 12 months (measured from date of hire); no carry over. No more than 2 weeks at a time. No less than 3 days at a time. 2 weeks notice to Webster and approval.

Holidays—Christmas day, New Years day, 4th July, Thanksgiving, either Friday before or Monday after Easter.

FMLA leave—policy described in "Family and Medical Leave Act Leave Act Policy" (which you drafted for her earlier). Incorporate by reference.

Other leave (for personal, religious, and other non-FMLA covered purposes)—without pay, 7 days per year—one week notice required, except in emergencies.

Insurance—covered by company's Blue Cross and Blue Shield medical insurance policy. No other insurance.

No retirement plan. Employees urged to have 401(k)s.

Contract will be for one year.

Employer may terminate early under two circumstances. 1) for "cause," including failure to perform job duties satisfactorily, any other breach of this contract, insubordination, refusal to follow instructions, absenteeism (beyond authorized leave), dishonesty, being intoxicated while on the job, etc. 2) Non-"cause" early justifications for terminations include elimination of job position, insolvency, economic and business reasons not related to employee's job performance. Employer may terminate at any time and for no reason at all if 2 weeks notice is given and employee is paid a full month's salary as severance pay.

Employee may terminate at any time, provided 2 weeks notice is given.

Contract automatically renews from year to year, unless terminated.

Normal work schedule. Monday–Friday, 9:00–5:00, with one hour for lunch. Employee may be expected to work additional hours, including on weekends, if the needs of the business dictate.

No arbitration!

Exercise 21: Apartment Lease

You have gone over the checklist developed for your client in Exercise 6 and the interview produced the following information. Some items on the checklist require no information from the client and should be included automatically. If information would be required for a checklist item but none is given, assume that it is unnecessary to include any reference of the matter (for example, these apartments have no out-of-unit storage areas).

You have also learned that the apartments are near the University Law School. The client informs you that most of the tenants, thus, will probably be law students—who, he notes from experience, have a penchant for wielding "their superficial knowledge of the law like three-year olds playing with the Excaliber Sword." Draft the lease agreement with that particular audience in mind.

Client Notes:

Name of Apartment. Collegiate Apartments, 248 Elm Street, Cambridge, Your state.

Landlord: Ronald Hawthorne de Trump, doing business as deTrump Realty, Inc., 1330 South Main Street, Cambridge, Your state.

Apartment Manager & Owner's Agent: Martha Marbles, Apartment 1–A, Collegiate Apartments, 248 Elm Street, Cambridge, Your state.

Appliances: Refrigerator, stove, dishwasher, disposal.

Cable available: tenant pays.

Parking: No campers, boats, trailers, or truck tops may be kept in lot.

Common areas—laundry room; coin operated. Other areas landlord will maintain are the two stairways, the small lobby where mailboxes are located, and hallways, the parking lot, and the grounds.

Utilities: Landlord pays electrical, gas, water, and garbage fee.

Garbage: Tenants must place general household garbage in dumpster; segregate paper, glass (clear, brown, green), plastic, and aluminum and put them in the bins marked as such.

Term: One year.

Renewal: Automatically renews for one year unless either party gives notice 30–days in advance of termination date.

Grounds for termination: [Advised client that you will incorporate the statutory grounds for termination as part of the contract.]

Security deposit: One month's rent in advance. [Advised client will incorporate the statutory requirements concerning return as part of the contract.]

Terms of rent: $550 per month.

Paid when: First day of the month, unless it is a Saturday, Sunday, or federal holiday, in which case it will be paid the next day. Before 5:00 p.m. Prepayment allowed, no more than one month's rent in advance. More than 5 days late="breach."

Where: manager's office.

Method: Check or money order; no cash.

Limits on occupancy:

Number: 2 or 3, depending on which apartment. Leave a blank. All permanent residents must be signatories to the lease.

Children: None.

Pets: None

Status of tenants: No limits.

Limits on use of premise: Residence only. No loud parties. No water beds.

Landlord's & tenant's obligations concerning maintenance of the property. [Advised client that you will incorporate the statutory requirements as part of the contract.]

Right of entry: [Advised client you will incorporate the statutory rule as part of the contract.]

Assignment: Tenant cannot assign. Landlord may if property is sold; buyer/assignee bound by terms of lease.

Household goods insurance: Responsibility of tenant. Landlord is not liable for any losses.

Exercise 22: No–Smoking Ordinance

TO: Staff Attorney

FROM: Senator Hector Garcia Gonzales, Chair
               Public Health & Welfare Committee

RE: Smoking Ban

I want to introduce a bill prohibiting smoking in all public buildings within the state and in public transportation.

I firmly believe that secondary smoke is detrimental to the health, well-being, and comfort of non-smokers and that we have a right to be free of this pestilence while working in or using public facilities. Indeed, non-smokers should not have to run the gauntlet of smoke in order to enter a public building, so I want a smoke-free zone outside the entrances as well.

I am not insensitive to the rights of smokers. Heavens no! Some of them even vote. They should, thus, be allowed to smoke in their own private offices, provided they are enclosed. Also exempt are designated lounges and break areas, provided that there is a separate and equivalent non-smoking area as well. These areas must contain signs indicating whether they are smoking or non-smoking. On the other hand, I think our hospitals should have the option of being totally smoke free in this regard.

Violation of the smoking ban should be a misdemeanor with a fine of $50 per violation.

Please draft a bill for my review. If you have any questions, no not hesitate to give me a call.

Exercise 23: Anti–Stalking Statute

You are an aide to State Representative Sharon C. Hopkins. Several women's advocacy groups have complained that although the state has an anti-stalking statute, the police are reluctant to arrest persons accused of stalking and that several district attorneys have made it quite plain that prosecuting a stalking case is low on their list of priorities.

The Senator investigated further and discovered that both the police and the district attorneys say that the stalking statute is virtually incomprehensible and possibly unconstitutional.

a. To help her better understand the existing statute and its possible defects, she asked you to prepare a written outline and critique (of both style and substance).

The statute is as follows:

```
1         Section 16–3–1070. Crime of Stalking.
2
3     (A) For purposes of this section:
4         (1) "Harasses" means a knowing and willful course of
5  conduct directed at a specific person which seriously alarms,
6  annoys, or harasses the person and which serves no legitimate
7  purpose. The course of conduct must be such as would cause
8  a reasonable person to suffer substantial emotional distress,
9  and must actually cause substantial emotional distress to the
10 person.
11        (2) "Course of conduct" means a pattern of conduct
12 composed of a series of acts over a period of time, however
13 short, evidencing a continuity of purpose. Constitutionally
14 protected activity is not included within the meaning of
15 "course of conduct."
16        (3) "A credible threat" means a threat made with the
17 intent and the apparent ability to carry out the threat so as to
18 cause the person who is the target of the threat to reasonably
19 fear for his safety. The threat must be against the life of, or a
20 threat to cause great bodily injury to, a person.
21
22    (B) It is unlawful for a person to willfully, maliciously, and
23 repeatedly follow or harass another person and make a
24 credible threat with the intent to place that person in
25 reasonable fear of death or bodily injury. A person who
26 violates the provision of this section is guilty of the crime of
27 stalking which is a misdemeanor and, upon conviction, must
28 be imprisoned not more than one year or fined not more than
29 one thousand dollars, or both.
30
31    (C) A person who violates subsection (B) when there is a
32 temporary restraining order or an injunction, or both, in effect
33 prohibiting the behavior described in subsection (B) against
34 the same party is guilty of stalking which is a misdemeanor
35 and, upon conviction, must be imprisoned not more than two
36 years or fined not more than one thousand dollars, or both.
37
38    (D) A person who is convicted of a second or subsequent
39 offense for a violation of subsection (B) within several years of
40 a prior conviction under subsection (B) against the same
41 victim and involving an act of violence or "a credible threat"
```

42 of violence as defined in item (3) of subsection (A), is guilty
43 of stalking which is a misdemeanor and, upon conviction,
44 must be imprisoned not more than three years or fined not
45 more than two thousand dollars, or both.
46
47   (E) This section does not apply to conduct which occurs
48 during labor picketing.

b. Draft a new anti-stalking statute that cures the problems of the old one and better addresses this troublesome phenomenon.

Exercise 24: The Waterfall

What follows is a complex provision from a real estate joint venture structured as a sale of property with so-called "seller-take-back" financing with an "equity kicker" in the form of a "waterfall" participating contingent interest in the profits from development. The terms in quotes above are shorthand for very detailed provisions in the transactional documents. The "waterfall" contingent participating interest provisions appears here. This is a very confusing provision when encountered for the first time. Try reviewing it in a number of "passes," like an airplane pilot surveying unknown territory. Make your first pass at 35,000 feet and spot the big things. The next pass is made at 10,000 feet, to see some specific features. Then decrease altitude and fly over it at 500 feet, reducing your speed, and understand the nuances.

Brief background: In this transaction, the original owner of the property in question is selling the property to the developer and taking back a note secured by a deed of trust on the property. The developer is going to build a golf course, clubhouse, lots, and infrastructure (streets, curbs, gutters, electrical, gas, cable and sewage systems), around the golf course. The developer does not plan to build houses. It will sell the lots and memberships in the golf club, which it will operate until all lots have been sold, at which time the club and course will be turned over to the homeowners' association. Homeowners or merchant builders that purchase the lots will build the homes, within the parameters of the covenant, codes, and restrictions that the developer will record against all lots to ensure a certain uniformity of style and use for the development.

The note that the seller is taking back in exchange for the land—the "seller-take-back-financing"—provides for payments of two sorts: sums certain payable at times certain and a participating contingent interest (a variable payment) that allows the original owner/seller to benefit if the development is a success. In order to allow the developer to obtain financing for construction on the property, the original owner/seller/lender has agreed to subordinate its deed of trust securing the note to allow another lender (who provides the "Permitted Senior Debt" referred to in the provision) to make a construction loan that will be senior and have a first priority lien on the property to secure its loan. Under the note, the original owner/seller is the "Lender" because it is taking the note and deed of trust in exchange for the property. The developer is the "Maker."

You may want to draw a picture or otherwise diagram this transactional structure in order to provide context for your analysis of the provision below. Beginning drafters often do not recognize the value that pictures, graphs, and charts can have for understanding and organizing complex facts, rights, and relationships. It is critical to understand the business terms and structure of a deal like this before drafting or reviewing the agreements that are supposed to memorialize it.

[Beginning of Provision]

11.1 *Payments of Participating Contingent Interest.* As additional consideration for the sale of the Property by Lender to Maker, Lender shall be entitled to receive certain additional payments based upon the cash flow generated from management, sales and operations of the Property. The payments received by Lender pursuant to this Section 11 are referred to herein as the "Participating Contingent Interest." For purposes of calculating payments of Participating Contingent Interest to Lender hereunder, Cash Flow and Excess Cash Flow (as defined hereinbelow) shall be deemed held by a third party and distributed from time to time to Lender and Maker in accordance with the following priorities. Excess Cash Flow (defined herein to mean Cash Flow remaining after payment of any required payments of Unpaid

Purchase Price under this Note or any optional payments made under section 6 hereof) shall be distributed from time to time as follows:

(a) First, to Maker until Maker has received distributions under this subsection (a) equal to Maker's Capital Investment plus an amount ("Preferred Return") sufficient to achieve an internal rate of return ("IRR") of 15% on Maker's Capital Investment (The Capital Investment plus Preferred Return are referred to collectively as the "Preference Capital"). Distributions of Cash Flow pursuant to this subsection (a) shall be deemed to be made first with respect to accrued and unpaid Preferred Return, with the balance applied and credited to Maker's Capital Investment.

(b) Next, Excess Cash Flow shall be distributed 75% to Maker and 25% to Lender until such time as Maker has been distributed an amount ("Additional Preferred Return") which, when added to amounts distributed to Maker pursuant to subsection (a) above, (x) is sufficient to achieve an IRR on Maker's total Capital Investment less Maker's Excess Capital Investment in the Property that is greater than or equal to twenty-five percent (25%), and (y) that is equal to 200% of Maker's total Capital Investment less Maker's Excess Capital Investment in the Property.

(c) Thereafter, Excess Cash Flow shall be distributed equally between Maker and Lender.

If distributions of Participating Contingent Interest are made pursuant to subsections (b) and (c) above, and Maker thereafter makes an additional Capital Investment ("Additional Capital Investment"), Preferred Return, Preference Capital and Additional Preferred Return with respect to such Additional Capital Investment shall be calculated from and after the date such Additional Capital Investment is made, and distributions of Excess Cash Flow shall be made in accordance with the priorities set forth in Section 11.1 with respect to the Preferred Return, Preference Capital and Additional Preferred Return payable with respect to such Additional Capital Investment. Notwithstanding the foregoing, in no event shall Lender be required to return any payments of Participating Contingent Interest theretofore paid to Lender on account of such Additional Capital Investment.

For purposes of this Promissory Note, the term "Internal Rate of Return" or "IRR" means the annual discount rate, determined by iterative process, which results in a net present value of approximately zero (0) when such discount rate is applied to Maker's Capital Investment from time to time and certain distributions in respect of Maker's Capital Investment from time to time. For purposes of determining Internal Rate of Return for purposes of this agreement, the formula below shall be utilized:

$$O \ = \ -CC + \ \frac{D^1 - C^1}{1 + r} \ + \ \frac{D^2 - C^2}{(1 + v\,r)^2} \ + \ldots \ \frac{D - C}{(1 + r)n}$$

"-C" = Maker's Initial Capital Investment.

"Cn" = Maker's additional Capital Investment invested in the period denoted in subscript.

"Dn" = All distributions to Maker in the period denoted in subscript.

"r" = Periodic discount rate expressed as a decimal equivalent to the annual "IRR" or internal rate of return.

For purposes of the above formula, Maker's Capital Investment made in any month shall be treated as having been made on the first day of such month and cash distributions in any month shall be treated as having been made on the last day of such month. In the event of a sale of all of the Property by Maker in accordance with the terms of this Note and the Deed of Trust, to the extent all of the consideration therefore shall have not been paid in cash, then the collection and distribution of Excess Cash Flow, as, when, and to the extent received, shall be administered by the Maker, or if Maker shall have been dissolved, by the former managing member of Maker, and distributed in accordance with the provisions of section 11.1 hereinabove.

Participating Contingent Interest, if any, shall be payable monthly on or before the fifteenth business day of each calendar month.

11.2 *Definitions.*

(a) *Capital Investment; Definition.* The term "Capital Investment" shall mean any and all capital (including Excess Capital Investment) contributed by the members of Maker in excess of Two Million Dollars ($2,000,000) as and to the extent expended by Maker on and after the Closing Date as defined in the Purchase Agreement with respect to the acquisition, construction, development, sales and marketing of the Property. Capital Investment shall also include any amounts borrowed by Maker and not secured by the Property as and to the extent such loan proceeds are expended towards the acquisition, construction, development, sales and marketing of the Property. Capital Investment shall also include letters of credit obtained by or on behalf of Maker and delivered in connection with Maker's acquisition and development of the Property ("Letters of Credit"); provided, however, that, with respect to any such letter of credit the collateral for which is limited to the Property and for which none of Maker's members has any liability, then unless amounts are drawn by the beneficiary of a Letter of Credit, the outstanding liability amount of such Letter of Credit shall not be deemed Capital Investment for purposes of calculating Preferred Return and Additional Preferred Return, and shall not be included in the principal amount of any Capital Investment.

(b) *Cash Flow; Definition.* "Cash Flow" for any calendar month is defined as Revenues during such month plus any cash reserves maintained by Maker which Maker reasonably, in the exercise of its good faith business judgment, determines to be unnecessary and therefore may be released, less the sum of:

(i) Costs during such calendar month;

(ii) Deposits into reserves (if any) made during such month; and

(iii) Payments required and made during such month under the Permitted Senior Debt Documents.

(c) *Costs; Definition.* "Costs" shall mean, for a given calendar month, the aggregate of the following which are properly chargeable to the operation of the Property and as determined under the cash method of accounting unless otherwise provided herein.

(i) Real estate taxes and insurance premiums paid;

(ii) Service payments, maintenance contract payments, development fees, on-site employees' wages and fringe benefits; costs of repairs and maintenance; promotional and advertising payments; public relations and similar expenses; reasonable accountants' fees; fees and expenses of third party operators of the "Facilities," as defined below; and other reasonable operating expenses of the Property accrued during such calendar month;

(iii) With respect to sales of the Property and Memberships, all reasonable and customary costs and expenses incurred by Maker in connection with the sales of the Property and Memberships, including but not limited to, reasonable attorneys' fees of Maker, Lender, and Senior Lender, title insurance, reasonable travel and entertainment expenses, and brokerage fees at prevailing market rates;

(iv) Justified and reasonable refunds paid by Maker during the calendar month of any Revenues received in an arm's length transaction;

(v) Reasonable administrative and general overhead expenses of Maker and its managing member for expenditures incurred directly in connection with the operation and development of the property;

(vi) The actual costs of restoration of the Property incurred following a casualty to the extent of the permitted deductible under the applicable insurance policy or where there are no insurance proceeds therefore and Maker is not required to and does not carry insurance therefore;

(vii) Costs of construction and other hard costs to the extent not paid with advances under the Senior permitted Debt; and

(viii) Actual fees and other costs of issuance paid to the Senior Permitted Debt.

"Costs" shall not included fees, expenses, interest, preferred return, or other consideration paid by Maker (or any of its affiliates) with respect to debt or equity capital contributed by members of Maker. "Costs" shall include market rate fees paid to the issuers in respect of the issuance and/or renewal of Letters of Credit.

(d) *Excess Capital Investment; Definition.* The term "Excess Capital Investment" shall mean any amount by which Maker's Capital Investment exceeds $.

(e) *Revenues; Definition.* "Revenues" shall mean, for a given calendar month, all Revenues from the Property and the operation thereof, as determined under the cash method of accounting, received by Maker or its authorized managing agent for the Property during that calendar month. "Revenues" shall include, without limitation, (i) all consideration (including, when converted into cash, promissory notes or any other form of consideration) actually received by Maker from all sales of the Property, which consideration shall also include any forfeited deposits retained by Maker (in the case of a terminated escrow), option fees to purchase lots or monetary settlements with prospective purchasers, (ii) fees and revenues generated to Maker from the operation of those certain country club and golf course facilities ("Facilities") to be developed on the Property, including receipts with respect to charges for merchandise, services, rents, license fees and from all other sources derived by Maker (or its Affiliates) from the Facilities; (iii) fees for lessons, greens fees, tennis court fees, public and private banquets held at Facilities, membership dues and all other fees or charges of any kind paid with respect to the use of the Facilities; (iv) brokerage commissions, fees and any proceeds retained by Maker (or its Affiliates, but excluding the Sales Company referenced at Section 16.1 of the Purchase Agreement) in the transfer or sale of memberships or interests in the Facilities; (v) charges for all food served and sold at the Facilities, including alcoholic and non-alcoholic beverages; (vi) fees and revenues generated to Maker (or its Affiliates) in respect of the sale of membership interests in the Facilities and the sale of the Facilities, as may be permitted under the Deed of Trust; (vii) proceeds from financing, refinancing and further encumbrancing the Property as and to the extent permitted under the Deed of Trust including, without limitation, the Permitted Senior Debt proceeds; and (viii) any other funds or proceeds received from any other source derived from the Property, including casualty insurance proceeds and condemnation proceeds not applied to restoration of the Property.

[End of Provision]

A.   Think about this provision and how it works. Can you describe it so that your non-lawyer client, the original land owner, knows what the super-slick developer is proposing? The developer has merely described this as an "equity kicker" that will allow them both to share the profit. Your client wants to understand what is actually being proposed.

B.   Who bears the risk if things do not go as well on the project as expected?

C.   What happens to Lender's participating contingent interest if, instead of getting a construction loan, Maker puts in its own funds (equity capital) to finance the development?

D.   Redraft these provisions in plain English to improve their clarity and precision.

Exercise 25: Attorney's Retainer Agreement

TO: Most Junior Associate

FROM: Most Senior Partner

RE: Retainer Agreement

Attached is a copy of a plaintiff's litigation retainer agreement we have used since my beloved Grandfather founded the firm in 1929. The Executive Committee, in their infantile wisdom, has suggested that we need to revise it— because of both style and substance. I think otherwise, but in this instance I will bow to their wishes.

You are supposed to be a reasonably competent drafter. Do something with it.

Time-log this as "Firm Work" and do not let it interfere with your billable hours.

AGREEMENT OF RETAINER AND EMPLOYMENT FOR THE RENDERING OF LEGAL AND RELATED SERVICES
KNOW ALL MEN BY THESE PRESENTS:

This agreement of retainer and employment for the rendering of legal and related services, made this the ____ day of _____, 19__, at _____, by and between _____ who is hereinafter known as "client" and _____ of the firm of Savage, Pillage, and Lute hereinafter known as "attorney," WITNESSETH:

Client employs and retains attorney to represent him as his attorney-at-law in a cause of actions against _____ regarding _____

_____

_____

_____

_____ and empowers him to effect a compromise in said matter or to institute such legal action as may be advisable in his judgment, and agrees to pay him for his services ___ percent (___%) of the total amount recovered, if said cause of action is settled without the institution of legal action; or ___ percent (___%) of the total amount recovered after suit if filed but before trial on said matter commences; or ___ percent (___%) of the total amount recovered under a verdict and judgment rendered in said matter by a court of competent jurisdiction. In addition, regardless of the outcome of the suit or settlement efforts, client shall be responsible for all costs, expenses, and disbursements.

Attorney is hereby given a lien on the said claim or cause of action, on any sum recovered by way of compromise or settlement, and on any judgment that may be recovered thereon, for the sum and share hereinbefore mentioned, as his fee; and it is further agreed that attorney shall have all general, possessory, or retaining liens, and all special or charging liens known to the common law; and it is further agreed that attorney may retain his share out of the amount finally collected by settlement, suit, or judgment in full of his services rendered.

Client agrees that he will enter into no settlement in said suit except with the prior approval and in the physical presence of attorney, and should he do so in violation of this agreement he agrees to pay attorney the sum and share hereinabove indicated.

Client agrees not to replace said attorney or terminate his services without the consent of attorney, except for misconduct or incapacity of said attorney to act; and if substitution or termination is effectuated in violation hereof, attorney shall be entitled to the full share and sum hereinabove indicated.

It is agreed that attorney has made no guarantees, warranties, or representations regarding the successful consummation or termination of said cause of action, and all expressions relative thereto are matters of opinion only.

Attorney accepts said retainer on the conditions hereinbefore enumerated.

In witness whereof the parties have set their hands and seals on the date first above mentioned.

Redraft the retainer agreement, adding or deleting provisions as necessary. Review the rules of professional conduct that have been adopted in your state. Make sure the agreement contains everything that is required and contains nothing that is prohibited.

Exercise 26: Association By–Laws

TO: Associate

FROM: Partner

IN RE: Lake Bueno Homeowner's Association

A group of homeowners living up on Lake Bueno has retained our firm to assist it in forming a homeowner's association. They will need to form a nonprofit corporation and get tax-exempt status from the IRS. Mr. Rehnquist, of our Tax Department, is working on the application for tax exempt status and Ms. O'Conner, in our General Corporate Department, will file the actual articles of incorporation with the Secretary of State. In both instances, however, they will need to attach a set of by-laws, which I want you to draft.

Lake Bueno is located in northeast McDonald County, on the Travis River. It runs from the dam near Pleasantville up to where the Buckhorn Creek feeds into the river. It is owned by the Consolidated Power Company, which generates power through the dam that forms the lake. Consolidated still owns about a fifth of the land contiguous to the lake. The rest has been divided into lots ranging from half an acre to two acres, which Consolidated has either sold outright or leases (usually 30 years) with an option to buy. The State maintains three public boat ramps on the lake.

The homeowners apparently have several specific concerns. Consolidated has not been cooperative in warning the homeowners of "draw downs" and its pier, seawall, and rip rap permitting process is slow. They also feel that the company has not done enough to fight hydrilla, which is choking several of the shallow coves. And they are real concerned over what Consolidated might want to do with the remaining land it owns and would like to at least have some input on that. Basically, they feel that Consolidated is oblivious to their interests and would like to have a united front in dealing with the company.

They are also concerned about pollution to the lake, specifically Tom's Hog Farm which is twenty miles upriver. They say that runoff from the hog pens is causing a problem and that the State Department of Environmental Control has pretty much ignored their complaints.

They also have complaints with the county—poor road maintenance, the three trash dumpster areas on the lake are filthy, slow response time by the sheriff, feral dogs running in the woods near the lake, failure to enforce the law against fishing from bridges (which they say causes serious safety problems), and so on.

At the very least, they say, an organization like this can keep the homeowners informed of things that are going on in their community that affect the value of their property and the quality of life on the lake. For example, they would like to put out a monthly newsletter.

Finally, they want an organization that can spearhead all kinds of community programs and events—a 4th of July boat parade and fireworks display, boating and swimming classes, Crime Watch, road and shore cleanups, and the like.

They want to limit membership to owners and permanent residents of lake front property.

Mr. Rehnquist says to be careful not to suggest that the association will engage in any partisan political activities. Indeed, I think you should have a provision specifically prohibiting it. Ms. O'Connor says that all she needs for incorporation purposes are that the by-laws have a board of directors, an annual meeting for the election of directors, and procedures for dissolution (including disbursement of remaining funds).

a.   On the basis of this information, make an outline of the substantive content of your by-laws.

b.   Draft the by-laws.

Exercise 27: Requirements Contract

TO: Senior Associate

FROM: Senior Partner

RE: Contract Revision

Once more, I must call upon your expertise as a drafter.

Attached is a contract that was drafted by one of our summer clerks. The substance of the contract accurately reflects the desires of our client, the Sooner Sand Company, but the style and format of the contract are atrocious! I have discovered that the clerk went to this client's file, found a contract my grandfather had drafted for this client back in 1929, and simply changed the dates and some minor details. That will not do.

Ironically, the contract the clerk relied on led to litigation. *McMichael v. Price*, 58 P.2d 549 (Okla. 1936). Although our firm won the case, we should not be producing documents that are ever susceptible of provoking litigation. You might read the case to see if you need to do anything to avoid a reoccurrence of that problem.

For the benefit of this hapless clerk: First, prepare a line-by-line critique of the contract. Then draft a revision. This will give the clerk a better idea of the quality work we demand in this law firm.

Contract

1   This Contract and Agreement entered into on this the
2   5th day of August, 1998, by and between Harley T. Price III,
3   doing business as the Sooner Sand Company, party of the first
4   part, and Page Peregrinus, party of the second part, witnesseth:
5
6   Whereas, the party of the first part is engaged in the
7   business of selling and shipping sand from Tulsa, Oklahoma,
8   to various points in the United States; and,
9
10   Whereas, the party of the second part is the owner of a
11 plot of ground hereinafter described as follows, to wit: Lot 65,

12 Section 10, Township 20 North, Range 15 East, Tulsa County;
13 and
14
15   Whereas, the party of the first part is desirous of buying
16 and the party of the second part is desirous of selling various
17 grades and qualities of sand from the plot of ground
18 hereinabove described;
19
31   Now, THEREFORE, in consideration of the mutual
32 promises herein contained, the said second party agrees to
33 furnish all the sand of various grades and qualities which the
34 first party can sell for shipment to various and sundry points
35 outside of the City of Tulsa, Oklahoma, and to load all of said
36 in suitable railway cars for delivery to said Frisco Railway
37 Company as said initial carrier. Said second party agrees to
38 furnish the quantity and quality of sand at all and various
39 times as the first party may designate by written or oral order,
40 and agrees to furnish and load same within a reasonable time
41 after said verbal or written order is received.
42
43   In consideration of the mutual promises herein
44 contained, first party agrees to purchase and accept from
45 second party all of the sand of various grades and quality
46 which the said first party can sell, for shipment to various and
47 sundry points outside the City of Tulsa, Oklahoma, provided
48 that the sand so agreed to be furnished and loaded by the said
49 second party shall at least be equal to in quality and
50 comparable with the sand of various grades sold by other sand
51 companies in the City of Tulsa, Oklahoma, or vicinity. First
52 party agrees to pay and the second party agrees to accept as
53 payment and compensation for Sand so furnished and loaded,
54 a sum per ton which represents sixty percent (60%) of the
55 current market price per ton of concrete sand at the place of
56 destination of said shipment. It is agreed that statements are
57 to be rendered by second party to first party every thirty days;
58 the account is payable monthly by first party with a discount
59 to be allowed by second party of four cents per ton for
60 payment within ten (10) days after shipment of any quantity of
61 sand.
62
56   This contract and agreement shall cover a period of ten
57 years from the date hereof, and shall be binding and effective
58 during said period, and shall extend to the heirs, executors,
59 administrators and assigns of both parties hereto.
60
61   Dated this 5th day of August, 1999.
62
63 _____   _____
64 Sooner Sand Company, by   Page Pregrinus,
65 Harley T. Price III,   Party of the second part.
66 Party of the first part.
67
68

Exercise 28: Independent Contractor Agreement

Terra Firma Real Estate Management Company, Inc., manages commercial real estate properties throughout the Southeast—shopping centers, strip malls, office buildings, apartment building, warehouses, and the like. Its headquarters are at 1861 Peachtree Lane, Atlanta, GA 39901. The Company is very dependent on computer technology. In its headquarters office it has 76 desktop computers, which are networked and connected to all the usual peripherals—CD–ROM towers, printers, scanners, FAX machines, and others. The Company also has on-site computers and various peripherals at most of the properties it manages. The Company uses over 35 different software programs and operates its own web page.

Needless to say, something is always going wrong with the hardware (with the causes ranging from a defect in the product to user abuse), the computers often refuse to *talk* to the various peripherals, and the net suffers from a lot of *down time*. Employees require training. Specific application questions are always coming up. Data is sometimes *lost* and must be retrieved. And the web page seems to need constant updating and attention.

Over the years, the Company has relied primarily on the service personnel of the various hardware and software vendors to take care of these problems. But this has proved to be expensive, slow, and unsatisfactory. It has also used several computer service companies, with a resulting hodge-podge of systems and incompatible solutions. Occasionally, employees who purport to have expertise have fixed (or attempted to fix) a problem on an emergency basis.

The Company has thus decided that it needs to hire its own computer expert to keep the entire company-wide computer system running efficiently. It estimates that on average it would have 20 to 25 hours of work for such a person each week, including travel time to locations out of Atlanta.

Dorothy Kham, known to her friends as Dot, recently graduated for Georgia Tech with a masters degree in computer technology and engineering. She has set herself up as a computer consultant, doing business as Kham Computer

Technologies, at 1289–b Butler Terrace, Atlanta, GA 39902. She charges $65 per hour. She has heard that Terra Firma is offered her services. Terra Firma is impressed and wants to retain her, but only as a independent contractor and not as an employee.

Terra Firma wants you to draft an appropriate contract. For the necessary substantive content of this contract, see Kenneth A. Jenero & Philip M. Schreiber, *Drafting Effective Independent Contractor Agreements*, 23 Employee Relations Law Journal, No. 4, p. 127 (Spring 1989), or materials supplied by your instructor.

Exercise 29: Confidentiality Agreement

You represent the Rearden Steel Company (listed on the New York Stock Exchange as "RSC"). Jack Rearden, President and major stockholder, has told you that he has received an inquiry from Carbolic Fabricators, through its CEO, John Galt, suggesting an interest in purchasing Rearden's stock. If the price is right, Rearden might be willing to sell. Galt, however, want to do a thorough investigation of Rearden Steel before it proceeds. This will necessarily involve making Carbolic personnel privy to confidential information about Rearden's finances, production techniques, customer lists, and other matters. Rearden wants to make sure that this information remains confidential. He has asked you to draft a confidentiality agreement.

a.   Using the following article for guidance, construct a substantive-content check list of matters that should, from the *disclosing party's* perspective, be included in such a document.

b.   Then construct a list of matters that, from the *interested party's,* should be deleted from or added to that list.

c.   Finally, draft an agreement for Rearden.

Drafting and Negotiating
Effective Confidentiality Agreements

By Brian D. Bowden[2]

Confidentiality agreements create the contractual framework within which one party discloses to another

2. 59 Texas Bar Journal 524 (1996).   Used by permission from the author and Copyright © 1996 by Brian D. Bowden.   the Texas Bar Journal.

confidential and proprietary information. These agreements typically arise in the context of business acquisitions or dispositions, in which the disclosure of such information is necessary or desirable to enable substantive discussions regarding a potential transaction to proceed. Although confidentiality provisions often are included in basic transactional documents, a free-standing agreement is preferable because (a) it is more comprehensive and thus may better protect the interests of the disclosing party, (b) its enforceability is not dependent on that of a more-encompassing document that includes other, unrelated provisions, and (c) it may be entered into before the parties have discussed any substantive issues regarding the proposed transaction. In addition, the use of a separate agreement requires the parties to focus on an important subject that often is given insufficient consideration.

Because most, if not all, of the obligations in a confidentiality agreement typically burden the recipient of the information (the "interested party"), the interested party generally favors the shortest and least-comprehensive agreement possible. Conversely, it is incumbent on the disclosing party to ensure that the agreement provides adequate protection in all relevant areas. Although the length of the agreement and its level of detail will vary depending on the relative sophistication of, and the degree of familiarity and trust between, the parties, it is possible to provide a disclosing party with effective protection in a concise agreement. This article presents the typical, salient provisions of a confidentiality agreement from the perspective of each party, together with commonly-negotiated compromises. . . .

Definition of Information

Central to the agreement is the definition of the information to which the agreement pertains. Not surprisingly, the disclosing party will want to define "information" as broadly as possible. A comprehensive definition should include all information actually disclosed, whether before or after the execution of the agreement, whether tangible or intangible, and in whatever form or medium provided, as well as all information generated by the interested party or by its representatives that contains, reflects, or is derived from the provided information. The definition should also include the fact that the confidentiality agreement exists and that discussions between the parties concerning the proposed transaction are taking place. Alternatively, the parties may choose to prohibit disclosure of these facts in a separate paragraph of the agreement. In either case, the interested party should make the obligation with respect to the nondisclosure of this portion of the information reciprocal.

The interested party should seek to exclude the following from the definition of "information":

(a) Information that is or becomes publicly available other than through acts by the interested party or by its representatives in violation agreement. In negotiating the precise language of this exclusion, it is important to the interested party that the term "publicly available" is used rather than "in the public domain," which connotes legal entitlement to use. The interested party also should avoid a requirement that the information be "generally known by" the public, as this language imposes an additional and difficult evidentiary hurdle to overcome. The interested party also will want to ensure that the acts negating the exclusion are only those done in violation of the agreement.

(b) Information that is already in the interested party's possession at the time of its disclosure by the disclosing party. The disclosing party may require that the interested party's possession be "rightful" or "lawful," but the interested party should avoid these terms because they signify legal entitlement to use. The disclosing party also may require that prior possession be "evidenced by the interested party's written records," which restricts the types of evidence that the interested party may use to support its reliance on the exclusion. Although, as a practical matter, it will be difficult for an interested party to avail itself successfully of the exclusion without written evidence, there is no conceptual justification for this restriction.

(c) Information that is disclosed to the interested party by a third party who, to the interested party's knowledge, is not prohibited from disclosing the in-

formation pursuant to a confidentiality agreement with the disclosing party. The disclosing party will prefer (i) to omit the knowledge qualifier so that the interested party guarantees that the source of the information was, in fact, entitled to disclose it and (ii) to expand the source of the prohibition on disclosure to any fiduciary, contractual, or other duty to any person. A well-accepted compromise is to impose on the interested party only a duty of due inquiry as to the right of the third party to disclose the information, but to accept the disclosing party's broader scope of the source of the prohibition on disclosure.

Subject to the negotiation of precise language, the three categories of exclusion set forth above are almost universally accepted. There are, however, two additional categories of exclusion that the interested party should attempt to obtain that may not be acceptable to the disclosing party.

(d) Information that the interested party develops or derives without the aid, application, or use of the furnished information. Although this exclusion is unobjectionable in concept, the disclosing party often perceives it as too broad and subject to abuse. Because of this perception, and because the exclusion imposes a difficult evidentiary burden on the interested party in any event, the disclosing party's position usually prevails.

(e) Information that the interested party is advised by legal counsel is required to be disclosed by law or by legal process. The disclosing party often objects to this category because the agreement typically contains a separate paragraph on legal process. From the interested party's perspective, however, the exclusion is desirable because it insulates the interested party from liability regardless of whether the interested party follows precisely the detailed requirements of the legal process paragraph. It is particularly important that the interested party include the words "is advised by legal counsel" to avoid becoming a guarantor of the legal obligation to disclose the information to a court or other judicial or administrative body.

Permitted Use of the Information

The agreement should specify the purpose for which the interested party may use the information and should specifically prohibit any other use. The best approach is simply to recite that the information may be used only to assist the interested party in evaluating the proposed transaction, which the agreement may describe with the desired degree of specificity. This provision is usually not controversial, but the interested party should avoid ambiguous language regarding prohibited uses, such as "use in any way detrimental to the disclosing party."

Permitted Discloses

It is important to both parties that the agreement establish clearly the categories of persons to whom the interested party may disclose the information and to what extent the interested party will be liable for acts by any such persons in violation of the agreement. The agreement should define such persons (who typically include officers, directors, partners, employees, affiliates, agents, and representatives) as the "representatives," or some similar term, of the interested party. To insulate the interested party more effectively from liability, the interested party should omit from this definition persons who are not within its control and have them enter into separate and independent confidentiality agreements with the disclosing party. Potential co-investors, in particular, should be excluded because they are not agents of the interested party and their interests may be inconsistent. By defining "representatives" generically, the term also can be applied to the disclosing party with respect to its obligations under the agreement.

Following a description of permitted discloses, the agreement typically provides that the interested party will provide the information only to those of its representatives who (i) need it to assist the interested party in evaluating the proposed transaction, (ii) are provided with a copy of the confidentiality agreement, and (iii) agree to be bound by the confidentiality agreement to the same extent as if they were signatories thereto. The disclosing party should include a provision making the interested party fully liable for acts by its representatives in violation of the agreement and may also with to require a written undertaking of the representatives to be bound by the confidentiality agreement, but this latter requirement is burdensome to the interested party and is not usually imposed. Similarly, the interested party may attempt to exculpate itself from liability for the acts of its representatives once it has complied with the specified conditions, but this attempt is rarely successful. The disclosing party may include an additional requirement that the interested party take all reasonable measures to prevent its representatives from violating the agreement. Assuming that the interested party should strike the word "all" so that is may more easily defend its actions to prevent such disclosure if they prove to be unsuccessful.

Return of the Information

The agreement usually obligates the interested party to return the information once the interested party has determined not to pursue the proposed transaction, or anytime at the request of the disclosing party. The interested party should (a) obligate itself to return the information only upon the disclosing party's request, so that the disclosing party has the burden of initiating the return process, (b) require the disclosing party's request to be in writing, and (c) be permitted to destroy information not furnished by the disclosing party rather than deliver it to the disclosing party. The disclosing party reasonably may require that an officer of the interested party certify the destruction in writing, and that the furnished information be returned to it within a specified length of time, commonly five days after receipt of the notice.

Legal Process Seeking Disclosure of the Information

The disclosing party should obligate the interested party to follow certain procedures if it is requested to disclose any of the information pursuant to legal process. As typically drafted by the disclosing party, the agreement provides that, in such event, the interested party (a) must give the disclosing party as much notice as possible to enable the disclosing party to attempt to avoid the disclosure, (b) must use its best efforts to cooperate with the disclosing party in any such attempt, and (c) may disclose only that part of the information that, in the written opinion of its legal counsel, it is required to disclose. The interested party should (a) avoid any requirement that the legal process be valid: or that the subpoena or order be issued by a court of "competent jurisdiction," as these are legal determinations that the interested party will not necessarily be in a position to make,

(b) ensure that the opinion of its counsel is not required to be written to avoid the expense and difficulty of obtaining a formal legal opinion quickly, (c) agree to use reasonable, rather than best, efforts to ensure that the confidentiality of the information is maintained, and require that all such efforts be at the sole cost and expense of the disclosing party, and (d) avoid any requirement that the interested party be subject imminently to contempt or other penalty before disclosing the information.

Disclaimer of Accuracy and Completeness

The disclosing party often includes in the agreement a disclaimer as to the accuracy and completeness of the information. While this is usually acceptable, the interested party should seek to include the disclosing party's representation that is believes is good faith that the furnished information is in fact accurate. The disclosing party likely will be more reluctant to represent that the furnished information is complete.

Attorneys' Fees

Because the interested party has the great majority of the obligations in the agreement, the disclosing party will want to make the interested party responsible for the disclosing party's costs and expenses in the event of a breach or threatened breach of the agreement. The interested party should (a) make the obligation reciprocal, (b) limit the obligation to those expenses actually and reasonably incurred by the prevailing party in successful litigation, so that the disclosing party must prevail in court to recover under this provision and so that investigatory and other pre-litigation costs and expenses are excluded, and (c) delete the reference to threatened breaches.

No Obligation To Proceed with the Proposed Transaction

To protect itself against potential claims that it has agreed to consummate the proposed transaction with the interested party as a result of, among other things, the execution of the confidentiality agreement, the disclosing party should include a specific statement that, until the execution and delivery of a definitive agreement, the parties are under no obligation with respect to the proposed transaction by virtue of the confidentiality agreement of any other written or oral understanding or agreement, except with respect to the matters specifically addressed in the confidentiality agreement. This provision should be acceptable to the interested party if it does not include blanket waivers of claims against the disclosing party.

Waiver of Right To Jury Trial

The disclosing party should require the interested party to waive its right to a jury trial. From the perspective of the disclosing party, who is the likely plaintiff in any court proceeding, the waiver serves to expedite the trial and to increase the likelihood that any technical issues, particularly with respect to the nature of the information and to the damages flowing from breach of the agreement, will be understood fully and given adequate consideration. The interested party, of course, should avoid this waiver. Even if the disclosing party prevails on this point, however, the disclosing party should include a severability clause in the agreement to protect itself against a court finding that the waiver is unenforceable on public policy grounds.

Representation of Rightful Disclosure

The interested party should include in the agreement (a) the disclosing party's representation that it is entitled to disclose the information, and (b) an indemnity for any breach of such presentation. This provision is particularly important when the information relates to another party who is not a signatory to the confidentiality agreement and there is no clear and substantiated agency relationship between the disclosing party and such other party. This issue typically arises when the disclosing party is an investment banker who has been retained to assist a client with the disposition of its business or assets.

. . . .

Prohibition on Solicitation of Employees

Depending on the particular circumstances, the disclosing party may want to prohibit the interested party from hiring any of the disclosing party's employees for a specified period of time. The interested party should attempt to limit the prohibition (a) to the solicitation, but not the hiring, of key employees who were identified by the interested party pursuant to its evaluation of the proposed transaction, and (b) to personal, as opposed to general, solicitation. Acceptable time periods for the prohibition typically range from six months to two years.

Forum and Venue Provisions

If a disclosing party is entering into agreements with one or more interested parties in different geographical locations, it is a good idea to provide for exclusive forum and venue in a court of its choice and to include the interested party's consent to personal jurisdiction and waiver of its right to invoke the inconvenient forum objection. The interested party may lessen the effect of these provisions simply by making the forum and venue selections non-exclusive.

Right to Equitable Remedies

Disclosing parties commonly include the interested party's acknowledgment that the disclosing party will be entitled to specific performance and other equitable remedies in the event of a breach or threatened breach of the agreement without the posting of any bond and without proof of actual damages. Because equitable remedies are by their nature within judicial discretion, however, the effectiveness of this provision is questionable. Rather than arguing for deletion of the entire provision an interested party may prefer to nullify its effect simply by stating that the disclosing party will be entitled to *seek* equitable remedies. Although the effect of this change should be transparent to most readers, counsel to disclosing parties have accepted it more often than one might expect. In any event, the interested party should attempt to delete the references to the posting of bond and to proof of damages.

. . . .

Term of the Agreement

As typically drafted by the disclosing party, the agreement specifies no term, and this position should prevail on the merits. A specified term is unjustified for information that consists of trade secrets and, to the extent that it consists of financial information, such information will become stale over time in any event. In addition, financial information pertaining to a public company will be publicly-disclosed on a periodic basis pursuant to securities laws requirements. Finally, the disclosing party justifiably will not want any contractual time limit on its remedies.

Conclusion

Too often parties give insufficient consideration to maintaining the confidentiality of proprietary information in the rush to negotiate and complete a proposed transaction. Careful attention to this issue at the beginning of discussions will better protect the disclosing party, in particular, if the relationship between the parties becomes adversarial.

Exercise 30: Structuring the Deal for the Right Remedy

Listed below are the desired results of a contract provision or provisions. For each, (a) describe the type of provision that is most appropriate to use to achieve that result and explain why that type of provision is the most appropriate and (b) draft the provision, making sure that the final provision is of the correct type, is of an appropriate scope, and will trigger the appropriate remedy when needed.

A. The buyer's right to terminate a real estate acquisition and obtain a refund of all down payments and deposits prior to closing if the buyer's inspections disclose the presence of environmental contaminants on the property.

B. A seller's right to recover damages from a corporation's sole shareholder if the corporation fails to meet its obligations under its contract of sale to the seller.

C. A buyer's right to terminate an asset purchase agreement if, prior to closing, it is determined that the assets total less than a certain number of items.

D. A buyer's right to reduce the purchase price payable as part of the sale on a pro rata basis if, prior to closing, it is determined that the assets total less than a certain number of items.

E. A seller's statement, meant to induce a buyer to enter into a transaction and engage in due diligence, that the earnings of a particular division are above a certain level.

F.   A lessee's promise to use the leased equipment for its own internal uses and not to lease or otherwise permit third parties to use the equipment.

G.   A buyer's commitment to resell goods abroad and not in the domestic market.

H.   A buyer's obligation to make an initial deposit of 5% of the purchase price at the time of signing a purchase agreement, with this deposit to represent the limit of the seller's damages should the buyer fail to consummate the sale.

I.   A provision making an agreement non-assignable.

J.   A provision limiting a party's remedies to monetary damages.

K.   A requirement that a buyer obtain a seller's approval for all announcements and statements to third parties regarding the transaction that are made prior to closing of the transaction.

L.   A provision making an agreement contingent upon approval of the state and local government.

M.   A provision making a buyer's obligation to purchase contingent upon the buyer obtaining financing in a certain amount and on certain terms.

*

APPENDIX

The following publications are among those that have influenced or contributed to the content of this book.

Adams, Kenneth A., *A Manual of Style for Contract Drafting* (ABA 2004).

Aitken, J.K., *Piesse, The Elements of Drafting* (9th ed. 1995).

Brody, Susan L., Rutherford, Jane, Vietzen, Laurel A., Dernbach, John C. *Legal Drafting*. Boston, MA: Little, Brown and Co. Copyright 1994.

Burnham, Scott J., *Drafting Contracts*. Charlottesville, VA: The Michie Co., 2nd ed. Copyright 1987, 1993.

Child, Barbra, *Drafting Legal Documents, Principles and Practices*. St. Paul, MN: West Publishing Co., 2nd ed. Copyright 1992.

Darmstadter, Howard, *Hereof, Thereof, and Everywhereof: A Contrarian Guide to Legal Drafting*. Chicago, IL: American Bar Association. Copyright 2002.

Dick, Robert L., *Legal Drafting* (1972).

Dickerson, Reed, *The Fundamentals of Legal Drafting*. Boston, MA: Little, Brown and Co. Copyright 1965, 1986.

Dickerson, Reed, *Materials on Legal Drafting* (1981).

Felsenfeld, Carl, & Siegel, Alan, *Writing Contracts in Plain English* (1981).

Field, Arthur N., *Legal Opinions in Business Transactions* (PLI 2006).

Filson, Lawrence E., *The Legislative Drafter's Desk Reference* (1992).

Fox, Charles M., *Working With Contracts* (PLI 2002).

Garner, Bryan A., *A Dictionary of Modern Legal Usage* (2nd ed. 1995).

Garner, Bryan A., *Advanced Legal Drafting*. Dallas, TX: Bryan A. Garner and LawProse, Inc. Copyright 1993.

Garner, Bryan A., *Advanced Legal Writing and Editing*. Dallas, TX: LawProse, Inc. Copyright 1993.

Garner, Bryan A., *Guidelines for Drafting and Editing Court Rules* (1997).

Garner, Bryan A., *The Red Book, A Manual on Legal Style.* St. Paul, MN: West Group. Copyright 2002.

Garner, Bryan A., *The Scribes Journal of Legal Writing.* New York, NY: Matthew Bender, vol. 7, 1998–2000. Copyright 2000.

Garner, Bryan A., *The Scribes Journal of Legal Writing.* St. Paul, MN: West Publishing Co., vol. 5, 1994–1995. Copyright 1996.

Gentle Jr., Terry W., and Heminway, Joan MacLeod, *Bank Mergers in Tennessee: An Annotated Model Tennessee Bank Merger Agreement. Transactions: The Tennessee Journal of Business Law*, Buffalo, NY: William S. Hein & Co., Inc., vol. 5 Spring 2004 Number 2. Copyright 2004.

Haggard, Thomas, R., *UCC 2–207 A Suggested Analysis,* 10 J. LAW & COMMERCE 257 (1991).

Haggard, Thomas, R., *The South Carolina Rules of Statutory Interpretation*, SOUTH CAROLINA LAWYER, November/December 1991.

Haggard, Thomas, R., *Tips on Drafting and Enforcing a Policy Against Sexual Harassment*, 36 INDUSTRIAL MANAGEMENT, No. 1 (January/February 1994) (with Alexander).

Haggard, Thomas, R., *The South Carolina Anti–Stalking Statute: A Study in Bad Drafting,* SOUTH CAROLINA LAWYER (March/April 1994).

Haggard, Thomas, R., *The Lawyer's Book of Rules for Effective Legal Writing* (1997).

Haggard, Thomas, R., *Contract Law from a Drafting Perspective—An Introduction to Contract Drafting for Law Students* (2003) (with instructors manual).

Hayakawa, S.I., *Choose the Right Word, A Modern Guide to Synonyms.* New York, NY: Harper and Row, Publishers. Copyright 1968.

Heminway, Joan MacLeod and McLemore, Timothy, *Acquisition Escrows in Tennessee: An Annotated Model Tennessee Acquisition Escrow Agreement. Transactions: The*

Tennessee Journal of Business Law, Buffalo, NY: William S. Hein & Co., Inc., Vol. 7 Spring 2006 #2. Copyright 2006.

Kuney, George W. and Lloyd, Robert M., *Contracts: Transactions and Litigation*. St. Paul, MN: West Publishing Co. Copyright 2006.

Kuney, George W. and Looper, Donna C., *California Law of Contract* (CEB 2007).

Kuney, George W., *The Elements of Contract Drafting, 2d Edition*. St. Paul, MN: West Publishing Co., Copyright 2006.

Lloyd, Robert M., *Making Contracts Relevant: Thirteen Lessons for The First Year Contracts Course*, 36 Ariz. St. L.J. 257 (2004).

Lloyd, Robert M., *Hard Law Firms and Soft Law Schools*, 83 N.C.L. Rev. 667, Copyright 2005.

Martineau, Robert J., *Drafting Legislation and Rules in Plain English* (1991).

Mullins, M.E., *A Handbook for Legislative Drafters* (1996).

Oates, Laurel C., Enquist, Anne, Kunsch, Kelly, *The Legal Writing Handbook*. Boston, MA: Little, Brown and Co. Copyright 1993.

Ray, Mary B., Cox, Barbara J., *Beyond the Basics, A Text for Advanced Legal Writing*. St. Paul, MN: West Publishing Co. Copyright 1991.

Ray, Mary B., Ramsfield, Jill J., *Legal Writing: Getting It Right and Getting It Written*. St. Paul, MN: West Group, 3rd ed. Copyright 2000.

Schultz, Nancy L., Sirico, Jr., Louis J., *Legal Writing and Other Lawyering Skills*. New York, NY: Matthew Bender, 3rd ed. Copyright 1998.

Shertzer, Margaret, *The Elements of Grammar*. New York, NY: Macmillan Publishing Co., Inc. Copyright 1986.

Statsky, William, *Legislative Analysis and Drafting* (2nd ed. 1984).

Strunk, Jr, William, White, E.B., *The Elements of Style*. Macmillan Publishing Co., Inc., 3rd ed. Copyright 1979.

Drafting Business Contracts: Principles, Techniques and Forms. Berkeley, CA: The Regents of the University of California. Copyright 1994, 1996.

*

Index

References are to Pages

413

†